Upland communities

Environment, population and social structure in the Alps since the sixteenth century

PIER PAOLO VIAZZO

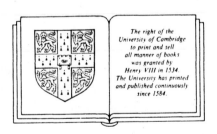

The right of the
University of Cambridge
to print and sell
all manner of books
was granted by
Henry VIII in 1534.
The University has printed
and published continuously
since 1584.

CAMBRIDGE UNIVERSITY PRESS

Cambridge
New York   New Rochelle
Melbourne   Sydney

Published by the Press Syndicate of the University of Cambridge
The Pitt Building, Trumpington Street, Cambridge CB2 1RP
32 East 57th Street, New York, NY 10022, USA
10 Stamford Road, Oakleigh, Melbourne 3166, Australia

First published 1989

British Library cataloguing in publication data
Viazzo, Pier Paolo
Upland communities: environment,
population and social structure in the
Alps since the sixteenth century –
(Cambridge series in population, economy
and society in past time, 8)
1. Europe. Alps. Social change, *1600* –
I. Title
303.4'09494'7

Library of Congress cataloguing in publication data
Viazzo, Pier Paolo.
Upland communities: environment, population, and social structure
in the Alps since the sixteenth century/Pier Paolo Viazzo
p. cm. – (Cambridge studies in population, economy, and
society in past time: 8)
Bibliography
Includes index.
ISBN 0 521 30663 9
1. Alps, Western – Population – History. 2. Alps, Western – Economic
conditions. 3. Alps, Western – Social conditions. 4. Human ecology – Alps,
Western – History I. Title. II. Series.
HB3581. V53 1989
304.6'09494'7 – dc 19 88–18973

ISBN 0 521 30663 9

Transferred to digital printing 2004

Cambridge Studies in Population, Economy and Society in Past Time

---

Series Editors:

PETER LASLETT, ROGER SCHOFIELD AND E. A. WRIGLEY

ESRC Cambridge Group for the History of Population and Social Structure

and DANIEL SCOTT SMITH

University of Illinois at Chicago

Recent work in social, economic and demographic history has revealed much that was previously obscure about societal stability and change in the past. It has also suggested that crossing the conventional boundaries between these branches of history can be very rewarding.

This series will exemplify the value of interdisciplinary work of this kind, and will include books on topics such as family, kinship and neighbourhood; welfare provision and social control; work and leisure; migration; urban growth; and legal structures and procedures, as well as more familiar matters. It will demonstrate that, for example, anthropology and economics have become as close intellectual neighbours to history as have political philosophy or biography.

1 *Land, kinship and life-cycle* Edited by RICHARD M. SMITH
2 *Annals of the labouring poor: social change and agrarian England 1660–1900* K. D. M. SNELL
3 *Migration in a mature economy: emigration and internal migration in England and Wales 1861–1900* DUDLEY BAINES
4 *Scottish literacy and the Scottish identity: illiteracy and society in Scotland and northern England 1600–1800* R. A. HOUSTON
5 *Neighbourhood and society: a London suburb in the seventeenth century* JEREMY BOULTON
6 *Demographic behavior in the past: A study of fourteen German village populations in the nineteenth century* JOHN E. KNODEL
7 *Worlds within worlds: the structures of life in sixteenth-century London* STEVE RAPPAPORT
8 *Upland communities: environment, population and social structure in the Alps since the sixteenth century* PIER PAOLO VIAZZO

For Davide and Giuliana

Contents

Illustrations

MAPS

Tables

Abbreviations

ACA	Archivio Comunale di Alagna
AFA	Archivio Farinetti, Alagna
APA	Archivio Parrocchiale di Alagna
ASDN	Archivio Storico Diocesano, Novara
ASN	Archivio di Stato di Novara
AST	Archivio di Stato di Torino
BRT	Biblioteca Reale, Torino

Acknowledgements

More than ten years have elapsed since Mary Douglas, back in June 1977, bought me half a pint of bitter in a pub not far from University College London and encouraged me to choose an Alpine village for my Ph.D. project and to integrate anthropological fieldwork with historical analysis. Since then my research has trodden unexpected paths. My Ph.D. dissertation still provides the foundation for the present volume – but more in terms of questions raised, perhaps, than in terms of conclusions arrived at. In particular, I gradually realized the crucial importance of investigating population dynamics in order to test models in ecological anthropology, and also became aware of the usefulness of going beyond the boundaries of community study and engaging in a comparative analysis covering the whole Alpine area. The broadening of the thematic and geographic scope of my study has led me to incur many intellectual and personal debts. I am grateful first of all to Phil Burnham, Rosemary Harris and Sally Humphreys, who supervised my work at the Department of Anthropology, University College London, and to the Italian National Research Council, the Central Research Fund, University of London, and the Folklore Fund, University College London, for supporting my field research in the Italian Western Alps. My first contacts with the Cambridge Group for the History of Population and Social Structure were instrumental in giving a marked historical-demographic orientation to my research. This orientation has then become even stronger through my close association with the Group since 1982. My greatest and sincerest thanks are due to Peter Laslett and Tony Wrigley, who both encouraged me to write this book and have been supportive all the way through. But I am also very grateful to all the other members of the Group, and particularly to Jim Oeppen for his help in statistical matters, and to Richard Wall who read large portions of the first version of this book in his usual careful way. I would like to extend my thanks to all the friends and colleagues who helped me by directing my attention to problems and evidence I was not aware of, by sending published and unpublished material which often proved invaluable and by reassuring me that some of my arguments were at least plausible, if not necessarily valid. I would like to mention at least Josef Ehmer, Anne M. Jones, Alison Keymer, Jon Mathieu, Sheilagh Ogilvie, Christian Pfister, Othmar Pickl, David Siddle, Richard Smith, Maria Todorova, Chris Wilson. Finally, debts of a special kind I owe to Mariangiola Bodo, whose help was decisive in the first years of my research, and to Dionigi Albera, who joined forces at a critical stage in my work and shared his expertise on the ethnography and historical demography of the Western Alps.

Introduction: anthropology, historical demography and the study of mountain societies

The question of the relations between the physical environment and human social organization is a very old one. It has fascinated many generations of scholars and stirred up acrimonious debates. And in the course of these debates, as Lucien Febvre remarked in his *Geographical introduction to history*, the advocates of environmental primacy have constantly placed a strong emphasis on 'the influence of mountains on man, and the special characters which they imprint on mountain societies – characters in every respect dissimilar to those of societies on the plains, being affected by a natural environment peculiarly oppressive and tyrannical'.[1]

This was particularly the case in the late nineteenth and early twentieth centuries, when the laudable attempt to counteract the dangers of racial determinism led some of the pioneers of human geography to espouse a no less extreme form of environmental determinism. The method associated with the names of Friedrich Ratzel and Ellen C. Semple consisted in comparing peoples of different ethnic stocks but living under analogous geographical conditions. If these peoples were found to display similar social and economic features, then it seemed legitimate to infer that such similarities were due to environment rather than to race.[2] The fact that similarities in economic and social organization appeared to be especially marked in mountain areas was taken as evidence that virtually no alternative was available to people inhabiting regions in which the beauty of nature belies extraordinarily difficult living conditions. Indeed, Semple had little hesitation in arguing that upland populations all over the world were bound to be culturally and intellectually backward, for the mountains are just 'regions of much labor and little leisure, of poverty to-day

[1] Febvre, *Geographical introduction to history*, p. 194.
[2] See Ratzel, *Anthropo-Geographie*, and Semple, *Influences of geographic environment*.

1

and anxiety for the morrow, of toil-cramped hands and toil-dulled brains'.[3]

Ratzel's determinism soon came under attack in France, where the geographer Paul Vidal de la Blache warned his colleagues not to underestimate the human ability to affect and modify the natural environment and urged them to concentrate their studies on what he called the 'reciprocal exchanges' between geographical conditions and social facts.[4] These ideas exerted a powerful influence on some key figures in French human and historical geography, including Philippe Arbos, one of the founding fathers of Alpine human geography, and Febvre, an historian with a deep interest in geography who became the most trenchant critic of environmental determinism. Vidal and his followers would not deny that upland populations displayed similar economic and social arrangements, but feared that Ratzel's emphasis on similarities could obscure the existence of significant differences and therefore the historical originality of the various mountain areas. Differences were in fact believed to be far more revealing, since they demonstrated that human populations were not faced by inescapable environmental imperatives but rather by a range of possibilities.

In the period between the two world wars this doctrine (which is generally known as 'possibilism', in opposition to Ratzel's 'environmentalism') was dominant on both sides of the Atlantic. By 1950, however, a reaction against it was already apparent. Ironically, in history such a reaction is perhaps most evident in the work of Febvre's best-known pupil, Fernand Braudel, whose notions of *'longue durée'* and 'geographical time' border on environmental determinism.[5] But a similar swing of the intellectual pendulum can also be detected in the writings of geographers and anthropologists, who felt that Febvre's epigrammatic statements ('Des nécessités, nulle part. Des possibilités partout')[6] were in the long run stultifying and distracted

[3] Semple, *Influences of geographic environment*, p. 20. Cf. Ratzel, *Anthropo-Geographie*, vol. 1, pp. 199–204.

[4] Vidal de la Blache, 'Les conditions géographiques des faits sociaux', pp. 21–2.

[5] Braudel's penchant for environmental determinism is particularly clear in his well-known 1958 article on the *longue durée*, where he emphasizes the role of geographical constraints and writes that 'l'homme est prisonnier, dès siècles durant, de climats, de végétations, de populations animales, de cultures, d'un équilibre lentement construit, dont il ne peut s'écarter sans risquer de remettre tout en cause'. Braudel, 'Histoire et sciences sociales', p. 731. However, the notions of *longue durée* and 'geographical time' (discussed in Chapter 2 below, pp. 35–8) had been proposed by Braudel a few years earlier, in the first edition of his *Méditerranée* (1949). It is interesting to note, in this respect, that in his otherwise highly complementary view of Braudel's book, Febvre warned against the dangers of 'une sorte de permanence géographique qui confinerait à l'éternité'. See Febvre, 'Un livre qui grandit', p. 220.

[6] Febvre, *La terre et l'évolution humaine*, p. 284.

attention from the fact that the range of possibilities greatly varied from one milieu to another, and in some circumstances could be very limited indeed.[7]

As the geographer A. F. Martin noticed in 1952, the older determinists had oversimplified the physical as well as the human world and had been apt to skip several links in the chain of causation by jumping directly from climate to civilization – or even to the genius of the peoples. But it could hardly be disputed, he maintained, that 'through its control on agriculture climate does have a considerable indirect effect on civilization'.[8] Important empirical support to this view has come especially from the geoecological approach pioneered by Carl Troll, whose work has been – significantly – mainly concerned with upland regions. Geoecological research in the Andes and other tropical mountain areas has shown how the interaction of altitude, climate and soil fertility sets upper limits to agriculture and pastoralism and, within the range for agriculture, upper limits on types of crops.[9] In particular, Troll has argued that 'the diurnal temperature climate with nightfrost in greater heights was an important factor for the agricultural conquest of the high Andes of Bolivia and Peru', and has indeed gone so far as to claim that 'in fact, it was this peculiar climate which was a decisive factor in the history of the Andean civilizations of the Indians'.[10]

In anthropology, the possibilist position of such leading scholars as Alfred Kroeber in the United States and Daryll Forde in Britain lost ground to the 'cultural ecology' of Julian Steward, whose aim was to determine the extent to which modes of subsistence and, ultimately, forms of social organization were shaped by certain characteristics of the environment.[11] The method advocated by Steward was reminiscent of Ratzel's comparative approach, for Steward too was particularly interested in finding what he called 'regularities', or similarities between cultures that recur in historically separate areas and may therefore be explained as a result of similar environmental features. Indeed, some of the criticisms levelled by Vidal and Febvre against Ratzel surely apply to cultural ecology as well. For one thing, there is little doubt that according to cultural ecologists human social and cultural behaviour is to a large extent determined, in a mechanistic

---

[7] Cf. Spate, 'Environmentalism', pp. 94–5.

[8] A. F. Martin, 'The necessity for determinism', p. 8.

[9] See especially Troll, *Die tropischen Gebirge*, and Troll (ed.), *Geo-ecology of mountainous regions*.

[10] Troll, 'The cordilleras of Tropical Americas', p. 32.

[11] The aims and methods of 'cultural ecology' are expounded in Steward, *Theory of culture change*.

way, by the natural habitat. Secondly, it can scarcely be denied that Steward's approach is distinctly ahistorical.

But it should be observed that according to Martin the older determinism of Ratzel and Semple was discredited 'not because its principles were disputed, but empirically, because its examples were disputed'.[12] The comparative studies conducted by Steward and his followers were, on the other hand, based on the far more detailed and reliable empirical evidence collected in the course of intensive anthropological fieldwork. Moreover, although Steward's approach was deliberately ahistorical, it directed attention to a number of functional relations between environmental conditions and forms of economic and social organization which historians are now finding increasingly relevant to their own work.[13]

However, while Ratzel and his disciples had displayed a certain interest in the ways in which especially mountain populations managed to keep their numbers in balance with their resources, cultural-ecological models are conspicious because of the virtual absence of demographic variables. This may at first sight appear surprising, but is a logical consequence of the fact that cultural ecologists were (and are) essentially concerned with those aspects of social structure and organization that are most closely related to subsistence activities. Such a focus on subsistence patterns and their social-organizational correlates has discouraged a serious exploration of those sectors of social structure which are related not so much to production strategies as to the preservation of a balance between population and resources.

Things have changed dramatically since the 1960s because of the growing popularity which the concept of ecosystem has enjoyed among ecological anthropologists. The term 'ecosystem', initially introduced in the literature on general ecology,[14] designates a biotic community of interrelated organisms together with their common habitat. Two attributes of this concept have proved particularly attractive to anthropologists and other social scientists. The first one is the emphasis it lays on the web of material exchanges and interdependences among the group of organisms which form the community and the relevant physical features of the setting in which they are found. The second one is that ecosystems in a steady state possess a property of self-regulation which is closely reminiscent of homeostasis in living organisms, of feedback principles in cybernetics and of

---

[12] A. F. Martin, 'The necessity for determinism', p. 8.
[13] Cf. Ehmer and Mitterauer, 'Einführung', pp. 10–11.
[14] On the historical development of the notion of ecosystem, see Golley, 'Origins of the ecosystem concept'.

the functioning of servomechanisms in systems engineering.[15] The adoption of an ecosystemic approach has led anthropologists, human geographers and archaelogists to a new formulation of ecological problems. On the one hand, as Roy Ellen has noticed, the description of ecological interactions has become more sophisticated, involving computations of carrying capacity and estimates of energy intake, output and efficiency for different groups and activities. On the other, anthropologists especially have developed an interest 'in the way in which cultural institutions might serve to regulate certain systems of which human populations are part'.[16] These problems have been explored through functional analyses designed to specify empirical ranges of tolerance limits within which stability is maintained and to describe the operation of the homeostatic mechanisms which enable a system to preserve an equilibrium state, or to revert to it after a temporary disturbance.[17]

The point to be stressed is that in anthropology the adoption of an ecosystemic approach has entailed a shift in the focus of research from a concern with the relations between environmental features and modes of subsistence to the analysis of the relations between population and resources. In particular, the proponents of this approach (which is commonly known as 'neo-functionalism', to distinguish it from earlier forms of anthropological functionalism) have borrowed from biological models of the ecosystem the notion that the successful local population is one which adjusts its numbers in such a way as to maintain local resource stability. The study of population regulation has therefore acquired a crucial importance, and in the past twenty years a large number of anthropological investigations have tried to determine whether social practices ranging from marriage and infanticide to ritual and warfare could be related to the end of maintaining population equilibrium.[18] Yet 'it is paradoxical', as Emilio Moran has recently remarked, 'that ecological anthropological studies have only rarely explored the changing population variable over time given the importance of demographics in population ecology'.[19]

This paradoxical situation is largely explained by the fact that most

---

15 Cf. Stoddard, 'Organism and ecosystem', pp. 524–8, and Ellen, *Environment, subsistence and system*, pp. 180–1. Indeed, in the jargon of ecosystemic analysis the terms 'regulatory mechanism', 'feedback mechanism', 'homeostatic mechanism' and 'servomechanism' are often used synonymously.
16 Ellen, 'Ecology', p. 219.
17 Cf. Collins, 'Functional analyses'.
18 For a critical discussion of these studies, see Bates and Lees, 'The myth of population regulation'.
19 Moran, 'Ecosystems research', p. 17.

ecological anthropologists, like their colleagues in other sectors of anthropology, have mainly relied on ethnographic data collected during their fieldwork. This is best shown by the work which has had the greatest impact on the development of an ecosystemic approach in anthropology, namely Roy Rappaport's study of the Tsembaga people of New Guinea. The demographic data used by Rappaport to test his set of hypotheses only refer to the period covered by his fieldwork (which extended from October 1962 to December 1963) and on a few rough estimates covering the previous fifty years.[20] Admittedly, the notion of ecosystem has been very popular also in archaeological anthropology. But for archaeologists it has mainly proved a useful conceptual device which has encouraged them to think in terms of systemic interrelationships. As a concrete unit of analysis, however, the ecosystem has had little role in archaeological research, not least because knowledge of prehistoric populations can be at best circumstantial.[21]

Yet, it is increasingly being recognized that in anthropology ecosystemic models are bound to remain mere 'explanatory sketches'[22] unless population dynamics are studied in the long term. Therefore, the efforts of ecological anthropologists are now concentrated on the development of a 'processual' approach capable of overcoming what Benjamin Orlove has called 'the split between the excessively short and long time scales'.[23] There is, in particular, a growing consensus that hypotheses concerning ecosystemic regulation should ideally be tested over periods of two or three centuries and that in order to do so it is necessary to borrow the conceptual and methodological tools of historical demography.[24]

It is worth noting that, although ecological anthropologists are only now starting to borrow methods and techniques from historical demography, the two disciplines already share a number of major theoretical concerns. An important strand in contemporary historical demography is characterized by a strong interest in the behaviour of demographic systems when population size approaches or exceeds environmental carrying capacity. The question of homeostatic regula-

---

[20] Rappaport, *Pigs for the ancestors*, pp. 14–15, 116.
[21] Cf. Jochim, 'The ecosystem concept in archaeology'.
[22] This term has been used by philosophers of science like C. Hempel and P. Collins to characterize models which are formally valid and specify the relevant laws and initial conditions, but need quantification in order to turn into full-fledged explanations. See Collins, 'Functional analyses', pp. 275–6.
[23] Orlove, 'Ecological anthropology', p. 245.
[24] Cf. Adams and Kasakoff, 'Ecosystems over time', and Moran, 'Ecosystems research', pp. 16–19.

tion has received considerable attention, and an ecological and quasi-cybernetic approach very similar to that of the anthropologists has been used.[25]

It is of course true that, when historical demographers discuss the relationships between population and environment, they often refer to the economic rather than to the physical environment. Also, their interest in homeostatic regulation has its roots not so much in the biological models of the ecosystem as in Malthus's notion of marriage as a preventive check.[26] But it should not be forgotten that Malthus himself was convinced that a decisive test for his theory would come from the study of the relationships between population and resources in extreme physical environments and predicted that, 'since there is no land so little capable of providing for an increasing population as mountainous pastures', it is in the uplands that 'the necessity of the preventive check should prevail to a greater degree'.[27] Indeed, Malthus devised (as we shall see in Chapter 2) a model of demographic and ecological regulation in mountain environments which is strikingly similar to the ecosystemic models proposed by anthropologists. Thus, the terrain seems to be ready for closer collaboration and exchange between historical demographers and the anthropologists engaged in the study of mountain societies. But demographic history requires that the relevant documents survive to be analyzed, and this is not always the case in upland areas.

It is interesting to note, in this respect, that in his *Essay* Malthus remarked that in Tibet 'religious retirement is frequent, and the number of monasteries and nunneries is considerable', and among

[25] The term 'homeostatic regime' is used in demography to denote 'the existence of a system of relationships between the fertility characteristics of a community and its socio-economic circumstances such as any movement away from an initial position of equilibrium tends to provoke changes elsewhere in the system which restore the original state'. Wrigley, 'Homeostatic regime', p. 97. Studies testing and discussing the hypothesis that demographic regimes in the past were homeostatically regulated include Ohlin, 'Growth in pre-industrial populations'; Dupâquier, 'De l'animal à l'homme'; Schofield, 'Demographic structure and environment'; Scott Smith, 'A homeostatic demographic regime'; Lesthaeghe, 'Social control'; and Wrigley and Schofield, *Population history of England*, pp. 454–84. A comprehensive survey of the historical-demographic and anthropological literature on population regulation is provided by Coleman, 'Population regulation'.

[26] It should be noticed, however, that leading historical demographers like E. A. Wrigley and J. Dupâquier have been strongly influenced (like Rappaport and others in anthropology) by the theory of 'group selection' proposed in 1962 by the zoologist V. C. Wynne-Edwards, who has argued that it is highly advantageous for survival (and thus strongly favoured by selection) for animal species to control their population densities and to keep them as near as possible to the optimum level for each habitat they occupy. See Wynne-Edwards, *Animal dispersion*, pp. 8–9.

[27] Malthus, *Summary view*, pp. 213–14.

the laity 'all brothers of a family without any restriction of age or of numbers, associate their fortunes with one female, who is chosen by the eldest'. It seemed evident to Malthus that 'this custom, combined with the celibacy of such a numerous body of ecclesiastics, must operate in the most powerful manner as a preventive check to population'.[28] The survey of the ethnographic literature carried out by Pedro Carrasco in 1959 confirmed that a pattern of polyandry combined with monasticism and with a custom of impartible inheritance had been reported for most parts of Tibet. But the documentation he could use in his survey was, unfortunately, only qualitative. How frequently this ideal pattern was attained in practice remained, he stressed, an open question.[29]

Very interesting quantitative evidence has now been provided by the American anthropologist Melvyn Goldstein and his associates, who have established that in the Tibetan and Himalayan villages they have studied in the 1970s polyandry was actually the dominant form of marriage. This resulted in a very high proportion of women never marrying. Moreover, age at first marriage for women was also strikingly late by Asian standards. Thus, although marital fertility was rather high, overall fertility was low.[30] These findings are of considerable interest for at least two reasons. In a very influential essay published in 1965, John Hajnal demonstrated that for at least two centuries up to 1940 north-western Europe had been characterized by late age at marriage for both sexes and by a high proportion of people never marrying, and argued that this pattern was radically different from any other pattern found elsewhere in the world.[31] The data collected by Goldstein reveal, on the contrary, that a pattern of late and infrequent marriage can also be found in the high mountains of Asia. At the same time, these data challenge the view that the low oxygen level ('hypoxia') is the main cause of reduced fertility at high altitude.[32] What they suggest is that the low birth rates displayed by the populations studied by Goldstein are not caused by hypoxia-induced low fecundity, but are the product of socio-cultural factors leading to low nuptiality and therefore affecting the exposure of females to intercourse.

These findings have encouraged Goldstein to contend that the traditional social organization of Tibet and other parts of the Himalayas

[28] Malthus, *Essay on population*, p. 123.
[29] Carrasco, *Land and polity in Tibet*, pp. 28–77, 212.
[30] Cf. Goldstein, 'Fraternal polyandry and fertility', and 'New perspectives on Tibetan fertility'; and Goldstein *et al.*, 'High altitude hypoxia'.
[31] Hajnal, 'European marriage patterns'.
[32] Cf. Abelson, 'Altitude and fertility'.

(and in particular those institutions which, like polyandry, lead to low nuptiality) should be seen as a set of adaptations to a physical environment whose inelasticity severely restricts the potential for increased energy production.[33] This argument, however, and the related one according to which Himalayan populations were traditionally part of a homeostatic system regulated by low nuptiality and impartible inheritance, are unfortunately very difficult to test and prove. As Goldstein himself has emphasized, there is no demographic evidence on traditional Tibet, and the same is apparently true of the rest of the Himalayas as well as of the Andes.[34]

The case is different for European mountain areas such as the Pyrenees or the Alps. Although the evidence is still far from being fully exploited, a considerable amount of historical-demographic sources are known to exist. What is more, there is probably no better place than the Alps to test the hypothesis that nuptiality functioned as a decisive homeostatic mechanism. As Map 1 shows, the Alps are a mosaic of ethnic and linguistic groups ranging from Provençal speakers in the western sector of the crescent to Slavonic people in the easternmost ranges. Thus, the Alps represent a natural and cultural boundary between civilizations – between transalpine Europe, where Hajnal's 'European marriage pattern' was dominant, and the Mediterranean and Slavonic worlds, where different and distinctive marriage and family patterns are held to have obtained.[35]

Only a few years ago, broad comparative investigations of these topics would have been impossible. In 1975 Paul Guichonnet had to acknowledge that the historical demography of the Alps was still in its infancy – a statement echoed by Hanspeter Ruesch in 1979 and by Jean-François Bergier in 1980.[36] As to anthropology, some interesting studies had already been completed, but they hardly contained any quantitative evidence. In the last few years, however, the situation has changed considerably. A fair amount of data concerning the post-1850 period are now available in the demographic, anthropological

---

[33] Goldstein, 'Social matrix of Tibetan populations'.

[34] Goldstein, 'New perspectives on Tibetan fertility', p. 722. Interesting attempts have been made to assess whether pre-hispanic Andean populations were kept in balance with their resources by a set of 'preventive checks' including celibacy and late marriage. However, existing information on possible pre-Columbian checks on Andean populations is scanty and often contradictory. Cf. Rabell and Assadourian, 'Self-regulating mechanisms', and Cook, *Demographic collapse*, pp. 24–7.

[35] On demographic structures and cultural regions of Europe see Hajnal, 'European marriage patterns', and 'Two kinds of household formation'; Macfarlane, 'Demographic structures'; and Laslett, 'Family and household as work group', pp. 516–35.

[36] Guichonnet, 'Développement démographique', p. 143; Ruesch, 'Die Demographie der Alpen', p. 178; Bergier, 'Le cycle médiéval', p. 166.

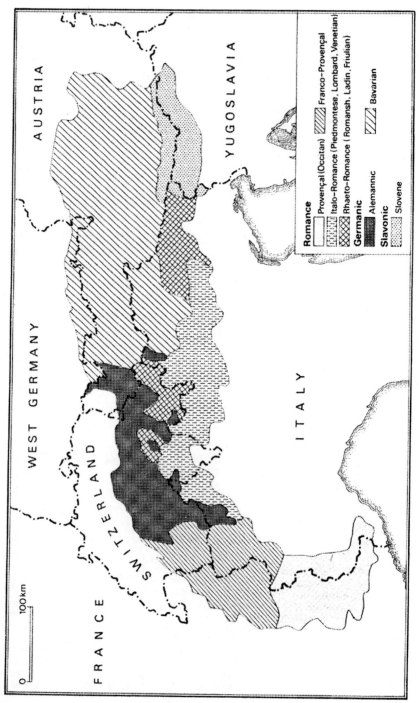

Map 1 Main linguistic groups in the Alps

Romance
☐ Provençal (Occitan)   ▨ Franco-Provençal
▨ Italo-Romance (Piedmontese, Lombard, Venetian)
▨ Rhaeto-Romance (Romansh, Ladin, Friulian)
Germanic
▨ Alemannic   ▨ Bavarian
Slavonic
▨ Slovene

100 km

and geographical literature, while historical-demographic research is increasingly shedding light on the more distant past. But it should be stressed that 1850 appears not only to be a chronological divide but also to mark a boundary between disciplines – a boundary which makes communication difficult and hinders the creation and the use of a common theoretical framework.

There is, however, one outstanding exception – namely the work of Robert Netting, which has indeed been saluted in anthropological circles as the best example so far of the kind of 'processual' approach mentioned above. Netting has provided a very competent ethnography of Törbel, a German-speaking village in the upper part of Canton Valais, in the Swiss Alps. But at the same time he has been one of the first anthropologists to realize that, if ecological models are not to remain 'distressingly hypothetical', it is necessary to go to the archives and to reconstruct the demographic history of the population living in the ecosystem under study. He has therefore engaged in a full demographic study based on the time consuming but highly rewarding method of family reconstitution.[37]

Although Netting's work is exemplary both theoretically and methodologically, it would obviously be unwarranted to accept and generalize all the conclusions he draws from his study. We may wonder, in particular, whether and to what extent Törbel can be taken as representative of Alpine communities (or, indeed, of all mountain communities). When Netting selected this village for his research, he certainly believed that it was quite representative.[38] In fact, Törbel tallied well with the canonical image of the upland community to be found in the then growing anthropological literature on the Alps. However, when I started my own anthropological fieldwork in Alagna, a village in the Piedmontese Alps,[39] I rapidly discovered that it hardly conformed with the received anthropological wisdom about Alpine communities, and certainly departed in many significant respects from the image of Törbel which emerges from Netting's studies.

This is all the more surprising if we consider that the two localities are very close both geographically and ethnically. Located at the top of the Sesia Valley, Alagna is one of the German-speaking communities (usually designated by the term *Walser*) which occupy the high valleys at the foot of the southern face of Monte Rosa. The foundations

---

[37] The results of Netting's research on Törbel (which started with a fourteen-month period of intensive fieldwork in 1970–1) are embodied in his book *Balancing on an alp. Ecological change and continuity in a Swiss mountain community*, published in 1981.

[38] Netting, 'Alpine village as ecosystem', p. 227.

[39] My field research in Alagna was conducted between April 1979 and September 1981.

of the Walser settlements date back to the second half of the thirteenth century, when these areas, like many other high valleys in a geographical range stretching from Savoy to Vorarlberg and Tyrol, were colonized by Alemannic settlers coming from the Upper Valais.[40] To be sure, when I did my fieldwork the village population was no longer ethnically homogeneous, the descendants of the original settlers having been joined by a large number of Italians. The German dialect was a dying language spoken only by some 80 elderly people out of a population of about 450. But a few decades earlier Alagna still shared with Törbel not only the same language but also the same material culture and the same legal tradition. The inheritance system, for instance, was very similar, being characterized by complete partibility and by the absence of dowry. Yet it was apparent that Alagna's demographic and economic history had been very different from that of Törbel.

Netting presents 'traditional' Törbel as a community closely approaching economic self-sufficiency, in which emigration was moderate and immigration virtually unheard of. By contrast, what first struck me in Alagna was the enormous importance of migration – emigration, in particular, both seasonal and permanent, but also immigration. This was in itself sufficient to make Alagna a more 'open' community than Törbel and to cast doubts on the image of the closed and isolated mountain community provided by the literature.

But there was another sense in which Alagna soon proved far more 'open' than I had expected. Students of mountain societies have commonly placed a heavy emphasis not only on the geographical and economic isolation of upland communities but also on the cultural consequences of this isolation. 'Mountain regions,' Semple had written in 1911, 'discourage the budding of genius because they are areas of isolation, confinement, remote from the great currents of men and ideas.'[41] And most anthropologists who have worked in the Alps, though arguing that the culture of mountain people possessed a dignity of its own, have not challenged the view that the mountains were backward. In fact, one of the main reasons why anthropologists have been attracted by the study of the Alps is that they assumed that this mountainous range located at the heart of Europe was a reliquary of old customs providing unique opportunities for glimpsing the social past of humankind and for investigating the transition from traditional to modernized society.

[40] The historical, linguistic and ethnological literature on the Walser is very large. An impressive survey is provided by Zinsli, *Walser Volkstum*.
[41] Semple, *Influences of geographical environment*, p. 20.

My perception of the question was radically modified when I realized that Alagna (contrary to Semple's assumption that artists could hardly be the product of uplands and mountains) had given birth not only to one of the most famous painters of the Italian *Seicento*, but also to a surprisingly large number of less well-known and yet competent painters and sculptors. I was particularly struck when, in the first period of my fieldwork, I came across a begrimed self-portrait of one of these painters, lying abandoned in what used to be a nice wooden house but had now been turned into a barn where a descendant of the painter kept his cows. That astonishing contrast between a dignified past and the shabby present strengthened my feeling that the interpretation of the historical evolution of mountain areas had probably been severely affected by insidiously anachronistic attitudes. It can scarcely be denied that mountain areas are socially, culturally and economically marginal – *now*. But what about the past? Moreover, it is unfair and incorrect to compare the mountains with the plains, when what is meant by 'the plains' is actually a sophisticated urban environment. Clearly, comparison should be made with *rural* areas. Indeed, if we consider that Alpine emigration was largely oriented towards the cities in the plains, it might be argued that mountain emigrants were more likely to come in contact with the 'great currents of men and ideas' mentioned by Semple than the plain dwellers living in the countryside.

It would of course be absurd to claim that findings from a single village can 'falsify' or turn upside down the dominant image of the Alpine community. Nevertheless, the discrepancy between what I had originally expected and what I actually found in Alagna was striking. This has been the stimulus to the comparative study whose results are reported in this book. I originally intended to conduct a detailed comparison between Alagna and Törbel, but the scope of the study has gradually broadened to encompass the whole of the Alpine area. It should be stressed, however, that the book makes no attempt at providing either a narrative or a systematic analysis covering all aspects of Alpine ethnography and demographic history. Rather, it concentrates on a set of related issues in order to reassess the models of the upland community proposed mainly by anthropologists and to test a number of theoretical propositions concerning the ways in which mountain populations achieved a viable balance with their resources.

These two aims are in fact connected to one another. Take, for instance, emigration. The dominant view still holds that emigration was essentially a 'safety valve'. The underlying model is that fertility was high and that the ceiling of resources was easily reached owing to the marginality of mountain agriculture. Upland societies are therefore believed to have been especially vulnerable to Malthusian positive checks unless they managed to get rid of the surplus population. The picture is one of localities stricken by poverty and constantly on the verge of mortality crises, where emigration was only caused by 'push' factors. My anthropological data on Alagna suggested, on the contrary, that emigration in this village owed more to pull than to push forces. This may not have been true of all Alpine emigrants, but comparative evidence from other localities suggests that in this respect Alagna was not exceptional either. Such a finding is a spur to reconsider the notion of the *poverty* of mountain areas and to reassess the *quality* of Alpine emigration. Moreover, the emphasis placed on the regulatory functions of marriage by writers as different as Malthus and Netting challenges the conventional view of mountain ecosystems being chiefly regulated by permanent emigration. This leads to the problem, so to speak, of the *quantity* of mountain emigration – and more generally to a full reconsideration of Alpine demography in historical perspective.

The structure of the book reflects rather closely the progression of my research, which started with a prolonged period of anthropological fieldwork in Alagna, went through a spell of intensive analysis of local demographic series extending back to the late sixteenth century, and finally ended up with a comparative analysis of a large body of empirical material supplied by studies of upland regions and communities in the French, Italian, Swiss and Austrian Alps.

The first two chapters introduce and discuss the models and theories which the book will try to test. Although I also present historical and geographical models as well as Malthus's own model, emphasis is mainly placed on the development of ecological models in anthropology and on the set of predictions they provide.

The aim of the next three chapters is twofold. They try, first of all, to give the reader an idea of the ethnographic conditions in which anthropological models have originated and have been tested. But at the same time they also attempt to use the evidence accumulated by anthropological, demographic and geographical studies to examine the demographic and economic evolution of the Alps since 1850, in order to provide at least some answers to the questions raised in the Introduction and in the first two chapters. But although both Chapter 4 and Chapter 5 document the spectacular changes occurring after the Second World War, they also show that the extent and direction of change are less easy to assess than is usually believed and that interpretations of recent changes in terms of 'modernization' theory can distort our perception of the Alpine past. As the final paragraphs of Chapter 5 suggest, it is therefore necessary to proceed to a straightforward historical investigation, which is what the second half of the book tries to provide.

The starting point of this investigation is the study of migration, which reveals the importance not only of emigration (whose nature and causes are reassessed in Chapter 6) but also of immigration (Chapter 7). A general discussion of the relations between population and resources in a long-term perspective is the theme of Chapter 8. The demographic evidence reviewed in this chapter indicates that the dominant notions about the demography of the Alpine *ancien régime* must be profoundly revised. Although this evidence lends some support to the view that nuptiality was an important and in some cases even decisive homeostatic mechanism, it also shows that other regulatory mechanisms could be at work. One such mechanism was emigration. But it is argued that the notion of permanent emigration as a safety valve is simplistic and obscures the importance of the effects of emigration on fertility. Another finding is that nuptiality varied both over time and from one region to another. This shows that some of the assumptions held by most anthropologists are untenable and vindicates the importance of cross-Alpine comparison.

Two regional comparisons are of special interest: the one between the French and the Italian sides of the Western Alps and the one between the Swiss and the Austrian Alps. These two cases are a stimulus to discuss, in the last two chapters, the importance of a few major social-structural variables. In Chapter 9, attention is focussed on the study of the domestic domain and an attempt is made to establish whether household forms are more decisively shaped by cultural or by environmental factors, and also to explore the possible effects of household forms on nuptiality and fertility behaviour. Chapter 10, which is mainly concerned with the Swiss and Austrian Alps, considers the influence of inheritance rules and communal structures on social stratification and its demographic correlates, and goes back to the fundamental problem of the legitimacy of conceptualizing Alpine communities as closed (eco)systems.

1

Environment, population and social structure: the Alpine village as an ecosystem

Universals in mountain habitats

When Lucien Febvre wrote, in 1922, that 'il n'y a point une sorte d'unité de la montagne',[1] he was reacting against those followers of Ratzel who stressed the similarities found in the social and economic life of upland populations in order to demonstrate that analogous geographical conditions always entail analogous developments. If too strong an emphasis is placed on general similarities, he rightly argued, the various mountain areas are inevitably stripped of their distinctive history. Yet neither Febvre nor Vidal de la Blache, the forerunner of geographical possibilism, would deny that in the mountains the impact of the natural environment on human populations is most dramatic and direct, especially in the high valleys.[2] Nor would they dispute that mountain habitats are universally characterized by a certain number of major physical and climatic features.

The outstanding feature of any mountain habitat is of course altitude, which powerfully affects such climatic factors as air pressure and composition, insolation, winds, evaporation, humidity, precipitation, and above all temperature. It is well known that with the rise from the sea level into the upper regions of the atmosphere the temperature decreases. It was been calculated, for instance, that on the northern side of the Swiss Alps the mean annual temperature drops from about 8.5° C at 500 m of altitude to 5.4° C at 1,100 m and to 0.3° C at 2,000 m.[3] As a result, mountain areas typically offer, within a few thousand feet, a vertical (altitudinal) duplication of the otherwise hori-

---

[1] Febvre, *La terre et l'évolution humaine*, p. 240.
[2] See Vidal de la Blache, 'Les genres de vie', p. 209, and Febvre, *La terre et l'évolution humaine*, p. 237.
[3] Veyret, *Les Alpes*, p. 39.

zontal (latitudinal) succession of climatic belts and vegetation zones. Indeed, as Roderick Peattie noticed, 'travelers among mountains delight in telling how their climb began amidst a splendor of tropical foliage. Then in succession they went from the evergreen broad-leafed zone to that of the deciduous trees, to the evergreen conifers, to an arctic heath, and so to eternal snow.'[4]

Although such patterns of 'vertical biotic zonation' are particularly complex and spectacular in equatorial mountains like the Paramo Andes, where they may stretch from tropical forest to snow cap,[5] they are highly impressive also in mid-latitude ranges like the Alps or the Himalayas. Thus, in the Alpine area it is usual to distinguish (on the basis of their characteristic vegetation) at least five successive climatic belts: a colline zone reaching the upper limit of the vine culture, which can vary from about 500 m to over 1,000 m on sheltered slopes favourably exposed to the sun; a montane zone and a sub-Alpine zone extending up to the limits of the deciduous and coniferous woods (800–1,700 m and 1,600–2,400 m respectively); an Alpine zone including the whole space between the uppermost limit of trees and the first appearance of permanent snow; and, finally, the snow and glacial zone, the region of heath and cryptogams.[6]

However, a simple distinction of major vegetation zones fails to convey the complexity of the environmental differentiation of the Alpine valleys. Two crucial points need to be stressed. It is essential to note, first of all, that any valley displays a *dual* pattern of vertical zonation. A cross-sectional succession of vegetation belts ranged in tiers up the slope from stream to crest can be observed on both sides of the valley. But a similar, if less rapid, succession can also be observed longitudinally – from mouth to head – on the valley floor, where settlements and arable land are usually located. Therefore, villages and fields in the same valley are subject to different climatic conditions. On average, in the villages placed near the mouth of the valley (at an altitude of perhaps 500 or 600 m) the awakening of the vegetation occurs towards the middle of March and a permanent cloak of snow will not settle down until the middle of December. In the villages placed at the head of the valley, on the other hand, snow often settles in early November to last for six or seven months.[7]

This accounts for a number of all important contrasts between high

[4] Peattie, *Mountain geography*, p. 79.
[5] Troll, *Die tropischen Gebirge*, pp. 45–9; Cuatrecasas, 'Paramo vegetation'.
[6] Veyret, 'Natural conditions', pp. 37–9.
[7] Peattie, *Mountain geography*, pp. 79–85.

valleys and low valleys. For one thing, high valleys have very long winters and a sometimes spasmodic concentration of agricultural activities in a much shorter growing season. Secondly, high valleys and low valleys display marked differences in the timing of harvest. It can be estimated, for instance, that at an altitude of 500–600 m winter wheat will be ripe by the middle of July, whereas in high-altitude fields (1,300–600 m) it will be harvested approximately one month later. Thirdly, the inhabitants of the high valleys can grow only those varieties of grains which, like rye or barley, are highly tolerant of cold. Moreover, they have no access to such fruits as chestnuts, which are seldom found over 1,200 m of elevation and have been for centuries a fundamental article of diet in many Alpine low valleys.

The other crucial point to be stressed is that altitude and its associated climatic factors are not the only determinants of vegetation. In fact, local (or, as environmental scientists say, 'edaphic') factors can prove almost as decisive. As a prominent feature of mountain topography is its ruggedness, some slopes are far more exposed to winds and sunlight than others; and especially in mid-latitude ranges, where the growing season is confined to the short summer period, exposure to sunlight is of paramount importance. This is perhaps best demonstrated by the striking contrast between the sunny and the shady sides of alpine valleys, which are conventionally designated by geographers as *adret* and *ubac*, the two terms used by the populations of the French Alps. The shady side, or *ubac*, is usually rocky, steep and densely forested, whereas the sunny slope, or *adret*, is gentler and much more fertile. As a consequence, Alpine populations have almost invariably selected the *adret* both for agricultural activities and for settlement.[8]

The macroscopic contrast between *ubac* and *adret* is, however, replicated infinite times on a smaller scale. In the Alps it is very common for beds of snow to give way in a few minutes' walk to sunny slopes covered with brilliant vegetation. If we add that soil characteristics are exceedingly variable and that areas exposed to air currents tend to receive a greater amount of rainfall, it becomes evident that in the Alps, and more generally in the mountains, edaphic factors are responsible for a multitude of interlocking micro-climates producing a variety of vegetational arrangements. Peattie was therefore not exaggerating when he observed that, although altitude gives a rough idea of vegetation and cultivation limits, nevertheless each field in moun-

---

[8] Burns, 'The Circum-Alpine area', p. 132; Peattie, *Mountain geography*, pp. 88–93, 184–91. The two terms *adret* and *ubac* derive from Latin *ad rectum* and *ad opacum*.

tainous terrain has its distinctive climatic and pedological characteristics.[9]

Mixed production strategies

In his recent critical appraisal of the subject, David Guillet has convincingly argued that the soundest and most fruitful starting-point for the ecological study of upland societies is still offered by the fundamental question of the extent to which what he calls 'production strategies' are constrained by environmental forces.[10] In mountain environments, as we have just noticed, agricultural activities are decisively constrained by the climatic effects of altitude; and the influence of edaphic factors, which determine a highly irregular biotic distribution, is also significant. In addition, it should be stressed that in mountain areas productive land is not only marginal but also scarce. It may be estimated, for example, that of the space lying between the summits of the Alps and the low country at least one-quarter is utterly barren, consisting of snow fields, glaciers, bare rocks, lakes and the beds of streams. Since roughly one-half is occupied by forests and high-altitude pastures, there remains only about one-quarter available for cultivation, divided between vineyards, fields and meadows. Needless to say, the balance worsens with altitude. In the Alps most high-valley communities occupy a territory of which less than 10 per cent is suitable for cultivation. Though critically important, the products of the crop fields located in the vicinity of the villages are thus hardly sufficient.

However, the steep gradient of the land makes it possible for mountain people to exploit several vegetation zones at different altitudes, and in particular the large expanses of grassland (botanically grading from steppe to tundra) which ring the valleys between the tree line and the glaciers. As is the case in most marginal areas, pastoralism provides the only way of making this non-cultivable land accessible to productive activities because of the animals' ability to convert the natural plant growth into nutritive products. Pastoralism is therefore most effective in complementing agriculture in mountain environments, and especially in the Alps and the Himalayas the dominant pattern of exploitation has indeed been, until very recently, a

---

[9] Peattie, *Mountain geography*, p. 85. For a recent discussion of the limitations of the notion of 'vertical zonation', see Thouret, 'Pour une perspective géographique de l'étagement'.

[10] Guillet, 'Cultural ecology of mountains', p. 563.

combination of cultivation and herding variously labelled as agro-pastoralism, mixed mountain farming or *Alpwirtschaft*.

Although the viability of a mountain farm requires access to a rather wide range of resources, the core of Alpine agro-pastoral systems is represented by two spatially segregated spheres of production: the fields and meadows near the village, which provide crops for food and hay for the winter stabling of animals, and the high-altitude pastures, which during the summer offer grazing for cattle, sheep and goats. These summer pastures are known throughout the Alpine crescent as 'alps': *alpages* in French, *alpi* or *alpeggi* in Italian, *Alpen* in German. It is important to stress that this term of pre-Roman origins (which has given the Alps their name) designates not simply the pasture but also the huts and stalls which are occupied for some three months a year by herders and animals. And it is also interesting to notice that it is extremely unusual for cattle and herders to move directly from the village to the alp and spend the whole grazing season there. Animals are generally first transferred to granges placed in the higher meadows, which are used for grazing in combination with haying and perhaps some agriculture. After a couple of weeks the cattle will be moved to the lower alps, where they will be fed for a period of two to four weeks, and then to the upper alps, where they will be pastured until the first snowfalls of early September. When cold weather begins to threaten the highlands, the herders descend to the lower alps, then to the granges, and finally to the villages.

This ladder sequence from the village to the granges and then to the lower and upper alps is fairly typical, but the ascent to summer pastures may be even more gradual. In some parts of the French Alps there is a separate set of huts for almost every week of the summer.[11] The presence of this chain of buildings placed at short intervals along the path leading to the alps is a tangible demonstration of the efforts made by the local populations to take maximum advantage of the various vegetation belts. It also nicely shows the extent to which the structure and seasonal rhythm of mountain pastoralism is shaped by altitude. But in the agricultural sphere, too, the role of 'verticality' is of the utmost importance, for a gradual up-slope progression also characterizes the reaping of grain in the fields and the ripening of hay in the meadows. Netting has reported that in Törbel observant farmers could distinguish a difference in relative plant growth with every twenty metres of altitude. This means that

---

[11] Peattie, *Mountain geography*, p. 135.

scattered land parcels located at slightly different altitudes are best suited to schedule the work load evenly and efficiently over the whole growing season, whereas 'if a family's land were concentrated in one zone, the highly labor-intensive cutting, raking, drying, and transport of the hay would come all at once, with a long slack interval before the next haymaking'.[12]

As a matter of fact, patterns of scattered tiny plots are a very typical feature of mountain agriculture. This system of highly fragmented landholding has been severely criticized by agricultural economists on several counts. It has been argued, in particular, that the dispersion of plots is the cause of inordinately high transportation costs, while their small size inhibits the use of machinery.[13] The realization that land parcels scattered at different altitudes favour the optimization of household labour suggests that economists may have been too harsh. Moreover, it should not be forgotten that mountain farming is an extreme example of marginal agriculture and that the probabilities of crop failure are consequently much higher than in the lowlands.[14] No less significantly, because of the ruggedness of mountainous terrains even adjacent fields may greatly differ in terms of fertility, moisture retention, accessibility, gradient of slope and exposure to sunlight. Most anthropologists and mountain geographers are therefore in agreement that at least in the past fragmentation represented a 'rational' and nicely adaptive response to the environmental imperatives of mountain habitats, for it allowed access to varied crops and minimized the risk of total failure by utilizing different microclimates.[15]

Environment and social organization

Comparative research has ascertained that mixed production strategies combining agriculture and stock-raising overwhelmingly prevail (or prevailed) all over the Alps as well as in the Himalayas and in the Andes.[16] This is an important but hardly unexpected finding, for it stands to reason that in mountain areas and other marginal

---

[12] Netting, *Balancing on an alp*, p. 19.

[13] For a useful discussion of these criticisms, see Loup, *Pasteurs et agriculteurs valaisans*, pp. 123–45.

[14] The probability of harvest failure has been found to increase exponentially with falling summer warmth and with elevation. See Parry, 'Secular climatic change', pp. 4–5.

[15] Burns, 'The Circum-Alpine area', p. 137; Friedl, 'Benefits of fragmentation'; Rhoades and Thompson, 'Adaptive strategies', p. 539; Netting, *Balancing on an alp*, pp. 18–21.

[16] Rhoades and Thompson, 'Adaptive strategies', pp. 536–9; Guillet, 'Cultural ecology of mountains'.

regions (where arable land is in short supply and crops yield fewer calories than cattle) recourse to pastoralism is scarcely avoidable. But anthropologists and human geographers steeped in Steward's tradition have also been impressed by a number of intriguing and less obvious similarities in some crucial institutions of mountain societies, and have advanced the argument that the necessity of co-ordinating agricultural and pastoral activities finds expression in analogous patterns of social organization.

Students of mountain farming broadly agree that the main reason why mixed production strategies are adopted is that no single vegetation zone seems to possess the necessary potential to support a human population for any length of time. Moreover, as we have just seen, exploiting only one vertical production zone would be an inefficient use of household labour, whereas 'a mixed, multicyclical production strategy optimizes labor use'.[17] Mixed strategies, on the other hand, clearly involve conflicting demands on household time and labour. As Lajos Vincze has remarked, 'synchronizing agricultural and pastoral work and dividing family labor accordingly poses serious problems, particularly when the two kinds of tasks coincide. Diverting manpower to one sphere of activity may lead to shortages in the other.'[18] If we consider that in the mountains the crop fields and the summer pastures are usually separated by considerable distances, we can easily see why the allocation of labour becomes so problematical during the summer, when labour is in greatest demand in both the agricultural and the pastoral sectors.

It is also relevant to note that in mountain areas the optimal ratio of herders to cattle can be as high as 1:30–40, and that the number of sheep which can be managed by a single shepherd is even higher.[19] In the Alps, however, the number of animals possessed by the average household was far smaller. Particularly in the Western sector of the crescent, the family herd typically included two or three cows, a couple of heifers, some sheep and a few goats. What is more, in the summer it was advantageous to split up the tiny family herds on the basis of the different grazing requirements of the various species and categories of animals. Milch cows were pastured in richer grasslands than heifers, whereas sheep and goats were moved to higher-altitude alps and browsed on the barren pastures near the snowline. Thus, although the importance of animals was critical, the small size of the

[17] Guillet, 'Cultural ecology of mountains', p. 565.
[18] Vincze, 'Peasant animal husbandry', p. 393.
[19] Vincze, 'Peasant animal husbandry', pp. 393–4.

family herd hardly warranted shifting one or more members of the household from agricultural work to herding.

In principle, the most efficient way of solving the problem consists in pooling animals and grazing resources and having the livestock cared for by an optimal number of herders. Forms of communal herding, either by rotation of owners or by specialized personnel hired jointly by them, are in fact very common in the Alps and in other mountain areas. By tending the cattle and taking charge of the processing of dairy products, some ten to fifteen individuals can relieve all the village households of many time-consuming chores. This, in turn, makes it possible for the rest of the working population to concentrate on the agricultural tasks. It is hardly surprising that anthropologists have regarded communal herding as a decisive answer to the thorny scheduling and integration problems posed by mountain agro-pastoralism and have emphasized the rationality and adaptive advantages of this practice.[20]

Releasing manpower for agricultural tasks and alleviating the problems which arise from the spatial disjunction of fields and alps are the two most evident advantages of communal herding. But geographers and anthropologists have pointed out several other reasons why alps should ordinarily be operated as a unit. There is little doubt that both the pastures and their accessories (huts and stalls, enclosures, etc.) are better and more economically cared for through communal management. In particular, the paths leading to the alps require construction and maintenance, an undertaking which calls for corporate efforts. It has also been suggested that, since the cattle enter the lower alp while the upper reaches still lie under snow, it is impossible or exceedingly difficult to parcel out land to individual households. Finally, only collective bodies such as village communities or alp syndicates may be able to mobilize the manpower needed to look after the water supply flowing from the alps.[21]

To sum up the argument so far, mountain geographers and cultural anthropologists essentially agree that mountain habitats impose mixed production strategies, but are also aware that agro-pastoralism (unlike specialized strategies such as pure pastoralism or intensive agriculture) has to face scheduling and integration problems which cannot find a solution within the household. They suggest, therefore, that

[20] Vincze, 'Peasant animal husbandry', pp. 396–7; Netting, *Balancing on an alp*, pp. 64–5.
[21] Peattie, *Mountain geography*, pp. 130–1; Rhoades and Thompson, 'Adaptive strategies', p. 540; Vincze, 'Peasant animal husbandry', p. 397; Guillet, 'Cultural ecology of mountains', p. 564.

'mixed strategies necessarily involve a suprahousehold sphere'.[22] More specifically, it is believed that 'the small garden plots and hay meadows are perhaps more efficiently exploited by individual households, while the requirements of successful pasturing of the village animals necessitate a coordinated effort'.[23]

This conclusion leads to a further step in the argument. If communal undertakings are to be properly accomplished, it is contended, then the dominant system of landholding must be expected to be compatible with such undertakings. In other words, different sets of tenure rights should be expected to prevail in different production zones. This argument is by no means new,[24] but has now received strong support from the findings of anthropological studies recently conducted in a number of Andean, Himalayan and Alpine communities. In all these villages communal tenure is reported to have been associated with high-altitude zones where grazing and gathering (for instance, in the form of firewood collecting) were done. By contrast, fields, meadows and other resources lying in lower-altitude production zones were subject to individual tenure.[25] To be sure, cases of localities where alps were privately owned and individually managed are known. But these cases have generally been dismissed as exceptions of little significance.[26] There is, indeed, little doubt that most anthropologists and many a geographer would subscribe to Peattie's statement that 'individual ownership of alps runs counter to the geographical set-up of the valley economy. The common ownership seems to have been decreed by nature.'[27]

After arguing that in mountain areas the natural environment not only constrains production strategies but also acts as a powerful force in moulding ownership patterns, the proponents of the cultural-ecological model take a final and bolder step. They claim that the economic and organizational requirements of mountain agro-pastoralism explain the evolution of a distinctive set of social and political institutions exhibiting the principles of consensual decision making and delegation of authority.[28]

Anthropologists have directed attention to the virtual ubiquity, crucial importance and formal structural similarities of village assemblies and councils of household heads in all mountain areas of the world.

[22] Guillet, 'Cultural ecology of mountains', p. 566.
[23] Rhoades and Thompson, 'Adaptive strategies', p. 540.
[24] It had already been advanced by Semple, *Influences of geographic environment*, pp. 575–6.
[25] Brush, 'Introduction', p. 130.
[26] See e.g. Netting, 'What Alpine peasants have in common', p. 141.
[27] Peattie, *Mountain geography*, p. 134.
[28] Burns, 'The Circum-Alpine area', pp. 146–7; Rhoades and Thompson, 'Adaptive strategies', p. 541; Guillet, 'Cultural ecology of mountains', p. 564.

To quote Guillet, 'the assembly provides a forum for face-to-face discussion and consensual decision making concerning a number of
issues including the scheduling of agricultural tasks, the construction
and maintenance of technological inputs, the delineation of ecologically sound production rules'.[29] They have also stressed that a considerable amount of power is conferred on local officials, whose task
is to compel the observance of the measures taken by the assembly
and counteract any individual attempt at reckless exploitation. It has
indeed been argued that the control exerted by the village officials
must be 'necessarily as demanding and restrictive as the harsh mountain environment itself',[30] for unless the number of cows on an alp
is strictly limited, overgrazing and destructive soil erosion will inevitably result. Also, the year's food supply of the whole community
may be put in jeopardy if the dates set for the departure and arrival
of the village animals are violated.[31]

Predictably enough, given the delicate balance of resources and
the high degree of interdependence between the households in the
community, corporate bodies also supervise land transfers. Indeed,
the community may maintain so strict a control over land use and
rights that lowland notions of 'private ownership' may prove misleading in the mountains. Land use tends to be reserved to the members
of the village community, and sale of land to outsiders is usually
discouraged or forbidden.[32] As the American anthropologist Robert
Burns has noted, the effect of these restrictions is to limit membership
and establish a relatively closed social frontier about the local group,
thus 'insulating it from abrupt or indiscriminate influences from the
outside, and thereby tending to stabilize it'.[33] The similarities between
these forms of social organization (which are seen as adaptations to
the mountain environment) and Eric Wolf's concept of the 'closed
corporate community'[34] are obvious and have been explicitly stressed
by several anthropologists.[35]

---

[29] Guillet, 'Cultural ecology of mountains', p. 564.
[30] Rhoades and Thompson, 'Adaptive strategies', p. 541.
[31] Peattie, *Mountain geography*, p. 133; Rhoades and Thompson, 'Adaptive strategies', p. 541.
[32] Burns, 'The Circum-Alpine area', pp. 145–6; Rhoades and Thompson, 'Adaptive strategies', p. 540.   [33] Burns, 'The Circum-Alpine area', p. 145.
[34] The notion of 'closed corporate community' was first proposed by Wolf in the mid-1950s. See Wolf, 'Types of Latin American peasantry', and 'Closed corporate communities'. This notion is discussed in detail in Chapter 10 below.
[35] See especially Burns, 'The Circum-Alpine area', pp. 144–8; Rhoades and Thompson, 'Adaptive strategies', p. 548; and more recently Sibilla, *I luoghi della memoria*, pp. 39–45. Cf. also Netting, 'What Alpine peasants have in common', pp. 136–7.

The village as an ecosystem

In the Alps one set of communal regulations is especially worth noting, namely the norms governing access to the summer pastures. As we have seen in the previous section, the exploitation of the alps was reserved for the members of the community, and the number of cows that could be fed on the summer pastures was often restricted in order to prevent overgrazing. But innumerable corporation statutes throughout the Alpine crescent also contained a clause prohibiting a cattle owner to 'carry' more animals on the pastures than he could winter. This is a clause of the utmost interest and several writers have recently emphasized its importance.[36] Its practical and theoretical implications, however, are not immediately apparent and can be properly appreciated only in the context of a fuller discussion of what human geographers mean by *Alpwirtschaft*.

We owe a clear formulation of this concept to the Swedish geographer John Frödin, who established it in the literature in 1940.[37] Like his predecessors, Frödin uses the term *Alpwirtschaft* to indicate a single economic, social and spatial system basically consisting of two kinds of productive soil (arable land and pasture) and their two corresponding kinds of settlement (the main village and the alp). But he draws a much sharper distinction between *Alpwirtschaft* and other exploitation systems such as settled agriculture, nomadism and transhumance, its distinctive feature being that during the winter the animals have to be fed in byres. The crucial implication is that hay becomes, in Frödin's theoretical framework, the link between the agricultural and the pastoral sectors and, in the last analysis, the element upon which the whole productive system is pivoted. On the one hand, it is on hay production (or, to put it differently, on the amount of meadowland possessed by the cattle owners) that the number of animals pastured on the alps ultimately depends. But hay also sets limits, on the other hand, to the amount of land which can be put under plough, for parcels that make good ploughland also make the best meadows. As Cole and Wolf have remarked, 'the peasant must therefore balance his requirements for crops against those for hay and divide his best lands accordingly'.[38]

In Frödin's elegant formulation, *Alpwirtschaft* can be conceived of

---

[36] Netting, *Balancing on an alp*, p. 61; Benetti *et al.*, *Uomini delle Alpi*, p. 144; C. Pfister, *Das Klima der Schweiz*, vol. 2, p. 51.

[37] Frödin, *Zentraleuropas Alpwirtschaft*, vol. 1, pp. xiv–xxi; cf. also de Planhol, 'Pression démographique', p. 534.

[38] Cole and Wolf, *The hidden frontier*, p. 123.

as a closed equilibrium system, whose empirical boundaries tend to coincide with the political and administrative boundaries of the village community. Although perfect equilibrium and complete closure cannot be expected in the real world, nevertheless the corporate regulations which are regarded to be typical of upland communal organization must have resulted, if properly observed, in forms of agro-pastoral exploitation closely approaching Frödin's ideal type. It is evident that the maintenance of the delicate balance between agriculture and pastoralism which is at the core of the model crucially depended on norms preventing the cattle owners from pasturing on the alps more animals than they could winter. Also, we have noticed that the members of village communities and similar corporate bodies enjoyed, like the Tsembaga people studied by Rappaport, 'common and almost exclusive access' to the resources of the territory they inhabited, and defended it against encroachment from outside.[39] It would therefore seem that the populations of mountain communities actively sought to keep local productive systems in a state of equilibrium and to reach a considerable degree of economic and demographic closure. This encourages the adoption of the notion of 'ecosystem' and, more specifically, invites the anthropologist to conceptualize the Alpine village as an ecosystem.[40]

As we have seen, since the mid-1960s, anthropologists have been increasingly attracted by the usefulness of the concept of ecosystem in focussing attention on patterns of functional interdependences between human populations, social institutions and natural environment. Its application to human ecology presents, however, serious difficulties. For analytical purposes any ecosystem must be closed.[41] But most ecosystems involving humans do not have clear-cut boundaries, and the drawing of them may become quite arbitrary. Nevertheless, anthropologists have found it expedient to consider the territory of a local group as an ecosystem, one important reason being that this enables them to apply an ecosystemic approach to 'units of sufficiently small size to permit convenient quantitative analysis'.[42]

Methodologically, this tendency for the ecosystem to be pragmatically identified with the anthropologist's traditional unit of analysis – a community of manageable size, usually a village – is probably more defensible in the Alps (and other mountain areas) than in most

---

[39] Cf. Rappaport, *Pigs for the ancestors*, p. 21.
[40] See Netting, 'Alpine village as ecosystem'.
[41] A useful discussion of the problem of ecosystemic closure is provided by Ellen, *Environment, subsistence and system*, pp. 177–203.
[42] Rappaport, *Pigs for the ancestors*, p. 227.

parts of the world. Indeed, Netting has explicitly argued that Alpine communities, particularly in Switzerland, offer 'several distinct advantages for the study of processes in ecological change and adjustment', because they are clearly bounded both geographically and politically.[43] Also, there is no doubt that from a theoretical point of view the adoption of the concept of ecosystem in Alpine anthropology marks an advance in two important respects. The first general advantage is that an ecosystemic approach provides models which describe the behaviour of complex systems, whereas cultural-ecological models only stress simple correlation and causality. A second advantage is that while cultural-ecological models tend to pay little attention to demographic variables, in the context of an ecosystemic analysis the role of population dynamics cannot be overlooked.

As we have noticed in the Introduction, a striking feature of even the most recent cultural-ecological models of upland social organization is the virtually complete absence of demographic variables. Cultural ecologists are, of course, deeply concerned with the broad patterns of population growth which are associated with long-term processes of expansion of resources and intensification of production.[44] But very few attempts have been made to investigate the demographic dynamics of population growth. Moreover, the emphasis is placed exclusively on expansion and intensification at the expense of a third major ecological strategy – regulation – which is, by contrast, a subject of crucial significance for anthropologists adopting an ecosystemic approach.

Netting has rightly observed that particularly in mountain areas, where the possibility of substantially expanding the agro-pastoral resources is severely limited and production cannot be intensified beyond a certain point, it rapidly becomes imperative for a community to devote major efforts to the regulation of the local ecosystem. As a consequence, the attention of Alpine anthropologists working within an ecosystemic framework is primarily directed towards the 'social servomechanisms' which are required to keep the village population in equilibrium with its environment: limiting immigration, encouraging emigration, delaying and restricting marriage in order to control fertility.[45]

Migration, nuptiality and fertility are demographic phenomena. But

---

[43] Netting, 'Of men and meadows', p. 132.
[44] These concerns are at the core of Burns's pioneering study of upland communities in the French Alpine region of Dauphiné. See especially Burns, 'Écological basis'.
[45] Netting, 'Of men and meadows', pp. 139–41; Friedl and Ellis, 'Celibacy, late marriage and potential mates', pp. 23–5.

their relationships with social-structural factors are obviously very close and have been explored by a large number of anthropological studies. These studies allow a set of predictions. Thus, it has been suggested that immigration of outsiders will be most effectively prevented when a village approaches the structural type which anthropologists call 'closed corporate community'.[46] As to emigration and nuptiality, it is something of an anthropological axiom that they decisively depend on the working of inheritance systems. As Jack Goody has contended, 'a different quality of relationships, varying family structures, and alternate social arrangements (e.g. greater or less migration, age of marriage, rates of illegitimacy) will be linked to differing modes of transmission'.[47] More specifically, systems of strict impartibility are expected to lead to low nuptiality, high migration and low population growth, whereas strict partibility should result, at the opposite end of the spectrum, in high nuptiality, low migration and rapid population growth.[48]

The study of inheritance has long been central to the anthropologist's analysis of social structure, mainly because of the importance of transmission rules in shaping the patterns of relations among kin. In ecological perspective, this traditional anthropological issue is supplemented by other questions, in particular by the problems of assessing the degree of adaptivity of the various systems of inheritance and their differential ability to work as homeostatic mechanisms. As far as Alpine research is concerned, two related but distinct predictions can be formulated. Spatially, impartible inheritance should be expected to prevail in mountainous regions and other marginal areas.[49] Over time, both kinds of inheritance system should be expected to react to changes in the balance between population and resources and to constrain nuptiality accordingly.[50]

The first of these predictions is easier to test, given the availability of a certain number of ethnographic reports. In the early 1970s, the hypothesis that impartibility fits better than partibility with the requirements of mountain ecosystems has indeed received some support from a statistical analysis of the comparative evidence which was

[46] See Burns, 'The Circum-Alpine area', pp. 145–6, and especially Netting, *Balancing on an alp*, pp. 76–82.
[47] Goody, 'Introduction', p. 1.
[48] Berkner and Mendels, 'Inheritance systems'; Brennan *et al.*, 'Inheritance, demographic structure, and marriage'.
[49] Wolf, *Peasants*, p. 75.
[50] Cole and Wolf, *The hidden frontier*, p. 151. Cf. Zubrow, 'Demographic anthropology', pp. 12–13.

then available.[51] But recent evidence shows that the question is more complex than it was previously believed, and still far from being settled. Difficulties in testing the second prediction (which is of crucial significance to any homeostatic model) are even greater, for that requires the ability to follow ecological and demographic processes over long periods of time. As Netting has rightly intimated, if ecological models are not to remain 'distressingly hypothetical', it is necessary to go to the archives and reconstruct the demographic history of the population living in the ecosystem under study.[52]

Indeed, this is what Netting himself has done in his study of Törbel, which has set an exciting paradigm for ecological investigations of Alpine villages. But in addition to providing a pioneering example of anthropological fieldwork combined with historical-demographic research, Netting's work has other merits. He has shown, for one thing, the usefulness of incorporating the more valuable contributions of cultural ecology into an ecosystemic approach. The model of the relations between population, environment and social structure outlined in this chapter is greatly indebted to the analytical framework proposed by Netting. Moreover, he has formulated in a clear and testable form a number of important hypotheses concerning the demographic correlates of agricultural intensification, the homeostatic functions of marriage and inheritance patterns, the functional relations between agro-pastoral economy and household structure, the demographic properties of the closed corporate community. These hypotheses constitute the core of the set of questions which this book will try to tackle by comparing the case of Törbel with that of Alagna and, whenever possible, with evidence from other Alpine localities. Before turning to this comparative ethnographic and historical inquiry, however, it is necessary to consider more critically some aspects of the models developed by ecological anthropologists and to examine a few significant similarities and differences between these models and those put forward by other students of upland society.

---

[51] Goldschmidt and Kunkel, 'The structure of the peasant family', p. 1065.
[52] Netting, *Balancing on an alp*, p. xii.

2

Open systems, open questions

Closed systems, homeostasis and history

A major feature of the ecological model of the upland community presented in Chapter 1 is that the sequence of arguments which has been outlined parallels the main stages in the development of ecological anthropology, from Steward's 'cultural ecology' to Rappaport's 'neo-functionalism' and the more recent 'processual' approach. This does not mean of course, that the development of ecological anthropology has consisted in a smooth accumulation of information and insights. As Benjamin Orlove has rightly stressed, 'each stage is a reaction to the previous one rather than merely an addition to it'. Nevertheless, each stage has been less a radical break from the previously dominant approach than an intellectual outgrowth of it.[1] This explains why, instead of repudiating Steward's legacy, a number of anthropologists adopting an ecosystemic approach have tried to build upon the achievements of cultural ecology. In the field of Alpine studies, this is most clearly demonstrated by Netting's work, which mainly focusses on regulation but incorporates the Stewardian concerns with irrigation systems and intensification strategies. It also shares with the explicitly cultural-ecological models proposed by Burns and by later writers a set of assumptions and claims about the adaptivity of communal forms of social organization and the crucial structural importance of closed corporate communities in mountain areas.

Admittedly, comparative work of the kind in which anthropologists like Rhoades and Thompson or Guillet have engaged inevitably presents considerable methodological problems. As Roy Ellen has observed, the larger the scale, the greater the number of variables

[1] Orlove, 'Ecological anthropology', pp. 235–7.

that may be involved in a single correlation.[2] When the units of investigation are the whole Alpine, Himalayan or Andean regions, testing causal hypotheses about the relations between environment and social organization becomes an arduous task. This is indeed the reason why anthropologists using an ecosystemic approach, whose aim is to validate hypotheses about the operation of selected variables through the use of extensive quantitative data, have adopted smaller units of analysis. Yet it would be a pity to reject on *a priori* grounds the idea that important, if broad, correlations may exist between major environmental variables on the one hand and distinctive social and economic arrangements on the other. On the whole, it seems fair to acknowledge that cultural ecologists' efforts to identify cross-cultural regularities have been successful in demonstrating that a number of such correlations are clearly detectable in the Alps and in the other mountain areas.

However, it must also be recognized that not all the arguments proposed by cultural ecologists are equally convincing. For instance, the claim that in upland areas the control exerted by communal bodies must be 'necessarily as demanding and restrictive as the harsh mountain environment itself',[3] appears to be rather suspicious. For one thing, the contrast which some anthropologists have established between the wisdom and rationality of communal bodies and the individual's proneness to 'wrong calculations' and 'reckless exploitation' of resources is highly questionable. Moreover, the assumption that the consensual decisions of communal councils are always 'ecologically sound'[4] implicitly subscribes to the romantic view (more or less consciously held by many anthropologists) that *Naturvölker* are so harmoniously integrated into their environment that it is unbelievable that they might damage it at all.[5]

These weaknesses cast some doubts on the more general arguments which have been offered to explain the presence of similar forms of communal organization in mountain ranges as distant from one another as the Alps, the Himalayas and the Andes. As we have noticed, cultural ecologists regard these communal forms as the product of processes of social evolution which are specific to mountain environments. Critics of cultural-ecological models have objected that this explanation cannot be accepted, because institutions like the assembly of household heads (or, indeed, the close corporate com-

[2] Ellen, *Environment, subsistence and system*, p. 5.
[3] Rhoades and Thompson, 'Adaptive strategies', p. 541.
[4] Guillet, 'Cultural ecology of mountains', p. 564.
[5] Cf. Ellen, *Environment, subsistence and system*, p. 39.

munity) are not restricted to mountain areas.[6] But criticisms of this kind are bound to leave the proponents of these models unscathed. Their position (as made clear by Rhoades and Thompson) is that the arguments advanced to explain the evolution of parallel social institutions in mountain environments 'obviously contribute nothing to the understanding of similar institutions in other environments', for these 'must result from a completely different set of causal factors'.[7]

This statement is symptomatic not only of cultural ecologists' environmental determinism but also of their avowedly ahistorical stance. Though not denying the importance of the environment, a less deterministically oriented anthropologist like Gérald Berthoud has suggested that 'the relationship between man and habitat in mountainous areas does not produce particular institutions, but results rather in an adaptation and a combination of general institutional elements which fit the natural environment'. It is indeed Berthoud's contention that the 'traditional' mode of production found in the Alps was not determined by the imperatives of mountain environment, but was the outcome of a particular dissolution of the feudal mode of production. Therefore, the unity of the Alpine area 'should not be defined *per se*, but rather by the specificity of its *historical process*'.[8]

Though framed in Marxist terms, Berthoud's argument brings us back to Febvre's point that too strong an emphasis placed on regularities found in mountain areas all over the world – or, for that matter, in all regions of the Alps – fatally obscures the distinctiveness of different lines of cultural and historical development.[9] In the preceding chapter we have noticed that the work of Steward and of his followers displays a deep concern with patterns of long-term social evolution. But the ultimate aim of cultural ecology remains the construction of 'cross-cultural types' consisting in regularities which are observed to recur several times 'in historical independence of one another'.[10] Rather than focussing on the outcome of the interaction between the environmental constraints typical of mountain areas and institutional arrangements common to the adjacent lowlands, the models proposed by cultural ecologists posit a dichotomy between similarities due to environmental causes and similarities due to historical diffusion. As

---

[6] Cf. Guksch, 'Comment to Guillet', p. 568.

[7] Rhoades and Thompson, 'Adaptive strategies', p. 548.

[8] Berthoud, 'Dynamics of ownership', pp. 119–20.

[9] This point is also made by Netting, *Balancing on an alp*, p. 57, who quotes approvingly Febvre's 'possibilist' contention that there can be no sort of mountain unity which would always be found wherever on the earth mountainous elevations exist. Cf. Chapter 1 above, p. 16.

[10] Steward, *Theory of culture change*, p. 89.

a consequence, these models tend to be not only general but also static – timeless constellations of cultural traits.

To be sure, similar criticisms can be levelled against the models favoured by neo-functionalist anthropologists. As we have seen in the Introduction, these models emphasize equilibrium, and it is almost axiomatic (as Netting has remarked) that 'equilibria annihilate history'.[11] However, if equilibrium models are simply used to provide 'a framework within which we can formulate propositions about the interdependence of elements', as Max Gluckman has suggested, they may still prove valuable in the study of change.[12] Even more significantly, it should be noticed that the concept of homeostasis, though close to that of equilibrium, implies somewhat greater variability and dynamism. Indeed, Vayda and McCay have denounced 'a tendency among some anthropologists to confuse homeostasis with concepts of static equilibria and unchanging systems', and have argued that the aim of ecological anthropology should be that of 'abandoning an equilibrium centered view and asking instead about change in relation to homeostasis'.[13] While neo-functionalist models expected regulatory mechanisms to function only to restore the original state and to maintain population at static levels, works published in the last few years are far more interested in studying the behaviour of these mechanisms in situations of population growth and in ascertaining their ability to assure a viable adjustment of population to changes in the environment.[14]

A different criticism of the models proposed by anthropologists adopting an ecosystemic approach concerns the closure of ecosystems and the identification of the local ecosystem with the village community. It is interesting to notice that the problem had already been seen in 1955 by Robert Redfield, who suggested that the concept of ecosystem is best applied to primitive communities which are 'closely dependent upon the land and the seasons. ... But as communities become more complex and more interdependent with other and distant communities it is less possible to use the concept of ecological system'.[15] Redfield's words were echoed some twenty years later

[11] Netting, *Balancing on an alp*, p. xiv.
[12] Gluckman, 'The utility of the equilibrium model', p. 221.
[13] Vayda and McCay, 'New directions in ecology', pp. 229–302.
[14] Cf. Orlove, 'Ecological anthropology', p. 250. A major influence in directing the attention of both anthropologists and archaeologists to the relations between demographic change and agricultural intensification has been E. Boserup's contention that population growth may stimulate technological progress. See especially Boserup, *Conditions of agricultural growth*.
[15] Redfield, *The little community*, p. 29.

by John Cole and Eric Wolf in their influential study of a high Alpine valley. Like Redfield, they maintained that ecological anthropology had been 'most successful in the study of relatively isolated, primitive societies'. But Alpine communities are, according to Cole and Wolf, neither closed systems nor homeostatic machines. They are part of complex societies, and in complex societies 'larger, "external" forces often dominate and shape the forces at work in creating the local ecology'.[16]

This criticism, too, can be countered by a number of arguments. It may be objected, first of all, that in the mountains social and economic life tends to be constrained by the physical environment to an unusual degree. Although the Alpine villages studied by anthropologists cannot be regarded as 'primitive' communities, it is reasonable to argue that until recently their economies were probably more 'closely dependent upon the land and the seasons' (to use Redfield's phrase) than those of most peasant communities. Also, we have seen that there are considerable analytical advantages in using the concept of ecosystem, and this requires closure at some point. But it is undeniable that this is a criticism of considerable force, for there is little doubt that particularly in complex societies local human groups can scarcely be expected to be economically, politically and demographically self-contained. To this crucial question we shall go back in the final pages of this chapter. But it is important to stress here that Cole and Wolf's 'externalist' argument is far more than a challenge to the ecosystemic approach. It also calls in question the image of the closed, self-sufficient upland community which has long been dominant not only among anthropologists and students of Alpine folklore but also in the works of historians and geographers.

Historical time, geographical time

In the historical and geographical literature, the economic evolution of the Alps is conventionally subdivided into three phases. The first phase is generally termed 'the age of autarky', and is believed to have lasted until the middle of the nineteenth century. It was then followed by a phase of transition lasting from 1850 to the Second World War (mainly characterized by the improvement of communications) and, after the war, by years of rapid and radical transformation.[17] When

---

[16] Cole and Wolf, *The hidden frontier*, pp. 21, 284.

[17] Cf. e.g. Veyret, *Les Alpes*, and Guichonnet, 'Développement démographique'. Slightly different periodizations are proposed by Merli-Brandini, 'Movimenti migratori', pp. 223–7, and by Raffestin and Crivelli, 'L'industrie alpine'.

dealing with the period before the last war and, even more, with the 'autarkic' past, the prevailing tendency is to assume that Alpine communities were socially and economically closed and virtually self-sufficient. Yet, even those works which place most stress on the closure and relative immutability of Alpine communities often provide (sometimes almost inadvertently) evidence which suggests that in the past some portions of the population pursued activities which can scarcely be described as autarkic and that the Alpine economy may have undergone considerable changes over time.

Perhaps the best-known example is the range of activities related to the flow of long-distance traffic through the Alpine passes. For nearly a century, traffic has been the favourite theme in Alpine historiography. The main achievement of the long series of studies unaugurated in 1900 by Alois Schulte's painstaking work on commerce and traffic between western Germany and Italy has been the demonstration of the crucial importance of Alpine traffic in the economic history of Europe, particularly in the Middle Ages.[18] 'The Alpine societies,' Braudel has written, 'seem to have existed for the express purpose of organizing the crossing of the mountains and furthering the progress of this profitable traffic in both directions, north and south.'[19] But these studies have also shown that Alpine traffic critically depended on the availability of local labour. The evidence we possess on the organization of transport suggests, indeed, that the inhabitants of hundreds of Alpine villages probably lived off the wages they gained by working as carriers and muleteers.[20]

But in many cases the mountain people appear to have been themselves involved in substantial commercial transactions with the people of the plains. In his classic regional study of the French Alps, for instance, Arbos had already observed that during the Middle Ages it was common for upland populations to engage in active commerce of cattle and cheese.[21] More recently, and more systematically, Jean-François Bergier has argued that the medieval history of the Alps is best conceptualized as a cycle. According to Bergier, in the fourteenth century the Alps shifted from a situation of cultural and economic closure to a phase of openness which represented a commercial

---

[18] Schulte, *Geschichte des mittelalterlichen Handels*. For a recent general discussion, see Bergier, 'Le trafic à travers les Alpes'.

[19] Braudel, *The Mediterranean*, p. 206.

[20] Cf. Schulte, *Geschichte des mittelalterlichen Handels*, vol. 1, pp. 357–484. However, the economic and demographic importance of Alpine traffic for the local populations have been questioned recently by Caroni, 'Zur Bedeutung des Warentransportes', pp. 97–8.

[21] Arbos, *La vie pastorale*, pp. 165–8.

high point for the whole area. In the late fifteenth century, when traffic lost part of its importance and the recovery of agriculture in the plains made Alpine cattle less necessary and less valued, the Alps reverted to a situation of economic closure.[22]

On a smaller temporal and spatial scale, many other cyclical movements of this kind can be detected throughout Alpine history, all pointing to changes in the degree of market involvement, in the importance of a wage economy, and so forth. These findings are not easy to reconcile with the still prevailing image of the immobile, self-sufficient upland village. But to what extent do they really undermine this image? On the one hand, there seem to be good reasons to play down, or at least to question, their significance. It might be argued, for example, that those villages which were peripheral to the trade routes (and they were by far the majority) must have been only moderately affected by traffic. But there are equally good reasons, on the other hand, to suspect that the notion of closed autarkic communities should be dismissed altogether, as just another myth about the past.

Our ability to answer this question depends in part on the results of further empirical research. But it is difficult not to form the impression that the frequent inconsistencies and ambiguities to be found in the historical and geographical literature may be largely due to a confusion of historical levels. It seems useful, in this connection, to go back to the distinction first formulated by Braudel in his famous work on the Mediterranean world in the age of Philip II. The history of the Alps as it emerges from works such as Bergier's study of the medieval cycle is, to use Braudel's words, one of 'slow but perceptible rhythms'. Braudel, however, also recognized the existence of a history 'whose passage is almost imperceptible, that of man in his relationship to the environment'[23] – the existence, that is, of a 'geographical time' whose tempo is regulated by immutable environmental constraints which make the Alpine communities of the early twentieth century significantly similar in many respects to those of the sixteenth century, and perhaps to those of prehistoric times.

Although these two levels are to be kept analytically separate, history is of course the outcome of the interaction of the two sets of forces to which they correspond – ecological on the one hand, political and economic on the other. Interestingly, Braudel clearly believes that, as far as the mountains are concerned, environmental constraints tend to have the upper hand. As we have seen, he is aware of the importance of traffic and of its impact on many an Alpine community.

---

[22] Bergier, 'Le cycle médiéval'.   [23] Braudel, *The Mediterranean*, p. 20.

Nevertheless, in general he maintains that 'the mountains are forced to be self-sufficient for the essentials of life, to produce everything as best as they can, to cultivate vines, wheat, and olives even if the soil and the climate are unsuitable'.[24] Thus, mountain economies inexorably tend, for Braudel, towards autarky. But the local populations' efforts to achieve a viable equilibrium are seldom sufficient and they are doomed to be backward and poor. A corollary of this view is that mountain areas become rapidly overpopulated in relation to their resources and that periodically the overflow has to be sent down to the plains. Mountain poverty – or, as he graphically writes, 'la faim montagnarde' – is the great spur of this journey downwards.[25]

This chain of arguments linking scarce resources to overpopulation, poverty and emigration has been widely accepted by historians with an interest in the Alpine world, not least because of the enormous prestige of Braudel's name. The impression one receives from the geographical literature, however, is rather different. For one thing, it is apparent that there is no consensus about the volume and the role of permanent emigration before the middle of the nineteenth century. Moreover, the whole approach to the study of the relationship between population pressure and emigration adopted by many geographers rests on a notion of overpopulation which departs considerably from the one used by Braudel.

Overpopulation, autarky and emigration

The prevailing view of the demography of the Alpine *ancien régime* owes much to the works of some distinguished members of the Grenoble school of Alpine geography, in particular of Raoul Blanchard, Paul Veyret and Germaine Veyret-Verner. One point is especially worth noting, namely that the approach of these scholars to the problem of demographic balance in mountain areas largely relies (as Veyret-Verner emphasized in an important article of 1949) on the concept of 'population optimum', a term by which they mean the population size at which average output per head is maximized.[26]

As is well known, maximization can hardly be achieved when a population is so small that its members are not allowed to benefit from economies of scale. In mountain areas, a typical illustration of

---

[24] Braudel, *The Mediterranean*, p. 33.
[25] Braudel, *La Méditerranée*, p. 42.
[26] Veyret-Verner, 'Équilibre démographique'. On the notion of 'population optimum', see Sauvy, *General theory of population*, pp. 36–41. For a useful discussion of the notion of overpopulation in relation to optimum population theory, see also Grigg, *Population growth and agrarian change*, pp. 11–19.

this general principle (whose importance has been made painfully evident by the recent experience of massive depopulation) is the impossibility of performing a number of vital communal activities if the local population falls below a critical lower threshold.[27] When a population is small, therefore, each increase in population gives a greater average output per head. However, if growth continues beyond the point at which average output is at its maximum, then an area is to be regarded as overpopulated.

The point most vigorously stressed by the Grenoble geographers is that, although these principles obviously apply to the mountains as well as to any other geographical setting, in the mountains the question is further complicated by the fact that their economy is characterized by an extreme seasonal contrast. As we have seen, during the summer the heavy concentration of agricultural and pastoral activities poses acute problems of labour allocation and availability. The mountains tend to be 'relatively underpopulated'. During the winter, on the contrary, any kind of agricultural activity comes to a complete halt, and the mountains suddenly become grossly 'overpopulated'. In a sense, the whole labour force is surplus. In order to increase the average output, it is thus mandatory for at least a portion of the population to engage in non-agricultural activities, or in agricultural activities elsewhere.

This raises a first major question, namely whether these supplementary activities are compatible with the notion of autarky. The answer provided by the Grenoble geographers is, to quote Veyret, that 'il s'agissait bien d'autarcie, en ce sens que les montagnards, à cause de leur pauvreté et du manque de transports, devaient produire presque tout ce qu'ils utilisaient, les objects et les vêtements aussi bien que la nourriture'.[28] The presence of some form of domestic industry is therefore seen as perfectly compatible with an autarkic economy, indeed as an organic part of it. The crucial requirement is that industrial activities must be primarily intended for the satisfaction of local needs. It is interesting to note, in this respect, that particularly Blanchard was at great pains to demonstrate that not only the textile industry but also mining (the other major kind of non-agricultural work to be found in the Alps) fell in most cases within the limits of

[27] A concise ethnographic account is provided by Friedl, *Kippel*, p. 95. Cf. also Sauvy's discussion of the notion of 'population minimum', in which he states that the adverse effects of 'minimum' population can be observed most often in mountain villages or in isolated small valleys. Sauvy, *General theory of population*, pp. 32–3.

[28] Veyret, *Les Alpes*, p. 70. A similar view is expressed by Merli-Brandini, 'Movimenti migratori', pp. 223–4.

autarky.[29] The same is true of seasonal emigration, which is assumed to be both complementary and subordinate to agriculture and pastoralism. Alpine peasants might well turn into emigrants every winter, but only to resume agricultural work in their villages as soon as the cold season was over.

Along with the issue of autarky, the other crucial point to be clarified is what the geographers of the Grenoble school mean when they state that rural industry and seasonal emigration were the best ways of solving the problem of mountain overpopulation. In spite of frequent allusions to the poverty of the mountains, which can easily lead the hasty reader astray, it is quite clear that they do not necessarily mean that these supplementary activities were indispensable to the survival of populations whose numbers tended to exceed the available resources and would otherwise be destined to famine and extreme indigence. Rather, they mean that both domestic industry and seasonal emigration were suitable responses to the 'chômage hivernal', the forced unemployment imposed by the rigours of climate, and helped increase the average output per head and approach the optimum.[30]

The notion of demographic equilibrium proposed by Veyret-Verner is definitely less concerned with the balance between resources and population than with the peculiar seasonal characteristics of mountain economies. As such, it is essentially ahistorical. Its time (to use Bell's helpful distinction)[31] is cyclical, not linear. One implication is that in principle permanent emigration (or any other form of population decline) is to be regarded as disadvantageous, because it makes summer underpopulation worse. Population growth, on the other hand, is tendentially advantageous, for it increasingly alleviates summer underpopulation, which is the problem to which priority is given. Moreover, population growth may even lead to an expansion of agricultural resources and stimulate the intensification of agricultural productivity. For some time, at least, marginal returns will also increase. During the winter, of course, mountains will be more severely overpopulated. But, provided that seasonal emigration and domestic industry help reduce unemployment and expand the total amount of resources, the problem can be overcome.

---

[29] Blanchard, *Les Alpes Occidentales*, vol. 6.2, pp. 493–517.

[30] Veyret-Verner, 'Équilibre démographique', pp. 333–4; Veyret, *Les Alpes*, p. 80. The notion of seasonal emigration as an effect of winter unemployment rather than of poverty is also prominent in the works of several historians of Alpine emigration. Cf. e.g. Châtelain, *Les migrants temporaires en France*, pp. 15–17, and Bergier, 'Le cycle médiéval', p. 255.

[31] Cf. Bell, *Fate and honor*, pp. 34–66.

Considerations of this kind suggest that even in mountain areas resources are not fixed. Nevertheless, it is evident that there must be limits to both intensification and expansion. Beyond these limits lies what Grenoble geographers sometimes call 'absolute' overpopulation, as opposed to the 'relative' or 'seasonal' overpopulation of the winter months. The point at which absolute overpopulation begins can be variously defined. One limit is the optimum population point, beyond which average output per head starts decreasing. Another limit is the subsistence level, beyond which the total carrying capacity of an area is exceeded. Population growth beyond the optimum point is 'irrational' but nonetheless feasible.[32] By contrast, when the subsistence level is crossed, Malthusian checks are called in to restore the balance. Whatever definition we adopt, it is clear that once limits are reached some form of regulation becomes unavoidable.

If we assume that the population of an Alpine community is growing and its resources cannot be expanded any further, the only manner in which it can respond to the pressures of overpopulation consists in limiting its numbers. This can be achieved in more than one way, but students of the Alps have mostly paid attention only to permanent emigration, which is invariably described as the vital 'safety valve' allowing Alpine populations to escape the rigours of Malthusian positive checks. Impressed with Braudel's incisive characterization of mountains as 'factories' producing migrant labour for other people's usage ('fabriques d'hommes à l'usage d'autrui'),[33] many historians and geographers have indeed taken for granted that massive permanent emigration must have been an endemic features of Alpine demography, thereby also accepting the notion that in the Alps the number of births tended to exceed the number of deaths by a large margin.

However, some leading authorities in the field have expressed diverging views. In spite of some similarities, the demographic model underlying Braudel's discussion of overpopulation and emigration in mountain areas is significantly different from the model proposed in 1975 by Paul Guichonnet. Like Braudel, Guichonnet believes that fertility was high. Crude birth rates, he suggests, were often higher than 30 per thousand and could exceed 40 per thousand. But while Braudel's model implies the existence of a high rate of natural increase, Guichonnet maintains that fertility was nearly offset by very high levels of both infant and adult mortality. As a consequence, natural

---

[32] C. Frödin, *Zentraleuropas Alpwitschaft*, p. 268.   [33] Braudel, *La Méditerranée*, p. 46.

increase was restriced and the size of permanent emigration relatively modest.[34] Indeed, according to Guichonnet one of the main features of Alpine demography in the 'age of autarky' is the lack of massive permanent emigration. Until 1850, he states, 'les abandons définitifs sont l'exception'.[35]

In this respect, Guichonnet's position is similar to that of Elizabeth Lichtenberger, one of Austria's most influential geographers. Reacting against what she regards as extreme and preconceived ideas about the Alpine world, she has argued that the Alps can hardly have constituted an important reservoir of people for urbanization or industrialization because their rate of natural increase has always been moderate. Like Guichonnet, she thinks that this is partly explained by the high level of infant mortality. But the main reason – and here she departs very significantly from Guichonnet's views – is that 'the average age at marriage has always been high, and the percentage of married people has remained low'. As a consequence, birth rates were comparatively low.[36] Lichtenberger suggests, in other words, that the Alps were characterized not by a 'high-pressure' but by a 'low-pressure' demographic regime hanging on low nuptiality. This may well reflect her greater familiarity with the rather distinctive social-structural and demographic features of the Eastern Alps. But it is remarkable that the system she outlines fits very closely with the model proposed, nearly two centuries ago, by Malthus.

Population and resources in mountain environments: Malthus's model

In the second and later editions of his *Essay on the principle of population*, Malthus discussed at length the case of Switzerland, whose distinctive demographic features, he reckoned, provided the clearest illustration of the general principles of his work. As he remarked, the available body of evidence suggested that in the last two centuries mortality had considerably improved throughout the country. This, however, had produced different effects in the various natural regions. 'Though the population ... in the flat parts of Switzerland has increased during the last century,' he wrote, 'there is reason to believe that it has been stationary in the mountainous parts.' For Malthus, the causes of such a difference were almost self-evident. In upland

---

[34] Guichonnet, 'Développement démographique', pp. 157–8.
[35] Guichonnet, 'Développement démographique', p. 161. The same view is expressed by Veyret, *Les Alpes*, pp. 80–3.
[36] Lichtenberger, *The Eastern Alps*, p. 7.

regions, he maintained, the limits to population growth were 'strikingly obvious'.[37]

It is relevant to note (particularly in the light of what has been said in the previous chapter about Frödin's notion of *Alpwirtschaft*) that Malthus stressed that in the mountainous districts of Switzerland the crucial requirement was 'to procure a sufficient quantity of fodder for the winter support of the cattle which have been fed on the mountains in the summer'. As 'the improvement of the lands in the valley must depend principally upon the manure arising from the stock, it is evident that the quantity of hay and the number of cattle will be mutually limited by each other; and as the population will of course be limited by the produce of the stock, it does not seem possible to increase it beyond a certain point, and that at no great distance'.[38] In these circumstances, the preventive checks of high celibacy rates and late marriage should be expected to prevail to an unusual extent, for the upland populations 'must adopt it or starve'.[39]

An excellent example of this mechanism at work was offered by the Alpine village of Leysin, in Canton Vaud, whose population appeared to be virtually unaffected by emigration and to rely entirely on the exploitation of agricultural and pastoral resources. An impressive feature of Leysin's demography around the middle of the eighteenth century was a probability of life which was, by contemporary standards, exceedingly high. But nuptiality and, consequently, fertility were also very low: 'the births were only about a forty ninth part of the population; and the number of persons above 16 was to the number below that age nearly as 3 to 1'.[40] No less interestingly, the average number of births had been for a period of thirty years 'almost accurately equal to the number of deaths'.[41] Fixed resources and improving mortality had apparently led to a decline of fertility and the population of Leysin had reached a stationary state, with crude birth and death rates in the region of 20 per thousand.

The case of this Swiss parish clearly does not conform with the picture suggested by Guichonnet. Leysin unmistakably displays a low-pressure demographic regime. In this connection, it is relevant to stress a point which, as Roger Schofield has rightly observed, is seldom made when the relationships between population and the environ-

---

[37] Malthus, *Essay on population*, p. 212. Malthus's chapter on Switzerland is largely based on the *Mémoire sur l'état de la population dans le pays de Vaud* published in 1766 by J. L. Muret. On Malthus and Muret, see now Behar, 'Malthus', p. 148–9.

[38] Malthus, *Essay on population*, p. 212.

[39] Malthus, *Essay on population*, p. 206.

[40] Malthus, *Essay on population*, p. 207.

[41] Malthus, *Essay on population*, p. 206.

ment are discussed – namely that, although a static (or slowly growing) population may result from both high-pressure and low-pressure regimes, the latter allow for a more favourable ecological balance. For one thing, replacement is more efficient, because the number of people who live for a short time consuming resources and then die without realizing their full potential for production is smaller. Secondly, as Malthus noticed for Leysin, the proportion of people under, say, sixteen years of age depends on fertility levels. As a consequence, late marrying populations with low fertility will have a more advantageous 'dependency ratio' of children to the working population.[42]

Another point of considerable theoretical interest is that Malthus regarded Leysin and more generally the Pays de Vaud and Switzerland as providing a striking demonstration of what he called 'the dependence of the births on the deaths'.[43] Once reached the ceiling of its resources, he reasoned, Leysin could only afford a fixed number of economic slots.

Under such circumstances, how would it be possible for the young men who had reached the age of puberty to leave their fathers' houses and marry till an employment as herdsman, dairyman, or something of the kind became vacant by death? And as, from the extreme healthiness of the people, this must happen very slowly, it is evident that the majority of them must wait during a great part of their youth in their bachelor state, or run the most obvious risk of starving themselves and their families.'[44]

Leysin is presented by Malthus as a system with a steady state, closed subsistence economy, where a social rule exists prescribing that in order to marry men must first achieve economic independence. Since marriage will only be possible when an economic position becomes vacant through death, in systems of this kind nuptiality and fertility will obviously depend on mortality, as Figure 2.1 shows.

It will be noted that declining mortality leads, on the one hand, to an increase in population size. But the lower the levels of mortality, the less economic slots are vacated and the lower the nuptiality. As Schofield has observed, 'demographically this is a very efficient system, because it works through an instantaneously adjusting mechanism, in which the age at marriage varies in response to fluctuations in mortality so that the population size is kept more or less constant'.[45]

---

42 Schofield, 'Demographic structure and environment', pp. 148–9.
43 Malthus, *Summary view*, p. 212.
44 Malthus, *Essay on population*, pp. 206–7.
45 Schofield, 'Demographic structure and environment', p. 152.

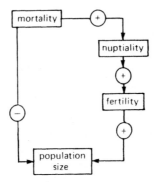

Figure 2.1 Malthus's 'closed system' model
Note: Adapted from Schofield, 'Demographic structure and environment',
p. 152

But Malthus also remarked that Leysin's 'extraordinary degree of healthiness could not *possibly* have taken place under the actual circumstances of the parish with respect to the means of subsistence, if it had not been accompanied by a proportionate action of the prudential restraint on marriage'.[46] In other words, mortality and nuptiality 'must constantly act and react upon each other'[47] if the right balance between resources and population is to be achieved and preserved and the scourge of 'positive checks' is to be avoided.

Malthus believed that his remarks on Leysin and the other upland parishes of the Pays de Vaud could safely be applied to all mountain villages where population was closed and the economy essentially agro-pastoral. Their main demographic features he expected to be low mortality and the absolute necessity of the preventive check. But he was also aware that the situation would be entirely different where these circumstances had been altered 'by a more than usual habit of emigration, or by the introduction of manufactures'.[48] In particular, Malthus dealt at some length with the effects of cottage industry, which had furnished 'a greater quantity of employment, and at the same time a greater quantity of exports for the purchase of corn'.[49] Reports from Swiss observers, and also some oral testimonies collected by Malthus during his trip to Switzerland, suggested that, where manufactures had been introduced in some substantial scale, the

---

[46] Malthus, *Summary view*, p. 214.   [47] Malthus, *Summary view*, p. 214.
[48] Malthus, *Essay on population*, p. 211.   [49] Malthus, *Essay on population*, p. 212.

increased opportunities of employment had led to a habit of early marriage and a considerable increase in population.

It is instructive to notice, in this respect, that in the model proposed by the Grenoble geographers the Alpine village constitutes a closed autarkic system even in the presence of domestic industry. There is, however, a marked difference between the nature and function of domestic industry as understood by the Grenoble geographers and the 'introduction of manufactures' described by Malthus. While Malthus is concerned with the effects of what we would now call 'proto-industrialization', the Grenoble geographers assume that domestic industry was subordinated to agro-pastoral activities and was simply a way of increasing the average output per head. Even seasonal emigration, as we have seen, is regarded by the Grenoble geographers to be compatible with their notion of autarky. In a Malthusian framework, by contrast, mountain villages seriously affected by cottage industry or emigration become *open* systems, both economically and demographically. Their demography, as suggested by Figure 2.2,

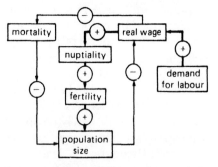

Figure 2.2 Malthus's 'open system' model
Note: Adapted from Schofield, 'Demographic structure and environment', p. 159

becomes dependent on exogenous factors, and local environmental constraints tend to lose any importance.

This suggests a few concluding considerations. Malthus's legacy to Alpine historical demography resides primarily in his prediction that mountain populations can be expected to reach a stationary state resting on a low-pressure demographic regime and in his elegant model of a closed homeostatic system with fixed resources. The similarities with the arguments put forward by Lichtenberger and with the models advanced by neo-functionalist anthropologists are striking.

But the similarity between the alternative Malthusian model illustrated by Figure 2.2 and the 'externalist' model proposed by Cole and Wolf is equally remarkable. Malthus, however, believed that different models were needed to investigate different kinds of upland community. Cole and Wolf, by contrast, seem to imply that since in complex societies local human groups can scarcely be expected to be economically, politically and demographically self-contained, then there can be no justification in conceptualizing Alpine communities as closed systems.

This is a serious and challenging criticism of the ecosystemic approach. Yet it would be dangerous to accept the objections raised by Cole and Wolf as a final demonstration that ecosystemic models cannot be legitimately or usefully applied to the study of the relationships between environment, population and social structure in the Alps. In human ecology, closure is inevitably a matter of degree, and it is only when closure is demonstrably weak that local ecosystems cease to be legitimate units of analysis and explanation. In fact, the validity of Cole and Wolf's 'externalist' model (like that of the competing ecosystemic model) is bound to remain undecided until its assumptions and predictions are properly tested. And to do so, it is necessary to determine empirically the degree of demographic and economic closure exhibited by local populations, their levels of fertility and mortality, and the extent to which nuptiality and migration acted as regulatory mechanisms.

As we have observed in the Introduction, until recently our knowledge of the economy and especially of the demography of Alpine communities in the past had not progressed very far since Malthus's days. In the last few years, however, the situation has improved very considerably. Although a great deal of research is still needed before the difficult questions raised in this chapter can receive a conclusive answer, we now dispose of a body of evidence which at least allows us to explore some of these questions and to test the various models which have been proposed. This is the aim of the remaining chapters of this book, and we shall start from a consideration of the changes which have occurred after the end of the 'age of autarky'. Chapter 4 will discuss the data on the changing social demography of Alpine communities which have been recently assembled by geographers, demographers and especially anthropologists, whose work has been largely concerned with the problem of change and continuity in marriage patterns and family forms. Chapter 5 will then tackle the question of ecosystemic closure by examining some crucial aspects of the traditional economy and of its recent transformations through an ethnographic comparison between Alagna, Törbel and other Alpine villages. But, in order to provide a context to these two chapters, it will be first necessary to discuss at greater length the reasons which have drawn anthropologists to the Alps and the conditions in which their ethnographic investigations have been conducted.

3

Anthropologists in the Alps

The Alps, 'a magnificent laboratory'

Although Alpine anthropology has established itself only in the last few decades, it had a distinguished forerunner. In the summer of 1912 Robert Hertz, one of Durkheim's most gifted pupils, was spending his holidays in Cogne, a village in the Aosta Valley. His six-week vacation, however, soon turned into a short but industrious period of fieldwork when he became aware of the existence of an old religious tradition whose sociological features immediately intrigued him: the festival of Saint Besse, the patron saint of Cogne and of the adjacent Soana Valley, which took place every year on 8 August in a remote corner high in the mountains, at over 2,000 m of altitude. During the summer, Hertz was able to observe the pilgrimage to the saint's shrine and to attend the festival itself. In addition, he collected from the people of Cogne the local variants of the legends surrounding the saint, which shed revealing light on the web of social relationships that linked the various communities which congregated at the festival. Back in Paris, this material was supplemented by historical, philological and iconographic research. The resulting article, published in 1913, may well be seen as the first anthropological contribution to the study of the Alps.[1]

This article clearly shows that Hertz regarded the Alps as an especially suitable terrain for the evolutionary study of society, and in particular of those 'elementary forms of religious life' which were at that time the central preoccupation of Durkheim and his school. The mountains, he maintained, are 'un merveilleux conservatoire ... dans les hautes vallées, des croyances et des gestes rituels se

---

[1] Hertz, 'Saint Besse'. For an evaluation of Hertz's work and its impact on the development of social anthropology, see Evans-Pritchard, 'Introduction'.

perpétuent depuis plusieurs millénaires, non point à l'état de survivances ou de "superstitions", mais sous la forme d'une véritable religion ... Le sociologue n'est pas ici moins favorisé que le zoologiste ou le botanique.'[2] In the late nineteenth century and up to the Second World War, this was a commonly held notion. In 1911 Ellen Semple had characterized the mountains as 'museums of social antiquities'. And twenty years later, in 1931, Adolf Helbok defined the Alps as 'the El Dorado of folklore studies', a reliquary of old customs, sayings and artifacts long disappeared in most other parts of Europe.[3]

This perception of the mountains as refuge areas for 'old habits, old costumes, old languages, old religions',[4] has obviously been greatly modified by the transformations which have followed the Second World War. When social anthropologists began to turn to the study of European peasantries, they found that the war had acted as a major catalyst of change and that important innovations were gaining a foothold in an ever-growing number of upland communities. Nevertheless, in his survey of the anthropological literature on Europe produced in the 1960s, Robert Anderson could still write that 'high in remote Alpine valleys, change comes more slowly than in villages on the plains. Peasant traditions hang on more persistently.'[5]

The survival of old traditions and habits was indeed the focus for some of the first anthropological studies of Alpine villages. It should be stressed, however, that the attitude of most anthropologists was rather different from that of the folklorists who had preceded them in the study of Alpine culture. The work of one of the pioneers of Alpine anthropology, John Honigmann, was largely concerned with the study and explanation of cultural survivals. But his aim was, in fact, to demonstrate the limitations of the 'geographic marginality' theory favoured by folklorists, and also of the economists' view that in the Alps modernization and economic rationalization were hampered by the conservatism of the local populations.[6]

An even greater difference separates previous studies of mountain folklore from the ecological approach which has marked Alpine anthropology since its very beginnings. The two articles which Burns published in the *Anthropological Quarterly* in 1961 and in 1963 are

[2] Hertz, 'Saint Besse', p. 177.
[3] Semple, *Influences of geographic environment*, p. 599; Helbok, 'Zur Soziologie und Volkskunde des Alpenraumes', p. 102.
[4] This characterization is used sarcastically by Febvre, *Geographical introduction to history*, p. 198, in his critique of Semple and other writers who had placed a heavy emphasis on the backwardness of mountain societies.
[5] Anderson, *Modern Europe*, p. 102.
[6] Honigmann, 'Survival of a cultural focus', and 'Rationality and fantasy'.

indicative of the programme of ecological anthropology in the Alps.[7] The first article was concerned with the area directly studied by Burns (the valleys of the Dauphiné, in the French Alps, and in particular the village of Saint-Véran) and tried to demonstrate that the spatial and social-structural evolution of the Dauphiné communities had been decisively shaped by environmental constraints. The second article was an attempt to define the distinguishing features of the Alpine culture area. Its core was a general ecological model of the upland community, which is still very useful and provides the basis for the more articulated model presented in Chapter 1.

We have already noticed that one major objection which can be raised against Burns's model (and more generally against the subsequent attempts to establish sets of broad correlations between environmental constraints and forms of social organization) is that it tends to be ahistorical, or even antihistorical. But there is another danger. The focus on universals of mountain habitats entails that the stress will be placed on unity, or uniformity of response, while the astonishing linguistic, ethnic and also religious diversity of Alpine populations will retreat into the background. Yet, what makes the Alps so fascinating is that through these mountains run some of the great cultural frontiers of Europe, separating the cultural sphere of the Mediterranean from the transalpine cultures to the north and from the Slavonic world to the east. What is more, the Alps offer unique opportunities to observe the cultural contrast between these major civilizations in close-up, particularly when the same valley is occupied by different ethnic groups.

In most cases, the coexistence of different ethnic groups in the same Alpine valley goes back to the Middle Ages and is the legacy of the dynamic expansion of Germanic settlers like the Walser, who founded over one hundred settlements in an area ranging from Savoy to Vorarlberg, or the groups of Bavarian and Carinthian peasants who colonized the upper ranges of many valleys in the Italian and Slovene Eastern Alps.[8] One of these 'contact situations' is represented by St Felix and Tret, the two adjacent villages which were selected in the early 1960s by Eric Wolf for his Alpine fieldwork. St Felix and Tret lie in the upper Non Valley, which marks the transition between South Tyrol, whose valleys are overwhelmingly inhabited by German-

[7] Burns, 'Ecological basis', and 'The Circum-Alpine area'.

[8] Situations of language contact in the Italian and Slovene Eastern Alps have been studied in anthropological perspective by Denison, 'Sauris: a trilingual community', and by Brudner, 'Maintenance of bilingualism'. In addition to Zinsli, *Walser Volkstum*, pp. 17–48, detailed accounts of the Walser colonization are provided by Kreis, *Die Walser*, and by Rizzi, *Walser*.

speakers, and the Romance valleys of the Trentino. Only fifteen minutes walk from one another, the two villages had to cope with the same environmental constraints, but were separated by a linguistic and cultural boundary: the inhabitants of St Felix were Tyrolese German-speakers, while the people of Tret spoke a Ladin dialect belonging to the Rhaeto-Romance family and were oriented towards Italian culture.

Himself a pupil and former collaborator of Julian Steward, Wolf has aptly remarked that the Alps offer 'a magnificent laboratory' to the ecological anthropologist interested in relating variations in social forms to variations in altitude, slope, soil and other environmental factors.[9] But the Alps also provide an experimental setting where the relative significance of environmental pressures and cultural values can be assessed. This was admirably shown in an elegant and engaging paper which Wolf published shortly after his first spell of fieldwork, in 1962.[10] In a series of later works Wolf has considerably revised some of the contentions advanced in this paper, largely because of the results of further research in the Non Valley conducted by Wolf himself and by his junior colleague John Cole.[11] However, the issues raised in the 1962 paper remain very important. It is therefore useful to consider in some detail these issues and, more generally, Wolf and Cole's ethnography, which has been extremely influential in the subsequent development of Alpine anthropology.

Cultural frontiers

Travellers and geographers have repeatedly noticed that in the Germanic Alps of Austria, Bavaria and Switzerland, settlements tend to be more widely dispersed than in the French and Italian Alps.[12] This is a fascinating contrast. In a famous passage, quoted and endlessly dissected by the nineteenth-century scholars who engaged in the study of the old Germanic community, Tacitus stated that it was a distinctive custom of the peoples of Germany that their villages were not laid out in the Roman style, with buildings adjacent and connected. The Germans, Tacitus wrote, 'colunt discreti, ut fons, ut campus, ut nemus placuit; vicos locant non in nostrum morem, conexis et cohaerentibus aedificiis, suam quisque domum spatio circumdat'

[9] Wolf, 'Ownership and political ecology', p. 201.
[10] Wolf, 'Cultural dissonance'.
[11] Wolf, 'Inheritance of land', and 'Ownership and political ecology'; Cole and Wolf, *The hidden frontier.*
[12] Cf. Veyret, 'Alps', p. 679.

– they dwelled apart, dotted about here and there, wherever a spring, plain or grove took their fancy, and every man left an open space round his house.[13] What Tacitus reported of Roman and Germanic settlements in the first century A.D. is apparently still true in the Alps today.

The sudden shift from nucleated to dispersed settlements is, in many Alpine districts, the clearest indication of the existence of an ethnic boundary. This is perhaps nowhere better visible than in the valleys colonized by the Walser. Whereas the Romance villages lying at lower altitudes are characteristically compact, the Walser settlements still reveal their original spatial structure made up of individual families living in isolated farmsteads (or small hamlets) surrounded by the parcels of land these families used for agriculture.[14] But the contrast was hardly less striking in the upper Non Valley when Wolf and Cole conducted their research. In the 1960s Tret was a nucleated settlement of just under forty dwellings, each typically containing a number of apartments whose inhabitants bore no necessary relationship to one another. 'Since the south wall of one structure may well form the north wall of the next,' the two anthropologists inform us, 'the buildings extend in one continuous mass, interrupted here and there by a passageway or kitchen garden, until the village abruptly ends and the fields begin.' In St Felix, on the other hand, homesteads lay scattered over the landscape, 'each surrounded by a solid block of fields and meadows separating it from its nearest neighbor'.[15]

As Wolf observed, the starkly different outward appearance of the two villages was a first indication that St Felix and Tret, in spite of close physical proximity, constituted 'different cultural worlds'.[16] But the anthropological inquiry brought to light many more dimensions of this ethnic boundary. One such dimension was the very different degree of identification of people with houses. In St Felix each house, with its attached fields and meadows, had a name, usually derived from some significant features of the natural and cultural landscape: a rock, a spring, a bridge, a field. As is common in the Austrian Alps, in local usage the villagers were designated by the name of the homestead they occupied rather than by their surnames or by some personal nickname as was the case in Tret. Thus, if a homestead was called *Brunn* (spring), the farmer on *Brunn* was invariably referred to by everybody in the village as the *Brunnerbauer*, his wife as the

---

[13] *Germania*, 16.
[14] See Weiss, *Häuser*, pp. 274–96.
[15] Cole and Wolf, *The hidden frontier*, pp. 8–10, 141–3.
[16] Wolf, 'Cultural dissonance', p. 8.

Brunnerbäuerin, and his unmarried children as, say, the *Brunnerhans* and the *Brunnerlisl*.

This identification between the various homesteads and their occupants, Wolf argued, was most likely reinforced by the fact that in St Felix inheritance was impartible and there was, consequently, a normative expectation that house and attendant property would pass intact from father to son. In Tret, too, houses bore names, usually the names of the original founders. But in this village inheritance rules prescribed that property should be divided equally among men and women, and marriage residence tended to be a matter of convenience or availability of living space. Thus, the descendants of the ancestor who was believed to have built a house were dispersed over many houses and there was no normative expectation that homestead and family line should be closely associated.

Even more significantly, diverging inheritance rules led to very different patterns of authority within the domestic groups. In St Felix, Wolf found a classic form of stem family organization. When a farmer died or retired, he was succeeded by one of his sons, who could eventually marry and establish himself as manager of the estate. Unable to marry, since they did not possess claims to a homestead, the brothers and sisters of the heir had either to accept the traditional status of unpaid labourers on their brother's farm or, alternatively, to emigrate and sever their ties with family and homeland. In the homestead with indivisible inheritance, Wolf notes, the *Bauer* is king, 'wielding authority over wife, children and remaining younger siblings, until he hands over the property to his heir, who duplicates the pattern in the new generation'. In Tret, by contrast, authority was not vested exclusively in the male head of household. Because of partibility, both husband and wife were potential claimants to property, and this led to a much more balanced pattern of authority, with the two spouses complementing each other in its exercise. This radically different distribution of power and authority distinguished very clearly households whose composition could be formally identical. As in St Felix, also in Tret households could contain, along with the married couple, one or more unmarried siblings. But, although managerial authority tended to be yielded to the married brother, the other siblings did not renounce their rights to a share in the property and retained an active say in decision making.[17]

Although their influence was most evident in the domestic sphere, inheritance rules were important well beyond the confines of the

---

[17] Wolf, 'Cultural dissonance', p. 9; Cole and Wolf, *The hidden frontier*, pp. 239–43.

households and played a crucial role in structuring the whole social field – 'into exclusive lineages of homesteaders in St Felix, and into the creation of an open and interlaced network of relations in Tret'.[18] Kinship terminology, a traditional subject of anthropological investigation, offered hints that in St Felix the emphasis, in reckoning kinship as in reckoning the occupancy of a holding, was heavily placed on the lineal continuity of the stem family. Both the Tyrolese system used in St Felix and the Ladin system used in Tret distinguished collaterals from lineals. But, whereas the Ladin system carefully specified generation in collaterality, the people of St Felix lumped together all collaterals, apart from brother and sister, into an undifferentiated category: uncles, male cousins and nephews were all designated by the term *fetter*; aunts, female cousins and nieces, by the term *basl*.[19]

It is obviously dangerous and unwarranted to see kinship terminologies as exactly mirroring social structure. Nevertheless, this major feature of Tyrolese terminology suggested that ties with collaterals were less significant in St Felix than in Tret. The existence of such social-structural contrast was in fact confirmed by ethnographic observation, showing that labour exchanges between collateral and affinal kin were frequent in Tret, but not in St Felix. It was also apparent that in Tret ties with neighbours were of the utmost importance, and that over the years each household had formed a network of relations of reciprocal assistance with other households upon which it was possible to rely for help and cooperation. In St Felix, on the other hand, kin were either absent or unrecognized; and in a village settled in isolated farmsteads there was scarcely any notion of neighbourhood and neighbourliness. The inhabitants of St Felix conceived of their village as the sum total of spatially discrete and economically independent domains. Accordingly, each farmer strived for self-sufficiency and tried hard to avoid any form of help from other farmers. When this was absolutely necessary, strict accounting was maintained, in order to make sure that exchanges would cancel each other exactly.[20]

Wolf's paper cogently suggested that the differences displayed by Tret and St Felix both in their outward appearance and in most critical features of their social structure were largely explained by a basic contrast between diverging inheritance systems. This was a remarkable finding which invited further and much wider considerations. A look at the map of the geographical distribution of inheritance

[18] Cole and Wolf, *The hidden frontier*, p. 243.
[19] Cole and Wolf, *The hidden frontier*, pp. 240–1.
[20] Cole and Wolf, *The hidden frontier*, pp. 168–74.

systems is enough to realize that with only few exceptions impartibility was traditionally dominant all over the Germanic world, whereas western and particularly southern Europe were apparently characterized by a variety of systems, but with a clear prevalence of partibility.[21] It seemed therefore legitimate to Wolf to regard the system of impartible inheritance found in St Felix as the legacy of a pristine Nordic civilization, and to conclude that the field study of the ethnic boundary between St Felix and Tret shed light, from a humble but revealing angle, on the more general contrast between Nordic and Mediterranean civilizations.[22]

But this detailed local study also appeared to provide a distinct indication of the primacy of culture over environmental constraints. As in other marginal areas, in the high Alpine valleys land is in short supply, and the effective management of a farm depends on the availability of varied kinds of terrain. In such circumstances, anthropologists have maintained, impartible inheritance would seem to be eminently adaptive. Under partible inheritance, by contrast, land would tend to be continually fragmented until each holding becomes economically worthless. Also, the composition of the estate would change with each generation, thus threatening the delicate balance of arable land, meadows, pastures and forest that every farmer needs. The fact that in spite of these drawbacks the inhabitants of Tret had retained a system of partibility was, according to Wolf, evidence of their loyalty to a deeply rooted cultural heritage.[23]

Riddles in Alpine ethnography

Wolf's 1962 paper on 'Cultural dissonance in the Italian Alps' shows very clearly both the strengths and weaknesses of the nascent Alpine anthropology – its unusual potentialities as well as its inability to reach, on the basis of village fieldwork alone, solid conclusions about a number of important issues. The techniques of field research which anthropologists had developed in the study of 'primitive' societies were invaluable to the exploration of the functioning of kinship groups or to the pinpointing of the social-structural concomitants of ethnic difference at the local level. But the prominence granted to fieldwork tended to produce premature generalizations. Wolf's partial revision of his early position is indicative of the growing awareness, on the part of Alpine anthropologists, that several widely accepted notions

---

[21]   See the map in Pfeifer, 'Quality of peasant living', p. 257.
[22]   See Wolf, 'Cultural dissonance', and 'Inheritance of land', p. 103.
[23]   See Wolf, 'Cultural dissonance', p. 8, and *Peasants*, p. 75.

about the main ethnographic characteristics of the Alps could not stand a careful comparative and historical scrutiny. Indeed, Alpine anthropologists were among the first in the profession to stress the importance of acquiring more than a passing acquaintance with history – to such an extent, in fact, that some of their colleagues who had worked in other mountain areas even expressed the concern that the very richness of the historical records might lead Alpine anthropologists to be overcautious in generalizations.[24]

Let us consider, for instance, the problem of settlement patterns and the traditional notion, initially shared by Wolf, that dispersed settlements are a distinctive feature of Germanic populations. It is sufficient to examine the case of the Walser to realize that the question is actually much more intricate. We have seen that the Walser communities offer impressive examples of scattered settlements sharply differing from the nucleated Romansh villages lying at lower altitudes in the same valleys. Yet in the homeland of the Walser (the German-speaking upper part of Canton Valais) dispersed settlements are far from being the norm, which implies that the Walser pattern must be a product of the process of colonization.[25] Remarkably, a tendency for dispersed settlements to prevail in high-altitude areas of more recent colonization, and for nucleated settlements to prevail in the lower zones, can also be detected in the Austrian Alps, where the population is ethnically homogeneous. And, although the evidence is at times conflicting or unclear, it would seem that a similar tendency can be detected in other regions as well, from the French Alps of Savoy to the valleys of Alpine Slovenia.[26]

This has been noticed by Wolf, who has gradually modified his previous argument and has suggested, in the book written in collaboration with Cole, that dispersed settlements appear to be 'correlated more with colonization than with ethnicity'.[27] Once this correlation is accepted, however, it still remains to be explained why areas of recent colonization were mainly made up of isolated homesteads. The proposed explanations are mostly ecological. Some scholars believe that dispersed settlements are primarily a function of the predominantly pastoral orientation of populations settled at high altitudes.[28]

---

[24] Rhoades and Thompson, 'Adaptive strategies', pp. 535–6.
[25] See Weiss, *Häuser*, p. 280, and especially Zinsli, *Walser Volkstum*, pp. 86–110.
[26] Cholley, *Les Préalpes de Savoie*, p. 391; Blanchard, *Les Alpes Occidentales*, vol. 7, pp. 478–80; Fliri, *Bevölkerungsgeographische Untersuchungen*, p. 9; Thomas and Vojvoda, 'Alpine communities'.
[27] Cole and Wolf, *The hidden frontier*, p. 31. This view is shared by Weiss, *Häuser*, pp. 275–82.
[28] Weiss, *Häuser*, p. 278; Elsasser-Rusterholz, *Beiträge*, p. 37.

Others, including Cole and Wolf themselves, have remarked that in
the high valleys, where topography makes it difficult to establish compact masses of contiguous cultivated parcels, settlements made up
of scattered homesteads provide each householder with the best possible access to his lands.[29]

Whatever the merits of these broad ecological hypotheses, they still
do not account for the higher frequency of dispersed settlements in
the Germanic Alps. And on a smaller scale, but no less crucially,
they do not account for the striking differences between villages like
Tret and St Felix, which share the same high-altitude environment.
As we have just seen, a simple explanation in ethnic terms does not
hold. Nor does the notion that customs of undivided inheritance are
part of a pristine Germanic heritage. This once dominant view, as
Wolf acknowledged in an article of 1970, has now been abandoned
or strongly qualified by most scholars.[30] In order to overcome these
difficulties, Wolf and Cole have thus progressively moved towards
a set of historical explanations, suggesting that the differences between
the two villages have their roots in the circumstances of their foundation in the Middle Ages.

In Tret, they have argued, partible inheritance was favoured by
Romanic landlords who saw their interests better served by a prolifer-
ation of households (and therefore of taxation units) than by protecting
a constant number of landed estates. The later foundation of St Felix
was, on the other hand, part of a large process of settlement expansion
which was particularly important in the Germanic Alps but also affected many high valleys on the Italian side. Promoted by the Tyrolese
nobility, the colonization of St Felix took place in a period of growing
market involvement. Thus, instead of furthering the establishment
of a nucleated settlement surrounded by a belt of common land, the
feudal lords encouraged the colonists to found isolated farmsteads
in order to achieve a more intensive exploitation of all the unsettled
areas. Moreover, impartibility was imposed on the colonists as a
means of assuring the persistence of landed holdings capable of producing a surplus beyond household needs which could be marketed
in the lowlands.[31]

The view that different settlement and inheritance patterns are
related to diverging aims pursued by feudal lords is probably correct.

---

[29] Cholley, *Les Préalpes de Savoie*, p. 391; Cole and Wolf, *The hidden frontier*, p. 72.
[30] Wolf, 'Inheritance of land', pp. 103–4.
[31] See Wolf, 'Inheritance of land', p. 106, and especially Cole, 'Inheritance processes',
pp. 129–30.

But it is relevant to note that recent research indicates that it might be dangerous to place exclusive emphasis on the 'maximizing strategies' of the landlords. It is now becoming clear that, although the medieval colonization of the high valleys was mostly initiated by feudal lords, nevertheless several different types of settlement expansion can be identified. Where colonization was undertaken by groups of farmers, and merely tolerated by the landlords, there was usually a development of nucleated villages or large hamlets. And even where colonization did occur under manorial auspices, the imposition of impartible inheritance was not inevitable. This was particularly the case in the Western and Central Alps, but also in those eastern regions which were part of the Bishopric of Chur and therefore subject to the *Lex Romana Churiensis*, which set no limits to the subdivision of lots or buildings. All the Walser colonies, which are mainly concentrated in these regions or in other districts dominated by Roman law, do in fact display strict partibility. This explains, among other things, why Walser settlements look rather different from those found in Tyrol and in other areas where impartibility was the norm, such as the Emmental, several parts of Canton Lucerne and most Austrian regions. In these areas settlements still tend to consist of isolated homesteads (*Einzelhofsiedlung*), whereas in most Walser settlements partibility has led to the accretion of new houses near the original farmstead and to the formation of small hamlets (*Weilersiedlung*).[32]

This summary discussion of Alpine settlement patterns suggests that, although some historical and functional links can be detected, the overall picture looks extremely chequered. The same problems emerge when one examines other aspects of Alpine ethnography, and in particular the social and economic organization of the alps. Once again the Walser occupy a central place in the ethnological literature, mainly because of Richard Weiss's outstanding study of agropastoral practices in Canton Grisons. As Weiss showed, in this Swiss canton the Romansh villages have been traditionally characterized by an associative management of the alps: a team of hired male specialists, including a professional cheese-maker, was charged with the care of all the animals of the village, which were grazed in the undivided communal pastures while the owners and their families remained in the village to tend the fields and to mow the hay for the winter. In the Walser communities, on the other hand, the alps were individually managed. The grazing areas exploited by the Walser

---

[32] H. Becker, 'Medieval settlement expansion', pp. 28–9; Lichtenberger, 'Das Bergbauernproblem', p. 53. Cf. Wolf, 'Inheritance of land', p. 104; Wicki, *Bevölkerung des Kantons Luzern*, pp. 120–7; Braun, *Das ausgehende Ancien Régime*, pp. 70–5.

were no less large or compact than elsewhere, but were segmented into small private alps oriented towards the production of butter and low fat cheese for family consumption. Although there could be forms of communal herding, dairy operations were performed by the owners. One important consequence was that, since the men had to remain in the village to work in the fields, the alps were staffed largely, or exclusively, by women.[33]

The individual management of the Alps has long been a favourite target of agrarian economists, who have pointed out its incompatibility with the requirements of a successful commercialization of dairy products.[34] But it can hardly be denied that even in the context of a subsistence economy this way of managing pastoral resources entails a substantial waste of labour. Yet, a perusal of the geographical and ethnographic literature reveals that, in spite of their patent 'irrationality', forms of individual alp management were widespread all over the Alps and can therefore scarcely be dismissed as an oddity. Very frequent on both the French and the Italian sides of the Western Alps, they are solidly attested in many parts of Switzerland and are indeed dominant in the easternmost regions of the crescent.[35]

In order to account for the origins of this mode of pastoral organization and for its surprising persistence in many districts up to very recent times, geographers and anthropologists have been forced to resort (as with the question of settlement and inheritance patterns) to a combination of ecological, economic and historical explanations. Some scholars have suggested that individual alp management is a reasonable, if not 'rational', alternative in those areas where the pastures are relatively close to the village and allow family members to move fairly easily between the fields and the summer huts.[36] Others have noted that forms of individual management are mostly found in communities where rights in pastures were originally granted, at the time of the colonization, to single households or to individual

---

[33] Weiss, *Das Alpenwesen Graubündens*, pp. 88–95.

[34] Cf. Carrier, *Water and grass*, pp. 252–64; Frödin, *Zentraleuropas Alpwirtschaft*, vol. 1, pp. 387–93; Veyret-Verner, 'Équilibre démographique', pp. 338–9

[35] On the Western Alps, see Arbos, *La vie pastorale*, pp. 415–523, and Blanchard, *Les Alpes Occidentales*, vol. 6.2, pp. 468–9. On the Swiss Alps, see Loup, *Pasteurs et agriculteurs valaisans*, p. 538; Weinberg, *Peasant wisdom*, pp. 24–6; Friedl, *Kippel*, pp. 47–56; Lurati, 'Alpwesen im Tessin', p. 762; Bucher, *Bevölkerung des Amtes Entlebuch*, pp. 194–210; and of course Weiss, *Das Alpenwesen Graubündens*, pp. 88–95. On the Eastern Alps, see Frödin, *Zentraleuropas Alpwirtschaft*, vol. 2, pp. 95–8, 441–50; Novak, 'Alpwesen in Slowenien', pp. 653–6; Thomas and Vojvoda, 'Alpine communities', pp. 219–24.

[36] Frödin, *Zentraleuropas Alpwirtschaft*, vol. 2, pp. 447–8; Elsasser-Rusterholz, *Beiträge*, p. 59; Zinsli, *Walser Volkstum*, p. 87; Netting, *Balancing on an alp*, p. 66.

family corporations. This circumstance, it is argued, led to the development of private ownership not only of fields and meadows (which is the rule everywhere) but of the high pastures as well, and this in turn acted as a factor powerfully favouring individual management.[37]

Variability in alp organization has been the subject of a considerable number of ethnological and geographical studies since Philippe Arbos published in 1922 his pioneering work on pastoral life in the French Alps, in which he for the first time analysed in a systematic way the differences between communal and individual management. As his study showed, the geographical distribution of the two types could not be related to major variations in the physical environment. Sharing the antideterministic penchant of the French geography of the early twentieth century, he left the question of the causes of this distribution unsolved, and simply came to the conclusion that each type was to be seen as 'une manifestation originale de la spontanéité humaine'.[38] Very few scholars would now be prepared to adopt such an extreme 'possibilist' stand. But the evidence surveyed in this section shows that the attractive simplicity of the model outlined in Chapter 1 is spoiled by the baffling range of variation displayed by modes of alp management as well as by settlement and inheritance patterns. The welter of supplementary ecological and historical hypotheses which must be advanced to account for these 'anomalies' obviously weaken the explanatory power of the model.

Although broad ethnic or cultural explanations are no more tenable than sweeping ecological generalizations, this ultimately brings us back to the crucial problems raised by Wolf's study of Tret and St Felix. On the one hand, the variations we have briefly discussed demonstrate, to quote Ellen's apt remark that, 'because certain cultural traits have effects which make them ecologically adaptive, this in itself is insufficient to make them inevitable'.[39] Nevertheless, there is no question that the adaptive potential of the various forms documented in the Alps is different, and so is their degree of formal economic rationality. The origins of the system of individual management of pastoral resources found in a community may well go back to the particular conditions granted by feudal lords to groups of medieval settlers. But the fact remains that such a system entails a duplication of effort and creates severe problems of allocation of family labour.

[37] Arbos, *La vie pastorale*, p. 422; Liver, *Mittelalterliches Kolonistenrecht*, pp. 33–6; Carlen, 'Alpenlandschaft und ländliche Verfassung', p. 346.
[38] Arbos, *La vie pastorale*, p. 423. Cf. Parain, 'Esquisse d'une problématique', pp. 5–6.
[39] Ellen, *Environment, subsistence and system*, p. 64.

And the same is obviously true of different patterns of inheritance rules, since partibility should predictably result in higher levels of nuptiality and fertility than impartible inheritance, and in a more hazardous tendency towards land fragmentation.

Thus, a 'genetic' approach which merely explains the ethnographic riddles facing Alpine anthropologists in terms of historical origins is hardly sufficient. The problem of the persistence of a seemingly irrational or maladaptive trait is no less interesting and important than that of its origin. In fact, this problem has attracted the interest of the anthropologists who have moved to the Alps in the footsteps of Wolf, Burns and Honigmann, and has stimulated them to reassess the role of inheritance systems and other institutions as regulatory mechanisms and to study in more detail the relations (and tensions) between rules and actual practice. These are some of the questions to be tackled in the next two chapters, where ethnographic evidence from my own study of Alagna will be compared with the findings of other anthropological researches. But, before turning to that, it is necessary to say something more about the conditions in which most recent anthropological investigations have been carried out, for there is little doubt that the ethnographic setting has significantly affected the conduct of field research and has also influenced some of the conclusions reached by the anthropologists.

The study of change

Towards the end of the 1960s a considerable number of anthropologists began to flock to the Alpine valleys. Guided by F. G. Bailey, a group of British anthropologists selected a number of Alpine and Pyrenean communities to test the transactionalist models which had just been developed by Fredrik Barth and by Bailey himself.[40] In the same years, the rise of the neo-functionalist approach, with its emphasis on ecosystemic regulation, was setting an exciting agenda for students of mountain cultural ecology. But the Alpine scene, as most anthropologists quickly realized, was rapidly changing, and those who were mainly interested in the study of human ecology in particular experienced severe difficulties.

When the American anthropologist John Friedl left for the Swiss village of Kippel, in 1969, he planned to work almost exclusively on the topic of mountain ecology. Located in one of Switzerland's remotest and allegedly most traditional valleys, Kippel promised an

---

[40] The results of these researches are embodied in two collective volumes edited by Bailey, *Gifts and poison* and *Debate and compromise*.

ideal setting for this kind of research. Once settled in the village, however, Friedl soon discovered that its economy had gone through startling transformations, the most evident being the drastic decline of mountain farming. While in 1950 over 70 per cent of the working population of Kippel was engaged in agricultural activities, by 1970 the proportion had gone down to only 14.2 per cent. It became clear, Friedl writes, that 'it was not possible to study traditional agro-pastoral practices when only one or two farmers remained in the village, nor did it seem wise to lay undue emphasis upon the traditional, ignoring the obvious changes that had occurred through industrialization in recent decades'.[41] Thus, the focus of his research shifted from ecology to social and economic change.

Friedl's experience is exemplary in many ways. For the pioneers of Alpine anthropology it had been quite easy to observe men and women still tending cows and collecting potatoes, or to take photographs of villagers carrying hay on their shoulders and living in old wooden houses. Younger generations of fieldworkers have found this increasingly difficult, or utterly impossible. This is not to say that they have abandoned the many important questions still open in the study of Alpine ecology. But their accounts, as Friedl makes clear in the introduction to his book on Kippel, tend to rely more heavily on the reminiscences of old informants and on the picture of former times provided by works on local history than on direct observation and measurement. Moreover, when the focus of the anthropological study is on recent change, the reconstruction of the past tends to be rather selective, since it is merely intended as a backdrop for comparison with the contemporary styles of life directly recorded by the anthropologist.

Friedl's study of Kippel is essentially an ethnography of change, and indeed a most useful and informative one, its value being enhanced by the fact that the transformations occurred in the occupational structure of Kippel are very close to the general trends observed in the Alpine area as a whole. In Kippel, two distinct phases can be detected. In the period following the Second World War, Canton Valais (of which Kippel is part) experienced an industrial boom which opened up new opportunities for the population of the region. As a consequence, during the 1950s, the trend in occupational change in Kippel was out of agriculture into industry. Most men, however, were able not only to stay in the village and commute daily to work but also to retain agriculture as a sideline occupation. Kippel became

---

[41] Friedl, *Kippel*, p. 3.

what is commonly known as a 'worker-peasant' village. In the 1960s agriculture continued to decline, but this time the growth of tourism favoured a flow into the tertiary sector rather than into industry. In 1970 people occupied in commerce, transportation and other service-oriented jobs accounted for 54.2 per cent of the working population and clearly outnumbered those employed in industry.[42]

The case of Kippel epitomizes, in several important respects, the economic transformations that in the last few decades have changed the face of the Alps. Significant regional differences do of course exist, and economists have identified a number of major patterns of economic evolution. It is also well known that in the French and Italian Alps the decline of mountain farming has been even sharper than in Switzerland or Austria, where measures have been taken by the governments to counteract rural exodus. But on the whole it is apparent that all over the Alps the years immediately after the Second World War witnessed an increased involvement of the Alpine populations in industry at the expense of agro-pastoral activities, and that more recently tourism has become the dominant economic and occupational sector.[43]

It should be noticed, however, that economic evolution may have followed rather different paths in different communities. In many localities, for instance, tourist development had already begun in the nineteenth century. In most places it did not progress beyond the stage of élite tourism until fairly recently, but in some cases it had produced spectacular changes well before the outbreak of the last war. A case in point is Davos, one of the Walser colonies in the Grisons. Before the explosion of tourism in the second half of the nineteenth century, Davos was a fairly large village with a population hovering between 1,600 and 1,800 inhabitants. After a series of unsuccessful attempts to make the village into a spa, in the 1860s Davos eventually began to establish itself as a major health resort. A few years later it was among the very first resorts to start a winter season (skiing was tried out as early as 1873) and by the end of the century this Walser settlement had grown into the biggest mountain resort in Europe, with a resident population of over 8,000 people. In 1930 the number of overnight stays was in the region of 1,500,000 and the number of inhabitants had reached the no less impressive figure of 11,164 – an extraordinary size for a locality at 1,800 m of altitude.[44]

[42] Friedl, *Kippel*, pp. 76–118.
[43] De Rossi, 'L'economia agraria alpina'; Dorfmann, 'Régions de montagne'.
[44] Jost, *Der Einfluss des Fremdenverkehrs*; Zimpel, *Der Verkehr as Gestalter der Kulturland-schaft*, pp. 254–97; Bernard, *Rush to the Alps*, pp. 112–17.

The remarkable case of Davos can be seen as one of the two ends of a wide spectrum. At the opposite pole we find those communities where the majority of the population is still today predominantly engaged in farming. These communities are mostly situated in inaccessible high valleys. If the morphological features of their territory are unsuitable for skiing and hinder tourist development, they may have little alternative but agriculture, for distance and difficult communications often prevent the men from commuting to the industrial towns at the foot of the mountains. Particularly where mechanization has not gone very far, it would seem at first glance that the economy has changed very little from the past. But it is immediately apparent that the future of these communities is seriously threatened by depopulation.

In most tourist resorts as well as in many worker-peasant villages a decline in mortality and low rates of emigration have successfully counteracted the effects of falling fertility. Tourist development, as we have just seen for Davos, even tends to attract immigrants. The inhabitants of the more disadvantaged areas, on the other hand, must either resign themselves to the low standards of living afforded by agriculture and stock-raising or migrate, and most young people ultimately decide to abandon their home villages. What they leave behind are ageing populations of men and women who keep the farms going but are mainly supported by state pensions. As a consequence, a growing number of marginal Alpine villages are now becoming purely remnant communities, both economically and demographically. In the past, Bailey has remarked, 'the surplus population went away from the mountains in great numbers, but it was still a surplus population ... The mountain communities, at least, were left intact. But since the end of the Second World War all this has changed. Emigration has turned into depopulation.'[45]

This suggests that in the Alps very little remains today of the traditional way of life. Although 'modernized' villages inevitably produce a more striking impression of change, farming communities are also rapidly changing, and no less dramatically. Some anthropologists, however, have denied that the transformations recently experienced by the Alpine area have been as radical as most observers believe. While scholars like Bailey or Friedl have emphasized the magnitude of change and have singled out the Second World War as a decisive turning-point, other anthropologists who have worked in the Alps, like Daniela Weinberg and more recently Adriana Destro, have

---

[45] Bailey, 'Changing communities', p. 33.

brought to the forefront the elements of continuity they have discovered in the villages where their fieldwork was conducted. 'To document the history of Bruson,' Weinberg writes, 'is to be impressed by the continuity of social structure and belief system in spite of obvious changes in the economy.'[46]

Both Weinberg and Destro are in fact successful in showing that villages where most inhabitants are no longer engaged in agriculture or pastoralism can nonetheless retain a strong line of ideological continuity with their peasant past. And Weinberg goes as far as to maintain that in Bruson social structure has been largely unaffected not only by the substantial economic changes but also by the severe decline of the population, from 423 inhabitants in 1910 to just 250 in 1969. The continuing numerical dominance of the same patrinomial groups,[47] she argues, is an indication that 'the demographic depopulation of Bruson has not been accompanied by a social-structural extinction of the village. One can almost say that the Bruson of today is a scaled-down but not significantly altered version of the Bruson of the turn of the century.'[48]

We may wonder whether this is a sufficient indication of basic continuity in social structure. If one considers that the drastic shrinking of the population of a village like Bruson is bound to affect not only the vitality of communal institutions but also other key sectors of social structure (marriage and the family, for instance), Weinberg's claims would seem open to question. It must be recognized, however, that they help direct attention towards a number of important but neglected aspects of the relation between demographic and social-structural change. Also, they challenge the received anthropological wisdom and suggest that the whole question of change and continuity in Alpine society needs to be reassessed. The next two chapters of this study will attempt such a reassessment.

---

[46] Weinberg, *Peasant wisdom*, p. ix. Cf. Destro, *L'ultima generazione*.
[47] On the notion of 'patrinomial kin groups' (i.e. groups of people distinguished by family names transmitted patrilineally), see Firth, 'Bilateral descent groups', pp. 24–5.
[48] Weinberg, *Peasant wisdom*, p. 158.

4

The changing demography of
Alpine communities

'Traditional' communities and tourist resorts

Most of what we know about contemporary population trends in the Alps comes from studies that geographers, and some economists, began to pursue in the late 1950s in the attempt to better understand a process of economic and demographic transformation which was rapidly taking imposing dimensions.[1] Both these earlier studies and the subsequent literature are largely based on post-war census data, which have been used to work out helpful and at times sophisticated typologies. Different authors have relied on different classificatory and analytical criteria. Some have started from variations in the occupational structure, others have subdivided Alpine communities according to their rates of population growth or their altitude. On the whole, however, all these studies have proposed a sequence of types ranging from 'traditional' communities, where agriculture is still of primary significance and population is sharply declining, to the demographically much healthier tourist resorts, where increasing proportions of the inhabitants are engaged in service industries.[2]

The striking contrast between these two extreme types of Alpine community was made almost brutally evident to me when, in the first months of my field research, I began to realize how different the situation of Alagna was from that of Rima and Rimella, the two

---

[1] See e.g. Veyret-Verner, 'Population'; Golzio, 'Il fattore demografico'; Butz, 'Extreme Entvölkerungsgemeinden'. A major concern was obviously mountain depopulation, which appeared to be serious in some parts of Switzerland and virtually unstoppable in the French and Italian Western Alps. Recent analyses of demographic dynamics in the French Alps suggest, however, that the rate of depopulation is slowing down considerably. See Prost, 'Évolution démographique', and David et al., 'Dynamique démographique'.

[2] See e.g. Janin, Le Val d'Aoste, pp. 338–71; and Furrer and Wegmann, 'Bevölkerungsveränderungen in den Schweizer Alpen'.

other Walser colonies in the Sesia Valley. Rima, which had been a small village since its beginnings, was now completely abandoned during the winter and was inhabited by no more than a handful of people during the summer. Rimella, on the other hand, had previously been a fairly large village by Alpine standards. The total number of people living in its many hamlets amounted to nearly 1,300 in 1861 and was still over 1,000 in 1901. Since then the population had dropped dramatically, at an accelerated pace after the Second World War. In 1980 it was under 300, with a very high proportion of old people. The causes accounting for this massive depopulation did not seem hard to detect. The harsh climate had made agriculture uncompetitive, while the rocky and steep slopes, besides being detrimental to agricultural activities, had also thwarted any prospect of skiing development.

The climate is obviously no less forbidding in Alagna. As the Reverend S. W. King wrote in 1858, 'at Alagna, the snow often sets early in November, lasting for six or seven dreary months, while hardly a warm day is known until July or August'.[3] Indeed, an altitude ranging from 1,200 m for the lower hamlets to 1,600 m for the higher ones has proved as fatal to agriculture in Alagna as in Rima and Rimella. But the very fact that an English traveller was visiting Alagna around the middle of the nineteenth century is indicative of the much more favourable opportunities afforded to this village by its position. Whereas Rima and Rimella are situated at the top of two narrow and meandering lateral valleys surrounded by ridges of no distinction, Alagna is placed right at the foot of Monte Rosa. As such, it was destined to attract travellers, scientists and climbers, and to grow in the heyday of mountaineering into one of Europe's best-known Alpine resorts. Given its importance, in the last decades of the nineteenth century the village was even on the verge of experiencing that 'railway revolution' whose consequences have been so far-reaching in many other Alpine districts. Eventually the project was not realized, but a new road was nevertheless constructed which is still today much better than the winding roads leading to Rima or Rimella, endemically broken or blocked because of heavy snowfalls, avalanches and landslides.

Thanks to its solid tradition of tourism, it was quite easy for Alagna to shift from the 'monoseasonal' pattern of summer élite tourism to the economically far more rewarding 'biseasonal' pattern. A few years after the end of the Second World War an embryonic winter season had already been created through the construction of a cablecar. But,

---

[3] King, *The Italian valleys*, p. 374.

in spite of this early start, Alagna has not been able to live up to its reputation. Like other classic mountaineering centres, it has not profited as much as might have been expected from the spectacular changes stimulated by the development of skiing, and cannot be said to rank today very high among mountain resorts. Yet the distinct impression one receives is that the village lives almost exclusively from tourism: men are mainly occupied either as ski instructors and cablecar operators or in the building industry as masons or carpenters, while most women (as is common in Alpine resorts)[4] are busy taking care of the day-to-day running of shops, bars and restaurants.

This impression is confirmed by the statistics on the occupational structure. In 1980, when I took a census of the village, the tertiary sector accounted for about 60 per cent of the active population, while a further 20 per cent consisted of men employed in the building industry, which was entirely dependent on tourism. Statistics also confirm that tourism has not failed to exert in Alagna the beneficial influences which have made it so popular with governments as a source of income for areas of otherwise limited economic potential. With a *per capita* income of 967,000 Italian Lira a year, Alagna occupied in 1970 the fifth rank among the twenty-eight communes of the valley, and was topped only by another tourist resort and by three rich industrial towns in the lower valley. In sharp contrast, Rima came twenty-fourth with 341,000 Lira and Rimella twenty-eighth with just 225,000 Lira.[5] From the early 1970s onwards, tourist development in Alagna has gradually come to a standstill, but the general pattern has scarcely changed. If anything, recent estimates indicate that the gap between Alagna and Rimella is wider today than it was in 1970.[6]

Alagna's comparatively high level of prosperity has in its turn had stabilizing effects on both the size and the age structure of the population. Its age structure is typical of tourist-oriented mountain villages, with people under 20 still outnumbering people over 60 years. This suggests that at least in the near future the village is likely to suffer no more than the minor losses it has experienced for the last few decades. Since the end of the Second World War, the population has indeed tended to fluctuate between 400 and 500 inhabitants – 428 in July 1980 according to my census. When compared with the 648 inhabitants recorded in 1861, and even more with the 499 recorded in 1935, this figure indicates that Alagna has experienced nothing

[4] Cf. Hutson, 'Valloire', pp. 24–5, and Weinberg, *Peasant wisdom*, pp. 47–54.
[5] Grasso, 'I movimenti della popolazione in Valsesia', pp. 23–4.
[6] UCCP, *I redditi dei comuni del Piemonte*, pp. 49–50.

similar to the massive exodus which has depopulated Rima and Rimella as well as many other less favoured villages all over the Alps.

The contrast is striking and no doubt very real. It conceals, however, the existence of an important similarity, namely that both in a tourist resort like Alagna and in a still largely agricultural community like Rimella the spatial distribution of the population has radically changed, because of the partial or total abandonment of the higher or more disadvantaged hamlets. This is a widespread phenomenon. Reported for all parts of the Alpine area, the abandonment of outlying hamlets and isolated farmsteads has resulted in major ecological changes: the upper limit of permanent settlement has declined by up to 300 m, and the land surrounding the deserted hamlets is in most cases falling back to wilderness, sometimes covered by a secondary formation of scrub.[7] But consequences are not only ecological. Though less frequently studied, social-structural consequences are no less interesting and important. The case of Alagna, where spatial transformations have been accentuated by the growth of tourism, provides a particularly useful illustration of this major process of change.

Spatial changes

Around the middle of the nineteenth century Alagna consisted of scattered groups of between five to twenty wooden houses, each hamlet being surrounded by fields and meadows. In the last hundred years or so, this typically Walser settlement has been altered beyond recognition by the new stone and concrete buildings which have filled in the spaces between the string of hamlets flanking the terminal part of the new road. The luxury hotels clustered around the church were the first modern buildings to appear in Alagna, soon followed by the stylish villas of a few wealthy families. Many more have then been constructed in the years since the Second World War, mostly blocks of flats to be sold or rented to tourists. All these buildings have formed a commercial and touristic core, which is usually designated as the 'centre' (*centro*) and can hardly be distinguished from the traditionally more nucleated Romance villages of the lower valley.

The growth of the 'centre' has profoundly affected the local inhabitants' perception of the spatial and social structure of the community. Alagna used to be divided into four sectors, or 'wards', each consisting of a number of hamlets. The four hamlets lying on the plateau overlooking the rest of the settlement and the six on the left bank of the

---

[7] Lichtenberger, 'The crisis of rural settlement', p. 184.

Sesia River were virtually two small separate worlds. A rather more blurred boundary then separated, on the right bank, the hamlets on the valley floor (which roughly correspond to what is now the 'centre') from the ones perched on the adjacent slopes. Alagna – or, in local German, *ds Land* – was the name of no single place. It designated the dispersed village as a whole, and the now almost forgotten collective nicknames which indicated the inhabitants of the various hamlets bear picturesque witness to each hamlet's strong individuality.

The old quadripartite subdivision has now been supplanted by a dichotomy in which the *centro* is opposed to the *frazioni*, a term meaning 'hamlets' with connotations of isolation or even backwardness. Though accessible through tarmac roads, the hamlets which are not part of the new centre are mostly regarded as inconvenient and are progressively becoming, conceptually as well as spatially, a periphery. Because of housing problems in the centre, it is not uncommon for a newly married couple to settle in a *frazione* and reopen a family-owned house which has perhaps been kept boarded up for decades. But in general people tend to move away from the outlying hamlets towards the better serviced centre, which most villagers now simply call Alagna. In the years immediately before the Second World War the population of the hamlets still exceeded that of the centre, if only by a very thin margin: in 1935 there were 246 people living in the *centro* and 253 living in the *frazioni*. In 1980 only some 80 people, or less than 20 per cent of the total population, dwelled in the *frazioni*. Some of the 'hamlets' still retained a population of reasonable size and consequently a certain level of social life. Others were sadly depopulated, and two or three were totally deserted.

In the past, the few minutes' walk separating Alagna's hamlets from one another concealed a much greater social distance. Old villagers brought up, say, in the hamlets near the church may candidly admit that they only vaguely knew many of those living on the overlooking plateau because they had few kinship ties there. The siphoning of inhabitants from the outlying hamlets to the new centre has obviously changed this situation. By uprooting many families from houses and places they had inhabited perhaps for centuries, it has deeply affected the traditional residential arrangements and has brought about a broadening of each individual's network of social relations. Moreover, the abandonment or utter transformation of most hamlets has led to the collapse of the institutions which had previously characterized them, singly or in groups, as distinctive social and economic units.

As is typical of many Alpine communities, the framework of

Alagna's social structure consisted of a bewildering variety of corporate groups which regulated most aspects of economic, social and religious life – from access to agricultural and pastoral resources down to the right to use a communal oven or the obligation to perform some collective task. In Alagna these corporate groups were to a very large extent conterminous with the various hamlets or wards. Thus, although they have not completely disappeared, their functions have inevitably atrophied. Most of the surviving corporations are crumbling and their members are sometimes uncertain as to whether they should still be regarded as living organizations. What is clear is that in the course of this century the old social structure, mainly made up of corporate groups recruited on the basis of residence and descent, has been supplanted by a new kind of social structure – a 'replicate social structure', to use the anthropological term[8] – consisting either of local branches of nation-wide centralized institutions or of voluntary associations. All these new institutions have a common feature. They concern the whole village population, whereas the old corporate groups mirrored the characteristic fragmentation of Alagna's dispersed settlement.

The 'illusion of demographic stability'

The changes illustrated by the case of Alagna cast serious doubts on Weinberg's contention that Alpine communities can still display a surprising degree of social-structural continuity in spite of the economic and demographic transformations of the last decades. Corporate groups whose main function was to control access to agricultural or pastoral resources can hardly be expected to survive the imminent demise of mountain farming. And it seems also clear that the breakdown of the old communal institutions is unavoidable when the depopulation of a hamlet or, as is increasingly common, of a whole village goes beyond a certain minimal threshold.

However, Weinberg's study of Bruson has the merit of highlighting one dimension of social-structural continuity which is too often overlooked. The most interesting finding to emerge from a comparison between the village census taken by Weinberg herself in 1969 and a listing of inhabitants compiled in 1910 is the continuing numerical dominance of a stable group of fourteen family names present in both censuses, which accounted for 82 per cent of all residents in 1910 and 85 per cent in 1969. Since all fourteen families belonged to the

[8] See Anderson and Anderson, 'The replicate social structure'.

village's *bourgeoisie*, or community of the citizens,[9] it was very likely that they had been in the village for a very long time. To the villagers, Weinberg reports, the unity and uniqueness of Bruson was indeed epitomized by this set of 'core families', whose origins were placed 'in the distant past among a generalized group of village founders, the *ancêtres*'.[10]

During my fieldwork in Alagna I was impressed by the deep, even passionate interest that particularly the older generations showed when talking about family names and by the evident pleasure they took in introducing me to the intricacies of the local naming system. The practical importance of mastering this naming system in order to identify kinship groups and property relations was rapidly fading by that time. But a surname could still betray the relatively recent immigration of a villager's grandfather or testify that another villager belonged to a family which had been in Alagna for centuries. Among the people still bearing the old local surnames I found much the same conceptions as in Bruson. They were proud of being so evidently related to the founders of the village and no doubt regarded themselves as the true core of the population. But they were also aware that their numerical importance was continuously declining because of immigration. Immigration and mixed marriages, they felt, had already undermined the vitality of the German dialect. Thus, many villagers now looked with some anxiety at prospects of tourist development which might stimulate much further immigration and turn the original population into a minority with little weight in local affairs.

The different fate of the old descent lines in Bruson and Alagna brings out an important aspect of the social demography of Alpine communities that census data and general statements about the stabilizing effects of tourism tend to conceal. It is undeniable that the problems of tourist resorts are far less dramatic than those faced by localities virtually unaffected by tourism like Bruson or Rimella, which are on the verge of physical extinction. On the other hand, surprisingly little attention has been paid to the possibility that in tourist resorts immigration, while producing 'beneficial' demographic effects, may also

[9] All Swiss towns and villages are characteristically divided into two separate entities, the older community of citizens (*Bürgergemeinde*, or *bourgeoisie*) and the more recently established community of residents (*Einwohnergemeinde*, or *commune des habitants*). This dualism dates back to a law passed on 13 November 1798, when Switzerland was occupied by the French revolutionary armies. Although several important political prerogatives have been transferred to the community of residents, the community of citizens still retains control of the bulk of communal property, whereas the community of residents only possesses what is necessary for strict administrative purposes. See Carlen, *Rechtsgeschichte der Schweiz*, pp. 61–4.

[10] Weinberg, *Peasant wisdom*, 85.

cause changes in the composition of the population which break what most local people would regard as a vital line of continuity. Yet the Alps provide striking examples of resorts rapidly growing to many times their original size. The population of Davos, as we have seen in Chapter 3, jumped from 1,680 inhabitants in 1850 to 8,089 in 1900 and 11,164 in 1930. When growth is so spectacular, the proportion of 'locals' is bound to go down drastically. In 1850 the members of the community of citizens (who were mostly people of old local descent) represented about 85 per cent of the resident population of Davos, a century later just 15 per cent.[11] Their absolute number, however, had at least remained almost unchanged. Things may be worse in other resorts. From the locals' point of view, one of the sad realities of tourist development is that most of the better positions can usually be filled by specialists from outside. Thus, even a highly successful tourist development may largely pass over the heads of the locals, who are still forced to leave the village and are replaced by immigrant skilled labour.[12]

In approaching tourist resorts like Alagna, which appear not to have suffered the massive depopulation so common in many Alpine villages in recent years, one must therefore be very careful to avoid what Laurence Wylie has called 'the illusion of demographic stability'. In this respect, the case of Roussillon (the community in Southern France described by Wylie in his famous book *Village in the Vaucluse*) is indeed exemplary. Between 1946 and 1959, the population of Roussillon approximately retained the same size, only dwindling from 779 to 680. These global census figures suggested that a few people had left, but that most of the others had stayed as members of a permanent population core of about 700. Closer examination revealed, on the contrary, that of all the individuals living in Roussillon from 1946 to 1959 only 275 had lived there for all thirteen years, and 137 of these were not born in the village.[13]

An analysis of population turnover is unfortunately not possible for Alagna. But a detailed listing of inhabitants compiled by the parish priest in 1935 provides a cross-section of the village population in the years immediately before the Second World War and allows one to gauge the changes which have occurred subsequently. A comparison with the census I took during my fieldwork indicates that the number of inhabitants born outside Alagna had nearly doubled, from 67 (or

[11] Jost, *Der Einfluss des Fremdenverkehrs*, pp. 160–72.
[12] Cf. Janin, 'Le tourisme dans les Grandes Alpes italiennes'.
[13] See Wylie, 'Demographic change in Roussillon', and also his reflections in the 3rd edition of *Village in the Vaucluse*, pp. 340–83.

Table 4.1. *Place of origin of married couples: Alagna (1935, 1980) and Roussillon (1946)*

	Alagna 1935		Alagna 1980		Roussillon 1946	
	N	%	N	%	N	%
Both husband and wife born in the village	39	53.4	27	29.7	12	11.4
Only husband born in the village	15	20.5	29	31.9	14	13.3
Only wife born in the village	17	23.3	24	26.4	27	25.7
Both husband and wife born elsewhere	2	2.7	11	12.1	52	49.5
Total	73	99.9	91	100.1	105	99.9

Sources: For Alagna, APA, *Status animarum* of 1935, and my own census of 1980. For Roussillon, Wylie, 'Demographic change in Roussillon', p. 232.

13.6 per cent) in 1935 to 113 (or 26.4 per cent) in 1980, whereas the proportion of people bearing the old local surnames had declined from over 50 per cent to less than one-third. These figures leave little doubt that in Alagna immigration has been affecting the composition of the local population much more seriously than in villages like Bruson or Rimella. But they also show that even in 1980 the proportion of immigrants, though not negligible, was still far from attaining the astonishing levels of a community like Roussillon, where people migrating to and from the village constituted the overwhelming majority of the population.

If we consider another indicator of mobility and population turnover, namely the place of origin of married couples, we are led to the same conclusion. This is very neatly demonstrated by Table 4.1. Yet, this table also contains data which, on closer inspection, suggest that even in a place like Alagna the importance of immigration and exogamy should not be underestimated. It shows, in particular, that, although the rate of village endogamy has substantially declined in the last few decades, nevertheless exogamous marriages were already rather frequent before the Second World War. Further analysis reveals that the reasons for male and female immigration were different. The majority of the in-marrying wives came from other parts of the Sesia Valley, mainly from neighbouring communities, whereas most of the men came from the mining districts of several Italian regions.

Two crucial features of male immigration in Alagna are, therefore, that it started well before the advent of mass tourism in the 1950s and that at first the major force behind it was mining, the oldest and most typical of Alpine industrial activities. During my stay in Alagna the mining industry was not thriving and only some twenty men still worked in the copper and feldspar mines. But the many abandoned tunnels scattered all over Alagna's territory and the remains of the large buildings which had once been used to process the ore testified to the antiquity and past importance of mining. Among the older villagers there was still a vivid memory of a sequence of mining booms which had occurred in the course of their lifetime and had caused waves of immigration. These booms were characteristically short-lived, and after a few years most miners would leave. But some of them married local girls and decided to remain.

As a result, immigration did not simply consist of a shifting fringe of individuals moving into and out of the village. The fact that in 1935 over 85 per cent of the inhabitants of Alagna were native-born suggests a very high degree of closure. But the picture changes when we look at the data from a different angle and realize, for instance, that about one-quarter of all households were headed by immigrants. What is more, the economic, social and cultural background of these men was completely different from that of the rest of the population. Before the Second World War most exogamous marriages were also ethnically and linguistically mixed; and in those families in which either the father or the mother was from outside, the children did not learn the German dialect. A detailed analysis of language transmission patterns demonstrates, in fact, that the rise in the number of mixed marriages in the period between the two world wars has been by far the single most important determinant of the decline of the Walser dialect, which has now reached its final stage.[14]

Geneticists working on Alpine populations have become increasingly aware that even high endogamy rates may not be sufficient to create the conditions of a genetic isolate. Recent research has shown that small numbers of in-marrying spouses can be responsible for a surprisingly high proportion of the gene pool.[15] It would seem reasonable to assume, on the other hand, that the cultural and linguistic closure of a community will come under serious threat only in the presence of massive immigration. When immigrants are few in number, it is believed, they are easily integrated. That reality may be more complex than these assumptions suggest is demonstrated by comparing Alagna with Davos. As a consequence of its spectacular growth as a tourist resort, Davos has been flooded with successive waves of immigration since the mid-nineteenth century. The level of intermarriage, however, has remained fairly low. Moreover, the

---

[14] Viazzo, 'Ethnic change in a Walser community', pp. 94–129.
[15] See Hagaman *et al.*, 'Genetic and demographic impact'; and for a general discussion of this problem, Jacquard, 'Concepts of genetics', pp. 36–7.

locals have also retained some degree of spatial segregation from the immigrant hotel personnel. This explains why in Davos the Walser dialect has displayed (at least until very recently) a vitality which is remarkable in a locality so massively affected by immigration.[16] In Alagna, the penetration into the community of a comparatively small number of outsiders has had, from this point of view, much more devastating effects.

Structural transformations

The preceding sections have shown that, although the size of Alagna's population has remained rather stable, in the course of the twentieth century its spatial distribution has enormously changed, while its ethnic composition has been deeply affected by the decline of village endogamy and, well before the advent of mass tourism, by immigration. In these respects, the 'demographic stability' suggested by the almost constant number of inhabitants is largely an illusion. But what about demography as it might be more conventionally understood? Have fertility, mortality, nuptiality and the age-sex structure also changed so radically?

It should be noticed that, along with the brute fact of emigration, the main demographic threat to the future of a great number of Alpine villages has been, since the end of the last war, an increasingly rapid process of population ageing. The two processes are of course closely related. Although the lowering of marital fertility and also the return of retired emigrants have played a part,[17] there is no doubt that the ageing of Alpine populations has been chiefly due to the exodus of young adults. Besides swelling the proportion of the older age groups, this has produced a fall in marriage and birth rates and caused a further erosion of the base of the population pyramid. In some extreme cases, elderly people may be two, three, or even ten times more numerous than children under fifteen years of age.[18] Such an acute disequilibrium is found in most of the so-called 'traditional' communities, but also in a growing number of peasant-worker villages, whose inhabitants are irresistibly attracted by the industrial towns of the lowlands.

Tourist resorts like Alagna seem, on the other hand, to have mostly escaped this fate. If we compare the structure of Alagna's population in 1980 with the age pyramid derived from the listing of 1935, we find that Alagna is today only slightly 'older' than in the years before

---

[16] Cf. Viazzo, 'Ethnic change in a Walser community', pp. 351–5.
[17] Veyret-Verner, 'Population', p. 177.
[18] UCCP, *I redditi dei comuni del Piemonte*, pp. 112–42.

the Second World War. The value of the ageing population index obtained by relating the number of people over 60 years of age to the number of those under 20 years[19] has merely increased from 0.79 to 0.84. This is a remarkably modest change, showing the effectiveness of tourism in 'stabilizing' Alagna's demography. It should not be overlooked, however, that in 1935 the base of the pyramid was already rather narrow. A quick examination of the birth registers reveals that the First World War had marked, some twenty years before, a turning-point in the recent demographic history of the village. The first year of war (for Italy, 1915) recorded a sudden and drastic drop in natality, from a crude birth rate in the region of 25 per thousand to the rate of 15 per thousand which still persisted in the 1970s.

The effects of tourist development are no less visible if we turn to the sex ratio. In most Alpine areas, and particularly in those which have failed to transform their economy, women tend to leave in greater numbers than men. As the anthropologist F. G. Bailey has remarked, in the Alps even more than in other rural regions of Europe young women are unwilling to marry into farming families, 'for these both fail to provide the comforts of modern life and inflict upon the house-wife the arduous routine of cattle, hens and heavy manual work on the farm or on the mountainside'.[20] As a result, farming communities display severely unbalanced sex ratios, young women being heavily outnumbered by men fatally destined to celibacy. In Alagna, by contrast, the sex ratio is today very balanced. In 1980 the village numbered 219 men and 209 women.

Figure 4.1 shows, however, that the sex ratio itself has greatly changed since 1935, when women outnumbered men by a ratio of 132 to 100. To some degree this is attributable to differential mortality. The rather more balanced ratios for the older age-groups found in 1980 seem to suggest that male mortality has somewhat improved. But the prevalence of women in 1935 is no doubt primarily explained by the massive permanent emigration of men, whose extent is even partly obscured by the simultaneous immigration of miners. A striking indication that the previous pattern of permanent male emigration is now a thing of the past, this alteration in the sex ratio is of great significance. And so is one of its predictable concomitants, namely the decrease in the number and proportion of women never marrying.

Besides showing that late marriage and a high proportion of permanent celibates are the two main features of the 'European marriage

[19] This is the index commonly used by Alpine geographers. It was proposed in 1961 by Veyret-Verner, 'Populations viellies'.
[20] Bailey, 'Changing communities', p. 35.

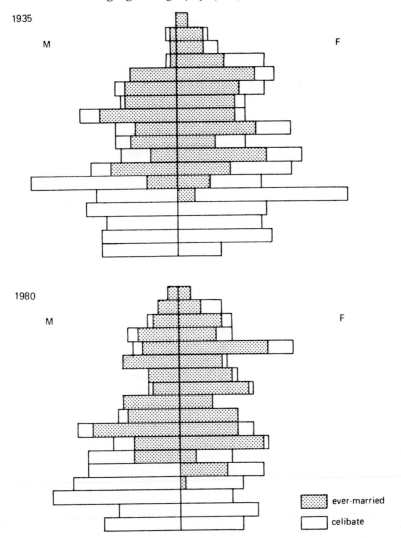

Figure 4.1 Population by age, sex and marital status in Alagna, 1935 and 1980

pattern', in his classic essay John Hajnal has argued, more specifically, that by the end of the nineteenth century 'the proportion of women never marrying rose to levels probably unprecedented in much of north-western Europe', primarily because of emigration being predominantly a male affair.[21] The pattern displayed by Alagna seems to

[21] Hajnal, 'European marriage patterns', p. 130

fit well with this general picture, and also with Hajnal's suggestion that the high rate of celibacy has been disappearing since the Second World War. In 1980, the proportion of unmarried women over sixty was still fairly high: 24.6 per cent, in comparison with 30.4 per cent in 1935. The proportion was, however, much lower among the younger women aged between thirty and fifty-nine. In 1980, only six women out of 73 belonging to this age group were spinsters (8.2 per cent), while in 1935 spinsters accounted for over one-third of the same age group (36 out of 107, or 33.6 per cent). Interestingly, the proportion of bachelors over thirty years of age has also declined, from 24.1 per cent in 1935 to 13.6 per cent in 1980. A comparison between the two pyramids suggests that age at marriage has also fallen, though less markedly than the rate of celibacy. This impression is corroborated by marriage records. In the period between 1901 and 1950, the mean age at first marriage was 29.3 years for men and 26.1 for women. In the following three decades, from 1951 to 1980, it has dropped respectively to 28.6 and 24.9 years.

To sum up, the figures briefly presented in this section demonstrate that also from a strictly demographic point of view the population of Alagna, in spite of retaining a fairly stable size and a similar age structure, has undergone a number of crucial transformations. Since 1935 the sex ratio has radically changed, male emigration has ended, permanent celibacy has almost disappeared and marriage age has declined to some degree. A couple of decades earlier, the outbreak of the First World War had coincided with a sudden and irreversible drop in birth rates. These changes seem to epitomize Alagna's modernization and its departure from an old economic and demographic order, in which the pressure of population on the local resources was controlled and alleviated by the check of nuptiality and by the safety valve of emigration. These findings, however, only refer to one village and to a fairly limited time-span. This obviously raises two broad and difficult questions, which it will be necessary to tackle in the remaining sections of this chapter. The first is whether, and to what extent, the trends detected in Alagna can also be found elsewhere in the Alps. The second and no less significant question is whether it is legitimate to use data from the late nineteenth and early twentieth centuries to make inferences about the demography of the Alps in a more remote past.

A late demographic transition

Placing Alagna's recent demographic history in a wider Alpine context is no easy task, since several factors make any comparative investigation of demographic trends in the Alps surprisingly difficult. One major problem is that criteria defining 'Alpine regions' or 'mountain communities' vary rather considerably from one country to another and from one study to another. What is more, for over a hundred years the population of upland areas has been continuously decreasing relative to the total population of the regions or provinces of which these areas are part. Since data are often available only for the whole regions or provinces, diachronic analyses are bound to be very tentative. Finally, in those cases in which one can only rely on crude birth or death rates, interpretation is made highly problematic by the anomalous changes which have occurred in the sex and age structure of Alpine populations. However, what evidence we do possess clearly indicates that in the course of the twentieth century all Alpine areas have experienced, although at a different pace, a very substantial decline of both mortality and fertility – a long-delayed demographic transition, one would be tempted to say.

To be sure, crude death rates are today fairly high and above national averages, particularly in France and Italy. But this is easily explained by the high proportion of elderly people in the population. Indeed, it is remarkable that in spite of the considerable ageing of the population they are much lower than the death rates recorded before the First World War, which were usually over 20 or even 25 per thousand. A clearer impression of the improvement is given by the estimate that between 1920–1 and 1969–72 the expectation of life at birth increased in the Alpine cantons of Switzerland from 52.1 to 69.2 years for men and from 54.6 to 75.1 years for women.[22] Comparable data are not available for the rest of the Alps, but improvements have probably been even greater in Austria, where it had been customary not to breast-feed babies and infant mortality had consequently been higher than the Alpine average.[23]

When one turns to fertility, a major divide soon emerges between the two halves of the Alpine crescent, for it is apparent that fertility dropped much more suddenly and much more markedly in the Western Alps than in Austria and in most Swiss mountain cantons. The decline was particularly dramatic in the Piedmontese Alps, where

---

[22] Hagmann and Menthonnex, 'Éléments de démographie alpine', p. 223.
[23] See Fliri, *Bevölkerungsgeographische Untersuchungen*, p. 54; Knodel and van de Walle, 'Breastfeeding, fertility and infant mortality', pp. 118–19; Helczmanovski, 'Die Entwicklung der Bevölkerung Österreichs', p. 138; and Bolognese-Leuchtenmüller, *Bevölkerungsentwicklung*, Tables 36 and 40. The relation between feeding practices and infant mortality in the Alpine area is discussed more extensively in Chapter 8 below, pp. 216–19.

the crude birth rate decreased, according to Blanchard's calculations, from 34.2 per thousand in the period 1881–1900 to 16.2 per thousand in the decade 1931–40.[24] In Alagna, as in several other sectors of the Western Alps (most notably in the French Alps), the birth rates of the years around the turn of the century had been rather lower. The decline was, therefore, proportionately less substantial. But the pattern was essentially the same: the First World War marked a rapid transition to fairly low rates which were destined to remain more or less stationary in places like Alagna and to decrease even further in the most severely depopulated and ageing communities.[25]

In the Central and Eastern Alps, on the other hand, fertility levels remained comparatively high. Because of the contemporaneous decline of mortality, in several areas population even increased. The case of one of the highest and harshest valleys of Tyrol, the Oetztal, whose population increased by 52 per cent from 1900 to 1960, has become classic in the geographical literature.[26] In the early 1950s the crude birth rate was still as high as 24.4 per thousand, and similar rates have been reported for other Austrian districts.[27] Although rates may have been slightly lower, the situation was no different in Switzerland, where throughout the twentieth century fertility has consistently been higher in the Alpine cantons than in the rest of the country. In 1960 the aggregate crude birth rate for the mountain cantons was still over 20 per thousand, a threshold which the other cantons had crossed immediately after the First World War.[28] Interestingly, in 1960 birth rates of 20 per thousand or more, well above the Italian national average, could still be found in a few mountain districts in the Italian Central and Eastern Alps.[29]

In the last twenty-five years, however, crude birth rates have been rapidly falling also in the Central and Eastern Alps. This is only in part the effect of the ageing of the population. Fertility rates have themselves declined quite abruptly. A study published in 1979 pointed out that in 1977–8 the Alpine cantons of Switzerland had for the first time reached the fateful threshold of just two children per woman

---

[24] Blanchard, *Les Alpes Occidentales*, vol. 6.1, pp. 330–46.
[25] Cf. Golzio, 'Il fattore demografico', p. 19, and Guibourdenche, 'Naissances et taux de natalité', p. 187.
[26] The case of the Oetztal is singled out by de Planhol, 'Pression démographique', p. 542, and by Guichonnet, 'Développement démographique', p. 190.
[27] See e.g. Kullen, *Wandlungen der Bevölkerungsstruktur*, p. 26; Arnold, 'Der Umbruch des generativen Verhaltens', pp. 417–8; Keller, 'Die Bevölkerungsentwicklung im Ausserfern', pp. 372–7.
[28] See Hagmann and Menthonnex, 'Éléments de démographie alpine', p. 218.
[29] Golzio, 'Il fattore demografico', p. 19.

and expressed the concern that even the 'legendary fertility' of Alpine people might no longer be able to assure the full replacement of the population.[30]

This last phase of the Alpine demographic transition has been witnessed also by some anthropologists. Writing in the early 1970s of a village in East Tyrol, one of them reports that 'the contrasts are spatially and chronologically startling. Within a single generation and within a quarter of a mile, the average family size has swung from the eight-ten child "labour-accumulating" farming family to an approximate ideal of two or three ... an outlying hamlet a quarter of a mile from the main village, equally near the road but as yet untouched by tourist development, shows no change from earlier generations.'[31] As this passage suggests, anthropological accounts may prove helpful to understand the links between economic diversification and demographic change. What is even more important, they are able to locate fine-grained differences in reproductive behaviour that can easily escape the demographer's notice. At times, however, some of the anthropologists and oral historians who have worked in the Alps, perhaps in the attempt to stress more vigorously the contrast between the traditional peasant communities of the past and the modernized villages of today, seem to have placed too much emphasis on oral evidence suggesting that in the past very large families were the norm.[32] At first sight these studies appear to bring support to the view that Alpine people used to be exceptionally prolific. But on closer inspection it becomes clear that their evidence, though often enlightening, tends to be highly impressionistic and cannot be seen as a final demonstration that the Alps had a 'primitive', high-pressure demographic regime. In fact, other data contained in the anthropological literature put this in question.

The check of nuptiality

Although they have only exceptionally provided data on fertility, Alpine anthropologists have often discussed at some length two of its major determinants, namely age at marriage and permanent celibacy. Thus, some quantitative information has at last become available on a subject which had previously been explored at village level only by a handful of Austrian geographers like Franz Fliri and Adolf Lässer

---

[30] Hagmann and Menthonnex, 'Éléments de démographie alpine', pp. 219–20.
[31] Heppenstall, 'East Tyrol', p. 144.
[32] See e.g. Benetti *et al.*, *Uomini delle Alpi*.

Table 4.2. *Age at first marriage in Alpine localities during the first half of the twentieth century*

Locality	Language	Period	Men	Women
Alagna (W. Italian Alps)	German	1901–50[a]	29.3	26.1
Festiona (W. Italian Alps)	Occitan	1911–50[a]	31.5	26.2
Vernamiège (Swiss Alps)	French	1906–55[b]	26.9–28.8	25.4–26.6
Lötchental (Swiss Alps)	German	1910–39[a]	33.5	30.1
Kippel (Swiss Alps)	German	1900–49[b]	29.9–33.4	27.4–29.7
Törbel (Swiss Alps)	German	1900–49[a]	32.6	28.8
Tret (E. Italian Alps)	Ladin	1900–49[c]	38	24
St Felix (E. Italian Alps)	German	1900–49[c]	34	28
St Georgen (Austrian Alps)	German	1892–33[b]	29.2–31.6	25.5–27.2
Unterinntal (Austrian Alps)	German	1900–39[a]	33.0	27.9
St Leonhard (Austrian Alps)	German	1901–48[a]	35.2	30.0
Oest. Sannitz (Austrian Alps)	Slovene	1900–49[a]	33.1	29.3

Key: a = mean; b = range of decennial means; c = median.
Sources: Anthropological studies. Alagna: Viazzo, 'Illegitimacy and the European marriage pattern', p. 109; Festiona: Destro, *L'ultima generazione*, p. 165; Vernamiège: Berthoud, *Changements économiques*, p. 219; Lötchental: Macherel, 'La traversée du champ matrimonial', p. 12; Kippel: Friedl and Ellis, 'Celibacy, late marriage and potential mates', p. 27; Törbel: Netting, *Balancing on an alp*, p. 135; Tret and St Felix: Cole and Wolf, *The hidden frontier*, p. 254; St Georgen: Khera, 'Illegitimacy', p. 312.
Geographical studies. Unterinntal: Fliri, *Bevölkerungsgeographische Untersuchungen*, pp. 30–2; St Leonhard: Lässer, *St. Leonhard im Pitztal*, p. 34; Oest. Sattnitz: Arnold, 'Der Umbruch des generativen Verhaltens', pp. 429–31.

or, more recently, Klaus Arnold.[33] These anthropological studies are all the more valuable because they place Alpine nuptiality much more firmly in the social and cultural context than is usually the case in the demographic and geographical literature. Unfortunately, periods of observation, statistical measures and methods of tabulating the data are not homogenous. A general picture does nonetheless emerge both for the first half of our century and for the years after the Second World War.

Even if the localities listed in Table 4.2 cannot by any means be regarded as a random sample of Alpine villages, the figures contained in this table strongly suggest that between 1900 and 1950 marriage tended to be late throughout the Alpine crescent. Table 4.3, on the other hand, seems to indicate that after the war marriage age, though

[33] Fliri, *Bevölkerungsgeographische Untersuchungen*; Lässer, *St. Leonhard im Pitztal*; Arnold, 'Der Umbruch des generativen Verhaltens'.

Table 4.3. *Age at first marriage in Alpine localities in the years after the Second World War*

Locality	Language	Period	Men	Women
Alagna (W. Italian Alps)	German	1951–80[a]	28.6	24.9
Festiona (W. Italian Alps)	Occitan	1951–65[a]	30.0	25.7
Vernamiège (Swiss Alps)	French	1956–63[a]	26.2	25.1
Bruson (Swiss Alps)	French	1969[b]	29.0	27.6
Lötchental (Swiss Alps)	German	1940–69[a]	31.8	28.2
Kippel (Swiss Alps)	German	1960–69[a]	27.1	26.0
Törbel (Swiss Alps)	German	1950–74[a]	30.6	27.1
Fersina Valley (E. Italian Alps)	German	1970s[a]	ca 32	ca 25
Tret (E. Italian Alps)	Ladin	1950–69[c]	31	25
St Felix (E. Italian Alps)	German	1950–69[c]	28	26
Oest. Sattnitz (Austrian Alps)	Slovene	1950–68[a]	31.2	26.3

Key: a = mean; b = SMAM; c = median.
Sources: For Alagna, Festiona, Vernamiège the Lötchental, Kippel, Törbel, Tret, St Felix and the Oest. Sattnitz, see Table 4.2. For Bruson, see Weinberg, *Peasant wisdom*, p. 32; for the Fersina Valley, see Sellan, 'Système familial', p. 55.

remaining rather high, has somewhat declined for both men and women. Roughly the same is apparently true for permanent celibacy. Comparative evidence clearly shows, indeed, that the very high proportions of celibates recorded in Alagna in the period between the two world wars were far from being exceptional. The combined celibacy rate for men and women ranged, in the first half of the century, from about 20 per cent in Festiona[34] and approximately 30 per cent in Törbel, Tret and St Felix[35] to even higher figures in such districts as the Val Maggia in the Swiss Canton Ticino, where almost 50 per cent of all women did not marry.[36] In several localities (Alagna is a good example) the incidence of permanent celibacy has now greatly declined, but in others it remains very substantial: in the 1970s the rate was still as high as 30 per cent in Kippel and approximately 40 per cent in the Fersina Valley.[37]

[34] Destro, *L'ultima generazione*, p. 171.
[35] Netting, *Balancing on an alp*, p. 132; Cole and Wolf, *The hidden frontier*, pp. 162–3.
[36] F. van de Walle, 'Migration and fertility in Ticino', p. 456.
[37] Friedl and Ellis, 'Celibacy, late marriage and potential mates', p. 34; Sellan, 'Système familial', p. 37. It is unfortunate that most studies only provide combined celibacy rates for men and women. Combined rates may hide critical compositional changes due to the decline of previous patterns of male permanent emigration and to the recent tendency for women to leave in greater numbers than men.

Table 4.4. *Age at first marriage in Alpine localities in the second half of the nineteenth century*

Locality	Period	Men	Women
Alagna	1851–1900[a]	27.2	24.2
Festiona	1871–1910[a]	30.4	24.5
Vernamiège	1876–1905[b]	26.0–29.8	24.9–26.8
Lötchental	1850–1910[a]	33.7	30.2
Törbel	1850–99[a]	33.4	29.1
Tret	1850–99[c]	30	24
St Felix	1850–99[c]	31	30
Unterinntal	1850–99[a]	35.4	29.9
St Leonhard	1851–1900[a]	32.4	29.2
Oest. Sattnitz	1850–99[a]	30.5	27.8

Key: a = mean; b = range of decennial means; c = median.
Sources: See Table 4.2.

Predictably enough, anthropological studies are rather less informative about the years before 1900, particularly as far as permanent celibacy is concerned. Nevertheless, some researchers have been able to establish marriage ages for at least the second half of the nineteenth century. Table 4.4 shows that in some villages marriage age was somewhat lower than in the first half of the twentieth century, whereas in others it appears to have slightly declined after the turn of the century. But on the whole the impression is that Alpine nuptiality was considerably low throughout the period between 1850 and the last war. Fragmentary as they are, the figures presented in these tables are therefore extremely interesting, for they unmistakably point to a pronounced version of Hajnal's European marriage pattern. Since moderate levels of nuptiality imply the existence of a low-pressure demographic regime, we may wonder how these figures can be reconciled with the image of a 'traditional' Alpine pattern of high fertility proposed by, among others, Guichonnet.[38] This is a complex problem, as we shall see. But there are reasons to believe that the contradiction is, to some extent at least, more apparent than real and that it is due to a confusion between marital and overall fertility.

In this connection, Massimo Livi-Bacci's analysis of the Italian censuses of 1881 and 1911 is particularly instructive. These two censuses are very precious because they are the only ones to provide data not simply by province but also by *circondario*, a smaller and geographically

[38] Guichonnet, 'Développement démographique', pp. 157–8.

far more homogeneous administrative unit. This gives a much more precise idea of the geography of Italian fertility, all the more so for the Alps, whose distinctive demographic features tend to be obscured by aggregate figures for provinces. Indeed, the most striking finding to emerge from Livi-Bacci's map representing the index of marital fertility (I_g) in the 284 Italian *circondari* in 1881 is that the whole range of Alpine districts forming the Italian border from the west to the east stands out because of its relatively high I_g, always above 0.600 and quite often above 0.700. High marital fertility, however, was coupled with a very low propensity to marriage, measured by I_m: in 1881 the Alpine districts were no less outstanding because of an I_m which was often below 0.450 and in some instances below 0.400.[39]

As Livi-Bacci himself remarks, this reveals the existence of 'a particular type of Alpine high fertility'. On the basis of the data provided by the Italian censuses of 1881 and 1911, this Alpine pattern can be seen as broadly characterized by an I_g in the region of 0.700 and by an I_m in the region of 0.400. Until very recently, little else was known about the components of Alpine fertility in the period between 1850 and the First World War. The information on age at marriage and celibacy rates offered by the anthropological literature suggested, of course, that nuptiality had been low all over the Alps. On the other hand, the figures on the Swiss Cantons Valais and Uri briefly presented by Francine van de Walle in 1975 indicated that in some parts of the Alps legitimate fertility could be much higher,[40] and it was also clear that levels of illegitimate fertility could vary quite considerably. In a paper written some years ago, however, it seemed reasonable to assume that the whole range of variations was largely encompassed

[39] Livi-Bacci, *History of Italian fertility*, pp. 153–74. The I_g and I_m indices are part of a set of interrelated indices devised by A. Coale in 1965 to show how close the fertility being measured comes to a theoretical maximum. The set includes three indices of childbearing $(I_f, I_g$ and $I_h)$ and one index of nuptiality (I_m). The three indices of childbearing relate the number of births observed in a population to the expected number of births which the women in that population would have produced had they been exposed to the childbearing rates of married Hutterite women in the decade 1921–30. (The Hutterites are an Anabaptist sect living in the High Plains of the United States and Canada and have been selected as standard population because their women had the highest fertility ever reliably recorded.) I_f is the index of the rate of childbearing by all women regardless of their marital status; I_g is the index of the rate of childbearing by married women; I_h is the index of the rate of childbearing by women not currently married. The index of proportion married (I_m) is the ratio of the number of births which currently married women would produce if subject to Hutterite fertility to the number of births all women would produce if subject to Hutterite fertility. The four indices are related by the following expression: $I_f = I_m \times I_g + (1 - I_m) I_h$. See Coale, 'Factors associated with the development of low fertility', and more recently Coale and Treadway, 'Summary', pp. 153–62.
[40] F. van de Walle, 'Migration and fertility in Ticino', p. 448.

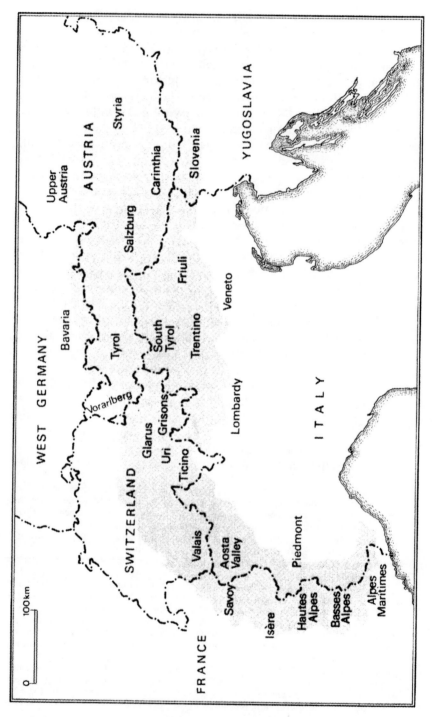

Map 2 Major regional subdivisions in the Alpine area

Table 4.5. *Components of Alpine overall fertility*

Model A.	High legitimate fertility, low nuptiality, low illegitimacy
	$I_g = 0.700$; $I_m = 0.400$; $I_h = 0.010$; $I_f = 0.286$
Model B.	High legitimate fertility, low nuptiality, high illegitimacy
	$I_g = 0.700$; $I_m = 0.400$; $I_h = 0.100$; $I_f = 0.340$
Model C.	Very high legitimate fertility, low nuptiality, low illegitimacy
	$I_g = 0.900$; $I_m = 0.400$; $I_h = 0.010$; $I_f = 0.366$

Note: The four indices are related by the following expression:
$I_f = I_m \times I_g + (1 - I_m) I_h$.
Source: Viazzo and Albera, 'Population, resources, and homeostatic regulation', p. 224.

by the three simple models proposed in Table 4.5. Model A was derived from Livi-Bacci's figures, whereas Model B was presumably close to the experience of the Eastern provinces of the Austrian Alps, where illegitimacy was known to have been very high in this period.[41] As to Model C, it could be expected to be typical of some parts of Alpine Switzerland.

These models suggested that, contrary to what was commonly believed, in the Alps overall fertility (measured by the index I_f) was bound by the check of nuptiality to range from very low (Model A) to moderately low (Model C). They were based, however, on very thin or uneven empirical evidence and a considerable amount of guesswork. The results of the Princeton European Fertility Project, recently published by Coale and Treadway,[42] now make it possible to test them, at least to some extent. It should be stressed that there are severe problems in doing so, particularly because the fertility and nuptiality indices have been calculated for administrative units which are fairly wide and often heterogeneous from a geographical point of view. This raises, first of all, the familiar problem of which cantons or provinces should be counted as 'Alpine' and which should not. No less seriously, Livi-Bacci's analysis of the Italian censuses shows how markedly different a map of fertility or nuptiality may result according to the administrative units considered in the computations. Nevertheless, some important indications do come out.

Table 4.6, which presents the earliest available data for Austria, shows that in 1880 Model B (the 'Austrian' model) was in fact closely approached by three of the eastern *Länder*, and in particular by Upper

[41] See especially Mitterauer, 'Familienformen und Illegitimität'.
[42] Coale and Treadway, 'Summary'.

Table 4.6. *Fertility indices: Austrian Alpine 'Länder', 1880*

	I_f	I_g	I_h	I_m
Upper Austria	0.342	0.683	0.107	0.408
Salzburg	0.318	0.706	0.134	0.322
Styria	0.317	0.643	0.128	0.367
Carinthia	0.340	0.660	0.218	0.276
Tyrol	0.305	0.827	0.025	0.350
Vorarlberg	0.316	0.896	0.029	0.330

Source: Coale and Treadway, 'Summary', p. 80.

Austria. It also shows, however, that the unmarried women's propensity to have illegitimate children, measured by I_h, could be much greater than assumed by the model. In Carinthia the value of I_h was astonishingly high, but it is remarkable that it was perfectly counterbalanced by an outstandingly low level of nuptiality.[43] As a result, the value of overall fertility was exactly the same as that predicted by the model and observed in Upper Austria.

Overall fertility was very much the same in the two western *Länder*, Tyrol and Vorarlberg, but the weight of the various components was considerably different, for both these provinces displayed very high legitimate fertility, whereas the contribution of illegitimacy was negligible. Thus, rather than the 'Austrian' model they tended to approach the 'Swiss' one (Model C). Table 4.7 shows, indeed, that in the 1880s Tyrol and Vorarlberg fitted the 'Swiss' model much better than most Swiss cantons. Apart from Uri and Valais and, at the opposite extreme, Glarus, the Swiss mountain cantons appear to be closer to Model A, the 'Italian' model. It is intriguing, in this respect, that Model A is best fitted by Ticino, the only Italian-speaking canton. But the values for Schwyz, Obwalden, Nidwalden and the Grisons are not too dissimilar.[44]

It should be noted, however, that in some cantons marital fertility had apparently declined rather substantially during the previous two or three decades. In 1860 the value of I_g was much higher in Uri (0.972), Schwyz (0.871), Obwalden (0.899) and Nidwalden (0.869).

[43] The causes of the higher levels of illegitimate fertility displayed by Carinthia are to be found partly in the steep increase in the number of consensual unions recorded in the second half of the nineteenth century and partly in the higher proportion of servants in the population. See Mitterauer, 'Familienformen und Illegitimität', pp. 149–56.

[44] Table 4.7 includes the Swiss cantons classified as 'totally Alpine' or 'mainly Alpine' by Carol and Senn, 'Jura, Mittelland und Alpen'.

Table 4.7. *Fertility indices: Swiss Alpine cantons, 1888*

	I_f	I_g	I_h	I_m
Uri	0.345	0.906	0.013	0.371
Schwyz	0.298	0.697	0.012	0.417
Obwalden	0.290	0.755	0.013	0.373
Nidwalden	0.318	0.744	0.012	0.417
Glarus	0.230	0.460	0.009	0.488
Grisons	0.263	0.653	0.017	0.386
Ticino	0.285	0.695	0.012	0.399
Valais	0.335	0.800	0.022	0.400

Source: Coale and Treadway, 'Summary', pp. 149–50.

This indicates that caution is needed in using late nineteenth-century evidence to make inferences about the demography of the Alpine *ancien régime*. Not only in Switzerland, but also in Austria and Italy the values of about 0.700 observed in the 1880s might be due to a decline from higher levels of marital fertility. Overall fertility need not have been higher, though. It is remarkable that in these Swiss Cantons higher marital fertility was more than balanced, in 1860, by exceedingly low values of the index of proportion married (I_m): 0.347 in Schwyz, 0.279 in Uri and Nidwalden, 0.258 in Obwalden.

The case of Canton Glarus is no less interesting. A major feature of the demographic evolution of Switzerland is that fertility began to decline much earlier in the Protestant section of the population than among the Catholics. In the period between the two world wars the gap was still very wide.[45] This suggests that the higher birth and fertility rates of the Alpine cantons in the twentieth century may have been due not so much to their backwardness as to the fact that their population is overwhelmingly Catholic. The only Alpine canton with a predominant Protestant component is, in fact, Glarus.[46] And it is significant that in the 1880s a low level of overall fertility was already achieved, in this canton, not by curbing nuptiality (which was actually definitely higher than in the other cantons) but through family limitation.

In the Central and Eastern Alps, Glarus is apparently an exception. But on the basis of what is known about France in general, one should

[45] See Bickel, *Bevölkerungsgeschichte der Schweiz*, p. 230.
[46] In the second half of the nineteenth century Protestants accounted for about 80 per cent of the population of Canton Glarus and just over 50 per cent of the population of Canton Grisons. All the other Swiss Alpine cantons were overwhelmingly Catholic.

Table 4.8. *Fertility indices: French Alpine 'départements', 1861 and 1901*

	I_f	I_g	I_h	I_m
1861				
Savoie	0.301	0.723	0.019	0.401
Haute-Savoie	0.298	0.735	0.027	0.382
Isère	0.271	0.526	0.020	0.496
Hautes-Alpes	0.333	0.645	0.017	0.497
Basses-Alpes	0.296	0.513	0.012	0.567
Alpes Maritimes	0.291	0.538	0.025	0.518
1901				
Savoie	0.265	0.501	0.028	0.501
Haute-Savoie	0.272	0.547	0.025	0.473
Isère	0.207	0.385	0.021	0.511
Hautes-Alpes	0.293	0.527	0.020	0.490
Basses-Alpes	0.256	0.462	0.014	0.540
Alpes Maritimes	0.199	0.349	0.043	0.510

Source: Coale and Treadway, 'Summary', pp. 94–107.

expect this 'post-traditional' pattern to have prevailed in the French Alps as well. The indices calculated a few years ago by Étienne van de Walle for three Alpine *départements* (Isère, Hautes-Alpes, Basses-Alpes) would indeed seem to confirm this.[47] Van de Walle's book, however, did not include data on the provinces which became part of the French state in 1860. These data are now available, and offer a rather more varied picture than it might have been supposed. Table 4.8 shows that at the time of their annexation to France both parts of Savoy displayed a pattern which was dissimilar to that of the other French Alpine areas and much closer to Model A. But in the subsequent decades a steady decline of marital fertility took place, accompanied by an increase in nuptiality. By the end of the nineteenth century Savoy had more or less aligned itself with the rest of France.

As one can easily see, the results of the Princeton study broadly agree both with the three simple models proposed in Table 4.5 and with the indications derived from the anthropological literature. It should be observed that the anthropological sample consists mostly of high-altitude communities, whereas the figures worked out by the Princeton Project refer to wider administrative units which also included the villages and towns of the low valleys and the pre-Alpine belt. Since these lower-altitude areas are ecologically and economically rather different from the high valleys, it is likely that they also dis-

[47] É. van de Walle, *The female population of France*, pp. 235–40, 331–3.

played demographic differences.[48] All in all, however, there can be little doubt that in the second half of the nineteenth century overall fertility was moderate all over the Alps and that apart from Canton Glarus and some French *départements* this was mainly explained by the very low level of nuptiality.

Inheritance systems, family forms and environmental constraints

Both the anthropological sample and the Princeton study also direct the attention to another point of the utmost importance. As we saw in Chapter 1, it has been repeatedly argued that impartible inheritance (which in peasant societies maintains a fixed number of openings on the land) logically limits the number of marriages, which will also tend to be late. Partible inheritance, on the other hand, is expected to result in high nuptiality. Interestingly enough, of all the localities in the anthropological sample only the Austrian villages (including St Felix) had impartible inheritance. Yet nuptiality was only marginally lower, if at all, than in the other communities. The same indication comes from the Princeton figures, which demonstrate that different levels of nuptiality were clearly related to different levels of fertility but hardly to different inheritance systems. A high frequency of celibacy and a late age at marriage for both men and women were virtually ubiquitous whatever the inheritance system.

Inheritance systems are generally deemed to influence not only marriage patterns but also household structure and composition. Comparative evidence on nuptiality suggests, however, that Alpine marriage patterns could be shaped more effectively by environmental constraints than by the formal properties of inheritance and succession rules. We may therefore wonder whether household structure could also be affected more decisively by environmental factors than by inheritance and whether there existed, as a consequence, a specifically 'Alpine' household type. In his pioneering attempt to identify the

---

[48] An interesting indication comes from the French Alps themselves, where studies conducted after the Second World War found that in the high valleys marital fertility was higher than in the low valleys, but crude birth rates were very much the same or even lower. This was explained by the fact that in the high valleys permanent celibacy was more frequent, whereas in the low valleys family limitation was more widespread. High celibacy rates were partly an effect of mountain exodus. But the higher rates of marital fertility suggested that the people of the high valleys were still largely relying on the prudential check of marriage and had been slower in shifting to 'more modern forms of malthusianism'. See Veyret-Verner, 'L'évolution des méthodes', pp. 410–11.

distinguishing features of the Alpine culture area, Burns had indeed argued that one such feature was the stem family, which appeared to have been dominant throughout the Alps and stood in marked contrast to the joint family of the Mediterranean. 'Its significance in pointing up the unity of the Alpine zone.' he contended, 'inheres in the fact that it has entrenched itself firmly as family type even on the southern flanks of the cordillera, in regions which otherwise have been affected by a wide variety of Mediterranean influences.'[49]

Formulated in 1963, when Alpine anthropology was still in its early stages, this was a bold generalization – seriously at odds, we may notice, with what had just been reported by Wolf about inheritance rules and family forms in Tret and St Felix.[50] In his first spell of fieldwork, however, Wolf had mainly focussed on inheritance ideologies. Further research carried out by Wolf himself and by John Cole gradually revealed that the marriage pattern, the size of the holdings and the composition of domestic units were, in spite of differing ideologies, remarkably similar in both villages. Cultural and ideological factors were crucial to explain the very different structures of power and authority within the household found in Tret and St Felix. But in both villages environmental constraints apparently made it imperative to avoid the division of the estate, in order to retain holdings of optimum or at least viable size. In its turn, this caused in Tret no less than in St Felix a very low level of nuptiality and was conducive to the formation of households approaching the stem family type.[51]

In Burns's view, the rationale underlying the prevalence of the stem family in the Alps was almost self-evident: 'because the quantity of land involved is rarely if ever capable of supporting more than one household, its division among heirs ... is inevitably disastrous'.[52] Although their evidence was not conclusive, Cole and Wolf's work ultimately came to support this ecological argument. Reviewing some years later the anthropological literature on the Alpine family produced in the 1960s and 1970s, George Saunders arrived at very much the same conclusion. But he added that particularly in mountain areas, where domestic groups had to exploit varied types of land, a stem family organization seemed to possess other adaptive advantages. Unlike nuclear families, he observed, stem families could use marginally productive persons (such as the very young or the elderly) for

[49] Burns, 'The Circum-Alpine area', p. 143.
[50] Wolf, 'Cultural dissonance'. See Chapter 3 above, p. 54.
[51] Cole and Wolf, *The hidden frontier*, p. 202.
[52] Burns, 'The Circum-Alpine area', p. 143.

household chores, child care and drudgery, thus freeing the able-bodied for more physically demanding tasks. In this fashion, 'the stem family maximised its productive labor while providing security to the elderly and training for the young'.[53]

This was the state of the problem when, in the spring of 1979, I began my study of Alagna. Like most anthropologists who have worked in the Alps, I soon discovered that direct observation was of little use to highlight the structure and composition of the household in the traditional past. In Alagna, as in the vast majority of Alpine villages today, neolocality was both the ideal and the norm. But one could hardly expect otherwise. For one thing, the two ecological rationales of stem family formation proposed by Saunders (the need to retain a holding of viable size and the labour requirements of the household in a mountain environment) have obviously lost their force with the waning of agro-pastoral activities. Moreover, in many Alpine localities household structure has also been seriously affected by depopulation and the exodus of young adults. This, it is claimed, has not only altered the composition of the households but has also made housing more available, thus favouring the formation of independent nuclear families.[54] In Alagna the situation was rather different, for depopulation had not been too severe and the problem of housing was complicated by tourist development. It was clear, on the other hand, that residential arrangements had been deeply affected by the major changes which had occurred in the spatial distribution of the population and by the abandonment of the outlying hamlets. Also, I was told that neolocality had already been common before the Second World War, largely because of the immigration and in-marriage of miners, who almost without exception formed new households at marriage.

If direct observation was of little use, my informants' reminiscences enabled me to restore in rich detail what they regarded to be the traditional inheritance and family patterns. Alagna's system of inheritance was said by all older villagers to have been characterized by complete partibility. As in German-speaking Valais, each heir was entitled to an equal share of the estate, regardless of sex and age.[55] My informants could not envisage the harsh impartible system of Tyrol, which they found unjust and inhuman. Yet the residential

[53] Saunders, 'Social change', pp. 210–13.
[54] See Saunders, 'Social change', p. 230, and Sibilla, *Una comunità walser*, pp. 133–4.
[55] On inheritance patterns in German-speaking Valais, see Friedl, *Kippel*, pp. 61–2, and Netting, *Balancing on an alp*, pp. 172–3.

pattern was not so different in Alagna from arrangements commonly
believed to be dependent on inheritance systems emphasizing impartibility. Custom demanded that the ageing parents 'must not be left
alone' and at least one of the sons was expected to stay with them
after his marriage. When there was an only daughter, an uxorilocal
marriage would take place. Moreover, it was almost mandatory for
unmarried siblings to continue to reside with their parents and married
brother, pooling the property and operating a single economic unit.
Given these residential rules, one can expect the formation of a good
number of complex households formally identical to the ones found
in Tyrol and other areas of impartible inheritance.

At first sight, this oral evidence appeared to strengthen the argument that, in spite of differing inheritance ideologies, Alpine households tended to approach the form of a stem family. The listing of
1935 recorded, in fact, several examples of co-residential arrangements
which could be seen as developmental stages of a stem family structure. But in Alagna support of the elderly seemed to have been a
more important *raison d'être* of stem family formation than the environmental imperatives posited by most Alpine anthropologists. What is
more, my informants' recollections of their family life suggested that
in Alagna there had been no rule preventing two married brothers
from living together in the same household and forming what is
usually called a 'joint family'. The listing of 1935 contained no instance
of co-resident married brothers, and there can be little doubt that
in the period between the two world wars such a residential arrangement was exceedingly rare. But it was hard to tell whether this was
a relatively recent change or whether joint families had been, even
in former times, far more exceptional than the fragmentary and anecdotal evidence provided by the older villagers implied.

Nevertheless, my data seemed to provide some quantitative corrob-
oration to the view (held by most Alpine anthropologists) that in the
past complex households were much more numerous than today.
As Table 4.9 shows, in 1935 the proportion of complex households
(types 4 and 5 in the Laslett-Hammel classificatory scheme), though
not really impressive, was considerably higher than in 1980. Further
support to this view has recently come from the researches of a number
of anthropologists who have worked in the Western Alps and have
applied the Laslett-Hammel typology to the analysis of late nineteenth
or early twentieth-century census material. The data they have published suggest that in the past the proportion of complex households
might have been very high indeed. For example, in the 1930s Festiona,
a village in the Piedmontese Alps, contained about 12 per cent of

Table 4.9. *Household structure in Alagna, 1935 and 1980*

	1935		1980	
	N	%	N	%
1. Solitaries	34	20.5	46	28.9
2. No family	15	9.0	7	4.4
3. Simple-family households	93	56.0	100	62.9
4. Extended-family households	18	10.8	4	2.5
5. Multiple-family households	6	3.6	2	1.3
Total	166	99.9	159	100.0
Complex households (4 + 5)	24	14.4	6	3.8
Mean household size	2.99		2.62	

Note: The typology is the standard one devised by the Cambridge Group for the History of Population and Social Structure. The term 'no family' designates households consisting of coresident siblings, coresident relatives of other kinds, or persons not evidently related. A 'simple-family household' is found when a conjugal family lives on its own. An 'extended-family household' consists in a conjugal family with the addition of one or more relatives other than offspring. Finally, 'multiple family households' comprise all forms of domestic groups which include two or more conjugal families connected by kinship or by marriage. For a fuller description, see Laslett, 'Introduction', pp. 28–32; and Hammel and Laslett, 'Comparing household structure'.
Sources: See Table 4.1.

complex households, slightly less than in Alagna. But in 1877 the proportion was as high as 25.7 per cent.[56]

However, the results of Netting's analysis of household structures in Törbel show very effectively that a long-term evolution from complex to simple forms, though not implausible in the Alps, cannot be taken for granted. In Törbel, a transition can be detected from the high proportion of complex households recorded towards the end of the nineteenth century (approximately 25 per cent, as in Festiona) to the overwhelming dominance of simple family households observed today. But in the first half of the nineteenth century simple family households were nearly as dominant as they are now, and the proportion of complex households fairly negligible. What Netting convincingly suggests is that the increase in the number of complex households was due to the impact of demographic factors, in particular the decline of mortality and the population expansion of the second half of the nineteenth century. Changes in household composition

[56] Destro, *L'ultima generazione*, pp. 111–23. See also Saunders, 'Social change', pp. 221–9, and Albera, 'I giovani e il matrimonio', pp. 65–97.

were, he maintains, a response to physical constraints limiting the formation of neolocal households.[57]

Netting's work is highly instructive in several ways. It is, first of all, a reminder of the need to take into full account, in the study of family forms in the Alps, the effects of changing demographic constraints and opportunities. Secondly, the empirical evidence he supplies confirms that the anthropological arguments concerning the predominance of the stem family and its adaptive advantages are still far from being conclusively demonstrated. But the most important lesson to be learnt from the case of Törbel is perhaps that the time span covered by anthropological investigations, even when these are not meant to be strictly synchronic, is usually too shallow for the anthropologist to be able to determine how old an allegedly traditional form of family organization really is and to judge its ecological merits in a broad evolutionary perspective. The authors of a recent and intriguing oral historical study of traditional family patterns in the Valtellina (in the Italian Central Alps) have thought it justified to assume that, because of the geographical and economic isolation of the valley, the picture provided by their informants must have changed very little from the Middle Ages.[58] But this is a very dangerous assumption, tantamount to stating that before the transformations of recent decades the inhabitants of this valley had been, to use a once favourite anthropological phrase, 'people without history'.

The same risk is involved in the explanation of the marriage pattern observed in most parts of the Alps between 1850 and the Second World War. It is obviously tempting to reason that since in mountain areas environmental constraints have been until recently by and large unchanging then late marriage and high celibacy rates must have been a central feature of Alpine demography for a very long time. However, what data we possess on age at marriage in the second half of the nineteenth century do not enhance our confidence. Although still within the limits of the European marriage pattern, in several villages (including Alagna) marriage ages were lower than in the first half of the twentieth century. Moreover, the possibility cannot be ruled out that in the late nineteenth and early twentieth centuries celibacy rates may have reached unprecedented levels, as Hajnal suggested for the whole of north-western Europe.

Some anthropologists have stressed the similarities between the Alps

[57] Netting, *Balancing on an alp*, pp. 214–17. A similar increase in the proportion of complex households during the nineteenth century is reported for two localities in the Resia Valley (Italian Eastern Alps) by Morassi and Panjek, 'Strategie familiari'.
[58] Benetti *et al.*, *Uomini delle Alpi*, criticized by Viazzo, 'Due nuovi libri', pp. 305–6.

and the classic anthropological example of post-famine Ireland, where celibacy was a means of avoiding the division of estates and at the same time, along with late marriage, a means of controlling population growth.[59] But Alpine anthropologists should clearly avoid the pitfall fallen into by Arensberg and Kimball in their famous and influential study of the Irish stem family, when they failed to realize that the traditional nuptiality and family patterns they were discussing were scarcely a hundred years old at the time of their research.[60] Tantalizing bits of evidence scattered in the anthropological literature suggest that, if Alpine anthropologists were able to dig more deeply into the demographic history of their villages, a number of surprising findings would probably emerge. In her study of the Austrian village of St Georgen, for example, Sigrid Khera reports that in the 1820s marriage age for both men and women was much lower than a century later.[61] Unfortunately, this may often prove a very hard task even for the historically minded anthropologist. In a few exceptional cases some data may be directly available, as in St Georgen. But in general it is necessary to proceed to family reconstitution, a time-consuming effort which not all anthropological investigators can afford. And yet, the important questions left unsolved by the evidence surveyed in this chapter indicate that it is only by adopting a long-term historical perspective that some major anthropological hypotheses about marriage and family organization in the Alps can be tested, and the role of environmental and demographic factors correctly assessed.

[59] See Friedl and Ellis, 'Celibacy, late marriage and potential mates', pp. 23–5.
[60] Arensberg and Kimball, *Family and community in Ireland*.
[61] In the decade 1822–31 the mean age at first marriage was apparently as low as 24.0 years for men and 22.6 years for women, whereas in the period 1892–1933 it ranged between 29.2 and 31.6 years for men and 25.4 and 27.2 for women. See Khera, 'Illegitimacy', p. 312.

5

The traditional economy and its demise

The decline of mountain farming

The preceding chapter has suggested that in the study of recent trends in Alpine demography it is sometimes difficult to distinguish between short-term fluctuations and deeper structural transformations. On the other hand, it would seem hardly open to question that in the economic sphere the spectacular changes which have occurred in the last few decades, and particularly the decline of mountain farming, represent radical departures from the past. To be sure, villages where the majority of the labour force is engaged in farming still do exist, but they are much less numerous now than they were only twenty or thirty years ago. Moreover, these villages are the ones where mountain depopulation has been most pronounced. Swiss studies, corroborated by recent data on the Italian Western Alps, indicate that predominantly agro-pastoral communities now tend to have less than 300 inhabitants.[1] If we further consider that people of prime working age are often outnumbered by pensioners, it becomes clear that in these villages the seeming stability of the occupational structure masks a crisis of agricultural and pastoral activities which is no less serious than in peasant-worker communities or in tourist resorts.

The census data used by geographers and economists in their analyses of post-war economic trends leave no doubt that in the last forty years the decline of mountain farming has been general (and, in all likelihood, irreversible) throughout the Alpine area. It should be noticed, however, that these studies not only rely on a useful set of types of community but also arrange them (more or less explicitly) along an evolutionary sequence. As we have seen in Chapter 4, those

---

[1] Cf. Furrer and Wegmann, 'Bevölkerungsveränderungen in den Schweizer Alpen', and UCCP, *I redditi dei comuni del Piemonte*.

communities where most people are still engaged in agricultural or pastoral activities are classified as 'traditional'. At the opposite end of the spectrum, communities where the majority of the working population is employed in industry or in tourism are classified as 'modernized'. This is an indication that the authors of these studies take it for granted that in the 'traditional past' the economy of Alpine communities was essentially agro-pastoral. Although it would be foolish to dispute the importance of agriculture and pastoralism in the Alpine past, there are reasons to believe that the acceptance of such an evolutionary scheme extrapolated from post-war census data can adversely affect our understanding of Alpine economy in former times and fetter our interpretation of change. In order to demonstrate some of the risks involved, this chapter will examine a few aspects of the recent economic history of the Alps and will focus in particular on the case of Alagna, a village which provides (as we have seen in the previous chapter) a good example of a 'modernized' community.

If we trust the 1951 General Census, in that year 61 out of Alagna's 156 employed men, and 80 out of 100 employed women, were engaged in agriculture or livestock raising. These proportions are probably somewhat lower than in most other high valleys at that time. But, in view of Alagna's long involvement with mining and tourism, it is not surprising to find a sizable proportion of people employed in the secondary and tertiary sectors. Agriculture was nevertheless the main occupation for both men and women. The following decades have witnessed, as Table 5.1 shows, a steady growth of the tertiary sector, which in 1980 accounted for 58.9 per cent of the active population – or even 80 per cent if we add the 36 men who worked in the building industry, which in the Alps is now almost totally dependent on tourism. In 1980 the number of miners had sharply declined from 39 in 1971 to just 11, and agriculture or pastoralism were the main activity of only 7 men and 17 women, mostly in their forties or fifities.

The decline of mountain farming in Alagna is no less clearly documented by the changes one can detect in the landscape. Photographs taken around the turn of the century show careful terracing and a still considerable extension of cultivated land. Today, the terraced slopes remind the visitor of the long struggle against a forbidding environment, but they are more and more neglected and the dry-stone walls are collapsing. Even more strikingly, the patchwork of tiny fields which is so notable a feature of Alpine scenery has almost completely disappeared. The cultivation of rye and hemp – the two symbols of mountain self-sufficiency – was already very much on the decrease in the years before the Second World War, and has since then ceased

Table 5.1. *Occupational structure in Alagna 1951–1980*

	1951		1961		1971		1980	
	N	%	N	%	N	%	N	%
Agriculture	141	55.1	82	37.3	35	16.4	24	13.3
Industry	50	19.5	67	30.5	81	38.0	50	27.8
Tertiary sector	65	25.4	71	32.3	97	45.5	106	58.9
Total	256	100.0	220	100.1	213	99.9	180	100.0

Sources: 1951–71: ISTAT, *Censimenti generali*. 1980: my own census.

altogether. Estimates for 1970 indicate that cultivated land (mostly planted with potatoes) amounted to about 13 hectares, a mere 4 per cent of all potentially cultivable land.[2]

In 1970 pastures and meadows still occupied 650 hectares, but the decline of pastoralism has in fact been no less dramatic. As Table 5.2 shows, the animal population decreased between 1845 and 1918 much more sharply than the human population. These figures do not necessarily imply that the pastures were exploited below their carrying capacity. From the end of the nineteenth century it became very common to lease alps to outsiders, mainly shepherds and herdsmen from a neighbouring mountain area. This makes it extremely difficult to distinguish, from the First World War onwards, between the total number of cattle pastured in Alagna's territory and the number owned by local residents. For the 1940s and 1950s, reliable informants gave me estimates of 2,000–2,200 head of livestock (including sheep and goats) and it is conceivable that no more than one-fifth or one-sixth of them belonged to people living in Alagna. In the last twenty years or so, the total number of cattle 'carried' by the summer pastures has greatly diminished, mainly because most alps have proved increasingly inadequate to handle the needs of professional herdsmen. As far as the local population is concerned, one owner after the other has dropped out. In 1970, thirty-three owners possessed 127 head of cattle and 42 smaller animals. In 1980 the number of animals was probably greater, but there were only some fifteen owners left. The overwhelming majority of the animals belongs today to three or four professional herdsmen possessing up to fifty head each.

The story of Alagna's recent social and economic changes is, at first sight, a very simple one. Supported by the statistics on land

[2] ISTAT, *Secondo censimento dell'agricoltura*.

Table 5.2. *Animals owned in Alagna 1845–1918*

Year	Inhabitants	Cattle	Goats	Sheep
1845	ca 700	1,000	500	1,000
1881	677	861	273	599
1908	ca 700	495	140	217
1918	ca 650	499	100	172

Sources: 1845: Gnifetti, *Nozioni topografiche*, pp. 8–9. 1881–1918: Spanna, 'Val Sesia', p. 140.

use and the number of animals, the data on the occupational structure strongly suggest that in the course of a single generation the advent of mass tourism has completely changed the face of a village which in the early 1950s was still an essentially agricultural community. The case of Alagna, it would seem, tallies well with S. H. Franklin's general picture of the transformations undergone by peasant society in Europe after the Second World War – a profound restructuring of rural life resulting in 'a final divorce from the existence of the preceding centuries'.[3]

This is, however, only part of the truth. From the very first talks I had with my informants in Alagna it became apparent that in the 'traditional past' agriculture and pastoralism had not been the only pillars of the economic and cultural system of the village. When I started inquiring about the agro-pastoral life of old, I was surprised to discover that virtually every activity, including the hard work in the fields, was carried out by women. As to men, an old woman told me, '... well, there were also a few of them who put up with working in the fields'. But these were mostly immigrant miners, who were temporarily unemployed and were hired as day-labourers by the local families. Otherwise, agriculture was a proper occupation only for retired men and for boys under thirteen or fourteen – 'then boys had to go abroad to serve their three-year apprenticeship'.

This characterization of agriculture as something a man had 'to put up with' had very little in common with the image of the proud *Bauer* which emerges from the anthropological literature on the German-speaking Alpine world.[4] Significantly, in Alagna the term *pur* (the local variant of *Bauer*) survived almost only in the phrase 'to work like a *pur*' to indicate a man working as hard as a beast. Agriculture

[3] Franklin, *The European peasantry*, p. 6.
[4] See Honigmann, 'Bauer and Arbeiter'; Khera, 'Social stratification'; Cole and Wolf, *The hidden frontier*, pp. 10–11, 267–9; and Gal, *Language shift*, pp. 56–8.

was the realm of women. Men's realm was emigration – a seasonal emigration which took place in summer and was therefore incompatible with the requirements of agricultural work.

The end of seasonal emigration

Most emigrants from Alagna were skilled, well-paid plasterers. After completing primary school, boys were expected for the next two or three years to attend the drawing school which had been founded in the village in 1869 to provide some useful preliminary training. Some gifted pupils could receive further instruction in Varallo (the valley's chief town) or even at the Academy of Fine Arts in Turin, in order to become professional painters and sculptors. The majority, however, went abroad to serve their apprenticeship with fellow villagers who ran small firms in Swiss and French towns.

It is very instructive to calculate the proportion of plasterers out of all the bridegrooms born in Alagna, as recorded in the municipal marriage registers since their inception in 1866 (Table 5.3). These figures take us back to the middle of the nineteenth century and substantiate the assertion, made by a local scholar in 1845, that about 140 men left every year in the spring to work abroad in the building industry.[5] This is an enormous number for a village of 700 inhabitants. It explains why, to quote another nineteenth-century local scholar, women were 'incredibly active, the younger ones tending their herds in the alps, the others working in the fields, reaping, sowing, and carrying the crops on their shoulders'.[6]

Table 5.3 also shows that the plasterer's trade came to an abrupt end in the 1930s. Mainly oriented towards France, the Alagnese emigration was decisively affected first by the measures taken by the French government in 1926 to curb immigration, and then by the restrictions placed on emigration abroad by the Italian government in 1927. By 1929 Italian emigration to France had dropped to one-quarter of what it had been in the previous years.[7] Instead of starting their period of apprenticeship, the batch of Alagnese boys who were due to go to France that year stayed in the drawing school for another one or two years, but they had eventually to resign themselves to other (less rewarding) crafts. The courses in drawing were discontinued and most boys were apprenticed to carpenters in the lower Sesia Valley. The older plasterers who had already worked abroad were not

---

[5] Gnifetti, *Nozioni topografiche*, p. 6.   [6] Giordani, *La colonia tedesca*, pp. 11–12.
[7] Faidutti-Rudolph, *L'immigration italienne*, pp. 5–9.

Table 5.3. *Proportion of plasterers out of all Alagna-born bridegrooms*
1866–1950

Years	All	Plasterers	%
1866–70	18	14	77.8
1871–80	39	24	61.5
1881–90	26	20	76.9
1891–1900	30	17	56.7
1901–10	28	17	60.7
1911–20	11	6	54.5
1921–30	22	9	40.9
1931–40	16	1	6.2
1941–50	20	0	0.0

Source: ACA, Marriage registers.

forbidden to emigrate, and a few of them managed to remain faithful to the traditional pattern of seasonal migration up to the threshold of the Second World War. Fearing that the situation could worsen, some decided to settle abroad on a permanent basis.

In all these respects Alagna is probably representative of general trends which can be detected not only in the rest of the Italian Alps[8] but also, to cite a well-studied example, in such regions of Austria as Vorarlberg and Western Tyrol. A distinctive form of labour migration from these Austrian regions was that of the so-called *Schwabenkinder*, children aged between seven and fifteen years who moved to Southern Germany to work there as herdsmen or shepherds in the summer pastures. But these regions had also been characterized, since at least the late eighteenth century, by the summer emigration of large numbers of masons and stone-cutters to Switzerland and some parts of Germany.[9] Both forms of emigration rapidly petered out after the end of the First World War, when Germany had little to offer to foreign workers and Switzerland also restricted immigration. As Adolf Lässer reports in his detailed study of St Leonhard im Pitztal, a village in Western Tyrol, for a few years those who had relatives or friends in Switzerland still managed to emigrate. But in 1949 there were in St Leonhard only three seasonal emigrants as compared to sixty or seventy in the years before the First World War.[10] In this

---

[8] Cf. e.g. Giusti, 'Note riassuntive', p. liii; and Riccarand and Omezzoli, *Émigration valdôtaine*, pp. 47–52.

[9] See Lässer, *St. Leonhard im Pitztal*, and Keller, 'Die Bevölkerungsentwicklung im Ausserfern'.

[10] Lässer, *St. Leonhard im Pitztal*, p. 76.

community, as in Alagna and in many other villages in the Alps, the barriers erected against immigration by France and Switzerland, the economic crisis of the 1930s, universal military conscription and, finally, the outbreak of the war all concurred in causing the end of seasonal emigration.

For a village like Alagna, whose population had long been accustomed to a certain level of prosperity, the joint effects of the Great Depression and of the forced end of emigration must have been especially painful. The 1930s are remembered as a period of unprecedented hardship, poverty and lack of security. In the years before the Second World War, and even more during the war and the immediate post-war years, Alagna had to revert to an existence which was probably more autarkic than it had ever been for at least a century. Remarkably, if not surprisingly, a few men even started to work in the fields. Indeed, in the decade between 1941 and 1950 we find five bridegrooms classified as 'peasants', an occupation which had previously occurred in the marriage registers only once since 1866. The high number of men in agriculture recorded in the 1951 census is partly explained by this novel development. (And partly, we may add, by the fact that in those years a certain number of artisans managed to be legally registered as agricultural workers so as to be entitled to receive a pension from the state.)

The war led to another accidental yet remarkable departure. In order to escape military service, several men volunteered to work in the local mines and therefore joined the immigrant miners who were already employed there. Within the memory of men, villagers of local descent had only exceptionally, if ever, engaged in mining. The *erzlit*, as the miners were called in the local German dialect,[11] had always been a category of people apart, surrounded by a somewhat legendary aura. According to a local tradition, the mines had originally been a convict colony, and I was shown the now dilapidated 'prison' where the convicts were allegedly detained. Whatever its historical merits, this tradition reflects a sometimes unfavourable, and always uneasy, perception of mining and miners. Alagna's men had gradually come to define their identity in opposition to both the *pur* who worked in the fields and the *erzmo* who worked in the mines – two categories not so far removed from one another in Alagna, since it was the *erzmo* who most easily turned into a day-labourer in agriculture. Ironically, the end of the plasterer's trade was sealed, for the local men, by their ephemeral transformation into peasants and miners.

---

[11] The literal meaning of the term *erzlit* (sing.: *erzmo*) is 'ore-people'.

The cultural significance of emigration

Aptly entitled 'Die Lage heute: die Zeit ohne Saisonwanderung', the last chapter of Lässer's study of St Leonhard leaves little doubt that in the recent history of many an Alpine valley the end of seasonal emigration must have been a watershed not only from an economic but also from a social and a cultural point of view. Whatever the causes that had induced the first emigrants to leave their homes for a few months every year, it is evident that in villages like Alagna and St Leonhard emigration had become a deeply rooted and 'undisputed' custom (as Lässer says) and that its disappearance was bound to leave a wide social and cultural gap.

Up to the 1930s, as we have just noticed, being an emigrant had been a crucial component of the ethnic identity of any Alagnese man *vis-à-vis* the immigrant miners coming from outside. Also, the period of apprenticeship to be spent abroad almost ritually marked a boy's passage to manhood. As soon as he was five or six, a boy started to help tending the family herd or was hired by other families needing some additional labour. For a few years he would spend the summers in the fields and the alps, thus becoming intimately acquainted with the places and with a wide range of agricultural and pastoral activities. But he knew that his destiny was to become a plasterer. When he left for the first time for France or Switzerland, he was joining the ranks of men, leaving behind both the dark world of the *erzlit* and agriculture, which was to remain the realm of women.

Not surprisingly, the theme of emigration pervades the whole corpus of Alagna's traditional songs. Indeed, the most popular of these songs, *D'Landra*, is a celebration of the coming home of the emigrants:

D'Landra sind lustig,	The Alagnese are merry,
sind lustig im Land.	are merry in Alagna.
Die trinchind champagne,	They drink champagne,
und schlofind fum stroh.	and sleep on straw.

Even more revealing is, however, a wedding song which was still sung in the years immediately before the First World War. It starts as follows:

Ich ging in ainem obend spoot	I went late in the evening
der liebstu vor dem loden ...	before my beloved's window ...

Everyone having some familiarity with Walser dialects will notice at once that this is not Walser-German. There are phonetic alterations throughout (a typically Alagnese *obend spoot* instead of *abend spät*, for instance), but this is evidently one of those 'German poems imported from Switzerland' which, it is reported, 'were read and learned by

heart by the youth'.[12] This is so, however, only as far as the first
fourteen lines are concerned. For the last lines are marked by a sudden
shift, both lexical and grammatical, to Alagnese German and by the
unexpected introduction of the theme of emigration:

Behut dich Gott mi schatzelain,	Will God protect you, my sweetheart,
ich muas in fremdi landen.	I must go abroad.
Wos ich und du geholdet hain	That I and you have made love
ist mir und dir kain schanden.	is for me and you no shame.

The social morphology of an Alpine community

It is appropriate for an Alagnese wedding song to end with a touch
of sadness. The bitterness of parting must have been experienced
very often by newly wed couples. Many young men were away for
most of the year. They were due back on St Nicholas' day on 6
December and had to leave after less than three months. It was therefore in the winter that most weddings took place. Of the 215 marriages
celebrated in Alagna from 1871 to 1920, sixty-nine took place in January
and as many in February. In spite of church regulations prohibiting
marriages during Advent, December came third with 16. Thus, about
three-quarters of all weddings were concentrated in the three winter
months. In the decade 1921–30 this pattern was still detectable (47.4
per cent of all weddings took place during the winter), but broke
down completely in the 1930s, when seasonal emigration also came
to an abrupt end.

It was not infrequent for three or four weddings to be celebrated
in the same month, with their surrounding rituals, the banquets, the
dances accompanied by the music of the violinist. It is easy to imagine
how greatly weddings added to the cheerful atmosphere of months
already studded with feasts. The cycle of major feasts lasted one
month, from St Nicholas' day on 6 December, which marked the coming back of the emigrants and the beginning of the winter season,
to the feast of the youth (*jungulittutanz*) on 6 January. Even more
than Christmas day, which was spent at home, the heart of this festive
period was represented by the great evening dance of St Stephen's
day and by the solemn high mass on the day of St John the Evangelist,
which is regarded by the villagers as the Patron Saint's day. Interestingly enough, Alagna's patron saint is actually St John the Baptist.

---

[12]   Giordani, *La colonia tedesca*, p. 7.

It is another demonstration of the importance of emigration that the village's principal religious feast was moved from 24 June to the winter so as to be celebrated also by the men.

The *fasnachtfir*, the carnival bonfire, marked not only the passage to the drab Lenten period but also a major transformation in Alagna's social life. For most men, it was time to emigrate. But the emigrants were not the only ones to leave the village. On 19 March, St Joseph's day, about one-third of the remaining population moved from the valley floor at 1,200 m of altitude to Otro, the upper segment of a small tributary glen of the main valley, at over 1,600 m. These people belonged to a group of about sixty or seventy households, which formed a corporation enjoying exclusive rights in the pastoral and agricultural resources of the Otro valley. Legally designated in the old Latin documents as *consortes Oltri*, they also had possessions in the main valley, including a little farm land and the houses where they spent the winter months. However, the land they owned in Otro was more valuable, and coveted by the other villagers. The shaded side of the Otro valley is steep and densely forested, with just a few clearings used as pastures. But the opposite side basks in the sun for more months of the year and for more hours in the day than any other area in the territory of Alagna. Moreover, it slopes down very gently to the stream and therefore provides excellent land for either cultivated fields or meadows. In the past Otro supported for nine months – from 19 March to the middle of December – approximately 200 people, who lived in six hamlets made up of wooden houses exactly like those on the valley floor. For nine months the inhabitants of these six hamlets formed a small community within the community, with a little church, a chaplain and even a school with a teacher. They celebrated their own religious festivals and sang songs they alone knew.

Alagna was not, therefore, as compact a community as it could appear during the winter months, when all its members attended the religious festivals and took part in the carnival processions. Its 'social morphology', to use Marcel Mauss's term, changed very significantly in the course of the year; and it is difficult not to conceptualize this change in classic Maussian terms as a period of aggregation – the winter – followed by a dispersal.[13] Such a phase of dispersal began with the leaving of the emigrants and the transfer of a sizable portion of the population to Otro but culminated in the summer when each household, already deprived of its young men, had to disperse

---

[13] Cf. Mauss and Beuchat, 'Variations saisonnières'.

to outbuildings in order to cope with the requirements of the agro-pastoral economy.

In April, as soon as the snow began to melt, the villagers who had remained at home had to start clearing the soil of stones and debris. Then, the fields had to be dug and manured, and potatoes planted. It was only towards the end of May that the cows were let out of their stalls to graze in the vicinity of their owners' houses. Added to such routine activities such as housekeeping, feeding and grooming livestock, cleaning stalls and churning butter, the first tasks of the agricultural year placed a heavy burden on Alagna's predominantly female labour force. Even the help of small children was badly needed. Until the First World War the school year did in fact end around the middle of April. It was in June, however, and even more in July that activities reached their climax.

In Alagna, as is typical of Walser colonies, each household individually exploited fairly small portions of pastureland. There is evidence that in the rather remote past, when they were still very numerous, sheep and goats were communally tended by hired shepherds. Cattle, however, were a very different matter. I was struck by how resolutely old villagers replied to my question as to whether communal herding of cattle had ever been practised: 'No, no, no!', was the characteristically vehement answer of an aged woman who had spent many a summer in the alps, 'we had each our share of pastureland marked by boundaries, and had to be very careful not to let the cows cross them, otherwise we had quarrels with our neighbours'. The idea of pooling the resources of all the households having grazing rights in an alp was rejected by my informants as nonsense. Sometimes, two or three households closely related through kinship could agree to have their animals tended by one member of the family. This was particularly advantageous for the weaker households, which in Alagna mainly consisted of widows or elderly maiden aunts living on their own and possessing only one or two cows. But, whenever possible, each domestic group took care of its animals. Thus, in early June the household had to split up. One or two women spent the summer in the alp, in charge both of the small family herd and of dairy operations. The others remained in the village to tend the fields and mow the hay.

In the Alpine regions, where the animals have to be fed in byres throughout the six or seven winter months, hay-making is obviously an all-important activity. It is also an arduous, time-consuming one. In Alagna, the various households could partly solve their problems of labour shortage by hiring a boy (*hirtij*, 'young herdsman') or a young woman (*jungfrowwa*, 'servant') for the whole summer season, while day-labourers were recruited locally from among the miners to perform especially hard work. But a considerable number of mowers (know as *ranzin*), often coming from distant Italian regions, had to be hired during the peak period of hay-making. In the pastoral sphere, the main tasks were entrusted to the *màsseira*, typically one of the unmarried household daughters. She could be helped by another member of the household (perhaps her mother, or a maiden aunt, or a younger brother) or by a *hirtij*. But, if the family herd was very small, or if the labour shortage problems had not been successfully overcome, she might spend the whole summer alone in the alp.

Since the alps were privately owned and individually managed, there was no fixed day on which all households were expected to move their animals. Much depended on the specific characteristics of the sector of Alagna's territory where the alp was situated. In general, however, the alp season began in early June, when the animals were moved to a hut placed at about 1,500 m of altitude and surrounded by a small grazing area where they were fed for a week. Around the middle of June the cattle moved upwards to the 1,700– 1,800 m of the 'lower alp' (*in d'undrun alpu*), and at the end of July to over 2,000 m on the 'upper alp' (*in d'oubrun alpu*), where they were pastured until the first snowfalls of early September.

In early September, roughly six months after the *fasnachtfir*, another bonfire marked the beginning of autumn. The *fraidfir* ('joy-fire') was the highpoint of the feast celebrating the end of the alp season. Snow had already whitened the highest pastures, and it was time to go down to the lower alp, where the animals spent slightly more than one month, until the middle of October. Then, another week was spent in the same hut as in early June, and by the end of October the cows were back in the village, where they browsed on stubble and on the so-called 'third hay'. The main agricultural tasks were now the potato harvest, manuring the fields and sowing rye. It was also necessary to collect firewood, beech leaves to restuff the mattresses, and larch needles for animal litter.

This part of the year was, however, more characteristically associated with other kinds of activity. It was in autumn that each household butchered a pig, a sheep, and perhaps even a cow. The meat was processed into sausage or salted down and was used (along with boiled potatoes, carrots and onions) to prepare the *uberlekke*, the most traditional and substantial dish in the Alagnese winter diet. Pigs and cows are still butchered today by several households, but on a much smaller scale than in the past. Around the middle of the nineteenth

century, every year in the month of October about ninety pigs, fifty
or more head of cattle and 400 rams and goats were killed and salted
down among the different households.[14] The resulting diet, rich in
animal food, was 'generally an unaccustomed luxury elsewhere', as
an English traveller remarked.[15] It was also in autumn that the rye-
bread, which was made only once a year, was baked in the hamlets'
communal ovens.

The winter season properly began when snow forced the cows
indoors. Since the hay crop was insufficient to support all the animals,
many cows had to be dispatched to the lower Sesia Valley, or even
to the more distant plains of Piedmont and Lombardy, to spend the
winter there. Those cows which remained in the village were stabled
in local byres – 'and till May', as an old woman complained to me,
'there was no way of letting them out because of the snow'. In Alagna,
scattered snowfalls are likely to occur as early as the middle of October,
and they may sometimes be very heavy indeed. But they are short-
lived and it is usually not until the end of November or the beginning
of December that a permanent cloak of snow settles down over the
village. The three important saints whose days fall in this period (St
Catherine on 25 November, St Andrew on 30 November, and St Nicholas on 6 December) were called in Alagna *schneichreimra*, 'snow merchants'. And if St Andrew came only with his snow – *Sankt Andrei
chinnt mit sinem schnei*, as the proverb goes – St Nicholas also brought
back the emigrants and his day marked the real starting-point of a
new year.

Conclusions

Alagna is just one among thousands of Alpine villages, but I thought
it useful to rely at some length on my own ethnographic study of
this community for two opposite reasons. On the one hand, there
is little doubt that some of the major changes Alagna has experienced
in this century – such as the demise of mountain farming or the abrupt
end of seasonal emigration – are common to many other parts of
the Alps. It is also apparent that Alagna's agro-pastoral organization
displayed most of the basic traits which are taken to be typical of
Alpwirtschaft. Thus, the detailed ethnographic description of the
annual cycle of activities in this village gives a reasonable idea of
what life used to be like in many an upland community. It highlights,
in particular, one of the most distinctive and conspicuous characteris-

---

[14] Gnifetti, *Nozioni topografiche*, p. 6.   [15] King, *The Italian valleys*, p. 375.

tics of Alpine populations, namely their marked, sometimes extreme
spatial dispersion for long periods of the year.[16] But it is also clear,
on the other hand, that Alagna departs in several significant respects
from the ecological model of the mountain community outlined in
Chapter 1.

It should be noticed, first of all, that Alagna's local economy as
it can be remembered by even the oldest villagers was scarcely a closed,
self-contained system. From their recollections, it appears that well
before the First World War the major part of the grain supply was
purchased from outside. What is more, in spite of the shrinkage of
cultivated fields the hay crop was not sufficient to support the diminished village herd. Many cows therefore had to spend the winter
in the lowlands. Indeed, works by nineteenth-century local writers
report that around the middle of that century grain was already largely
imported from outside. In the same period, if our sources are to be
trusted, no less than one half of the cows were wintered in the lowlands following what is described – in 1845 – as 'an old custom'.[17]

Although the case of Alagna does not allow any easy generalization,
it should not simply be regarded as an anomaly. It is well known,
in particular, that in the nineteenth century 'inverse transhumance',
as geographers call the movements of cattle from the mountains to
the plains, was a widespread phenomenon.[18] Since winter stabling
is the linchpin of the notion of *Alpwirtschaft* as a closed equilibrium
system and establishes, in the last analysis, the legitimacy of treating
mountain villages as ecosystems, this raises fundamental questions
about the nature of the Alpine agro-pastoral economy. In Chapter
1 we have noticed that a great number of communities possessed
statutes which prohibited cattle owners to carry on the pastures more
animals than they could winter, and that several recent studies have
taken such statutes as a demonstration that the economy of these
communities was a closed system approaching equilibrium. In at least
one of these studies, however, oral evidence is also reported which
clearly indicates that in the late nineteenth century cows were, in
fact, largely wintered in the adjacent lowlands.[19] It is of course possible
to interpret such a discrepancy between norm and practice as a recent

---

[16] A general discussion of Alpine patterns of seasonal spatial dispersion is provided
   by Sölch, 'Raum und Gesellschaft in den Alpen', pp. 153–4. For a suggestive anthropological case-study, see Macherel, 'La traversée du champ matrimonial', pp. 14–21.
[17] Gnifetti, *Nozioni topografiche*, p. 6. See also Giordani, *La colonia tedesca*, p. 13.
[18] See e.g. Arbos, *La vie pastorale*, p. 563, and Blanchard, *Les Alpes Occidentales*, vol.
   6.2, pp. 471–3.
[19] Benetti *et al.*, *Uomini delle Alpi*, p. 190.

departure. But the example of Alagna (where 'inverse transhumance' was a long-established custom as early as 1845) makes one wonder about how frequently even before the end of the Alpine *ancien régime*, the state of closure and equilibrium predicted by the model was actually achieved and maintained.

The seductive image of the traditional upland community as a closed peasant economy is no less seriously challenged by the existence, in many parts of the Alps, of massive flows of seasonal emigration. In Alagna, to make things even more intriguing, the local men's seasonal emigration coexisted with the presence in the village of a sizable number of immigrant miners. Cases of manpower shortage in areas where men migrated in great numbers to work abroad are certainly puzzling and may not be very common. But they need not be exceptionally rare either. Similar situations have been reported for other Alpine mining districts[20] as well as for regions experiencing industrial development, such as the mountainous Swiss Canton Ticino in the late nineteenth century.[21] For the case of Ticino, Francine van de Walle has suggested that this seeming paradox becomes understandable once we consider that the Ticinese emigrants were landed peasants who fitted their migration schedules to the needs of their agricultural calendar, whereas the industries attracted landless immigrants. Such an explanation probably holds true for many situations of this kind. Yet it can hardly be applied to localities like Alagna (and, indeed, most valleys in Ticino itself), where emigration took place during the summer months. Once again, the case of Alagna cannot simply be dismissed as an oddity. Though less frequent than winter emigration, summer emigration is known to have been fairly common all over the Alps.[22] Its implications, however, have seldom been considered.

The most obvious consequence of male summer emigration is that the labour force left in the village will tend to be largely female, and in fact we have seen that Alagna's women are reported to have been 'incredibly active, the younger ones tending their herds in the alps, the others working in the fields'. But how could these women, though 'incredibly active', cope with the exacting tasks imposed by mountain farming? Were the agricultural and pastoral resources of a village like Alagna so restricted that even a reduced and predominantly female

[20] A well-documented case is that of Macugnaga, in the Anzasca Valley. See Schott, *Die deutschen Colonien in Piemont*, p. 74, and Mortarotti, *I Walser nella Val d'Ossola*, pp. 258–64.

[21] F. van de Walle, 'Migration and fertility in Ticino', p. 454.

[22] See Veyret, *Les Alpes*, pp. 80–2.

labour force was able to exploit them fully? An answer to these questions is a first step to assessing the degree of compatibility between male emigration and the requirements of mountain farming, and the respective importance of 'push' and 'pull' factors in causing male emigration.

One important point to be taken into account is that the Sesia Valley is a rather wet area receiving up to 2,500 mm of precipitation every year. As a consequence, Alagna did not need the irrigation works which are so prominent a feature in the agricultural landscape of much drier regions such as, for instance, the Aosta Valley or Canton Valais. Since activities related to irrigation are among the most onerous and time-consuming,[23] this means that a great deal of labour was saved. It has also been pointed out that the higher the settlement is, the more the emphasis tends to be placed on the pastoral rather than on the agricultural sector. As pastoral activities are less labour-intensive and more suitable to women and children, in the high valleys summer male emigration can be expected to be more compatible with the requirements of mountain farming than in the more autarkic villages at lower altitudes.[24] It seems therefore reasonable to conclude that the total amount of labour needed in Alagna was probably significantly lower than in other Alpine communities.

But, even if we accept this conclusion, the striking fact remains that in Alagna pastoral activities were carried out in a highly 'irrational' way. The waste of labour entailed by systems of individual alp management (which require a duplication of effort that could be avoided by means of communal herding) has often been emphasized. But this practice looks even more irrational in a village like Alagna, which had a reduced labour force mainly made up of women, old men and children. In mountain areas, as we have noticed in Chapter 1, the optimal ratio of herdsmen to cattle is probably in the region of 1:30–40.[25] In Alagna, it could be as low as 1:7–8. It is interesting to note, in this respect, that Vincze has recently suggested that a system of individual alp management can nevertheless be viable 'when a family is of the extended type'.[26] This is an important issue, to which we shall go back in due course.[27] But, although it is intriguing to speculate about the adaptive advantages of complex family households (and

---

[23] This point is emphasized by Netting, *Balancing on an alp*, p. 45.
[24] Weiss, *Das Alpenwesen Graubündens*, p. 94.
[25] Vincze, 'Peasant animal husbandry', pp. 393–4. Cf. Netting, *Balancing on an alp*, pp. 64–5.
[26] Vincze, 'Peasant animal husbandry', p. 398.
[27] See Chapter 9 below, pp. 246–9.

about a possible relation between their decline in Alagna and the parallel decline of agro-pastoralism), we should not forget that in Alagna many of these 'extended families' were deprived of their male members.

Vincze has alternatively suggested that a system of individual alp management can be viable 'when agricultural tasks are minimal ... because of the extreme scarcity of arable land'. The question is, therefore, whether arable land was so scarce in Alagna. As is typical of settlements placed at the top of high valleys, the territory of Alagna is very large, but about 35 per cent of its 7,278 hectares (distributed over altitudes extending from 1,100 m to the 4,500 m of the spires of Monte Rosa) are too high, steep or rocky to be used. According to the most reliable estimates, cultivable land (including meadows) amounts to only 307 hectares – a small area by comparison with the over 4,400 hectares of pastures, and clearly inadequate to supply hay for the number of animals these pastures can theoretically support.[28] Nevertheless, though representing just 4 per cent of the whole territory, the 300 hectares of cultivable land were likely to prove too heavy a burden for Alagna's diminished labour force. In Törbel (which in the period between the two world wars numbered about 650 inhabitants, roughly the same as nineteenth-century Alagna) animals were communally herded by some fifteen individuals, who relieved over one hundred households of the daily chores of feeding and milking the livestock. Yet Netting was told that the total effort of the whole local population was required to work 63 hectares of ploughland and 226 hectares of meadowland. The recent transition to a peasant-worker regime has left women almost alone to cope with agriculture, and 'everyone agrees that only by substituting mowing machines for absent male labour have the meadows been kept in use'.[29]

These machines were obviously not available to Alagna's women. But they could rely, as we have seen, on help from the day-labourers and the immigrant mowers, the *ranzin*. It is doubtful, however, whether these hired men could totally compensate for the absent male members of the household. And it is in any case significant that they were hired while a high proportion of the local labour force was 'wasted' in the alps. This implies not only that in Alagna most families found it profitable to replace the absent males by hired workers, but also that they could afford to retain a system which was 'irrational' yet eminently suitable to that pronounced individualism which is

[28] Spanna, 'Val Sesia', pp. 137–8.   [29] Netting, *Balancing on an alp*, p. 48.

(according to some ethnographers) a major distinguishing feature of Walser populations.[30]

All in all, this ethnographic sketch provides a picture which is in several ways reminiscent of the controversial account of medieval and early modern England proposed a few years ago by Alan Macfarlane. To apply Macfarlane's characterization to Alagna, one might say that 'traditional' Alagna, like medieval England, 'may have been rural and ultimately dependent on agriculture, but strangely it was almost certainly not a subsistence society where land and its ownership was the only means of wealth'.[31] This is all the more interesting if we consider that at first glance Alagna could easily be mistaken, on the sole evidence of relatively recent statistics on occupational structure and land use, for a conventional farming community.

The case of Alagna suggests that data of this kind, which have provided much of the empirical basis for the typological efforts of geographers and agrarian economists, are somewhat distorted by the process of 'peasantization' undergone by many Alpine communities in the course of the last one hundred years. The economic changes of recent decades have no doubt been magnified by the fact that during the Second World War the Alps, like most other rural areas all over Europe, suddenly reverted to a much more autarkic existence. In a tourist resort like Davos, to quote just one example, cultivated land increased by nearly 500 per cent between 1939 and 1945.[32] But in other regions similar processes had started rather earlier and had changed more deeply the face of local economies.

An instructive example is offered, once again, by the Pitztal. As we have seen, in this Austrian valley the aftermath of the First World War had determined the rapid decline of seasonal emigration. Thus, land had to be increasingly called upon to support many who would have emigrated and were now unable to find work. At the time of Lässer's study, in 1949, the valley had fallen on subsistence production and its inhabitants were trying hard to develop some form of tourism to survive.[33] That this process of 'peasantization' may have led several observers astray is indicated by a study of tourist development conducted in the same valley some twenty years later. What had been an area of massive seasonal emigration was portrayed as the very epitome of peasant economy and culture, a remote region which was

---

[30] On Walser individualism, see Weiss, *Das Alpenwesen Graubündens*, pp. 93–4; Tomamichel, *Bosco Gurin*, pp. 59–60; and Ilg, 'Walservolkstum in Vorarlberg,' p. 13.

[31] Macfarlane, *English individualism*, p. 123.

[32] Senn, 'Die Alpwirtschaft der Landschaft Davos', p. 314.

[33] Lässer, *St. Leonhard im Pitztal*, pp. 107–17.

just starting to emerge from a state of isolation which had prevailed for centuries.[34]

The conceptual framework used in this study of tourist development in the Pitztal, and its shortcomings, are common to a large sector of the literature on Alpine modernization produced by geographers, economists and other social scientists, including anthropologists. This invites a few final considerations. When anthropologists began to do fieldwork in the Alps, they were not all pursuing the same aims. 'Social' anthropologists, most notably Bailey and his pupils, were mainly looking for villages where minute interactions and social transactions between members of the same moral community could be observed and analyzed in a sort of anthropological laboratory. The aim of the more nomothetically oriented 'cultural' anthropologists was, on the other hand, to collect ethnographic data on mountain farming and traditional social organization, in order to test and further articulate broad evolutionary models of the upland community. Both, however, expected to find villages still largely 'unspoiled' by modern life. What they discovered was, on the contrary, that farming was rapidly declining, that communal institutions were crumbling, that village endogamy and large families were mainly things of the past. Understandably, most anthropologists found it both convenient and commonsensical to conceptualize the changes they were observing as a transition from the closure of the traditional past to the openness of the present situation.

It is a truism that in order to establish the extent, direction and causes of change, it is essential to have a sound knowledge of what was going on before. It is unfortunate that particularly in the studies carried out by Bailey and his pupils the main features of the traditional past are simply postulated (or reconstructed in a highly impressionistic way) rather than carefully investigated. When they describe the 'politics of innovation', with its factional disputes and its petty intrigues, their studies are lively and often very perceptive. But their general interpretation of social change and the effects of innovation looks suspicious. This is most evident in Bailey's own work on 'Losa', a village in the Piedmontese Western Alps. His whole analysis rests on the belief that until the last war this village was a closed, economically self-sufficient community with minimal contact with the outside world.[35] In fact, recent research shows that between the middle of the nineteenth century and the Second World War the economy of 'Losa', like that of Alagna, had been characterized by massive seasonal

[34] Béteille, 'Tourisme et milieu rural montagnard'.
[35] See especially Bailey, 'What are *Signori*?', pp. 248–51.

and temporary emigration and had relied on very substantial food imports.[36] What is more, a part of the territory of this community was a royal game reserve, and particularly in the second half of the nineteenth century the royal family used to spend the summer in 'Losa' with a large number of attendants. This had, among other things, marked seasonal effects on the local labour market.

The finding that communities like Alagna or 'Losa', and no doubt many others, were far from being closed economic and social systems raises thorny problems also for the proponents of ecosystemic models, for it suggests that the relationship between resources and population may have been more complex than they assumed, and the role of the regulatory 'social servomechanisms' much less important or obvious. It is indeed tempting to conclude that the model of the Alpine village as an ecosystem outlined in Chapter 1 should be rejected in favour of 'externalist' models such as the one proposed by Cole and Wolf, in which the local community is conceived of as an open system dominated by outside economic forces.[37] Yet it would be premature, and probably unwarranted, to argue that the ecosystemic model is wrong. It cannot be ignored, for instance, that a competent fieldworker like Netting was satisfied by his ethnographic evidence that Törbel had traditionally been a largely self-contained economy. What the striking contrast between Alagna and Törbel seems to indicate is that Alpine communities could differ very markedly from one another and that no single model is likely to do justice to their economic, social and cultural diversity.

But there is another point to be stressed. Many anthropologists, geographers and agricultural economists have been inclined to place too much emphasis on the Second World War as a unique turning-point, thereby implying that up to then Alpine communities had remained, to all intents and purposes, closed natural economies. The weaknesses of this stereotypical view of the Alpine past can easily be laid bare by showing, for instance, that the economies of communities like Alagna, St Leonhard or 'Losa' critically depended on seasonal migration and on substantial imports of food supplies. However, the evidence presented in this chapter cannot bring us far back into the past. It tells us nothing about, say, the beginning of seasonal emigration in these villages and its development over time. Thus, we

---

[36] According to the 1921 census, in the winter of that year no less than 968 out of Losa's 3,012 inhabitants were away as temporary or seasonal emigrants. Also, documents preserved in the Communal Archives record, for the decade 1915–24, a mean annual import of 350,000 kg of meal, 300,000 kg of maize, 80,000 Kg of rice and 200,000 kg of pasta. See Albera, 'Open systems.'

[37] See Chapter 2 above, pp. 46–7.

can be sure that in Alagna being an emigrant has been the destiny (and, presumably, the aspiration) not only of the oldest villagers still alive today, but also of their fathers, grandfathers and great-grand-fathers. And yet we know that when Alagna was founded, in the thirteenth century, its first inhabitants were proper mountain peas-ants. Although anthropology provides much of the theoretical frame-work which is needed to test competing models of the Alpine com-munity, the ethnographic material collected by the anthropologists in the field cannot help us to cross the deceptive threshold of the so-called 'traditional past'. To do so, it will be necessary to turn, in the next chapters of this book, to a straightforward historical investi-gation of the relationships beween environment, population and social structure in the long term.

6

The causes and consequences of
Alpine emigration

The medieval colonization of the high valleys

Current debates among ecological anthropologists clearly indicate that a shift from a synchronic to a long-term analysis of the relationships between environment and population is increasingly perceived as a crucial and urgent task. As Emilio Moran has recently remarked, a major limitation of ecological anthropology (and a rather paradoxical one, in view of the importance of the concept of 'population' in ecosystemic research) is that 'ecological anthropological studies have only rarely explored the changing population variable over time'. The remedy, Moran has argued, can only be 'an extension of the tools of ecological study to include also the tools of historical demography'.[1]

That such an extension of method and theory can mark a very significant advance in ecological anthropology is, indeed, one of the main contentions of this book. But there is a fundamental problem which cannot be overlooked, namely that even in Europe demographic series usually go back for at most three or four centuries. In the case of the Alps, as we shall see, we are reasonably well informed about the period between 1700 and 1850, and for a few localities some data are available also for the sixteenth and seventeenth centuries. Moreover, useful information about the late Middle Ages can be gleaned from the historical literature, especially as far as settlement expansion is concerned. The penetration of the Alpine region by man, however, started some 100,000 years ago, and for this vast time span we can only rely on scanty and largely inadequate archaeological evidence.

The chapters which follow will concentrate on the relatively recent periods for which a richer documentation is available. Nevertheless, it is essential that the much longer and mostly uncharted period

[1] Moran, 'Ecosystems research', p. 17.

121

between the end of the Ice Age and the sixteenth century A.D. is at least briefly surveyed, not so much for the sake of an impossible completeness as to gain a more correct perspective on a number of central questions. This is particularly necessary when the subject is the human ecology of a mountain area like the Alps, since the existence of obvious and largely immutable environmental constraints easily leads one inadvertently to turn the *longue durée* into eternity. Scanty as it is, the evidence we possess about prehistoric, Roman and medieval times shows, on the contrary, that the demography and human ecology of the Alps went through a number of critical changes.

Archaeologists seem to agree that the penetration of the Alps by human populations started some 100,000 years ago, in what is known as the Riss-Würm interglacial period. Traces of Mousterian hunters have been found in caves often situated at very high altitude, such as the 'Drachenloch' (Swiss Alps) at 2,445 m.[2] However, it was only some 10,000 years ago, at the end of the Ice Age, that groups of people began once more to move towards the Alpine valleys. The oldest remains concern parties of hunters who ventured into the uplands during the summer, following the seasonal migrations of wild animals. But in the course of the Middle Neolithic Age, and even more in the Bronze Age, several circumstances apparently encouraged people living in the plains to move to higher areas and to settle there on a more permanent basis. The fact that the remains of domesticated animals progressively come to outnumber those of wild animals and that corn-pollen grains begin to be attested at fairly high altitudes indicates that hunting was being gradually replaced by cattle-breeding and agriculture. It seems therefore legitimate to conclude that the Neolithic marks 'le vrai début du peuplement des Alps par des groupes pratiquant l'économie productrice qui est encore la nôtre'.[3]

The two main sets of factors behind this expansion were technological and climatic. If a warm and rather dry climate enabled more people to live a tolerable existence even at relatively high altitudes, improvements in toolmaking techniques (and later the adoption of bronze axes and knives) made it possible to clear the valley slopes more thoroughly. But it should be noted that during the Bronze Age the realization that rich copper deposits were to be found in the Alps also stimulated a remarkable growth in mining. In the Eastern Alps copper deposits were exploited on a comparatively large scale for about a milennium, up to the eighth century B.C., and in Tyrol the first

---

[2] Cf. Sauter, 'Chausseurs moustériens', pp. 126–7, and Pauli, *The Alps*, pp. 11–12.
[3] Sauter, 'Chausseurs moustériens', p. 133.

attempts to establish permanent settlements at high altitudes were indeed made by small groups of miners.[4]

To sum up, the intensification of both agro-pastoral and mining activities witnessed by the Bronze Age resulted in a denser settlement and, presumably, in an increase in the population. Since this tendency towards settlement and population expansion persisted during the Iron Age, when Celtic tribes are known to have moved to the Alps, Polybius was no doubt correct in writing that at the time of Hannibal's crossing (218 B.C.) the Alps had 'a considerable population'.[5] How numerous this population was, however, it is difficult to assess. Thanks to recent advances in paleodemography, life expectancy can now be estimated for a number of skeletal populations.[6] But, although these estimates can be used to form a notion of the size of population for a few localities at a given point in time, they hardly allow any generalization to larger regions, let alone to the whole Alpine area. To do so, one has still to rely on the meagre and highly elusive evidence contained in the works of Greek and Roman writers or, more solidly, on the study of place names.

As is well known, a few details have come to us of the conquest of many of the Alpine tribes by Augustus, though usually not much more than their names.[7] The only significant exception is the rather extended account of the Salassi (the inhabitants of present-day Aosta Valley) provided by Strabo in his *Geography*, and in particular his assertion that, when this population was defeated by the Romans in the year 25 B.C., no less than 8,000 fighting men and 36,000 non-combatants were captured and sold as booty.[8] As Peter Garnsey has recently noticed in his perceptive study of mountain economies in classical times, Strabo was 'a most casual collector and dispenser of information'.[9] Nevertheless, most students of the Western Alps have been inclined to give credit to these figures, mainly because they seem to tally with the general impression of dense pre-Roman settlement which is suggested by the study of place names. Topono-mastic research has in fact revealed a very substantial amount of place names of Ligurian, Celtic and (in the Eastern Alps) Rhaetic origin, which has led more than one scholar to the conclusion that before the Roman conquest the size and density of the population of the

---

[4] Pauli, *The Alps*, pp. 17–21.
[5] *Hist.*, 3, 48, 7.
[6] Cf. Pauli, *The Alps*, pp. 111–12.
[7] See especially Pliny, *Nat. Hist.*, 3, 132–7, and Strabo, *Geog.*, 4, 6, 2–9.
[8] *Geog.*, 4, 6, 7.
[9] Garnsey, 'Mountain economies', p. 9.

Alps were, especially in the western sector of the crescent, not very different from those recorded for much later periods.[10]

This is, however, hard to believe. There is, for one thing, little doubt that classical sources should be used with the greatest caution. The German archaeologist Ludwig Pauli, for instance, has recently argued that the crucial passage by Strabo is equivocal and lends itself to different interpretations, and that the figure of 44,000 people looks in any case implausibly high for the Aosta Valley.[11] No less caution is needed in the use of toponomastic evidence. Toponyms of pre-Roman origin are an indication that mountain areas have been known, exploited and to some extent inhabited by man for a long time. But the inference that the Alps must have been densely populated at a very early date clashes with all we know for the period in which our documentation becomes more abundant and reliable, namely the late Middle Ages.[12]

As we have briefly seen in Chapter 3, in the Alps the late Middle Ages were characterized by an imposing process of colonization and settlement expansion. Although several hypotheses have been put forward, it seems now beyond dispute that colonization was mainly promoted by the landed aristocracy and by the monasteries, anxious to exploit more intensively the marginal lands they possessed in the high valleys.[13] We have also observed, however, that recent research has identified several different types of settlement expansion and the possibility cannot be ruled out that in some cases colonization, though still regulated by feudal lords, may have been primarily a response to growing demographic pressure in the lower regions. What is certain is that the population of most high valleys was very sparse and scanty, not only in the Eastern Alps (where colonization was more widespread and intense) but also in the Western and Central Alps.[14]

The foundation of Alagna offers, in this respect, a typical example. When the first handful of Walser families settled in what is now Alagna, in the second half of the thirteenth century, the upper Sesia Valley was a distinctly underpopulated land. The whole of its territory, which was later to be subdivided into seventeen parishes, still formed

[10] Cf. e.g. Blanchard, *Les Alpes Occidentales*, vol. 7, p. 530, and Janin, *Le Val d'Aoste*, pp. 119–20.

[11] Pauli, *The Alps*, p. 172.

[12] For a balanced discussion of this issue, see Cholley, *Les Préalpes de Savoie*, pp. 385–98.

[13] To quote the Latin text of a typical agreement (excerpted in Kreis, *Die Walser*, pp. 126–7), the lords entrusted to the colonists 'nemora et terrae de quibus parvam recipiunt utilitatem et reditus et proventus ... [ut] ex ipsis terris suis possint utilitatem maiorem habere'.

[14] Cf. Pickl, 'Wirtschaft und Gesellschaft in den Ostalpenländern', pp. 41–8; and Viazzo and Bodo, 'Presenza walser'.

one large parish. Riva Valdobbia, the highest permanent settlement in the valley, was just a small village surrounded by vast grazing areas belonging to two monasteries. As was the case in many other parts of the Alps, these monasteries had long played a central role in regulating the movements of transhumant herds from the plains or from the lower valleys to the summer pastures of the high valleys. They possessed both the alps and the corresponding 'feet' (*pedes* in the Latin of medieval documents), the stations where the animals rested and were grazed for a while before moving upwards to the higher pastures. It is at the 'foot' of the various alps, a few miles from Riva Valdobbia, that the first Walser farmsteads originated: *Pe de Moyt*, at the foot of the Moyt alp, *Pe d'Olen*, *Pe d'Otro*. By the end of the fourteenth century more than half of the present-day hamlets are documented, and one source suggests that as early as 1306 the Otro alp was already beginning to turn into a semi-permanent settlement.[15]

Both toponomastic and documentary evidence amply demonstrates that in Alagna, as in most of the other areas settled in the late Middle Ages, the natural resources of the higher zones had been exploited well before the arrival of the colonists. However, by transforming what had been at most temporary herdsmen's camps into permanent settlements, and by pushing upwards the limits of pastureland, the medieval settlers powerfully shaped the cultural landscape of the Alps and decisively changed the demography and human ecology of the high valleys.

In prehistoric and Roman times, several Alpine populations certainly practised modest forms of transhumance involving the movement of flocks and herds over short distances from pastures in the plains to others on high ground. But it is remarkable that forms of long-distance transhumance similar to those attested for the Apennines in Roman times can be found in the Alps only towards the turn of the first millenium A.D.[16] This may at first look surprising. But it should be considered that long-distance transhumance requires the existence of a number of historical preconditions. As has been recently pointed out,[17] such preconditions include market demand for the products of pastoralism, political stability and – crucially – an élite possessing the resources in cash and in land to run sizable

[15] Cf. Rizzi, 'Sulla fondazione di Alagna', and Viazzo, 'Ethnic change in a Walser community', pp. 170–80.
[16] Cf. Arbos, *La vie pastorale*, pp. 564–77.
[17] Garnsey, 'Mountain economies'.

flocks and herds between properties in their possession or under their control. This was the role fulfilled in the Middle Ages by members of the landed aristocracy and above all by the numerous monasteries which had been founded at the foot of the Alps and endowed with property both in the mountains and in the adjacent plains.[18]

The development of long-distance transhumance represented a major historical change in the economy and ecology of the Alps. But after only two or three centuries, or less, the medieval colonization of the high valleys brought about a further shift, from a pattern of extensive land use based on transhumant pastoralism to a more intensive 'productive strategy' combining pastoralism and agriculture. The upland areas which had formerly been used as summer pastures were converted into fields and meadows, while new pastureland was created for the settlers' animals by cutting and burning forested land. No less significantly, the foundation and later growth of new settlements deeply affected the economy of the older settlements, whose inhabitants often found themselves deprived of the upland pastures where they had previously grazed their animals. In most cases they were forced to press into use the marginal land which was still available within the territory more directly controlled by their communities. Ecologically, this complex process of intensification led to a turning-point, since it would appear that, although rudimentary systems of mixed farming had been practised since prehistoric times, it was only as a consequence of the medieval colonization that a mature form of *Alpwirtschaft* came into being.[19]

This is a point of the utmost importance, for we have seen that the notion of *Alpwirtschaft* as a closed agro-pastoral system is at the core of the ecosystemic model outlined in Chapter 1. What is more, the medieval development of *Alpwirtschaft* was paralleled by the consolidation of the institutional form which is posited by the model, the so-called 'closed corporate community'. Alpine closed corporate communities have disparate origins. Some of them started as village councils, often enjoying substantial judicial prerogatives and serving as intermediaries between the landlord and the individual households. In other cases, they originated as corporate groups of households acting at first as rent-paying units and later on, when the feudal lords began to sell their possessions, as purchasing units. A common

---

[18] On the role of monasteries, see Bergier, 'Le cycle médiéval', pp. 176–213.
[19] Cf. de Planhol, 'Pression démographique', pp. 539–49, and Meyer, 'Wüstungen', pp. 256–8. For a recent discussion of the prehistoric evidence, see Pauli, *The Alps*, pp. 241–2.

feature is, however, the considerable degree of autonomy they even-tually achieved.[20] Such an autonomy allowed these groups to enforce measures regulating the behaviour of their members and, even more distinctively, to increase their institutional closure towards the outside by restricting membership and denying outsiders any access to local resources.

The colonization of the high valleys, the development of *Alpwirt-schaft* and the consolidation of the closed corporate community all concurred to produce, in the late Middle Ages, a fundamental disconti-nuity in the human ecology of the Alps. They brought about the confi-guration of economic and institutional traits which has then persisted until a very recent past and which invites a conceptualization of the Alpine village as a closed ecosystem. The balance of population and resources, however, no doubt changed very markedly in the course of this long period. It is apparent, in particular, that in the Middle Ages the Alps still contained large frontier areas and were therefore more likely to attract colonists than to expel surplus population. This raises the question of the beginning of Alpine emigration and of its relations with population growth, and in order to consider this ques-tion it will now be useful to go back to the case of Alagna.

Population growth and the beginnings of emigration

Like all the other Walser colonies, Alagna had certainly started from very small beginnings. Around the turn of the thirteenth century it presumably numbered less than twenty households.[21] The growth rate of this population of settlers was, on the other hand, very substan-tial. On 12 May 1475 seventy-eight household heads belonging to the hamlet communities of Alagna congregated in the church of St John the Baptist to sign a petition to the bishop of Novara, where they demanded that this church, which had been 'erected and built up by their ancestors', should be established as an autonomous parish church. The main reason adduced was that Alagna had grown into a large village and a full-time priest was therefore badly needed.[22] Since the notary tells us that the seventy-eight men represented over

---

[20] Cf. Bergier, 'Le cycle médiéval', pp. 192–221.
[21] Rizzi, 'Sulla fondazione di Alagna'. On the size of Walser settlements in the early stage of the colonization and in the first centuries of their history, see Zimpel, 'Entwicklung der Walserkolonien', pp. 130–9; Viazzo and Bodo, 'Presenza walser', pp. 149–52; and Rizzi, 'La colonizzazione walser'.
[22] ASDN 1–185, fols. 419r–426v.

two-thirds of all household heads,[23] it seems reasonable to reckon that Alagna consisted of a number of households ranging from 80 to perhaps 100 or 110, which leads to a conservative estimate of between 400 and 500 inhabitants. This shows that in the first two centuries after the colonization the population had increased at least fourfold and that the Alagnesi were right in claiming that in their village souls were now 'in copioso et maximo numero'.

From this point of view, Alagna's early demographic history is, as far as we can see, fairly representative not only of what we know about the growth of the Walser colonies and other areas of recent colonization, but more generally also of the population growth of the whole Alpine area in the late Middle Ages. In his pioneering contribution to Alpine historical demography, Wilhelm Bickel maintained that in 1400 the population of the Alps must have been very much the same as in the early eighteenth century, since resources had not significantly increased throughout this period.[24] This argument now seems highly dubious. What we have just seen about the colonization of the high valleys strongly suggests that in the fourteenth century large portions of the Alps were still severely underpopulated – an impression which is further reinforced by the admittedly scrappy evidence we possess for a number of Alpine regions. The most useful and reliable data concern Tyrol and show that the total population of this region markedly increased from just 45,000 in 1312 to 70,000 in 1427 and no less than 110,000 one century later.[25] In Tyrol the population growth of the late Middle Ages may have been greater and more persistent than in other areas, partly because its valleys had previously been less densely settled than elsewhere and partly (as we shall see in the next chapter) because of the massive immigration of miners which started in the fifteenth century. But the fourteenth-century enumerations which have survived for two regions of older and denser settlements like Savoy and the Aosta Valley, in the Western Alps, also provide figures which are much lower than those recorded or estimated for the eighteenth century.[26]

It should be noticed that the interpretation of these early enumer-

---

[23] '... maior pars immo plus quam duae partes ex tribus ex capitibus domus'.
[24] Bickel, *Bevölkerungsgeschichte der Schweiz*, pp. 41–6.
[25] Klein, 'Die Bevölkerung Österreichs', pp. 80–5.
[26] In 1368 the population of Savoy can be estimated in the region of 65,000 to 75,000 and that of the Aosta Valley in the region of 20,000 to 25,000. Eighteenth-century censuses suggest a conservative estimate of 275,000 inhabitants for Savoy in the 1750s and record a population of nearly 63,000 for the Aosta Valley in 1734. Cf. Rousseau, *La population de la Savoie*, p. 220, and Janin, *Le Val d'Aoste*, pp. 132, 169.

ations of the population of Savoy and of the Aosta Valley is rendered somewhat difficult by the fact that they were made in 1368, only a couple of decades after the ravages of the Black Death. Nevertheless, the prevailing view is now to see the late Middle Ages as a period of general population growth for the Alpine area, which seems to have been less disastrously affected by plague epidemics than the adjacent lowlands and to have enjoyed a comparatively higher degree of prosperity.[27] It is also agreed that it was in the course of the 'long sixteenth century' that the Alps reached a first demographic peak, followed by a period of stagnation or even decrease lasting until the mid-eighteenth century. When exactly this peak was reached, however, is still matter of debate.

Some leading scholars believe that in most Alpine areas this peak occurred around the year 1500, since it is towards the end of the fifteenth century that a rapid and substantial increase in both seasonal and, more importantly, permanent emigration can be observed.[28] This is taken as evidence that the Alps had become overpopulated and that the excess population had to be expelled and sent down to the plains. Although this is a plausible argument, it is also somewhat circular. The example of Alagna shows, in fact, that a great deal of caution is needed before the onset of emigration can be regarded as evidence that a demographic ceiling had been reached, or even as a symptom of overpopulation.

In Alagna the oldest reference to emigration is contained in a document of 1481, concerning two brothers who intended to move to an unspecified German-speaking area ('intendentes sese transfere ad partes Alamaniae').[29] Although our source does not inform us about their occupation, it is very likely that these two brothers were masons or stone-cutters. Also, there is little doubt that by the late fifteenth and early sixteenth centuries cases of long-distance emigration, mainly towards German-speaking areas, were far from being exceptional. The Swiss traveller Gilg Tschudi, who visited Alagna in 1524, described it as a village where 'all are stone-cutters and good masons who

---

[27] Bergier, 'Le cycle médiéval', pp. 221–6. The matter is, however, far from being settled, since the data provided by a number of studies suggest that in many upland districts the impact of the Black Death was no less devastating than in the lowlands. See especially Binz, 'La population du diocèse de Genève', p. 157; Fierro, 'Dauphiné et Faucigny', pp. 947–57; and Pickl, 'Wirtschaft und Gesellschaft in den Ostalpenländern', pp. 48–53. The problem of the effects of plague epidemics in the Alpine area is discussed more extensively in Chapter 8 below, pp. 210–11.

[28] Cf. Binz, 'La population du diocèse de Genève', pp. 158–9, and more recently Bergier, 'Le cycle médiéval', pp. 175, 254–6.

[29] Cf. Frey, 'Herkunft der Familie Bodmer', p. 459.

migrate widely around'.[30] And the painstaking researches carried out in the early 1930s by Rudolf Riggenbach have revealed, even more decisively, that from the beginning of the sixteenth century up to the late seventeenth century a very considerable number of master builders, masons and stone-cutters from Alagna were accepted as citizens by Swiss cities.[31]

It is surely intriguing that a steady and rather substantial flow of permanent emigration is attested for the first time towards the turn of the fifteenth century, when the population of Alagna had grown to such an extent that its inhabitants felt themselves justified to demand the establishment of their village as an autonomous parish. It would seem that in those years a crucial demographic threshold was crossed. But in order to understand better the causes and nature of emigration, and to assess its value as an indicator of overpopulation, it is necessary to consider the relation between permanent and seasonal emigration as well as the later evolution within Alagna's population.

Given the kind of sources he exploited (the registers of foreigners accepted as citizens by Swiss cities), Riggenbach was able to unearth only cases of permanent emigration. Predictably, the men from Alagna who were naturalized were either married to local women or unmarried. But the documents published a few years later by another Swiss historian, Siegfried Frey, demonstrate that married men also emigrated, although on a seasonal or temporary basis. One of these seasonal emigrants was Melcher Bodmer, the central character of Frey's study. After the death of his first wife, however, Melcher started to sever his connections with Alagna. He remarried in Zurich, and in 1543 he was naturalized by that city. Nevertheless, he remained active in the Alagnese land market for several years. Like other emigrants he had conferred powers of attorney upon a relative, and it was mainly through him that he bought and sold land until at least 1557. It is only in 1560 that he appears in Alagna in person to sell to his sister all the property he possessed in the village. Unlike his cousin Heindrich Bodmer, a bachelor who renounced his Zurich citizenship to return to Alagna as an old man, Melcher chose to break his ties with his homeland.[32]

---

[30] '... seynd alles Stein-Metzen und gute Maurer, welche weit herum wandeln.' Tschudi, *Gallia Comata*, p. 357. Tschudi visited Alagna in 1524, when he was nineteen years old, and briefly mentioned the village in his *Alpisch Rhetia* (1538). A more detailed description is contained in his later *Gallia Comata*. This work is known to have been finished by 1572, but was published only two centuries later, in 1758. Cf. Riggenbach, *Ulrich Ruffiner*, pp. 20–1.

[31] Riggenbach, *Ulrich Ruffiner*. Cf. also Guichonnet, 'L'émigration alpine', pp. 560–1.

[32] Frey, 'Herkunft der Familie Bodmer', pp. 7–15.

The set of documents concerning Melcher Bodmer collected by Frey are interesting in many respects. Besides recording in detail an instance of temporary emigration that gradually turns into permanent absence, they shed some light on property and kinship relations in sixteenth-century Alagna. They reveal, in particular, the existence of a busy land market in which the emigrants seem to have played an especially dynamic role. It is worth noticing that, unless they were acting through an attorney, transactions involving emigrants were overwhelmingly concentrated in the winter months. This led Frey to surmise that in the sixteenth century the seasonal rhythm of emigration might have been exactly the same as in the nineteenth and early twentieth centuries,[33] a guess that finds direct confirmation in a document I have found in the records of the Episcopal Tribunal in the Diocesan Archive of Novara. On 19 April 1581, the curate of Alagna reported to the examining judge that in his parish there were 'more than fifty men who for the most part go to Germany to work as masons and stone-cutters' and that they used to leave during Lent and come back on St Martin's day on 11 November.[34]

We have seen that in more recent times men tended to come back slightly later, on the day of St Nicholas. But, apart from this, the seasonal rhythm of emigration appears to have changed very little. However, the rough estimate of 'more than fifty men' given by the parish priest seems to indicate that in the 1580s the number of emigrants, though considerable, was much lower than in the mid-nineteenth century, when about 150 men were reported to emigrate every year. The question of whether the size of emigration, as distinct from its seasonal characteristics, was significantly different in the two periods is clearly of critical importance. In the nineteenth century emigration was the backbone of Alagna's social and economic life. We may wonder whether this was also true of the sixteenth century.

The key to solve, as far as possible, this problem is represented by a careful examination of the seasonal distribution of births and conceptions. As Francine van de Walle has shown in her study of the demographic effects of seasonal emigration in Ticino, this gives us an indirect but effective way to estimate the volume of seasonal emigration involving married men.[35] Indeed, the case studied by van

---

[33] Frey, 'Herkunft der Familie Bodmer', p. 9.

[34] 'Interrogatus respondit che de quella Cura di Alagna vi sono più de cinquanta huomini che per il più sogliono praticar nella alemagna facendo l'arte de muratori, et de scarpellini, quali si sogliono partir di quatragesima e ritornar a casa al S. Martino sequente.' ASDN XII, 2, 6, Foro eccl. Libri e registri. Criminalia, 1576–1583, fol.95r.

[35] F. van de Walle, 'Migration and fertility in Ticino.'

de Walle is highly relevant, for most emigrants from the Ticinese valleys were traditionally engaged in the building industry as masons, stone-cutters or plasterers and used to spend at home only the winter months. In Alagna we should therefore expect to find the same pattern as the one detected by van de Walle in nineteenth-century Ticino, where conceptions were much more frequent during the winter than in the rest of the year. It is unfortunate that the baptism registers start only in the May of 1582 and have a big gap from 1613 to 1677. But it is impressive to see that towards the turn of both the sixteenth and the seventeenth centuries nearly 50 per cent of all births took place in the three autumn months of September, October and November, corresponding to conceptions in December, January and February. Even if first births are not taken into account, so as to remove the distorting influence of the no less extreme seasonality of weddings,[36] the seasonality of births remains enormously pronounced (see Figure 6.1), thus pointing to an equally pronounced volume of seasonal emigration.

It is nevertheless intriguing that, if one looks in closer detail at the 1580s, the impression one receives is that in this decade the monthly distribution of births was not as strongly dominated by seasonal emigration as in the following decades. It is only in 1590 that seasonality steeply increases (11 of the 26 births of that year occurred in September only) and from then onwards the seasonal distribution of births is consistently shaped by emigration. The 1580s may just have been a slack period for Alagnese emigration.[37] Alternatively, one can surmise that the 1590s represented a turning-point. Because of the fragmentary and sometimes approximate character of our documentation, we are not in a position to decide ultimately. But the second hypothesis would certainly fit well with the findings recently reported by Paul Guichonnet, which suggest that the late sixteenth century saw a sudden spurt of Alpine emigration and that this was connected with climatic deterioration.[38]

The last decades of the sixteenth century were in fact marked by the abrupt beginning of the so-called Little Ice Age. This is most strikingly documented all over the Alps by the spectacular extension of the glaciers, which advanced several hundred metres within the span

---

[36] Over two-thirds of the marriages celebrated between 1618 and 1700 were concentrated in January and February.

[37] One might surmise, for instance, that emigration was affected by the decrees restricting travel to heretical lands promulgated in the 1570s and discussed in the next section.

[38] Guichonnet, 'Le partage politique des Alpes', pp. 282–5.

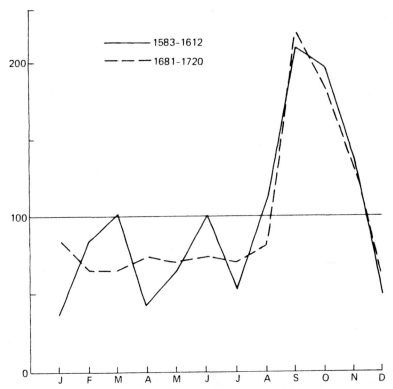

Figure 6.1 Monthly distribution of 2nd- and higher-order births in Alagna, 1583–1612 and 1681–1720

Note: The values plotted on the graph are index numbers. 100 represents the total that would be expected if births were evenly distributed throughout the year (taking the number of days in each month into account).

of few years. The Lower Grindelwald glacier, for example, expanded some 800 to 1,000 metres from 1580 to 1600.[39] The upper Sesia Valley was not spared by the climatic worsening. A note written by the parish priest of Riva Valdobbia provides a lively description of the exceedingly harsh weather of those years, characterized by very frequent and heavy snowfalls and, even more dangerously, by exceptionally long winters. In 1600 the snow cover lasted in Riva (which is placed at a slightly lower altitude than Alagna) until the end of May, and

---

[39] Cf. Le Roy Ladurie, *Times of feast, times of famine*, pp. 128–243, and more recently C. Pfister, *Das Klima der Schweiz*, vol. 1, pp. 144–9.

by late April snow was still four or five feet high.[40] As recent studies
have shown, conditions like this inevitably start catastrophic ecological
processes.[41] It is therefore reasonable to guess that their economic
consequences may have led an increasing number of men to join the
ranks of the seasonal emigrants.

These are, of course, only speculations based on a few shreds of
evidence. What we more positively know is that in Alagna the difficult
decades around the turn of the sixteenth century approximately coincide with the end of population growth. In the last third of the fifteenth
century, when Alagna was established as an autonomous parish and
emigration began to be documented, the village was still far from
attaining its maximum population. From less than 120 households
in 1475, Alagna had already grown to 160 households in 1594, when
it was visited by the bishop of Novara, Carlo Bascapè. But the ceiling
was apparently reached a couple of decades later. In 1617 Bascapè's
successor found in Alagna 180 households and 1,010 inhabitants, a
figure which was to remain roughly constant throughout the seventeenth century.[42]

This prompts two reflections. As we have seen, some scholars have
suggested that the population of the Alps reached a first peak in the
early sixteenth century. On the other hand, the climatological and
ecological data published in the last few years by Christian Pfister
would seem to indicate that conditions favouring growth persisted
until the beginning of the Little Ice Age.[43] In fact, the argument for
continuing and substantial growth in the course of the sixteenth century is supported by evidence concerning Savoy and the Austrian
Alps,[44] and even more convincingly by the new estimates recently
worked out by Markus Mattmüller for the Swiss Alps.[45] Whereas
earlier scholars like Bickel and Mayer had maintained that the population of Alpine Switzerland had remained more or less stationary,[46]
Professor Mattmüller now reckons that it increased very substantially
from 289,000 people in 1500 to 390,000 in 1600, and then only to 408,000

[40] '... nix erat alta ad collum viri honestae staturae.' This document is preserved
   in the parish archive of Riva Valdobbia and was brought to my attention by the
   late Professor E. Ragozza.
[41] Messerli *et al.*, 'Fluctuations of climate', pp. 258–9; C. Pfister, 'Changes in stability',
   pp. 292–4.
[42] See ASDN 1–24, fol. 89r, and 1–98, fol. 415v. Cf. also Bascapè, *Novaria*, p. 148.
[43] See especially C. Pfister, *Das Klima der Schweiz*, vol. 2, pp. 81–6.
[44] Cf. Binz, 'La population du diocèse de Genève', p. 161, and Klein, 'Die Bevölkerung
   Österreichs'.
[45] Mattmüller, *Bevölkerungsgeschichte der Schweiz*, vol. 1, pp. 351–68.
[46] Bickel, *Bevölkerungsgeschichte der Schweiz*, p. 46; Mayer, *The population of Switzerland*,
   p. 21.

people in 1700. On a more modest scale, this argument is corroborated by the demographic evolution of Alagna.

The case of Alagna also suggests that it might be dangerous to see the onset of emigration as an indication that Alpine population had reached or closely approached a peak. In Alagna a steady flow of permanent emigration is attested since the early sixteenth century, but population continued to grow for another hundred years. This is not to say, however, that during this period the population of Alagna lay below the limits set by its local agricultural and pastoral resources. Quite to the contrary, one strongly suspects that temporary and seasonal emigration allowed Alagna's population to grow well beyond the carrying capacity of the local ecosystem – which implies that the economic and demographic viability of this upland village was becoming increasingly dependent on the outside world. And to judge from the exceedingly pronounced seasonality of births, it would seem that at least from the early seventeenth century agro-pastoralism was in Alagna as strongly subordinated to emigration as it was in the nineteenth century.

The Alpine paradox

When the economic and demographic viability of a village depends very heavily on seasonal emigration, as seems to have been the case in Alagna, it is inevitable to regard it as an 'open system'. Yet, in some important respects, seventeenth-century Alagna still gives the impression of being a remarkably closed community. The terms of the problem were perceptively captured by bishop Bascapè in his account of the Walser parishes in his diocese. In the course of his pastoral visitations he had been struck by how successfully these parishes had managed to retain their German language and customs. This he attributed to their closure – to the fact that they had little contact with their Romance neighbours and married almost exclusively among themselves – but also to their habit of emigrating beyond the Alps.[47]

Indeed, data from Alagna show that at the time of Bascapè's visit the extent of village exogamy was extremely limited. On the basis of the baptism register we can safely estimate for the turn of the sixteenth century an endogamy rate exceeding 90 per cent. The proportion of babies born in the period 1582–1612 having one or both parents from outside is only 6.1 per cent (43 out of 700), and we arrive at

---

[47] Bascapè, *Novaria*, pp. 148–9.

exactly the same figure by calculating the proportion of 'family reconstitution forms' where at least one of the partners is not from Alagna
(only 14 out of 228). What is more, the few in-marrying women were
hardly a threat to the ethnic and linguistic homogeneity of the community, for they were almost without exception themselves Walser.
One century later, when family reconstitution can be resumed after
the wide gap in the baptism register, the proportion of wives from
outside is still very much the same. And the analysis of marriage
records (whose series runs unbroken from 1618 onwards) confirms
that throughout the seventeenth century endogamy rates remained
in the neighbourhood of 90 per cent.[48]

The very high rates of village endogamy and the no less extreme
seasonality of births epitomize the difficulties one finds in conceptualizing 'closure', 'isolation' or 'spatial mobility' in the Alps. In a sense,
it would not be unwarranted to describe Alpine village populations
as conspicuously immobile. Apart from rather anomalous localities
or periods, a researcher would look in vain for villages displaying
high rates of population turnover. What one is much more likely to
come across are levels of endogamy similar to those recorded in
Alagna, which inevitably reinforce the stereotyped image of the closed
mountain community.[49] But this is obviously only part of the truth.
With endogamy rates approaching or exceeding 90 per cent, seventeenth-century Alagna was almost certainly a genetic isolate. Yet one
half of the population – the male half – was constantly on the move.
Women would stay at home 'like moles', as an old Walser woman
from the village of Rima once put it to me. But their husbands and
their brothers, to use Tschudi's phrase, would 'migrate widely
around'.

It is not an overstatement to say that in Alpine communities men
and women typically formed, because of the exceptional extent of
emigration, two sharply distinct sub-populations. This point is of crucial importance to the understanding of some key features of Alpine
demography, as we have seen in Chapter 4 and shall see again in
the remaining chapters of this book. But emigration also explains a

[48] Of 447 marriages celebrated in Alagna between 1618 and 1700 no less than 412
were endogamous. This gives an 'endogamy rate' (defined as the ratio of the number
of endogamous marriages to all marriages) of 92.2 per cent. For a recent discussion
of the various definitions of 'endogamy rate' used in the literature, see Coleman,
'Marital choice', pp. 26–8.

[49] It may be relevant to note that in St Leonhard im Pitztal, a village which like Alagna
was characterized by high levels of seasonal emigration, the proportion of endogamous marriages was 91.2 per cent in 1785–1800, 90.9 per cent in 1801–1850, 89.9
per cent in 1851–1900, and 81.9 per cent in 1901–1945. See Lässer, *St. Leonhard
im Pitztal*, p. 51.

number of important cultural differences. For instance, all the linguists who have studied Alagna and the other German-speaking communities south of Monte Rosa have been unanimous in judging the dialect spoken by the women to be more archaic, and much closer to the common Walser stock, than that spoken by the men, which appeared to have been 'contaminated' by external influences. On the other hand, Alagnese emigration was largely oriented towards German Switzerland – overwhelmingly, in fact, until the middle of the seventeenth century. This opened the way to linguistic borrowings from both High German and *Schwyzertütsch*. But it also assured an unbroken contact with the Germanic world, and this was no doubt instrumental (as Bascapè had suggested) to preserve or even strengthen in the people of Alagna a feeling of ethnic and cultural difference *vis-à-vis* their Romance neighbours in the Sesia Valley.[50]

It should be noticed that for Bascapè this habit of 'emigrating beyond the Alps' was a matter of practical concern. Like most other Walser parishes in their diocese, in the sixteenth and seventeenth centuries Alagna represented a serious problem for the bishops of Novara. This diocese bordered upon land 'infected with heresy' and was within a few miles of the strongholds of Swiss Protestantism. It is therefore understandable that the bishops should keep a watchful eye on the threats posed by commercial relations with heretical lands and by transalpine emigration. The immediate aim of the bishops was to stem the danger of heretical contagion. From at least 1572, decrees restricting and regulating travel to heretical lands were promulgated by diocesan synods. Emigration towards areas infected with heresy was strongly discouraged. But, when it was absolutely necessary, the emigrants had to be given written permission by the bishop himself or by his vicar-general. No such permission could be given to men under twenty-five years of age, and the emigrants were expected to come back once a year to go to confession and receive Holy Communion or to send written proof that they had done so. The Church authorities' repeated complaints demonstrate, however, that in Alagna as well as in the other Walser parishes these regulations proved extremely difficult to enforce.[51]

The danger of heretical contagion was eventually stamped out, but in Alagna the impact of Protestant ideas may have been far from

---

[50] See Viazzo, 'Ethnic change in a Walser community'.

[51] Cf. Deutscher, 'Carlo Bascapè and Tridentine Reform', pp. 172–8; Mortarotti, *I Walser nella Val d'Ossola*, pp. 113–18; and Viazzo, 'Ethnic change in a Walser community', pp. 197–203.

negligible. Although this is a difficult point to prove, it is likely that religious reasons explain the decision taken by several Alagnese men to settle in Protestant cities, in spite of work opportunities being less favourable there than in Catholic areas.[52] One important consequence of these intense contacts with heretical lands was, in any case, the presence in Alagna of a considerable number of prohibited books in German, mainly translations of the Holy Scriptures. This is a complaint we find in the proceedings of pastoral visitations in the first half of the seventeenth century,[53] but by 1581 four local men had already been denounced to the episcopal tribunal for possessing Lutheran and Zwinglian books. The denunciation had come from Alagna's curate (a transalpine priest from the diocese of Constance), and we have previously mentioned the evidence he gave as providing direct information on the extent and seasonal rhythm of emigration. From it we also learn interesting details about the accused men and the difficult relations between the curate and his unruly flock, and particularly about one 'mastro Lorenzo maestro de lettere todesche', a teacher of German letters who 'has got both the New and the Old Testament of Martin Luther' and 'very often goes to Germany, whence he brings back many prohibited books'.[54]

The presence in Alagna of a teacher of German letters and of a sizable number of books inevitably raises questions about education and the spread of literacy, not only in this village but more generally in the Alps. It is relevant to observe that standards of scholastic achievement are today rather poor all over the Alpine area.[55] At first glance, it would seem obvious to regard such low standards as a legacy of the immemorial and fatal backwardness of traditional upland society. In fact, this is a popular but highly questionable view, and one of the first scholars to challenge it was the anthropologist Robert Burns, who went so far as to suggest that the Alpine area may have been traditionally characterized by an unexpectedly high degree of literacy and education. This suggestion originated from Burns's discovery that since the late Middle Ages the French Alpine village of Saint-Véran (where he did his fieldwork) had produced a large supply of notaries, who used to emigrate to the plains and offer their services not only as notaries and scribes but also as schoolmasters. They were apparently the product of a well-developed educational system

---

[52] Cf. Stucki, *Geschichte der Familie Bodmer*, pp. 31–4.
[53] See ASDN 1–117, fol. 227, and 1–134, fol. 430v.
[54] ASDN XII, 2, 6, Foro eccl. Libri e registri. Criminalia, 1576–1583, fol. 94.
[55] For a general discussion of current educational problems in the Alps, see Mériaudeau, 'L'enfant, l'école et la montagne'.

created by the village communities. In the Queyras Valley, of which Saint-Véran is part, all seven village communities had schools as early as the fifteenth century, and instruction was also sometimes offered in outlying hamlets.[56]

To Burns, who was writing in the early 1960s, it was doubtful how far his findings could be generalized to the entire Alpine region. Twenty-five years later the question remains difficult to answer, given the paucity of studies on this topic. Nevertheless, several instances supporting Burns's insights can easily be found in the literature. In both the Western and the Eastern Alps, cases are recorded of valleys whose inhabitants emigrated on a seasonal basis in order to travel as schoolmasters and teach the illiterate masses of the lowlands. The valley of Safien, in the Grisons, was actually known as the *Schulmeistertal*.[57] It is also apparent that particularly in the Western Alps notaries were familiar figures in even the most remote villages,[58] and many of them must have been natives of the uplands. In the course of the seventeenth century alone, Alagna gave birth to at least fifteen notaries.

It is worth noting that in Alagna a community school system similar to that of Saint-Véran is not attested until 1759, when a communal school was established for both boys and girls. We have seen, however, that a 'teacher of German letters' lived in Alagna in 1581, and there are several other indications that some form of teaching was offered in the village at an early date. Furthermore, we know that literacy (measured by the ability to sign one's name) was widespread well before the foundation of the communal school. As I have shown elsewhere, it can be estimated that in 1781 about 80 per cent of the men born in Alagna and aged between 60 and 79 years were able to write their names. The proportion of literates aged 40–59 reached 85 per cent, and among the younger age groups literacy was practically universal. The condition of the women was significantly different. For a long time they were probably taught to read but not to write, and it was only towards the middle of the nineteenth century, as the analysis of marriage records shows, that they acquired the ability to sign.[59]

[56] Burns, 'The Circum-Alpine area', pp. 149–51.
[57] Cf. e.g. Prato, *La vita economica in Piemonte*, p. 46; Fleury and Valmary, 'Les progrès de l'instruction élémentaire', p. 83; and Zinsli, *Walser Volkstum*, pp. 340–1.
[58] Cf. Prato, *La vita economica in Piemonte*, pp. 395–6, and Siddle, 'Cultural prejudice', pp. 22–3.
[59] Cf. Viazzo, 'Alfabetizzazione e istruzione scolastica'. Similar findings are reported for another Walser community south of Monte Rosa by Bodo, 'Issime', pp. 38–9.

Of course, it would be unwise to overlook the existence of contrary evidence. The Reverend King, for instance, noticed that in the 1850s virtually everyone in Alagna could read and write, and was impressed by the fact that boys were provided with instruction in French and Italian as well as in accounts, calligraphy and the elements of drawing which were so essential to the crafts practised by Alagna's emigrants. But he also made acid comments on the poor state of education in other valleys he had visited. 'The children are certainly taught gratis,' he remarked, 'but nearly all they generally learn is the Catechism, and portions of the mass and services.'[60] Testimonies like this suggest that in the field of education (as in many others) the Alps could exhibit a wide range of variation. However, it seems equally clear that educational standards were not as uniformly low as it is usually assumed. Indeed, what evidence we possess on literacy seems to indicate that the ability to write and read was rather more widespread in the Alpine uplands than in the surrounding plains.

Perhaps the best-known data are those analyzed by François Furet and Jacques Ozouf in their historical survey of literacy in France, which shows that literacy was widespread in large sectors of the French Alps at a very early stage, and particularly in what is today the *département* of the Hautes-Alpes. For this region, marriage records indicate that between 1686 and 1690 about two-thirds of all grooms were able to sign their names – the highest proportion in the whole of France.[61] But similar indications emerge from several other works. For instance, a very recent study of notarial records for a part of Savoy (one of the regions of the French Alps left out of Furet and Ozouf's survey) suggests that by 1766 over two-thirds of peasant owners were literate.[62] This evidence is admittedly rather circumscribed, and there is no guarantee that men signing notarial documents were representative of the entire population. However, the 1848 general census of the Kingdom of Sardinia (which included Savoy, Piedmont, Liguria and the County of Nice as well as Sardinia) demonstrates that in that year the provinces of Savoy were the ones with the highest proportion of literate people. What is more, this census shows that also in the Aosta Valley and in the other Alpine regions of the kingdom literacy levels were consistently higher than in the plains of Piedmont

---

[60] King, *The Italian valleys*, p. 197.
[61] The exact proportion was 64 percent. See Furet and Ozouf, *Reading and writing*, p. 31. Their study is largely based on the data collected by the Maggiolo survey in 1877–9 and already presented by Fleury and Valmary, 'Les progrès de l'instruction élémentaire'.
[62] Siddle, 'Cultural prejudice', pp. 23–6.

or in Liguria, not to mention Sardinia.[63] A very similar, and indeed even more striking contrast between uplands and lowlands is provided by Lombardy in the Napoleonic period.[64] And the impression of early and widespread literacy in the Alps is further reinforced by what evidence is available for Switzerland and especially for Austria in the late nineteenth century. In 1900, Vorarlberg was the Austrian region with the lowest rate of illiteracy (only 1 per cent), and Upper Austria, Salzburg and Tyrol also had an excellent record.[65]

Unfortunately, very few systematic efforts have been made to explore this question in greater detail. Nevertheless, a most intriguing line of inquiry has been recently indicated by the unforeseen results yielded by researches conducted on a cluster of Piedmontese valleys inhabited by mixed populations of Catholics and Protestants.[66] The expectation was that levels of literacy would turn out to be significantly higher in the Protestant areas, but this was only partially borne out by the analysis of marriage records. What these studies have revealed, instead, is a strong positive correlation between literacy and altitude – a finding which tallies very well with what we know about villages like Alagna or Saint-Véran (which happens to be, very fittingly, the highest settlement in the Western Alps).[67]

The surprising extent of literacy in many parts of the Alps has escaped most scholars, but has puzzled the few who have noticed it. One of the hypotheses which has been advanced is that in the Alps children received more education because the cold climate did not allow them any other activity in winter time.[68] But snow and

---

[63] Regno d'Italia, *Censimento degli Antichi Stati Sardi*, vol. 1, Tavola XIII. The high level of literacy of Savoy towards the middle of the nineteenth century has been recently noticed by Breschi and Livi-Bacci, 'Stagione di nascita', p. 99.

[64] In the early nineteenth century the proportion of spouses able to sign their names ranged in the mountain valleys of Lombardy between 45 and 70 per cent as compared to only 15–30 per cent in the plains. See Toscani, 'Scuole della Dottrina Cristiana e alfabetizzazione', p. 49.

[65] Cipolla, *Literacy and development*, pp. 16–22.

[66] Caffaro, 'Scolarità e alfabetizzazione in Val Pellice'; Cuoco, 'Scolarità e alfabetizzazione in Val Germanasca e Val Chisone'. The Pellice, Germanasca and Chisone Valleys are inhabited by a mixed population of Catholics and Waldenses, a religious group which originated in the south of France about 1170 through the preaching of Peter Waldo. To my knowledge, comparative studies of this kind are not available for other parts of the Alps. Billigmeier, *A crisis in Swiss pluralism*, pp. 75–6, 116–17, claims that in the eighteenth century literacy was high in both the Protestant and the Catholic areas of Romansh-speaking Engadine (Switzerland), but provides no quantitative evidence.

[67] A marked tendency for literacy to increase with altitude has been reported recently for another valley in the Piedmontese Western Alps by Allio, 'Emigrazione dalla Valle Maira', pp. 134–5.

[68] Cf. Fleury and Valmary, 'Les progrès de l'instruction élémentaire', p. 83.

cold weather, as Carlo Cipolla has remarked, can hardly be the only elements involved.[69] Even if much more work is needed on this topic, it seems likely that the tendency for literacy to grow with altitude is mainly explained by the fact that the incidence of seasonal emigration was much greater in the high valleys. So far we have talked about Alpine emigration in rather general terms. But it should be emphasized that the classic pattern of Alpine seasonal emigration, characterized by long journeys and lasting several months, was in fact to be found mostly in the high valleys. The inhabitants of the lower valleys also migrated, but, in the Western Alps particularly, their absence typically lasted only two or three weeks. Taking advantage of the slight difference in the timing of harvest due to a different altitude, they simply went to the adjacent plains to help with the harvest and then returned to their own fields.[70] It is evident that this was a completely different kind of emigration. As Jean-Pierre Poussou has shown,[71] it had a far more limited impact on the economy of mountain communities and on their social and demographic structure, and lacked, we may add, all those features which make seasonal emigration a factor favouring earlier and widespread literacy.[72]

This leads to a point of primary importance – to what we might call 'the Alpine paradox'. It would seem obvious to assume that it was in the geographically remoter high valleys, rather than in the less isolated areas at lower altitudes, that Alpine communities came nearest to a closed subsistence economy. This assumption, however, overlooks the fact that at higher altitudes the chances that a population has of approaching self-sufficiency are inevitably fewer. Moreover, the growing season is shorter, and the urge to 'optimize' labour correspondingly greater. Thus, the very marginality of the land has forced the communities of the high valleys to 'open' their economies to a greater degree than the communities of the low valleys. Some areas increasingly specialized in pastoral activities, as we shall see in Chapter 8, but a more important and indeed universal way of expanding local resources was represented by seasonal or temporary emigration. In some respects the villages in the high valleys probably remained more 'closed' than those placed nearer the mouth of the valleys. Endogamy rates, in particular, apparently tended to be

---

[69] Cipolla, *Literacy and development*, p. 74.
[70] Cf. Blanchard, *Les Alpes Occidentales*, vol. 7, pp. 547–53.
[71] Poussou, 'Les mouvements migratoires en France'.
[72] Cf. Furet and Ozouf, *Reading and writing*, pp. 164–5. The existence of a correlation between emigration and literacy has recently been stressed by Allio, 'Emigrazione dalla Valle Maira', p. 134.

higher,[73] and at first glance this may give the impression of more closed, inward-looking communities. But from an economic and a cultural point of view the communities of the high valleys were – paradoxically – more open than the villages at lower altitudes.

Was poverty the spur?

My contention that the conventional image of Alpine communities as closed subsistence economies and intellectual backwaters must be strongly qualified, and in some cases utterly reversed, largely rests on evidence that has surfaced in the last few decades. But in a way it simply restates a point made over sixty years ago by Febvre. 'Is the mountaineer,' he wrote, 'backward and slow as compared with the plain-dweller? ... These people, who have spread unceasingly over the great world routes; are they rivetted to the soil, deprived of outlook, and wrapped up in routine? It may be said that poverty has driven them; but poverty is the other name, or one of the other names, for a mountain environment.'[74]

This passage offers a useful starting point for a number of considerations. Quite sensibly, Febvre regarded emigration (and, indirectly, its economic and cultural benefits) as a consequence of the barrenness of upland areas. Indeed, it is hardly deniable that environmental factors have played a prominent part in causing large-scale emigration from the mountains and also in moulding those distinctive features which mark it out from other forms of spatial mobility. It is no accident, for instance, that in early modern France regular flows of seasonal emigrants travelling over long distances in groups, rather than just moving individually from one village to another, came almost without exception from the mountains.[75] In order to avoid the pitfalls of a static and ahistorical environmentalist approach, it is of course salutary to remember that the migratory imbalance between uplands and lowlands to which we are now accustomed is a relatively recent phenomenon. Until the late Middle Ages, as we have seen, people were more likely to move into the Alpine valleys than to leave them for good. Nevertheless, it may be generally accepted that, once a marginal area such as the Alps begins to be intensely colonized, the characteristic

---

[73] A well-documented case is the Ziller Valley (Tyrol), where in the period 1750–1850 proportions of endogamous marriages ranged from 75–90 per cent in high-altitude settlements to less than 40 per cent in the villages of the low valley. See Troger, *Bevölkerungsgeographie des Zillertales*, pp. 57–60.

[74] Febvre, *Geographical introduction to history*, p. 199.

[75] Cf. Poussou, 'Les mouvements migratoires en France', p. 63, and Poitrineau, *Remues d'hommes*, pp. 69–75.

inelasticity of mountain environments restricts so much the potential for increased productivity that the upper limits of the carrying capacity are fairly rapidly reached and emigration becomes unavoidable. But is it legitimate to conclude that from this moment the mountains become, to use Braudel's influential phrase, 'une fabrique d'hommes à l'usage d'autrui'?[76]

This is a very important issue. The characterization of mountain areas as 'factories' producing manpower on a large scale to be sent down to the plains implies, first of all, that in the mountains fertility was very high. It also conjures up the image of populations endemically exceeding the limits imposed by local resources only to be ruthlessly cut back. Furthermore, the allied notion of emigration as a safety valve mainly stresses the role of permanent emigration as a way of disposing of surplus population. To be sure, the existence of seasonal and temporary emigration is recognized by the proponents of this view, but their significance is generally minimized. To quote Michael Flinn, these forms of emigration 'merely mitigated and sustained the poverty of overpopulation. Lifting the ceiling a little does not solve the ultimate problem, and permanent out-migration was the only alternative to starvation at home.'[77]

Although the effectiveness of seasonal and temporary emigration as ways of expanding resources is likely to have varied considerably from one place to another, Flinn's argument that they provide no ultimate solution to the problem of overpopulation is obviously hard to dispute. The possibility still remains, however, that upland communities could at least approach a condition in which mechanisms lowering nuptiality and fertility kept natural increase within tolerable limits, thereby reducing the significance of permanent emigration as a safety valve. As we have noticed in Chapter 2, the image of the Alps as an important reservoir of people for urbanization and industrialization has been challenged by Lichtenberger; and the data presented in Chapter 4 show, in fact, that at least in the second half of the nineteenth century the overall fertility of Alpine populations was relatively moderate.

If we consider the question of regulation in a long-term perspective, what we should expect to find in the Alps are not constantly low levels of nuptiality and overall fertility, but rather an adjustment of demography to the worsening ratio of resources and population. We can safely assume, for instance, that in the first two or three centuries after its foundation Alagna must have displayed a 'frontier demogra-

[76] Braudel, *La Méditerranée*, p. 46. Cf. Chapter 2 above, p. 41.
[77] Flinn, *The European demographic system*, p. 74.

phy'. But towards the turn of the sixteenth century crude birth rates were already fairly low, ranging from 25 to 30 per thousand. This was most likely due to the effects of seasonal emigration itself, which entailed long periods of spousal separation,[78] and perhaps more decisively to low levels of nuptiality. There is unfortunately no way of measuring permanent celibacy, but marriage appears to have been late: men married on average at nearly 28 years of age and women at about 25 years.[79]

These figures suggest that some kind of homeostatic adjustment had occurred and seem to support the set of hypotheses about the role of nuptiality put forward in Chapter 4. To this important and complex problem we shall go back in due course.[80] What is necessary to stress here is that the undeniable fact that the poverty of the land was a major force behind Alpine emigration should not lead to over-hasty or surreptitious deductions. Thus, the greater relative importance of permanent emigration *vis-à-vis* other coping devices used by Alpine populations to strike a viable balance with their resources has to be demonstrated rather than merely asserted. Another major point is that whereas the poverty of the *land* was very real, the poverty of the *people* living in the mountains was simply potential. It only became real if population growth went unchecked and insufficient action was taken to expand shrinking local resources – a distinct possibility, perhaps, but by no means an ineluctable destiny. Students of the Alps, however, have mostly assumed that the inhabitants of barren high valleys were bound to be poor. In so doing, they appear to have confused two quite different kinds of poverty – a confusion, we may notice, very often exploited by the Alpine communities themselves in their petitions to central authorities, where their poverty was deliberately played up as part of negotiations to obtain exemptions from taxes and other tributes.[81]

The problem of mountain poverty clearly needs to be thought over again, and a consideration of the nature and proximate causes of

---

[78] On the effects of seasonal emigration on birth rates, see Menken, 'Seasonal migration and seasonal variation in fecundability'; Bongaarts and Potter, 'Fertility effect of seasonal migration'; and Massey and Mullan, 'Effects of seasonal migration on fertility'. Menken has estimated that a separation of eight months will lower birth probabilities between 33 and 43 per cent.

[79] Exact age at marriage can be established for 37 men and 48 women who married in the period 1618–29. The mean age is 27.85 and 24.83 respectively (median age: 27.70 and 25.25).

[80] Cf. Chapter 8 below, pp. 219–23.

[81] Cf. e.g. Blanchard, *Les Alpes Occidentales*, vol. 6.1, pp. 301–2, and Janin, *Le Val d'Aoste*, p. 173.

Alpine emigration constitutes a useful first step. It has been argued, to quote Flinn again, that 'we should be under no illusion about the forcible nature of emigration . . . People rarely leave their homes, holdings, and families for good willingly; only the direst pressures drive them to it.'[82] The decision to leave home permanently – or 'even for a short period', as Olwen Hufton has suggested in the influential pages she has devoted to emigration from the French Alps[83] – was enforced by sheer misery and desperation. Emigration was, in the words of yet another scholar, a 'fuite devant la misère'.[84] What is more, we are told that both permanent and seasonal emigrants lived a wretched existence also in the towns and villages to which they had moved, their way of life often being indistinguishable from that of beggars.

Such a dismal picture of Alpine emigration and Alpine society clearly does not fit with what we have seen for Alagna. When every year in the spring the Alagnese emigrants went back to their jobs in Switzerland and France, they left behind a prosperous village; and once in the plains, they could anticipate hard work but not a wretched and ignoble existence. This was certainly true of nineteenth-century Alagna, but things were probably not very different in the more distant past. It is remarkable that already in the sixteenth century many Alagnese emigrants were, like their nineteenth-century descendants,[85] building contractors employing several workers and gaining economic rewards that would have been unimaginable for a peasant. Melcher Bodmer, a master stone-cutter, normally had three *Knechten*.[86] But to build the church of St Theodore in Sion, the chief town of Valais, Ulrich Ruffiner employed twenty workers for eight years. As we know from a contract signed on 8 September 1514, he was paid 4,700 Rhenish florins in cash, plus 900 sextaries of wine, 200 bushels of rye and 16 good oxen.[87]

Ruffiner's case is admittedly rather special, for he was a distinguished architect. Yet, what is most impressive about Alagna in the sixteenth and seventeenth centuries is precisely the fact that Ruffiner's case, though unusual, was not isolated. A remarkable number

[82] Flinn, *The European demographic system*, p. 74.
[83] Hufton, *The poor of eighteenth-century France*, pp. 69–106.
[84] Guillen, 'Introduction', p. 2.
[85] In 1838, as the parish priest specified in introducing the *status animarum* of that year, there were in Alagna no less than 48 stone-cutters and plasterers 'who worked on their own account, that is who employed workers and called themselves building contractors'. APA, *Libri status animarum*.
[86] Stucki, *Geschichte der Familie Bodmer*, pp. 31–46.
[87] Riggenbach, *Ulrich Ruffiner*.

of architects emerged from the larger group of master builders, and Daniel Heintz was at least Ruffiner's equal. What is more, Daniel's son Joseph became Court Painter in Prague and was a major figure in European Mannerism. On the other side of the Alps, one of the outstanding personalities of the Italian *Seicento*, the painter Tanzio da Varallo, was in fact a native of Alagna, his real name being Antonio de Henricis. Along with his brother Giovanni, arguably the greatest sculptor in seventeenth-century Piedmont, Tanzio is the most eminent among a large number of lesser yet qualified painters and sculptors born in Alagna. Such a blossoming of artists is hardly what one would expect from a remote village in the mountains. Exceptional as it was in many ways, the de Henricis family was in other ways typically Alagnese. Of Tanzio's brothers, Giovanni was a renowned sculptor and Melchiorre a more than competent painter. But Enrico, Pietro and Giacomo were just *magistri lapicidae*, master stone-cutters.[88]

An impressive and highly relevant parallel is provided by the valleys of Canton Ticino, which were mostly characterized by a pattern of seasonal emigration which was exactly the same as that of Alagna. The hypothesis that the people of Ticino favoured seasonal emigration because it could be adjusted to the needs of agricultural and pastoral activities at home is unconvincing, since emigrants were mostly builders and were absent throughout the summer. It seems more appropriate to think that the benefits of summer emigration outweighed its costs. That in some cases these benefits could be startlingly high becomes clear when one realizes that in the sixteenth and early seventeenth centuries the building industry in Rome was dominated by a series of extraordinary architects coming from this hilly and mountainous region. The two brothers Giovanni and Domenico Fontana, Carlo Maderno, Francesco Borromini and Carlo Fontana were all born within a few miles of each other and are just the best known of a great number of masons and stone-cutters who went to Rome in search of work from Ticino.[89]

The builders from Alagna and from Ticino admittedly belonged to a skilled 'aristocracy of emigration'. Masons, stone-cutters and plasterers were paid much more than average on both sides of the Alps,

---

[88] I use here the names by which Alagnese artists are known to art historians – German names for those who worked north of the Alps, Italian names for the others. For a first bibliographical orientation, see Thieme-Becker, *Allgemeines Lexicon der bildenden Künstler*, and the more recent survey by Debiaggi, 'Gli artisti di Alagna'.

[89] The literature on the Ticinese architects is vast. For a first orientation, see Thieme-Becker, *Allgemeines Lexicon der bildenden Künstler*, and the more recent Macmillan Encyclopedia of Architects.

and their trades were highly respected ones.[90] As such they are not fully representative of Alpine emigration. On the other hand, it is far from certain that the fate of less skilled emigrants was as hopeless as is often assumed. Hufton has contended that in the second half of the eighteenth century the pedlars of Savoy and the other regions of the French Alps were just practising a sort of *économie de l'absence*. By spending a few months away from their villages they relieved the demographic pressure at home; but they 'did not expect to make a gainful livelihood from their trays and packs. They lived by their wits and often they were merely more elevated and thinly disguised beggars.'[91] This may have been true of Savoyard pedlars migrating to France in a particularly difficult period,[92] but can hardly be generalized to the whole of Alpine emigration or even to peddling, which was one of the most widespread and characteristic occupations among seasonal emigrants.

A striking counter-example is offered by Gressoney, one of the German-speaking communities south of Monte Rosa, only a few miles from Alagna. In Gressoney peddling was the main activity of seasonal emigrants for over four centuries, from the sixteenth century (when the valley of Gressoney was already known as the *Krämertal*, or 'valley of the pedlars') to the First World War. But the opportunities offered by this trade varied very considerably over this long span of time. Pedlars all over the Alps depended, as a rule, on urban-based merchants who not only supplied the goods to be sold but also advanced the money needed by the emigrants to support themselves during their journeys. However, many of Gressoney's pedlars gradually managed to by-pass these merchants and to become commercial entrepreneurs themselves, not rarely with astonishing success. Towards the end of the eighteenth century this made peddling so lucrative that in a few decades the people of Gressoney became spectacularly rich. In the second half of the nineteenth century Gressoney was one of the most affluent villages in the Alps and counted no less than twelve millionaires.[93]

The case of Gressoney offers a perhaps extreme but exemplary demonstration that Alpine emigration may well have been initially spurred

---

[90] Cf. Stucki, *Geschichte der Familie Bodmer*, pp. 31–46; Sella, 'Migrations montagnardes', p. 553; and Poitrineau, *Remues d'hommes*, pp. 104–11.

[91] Hufton, *The poor of eighteenth-century France*, p. 84.

[92] On the worsening of the economic condition of the French Alps in the second half of the eighteenth century and its effects on emigration, see Poitrineau, *Remues d'hommes*, pp. 6–48.

[93] Cf. K. Martin, *Einwanderung aus Savoyen*; and Riccarand and Omezzoli, *Émigration valdôtaine*, p. 20.

by the poverty of mountainous land (or, possibly, by the poverty of its inhabitants) but in the event may also have turned quite a few villages into well-to-do or even surprisingly wealthy communities. There is, indeed, a remarkable contrast between the vivid but exceedingly gloomy image of Alpine emigration conjured up by Hufton, Flinn and other historians and the much cooler view held by the French geographers of the Grenoble school, who simply regarded seasonal emigration as a maximizing strategy whereby average output per head was increased and 'optimum population' approached.[94] Such an attitude probably reflects these geographers' familiarity with the recent history of the numerous villages which up to the years between the two world wars owed to emigration a reasonable degree of prosperity.

The dramatic fall in living standards experienced by many an Alpine community after the abrupt decline of seasonal emigration in the first decades of the twentieth century is a useful reminder of the extent to which the poverty and prosperity of Alpine populations could depend not so much on their physical as on their economic and political environment. The final demise of seasonal emigration was of course an event of unique significance. But, throughout the five centuries of its history, Alpine emigration had been severely affected by wars, protectionist policies, economic crises and political upheavals. In 1556, to give just two examples, the City Council of Berne issued an edict which safeguarded the interests of the local guilds and prohibited the immigration of workers from several localities including Gressoney and Alagna.[95] And three centuries later, in the May of 1848, the curate of Alagna reported that only ninety-nine men were temporarily absent from the village 'because of the political changes that occurred in France in the month of February'.[96]

There is, to my knowledge, no comprehensive and systematic account of the ways in which Alpine emigration faced political or economic crises. However, important insights are provided by a study of immigration in Turin in the troubled first half of the eighteenth century.[97] This study shows that immigration was mostly seasonal and that the majority of the immigrants came from Alpine districts. But it also shows that different categories of immigrants were separated by strong geographical, occupational and economic boundaries. There were, first of all, groups of skilled and highly specialized

[94] See Chapter 2 above, pp. 38–41.
[95] Cf. Riggenbach, *Ulrich Ruffiner*, pp. 7–8, and Carlen, 'Der Rat von Bern'.
[96] APA, *Libri status animarum*.
[97] Levi, 'Mobilità della popolazione'.

workers, mainly stone-cutters and master masons from Ticino and from the Biellese, a district bordering on the Sesia Valley. There was, then, a category of semi-skilled or unskilled immigrants from Savoy and from the northern sector of the Piedmontese Alps. These were mainly odd-job men practising a variety of trades, the most characteristic occupation probably being that of carriers of wine-kegs (*brentatori*). Finally, there was a stream of beggars who poured into the city on a fairly regular seasonal basis. But the registers of people apprehended as beggars and vagrants reveal that they came almost exclusively from a few villages all located at rather low altitudes in the southern sector of the Piedmontese Alps, where begging is known from other sources to have been a recognized and perhaps dominant form of seasonal emigration.[98] No less interestingly, these registers also suggest that, even when Turin and Piedmont were affected by political, military or economic crises, people from the valleys supplying skilled and unskilled labour never joined the ranks of the beggars. They simply disappeared from the city for a while, to come back once the situation had improved.

Much more work remains to be done in this area, but the case of eighteenth-century Turin certainly gives cause to question the common view that reduced demand for seasonal labour readily turned Alpine migrants into beggars. In general terms, it is undeniable that the Alps sent fairly large numbers of beggars down to the plains. But begging appears to have been the extreme form taken by seasonal emigration in some Alpine districts, and one whose importance is easily overrated by focussing historical research on such sources as judicial records or the rolls of hospitals and charitable institutions. The marked difference found in Turin between the various groups and categories of workers also confirms that it is fallacious to assume that all the emigrants from the Alps were in command of only very limited skills. It is therefore vital to distinguish between what Guichonnet has termed 'les Alpes adonnées à l'émigration de qualité ... et les secteurs pratiquant des migrations "prolétariennes"'.[99]

Broad distinctions can primarily be drawn between geographical regions (such as, for instance, the northern and the southern sectors of the Piedmontese Alps) or between trades. But it should be stressed that significant differences could exist also among emigrants coming

---

[98] In addition to the data provided by Levi, 'Mobilità della popolazione', pp. 545–6, see Blanchard, *Les Alpes Occidentales*, vol. 7, pp. 314–19. Cf. also Bonnin, 'Les migrations dans les hautes terres dauphinoises', p. 38, and the balanced discussion by Châtelain, *Les migrants temporaires en France*, pp. 493–512.

[99] Guichonnet, 'Le partage politique des Alpes', p. 284.

from the same village and practising the same trade. Another serious consequence of equating emigration with poverty is, indeed, that this obscures the complex nexus linking emigration to the social and economic structure of the Alpine community. In its various formulations, this equation either conveys the impression that all emigrants were equally poor and hopeless or, alternatively, that emigrants overwhelmingly belonged to the poorer stratum of upland society. A growing amount of evidence suggests, on the contrary, that emigration was usually spread across the board and tended, if anything, to be more frequent among the richer than among the poorer inhabitants of Alpine villages.[100] In Alagna I was told that only poor men 'put up with working in the fields'. And this is also the conclusion emerging from a recent study by Laurence Fontaine, which is of special relevance because it concerns the activities of pedlars from a valley in the French Alps during the eighteenth and nineteenth centuries.

Seasonal emigration required careful planning. The emigrant needed a clear idea of where to go, a network of relatives and compatriots to rely upon, letters of introduction, and a passport if state boundaries were to be crossed. But emigration also required a fair amount of cash. Often this money was advanced by urban-based merchants, as we have seen. Alternatively, it could be borrowed from other sources: friends and relatives, local or urban moneylenders, possibly some communal fund especially established to enable emigrants to borrow money at low rates of interest. But, although conditions could vary considerably, as a rule the emigrant needed some kind of capital asset to be traded as security, and this was usually land.

What Fontaine is able to show very effectively is that in the communities of the Oisans Valley (where peddling was by far the dominant activity of seasonal emigrants) a major cleavage separated the landless, who could not afford to emigrate and were forced to work as agricultural day-labourers or herdsmen, and the emigrants, who were invariably landed and included in their numbers the members of the local élite. These social boundaries, however, could scarcely be fixed, for emigrants could easily be forced into debt and be dispossessed of their land, often to the benefit of other fellow villagers. This explains why the emigrants themselves were stratified into several categories. Indeed, some of the richer emigrants are better described as merchants than as pedlars. At the opposite extreme, other emigrants were heavily indebted and on the verge of joining the landless day-labourers. They

---

[100]   In addition to the study by Fontaine discussed in the next paragraphs, cf. Netting, *Balancing on an alp*, p. 103, and especially Albera *et al.*, 'Movimenti migratori'.

could still decide to migrate, but in that case they were in serious danger of living the impoverished existence of the 'thinly disguised beggars' described by Hufton.[101] In the final chapter of this book we shall go back to emigration and the credit system as mechanisms of social differentiation. But the brief remarks offered here suffice to show that emigration, far from being a mere 'survival strategy' dictated by the Alpine environment, was a major avenue of mobility up and down the village ladder, and also that the opportunities provided by emigration could lie beyond the reach of the very poor.

As Poussou observed over fifteen years ago, 'les causes de l'émigration saisonnière ou temporaire peuvent, à première vue, paraître simples: misère et surpeuplement. Lorsque l'on creuse un peu plus, on s'aperçoit que la réalité est beaucoup plus complexe'. In fact, his survey of the literature on migratory movements in France suggests that the condition of the emigrants was not always miserable and that they actually tended to be recruited more from amongst the rich than from amongst the poor. This led him to emphasize the importance of not lumping together quite different forms of emigration, 'car l'on a trop souvent confondu émigration de la misère et émigration du mieux-être'.[102] In these years Poussou's survey has been frequently cited and highly praised. But strangely enough, its main conclusions about the nature and causes of emigration from mountain areas have been largely ignored. Thus, most scholars have continued to characterize and explain Alpine emigration only in terms of poverty and overpopulation. In the Alps, as we have repeatedly noticed, generalizations are always hazardous and it is difficult for competing arguments to be established conclusively. But the evidence produced in this chapter surely indicates that the case of Alpine emigration needs to be reopened.

[101] Fontaine, 'Effets déséquilibrants du colportage', pp. 21–7.
[102] Poussou, 'Les mouvements migratoires en France', pp. 68, 70.

7

The wealth from the earth:
mining and immigration

Industrial employment and geographical mobility in the 'age of autarky'

Although the causes and nature of Alpine emigration have often been misunderstood, as the preceding chapter has tried to demonstrate, its significance has hardly been questioned by any scholar. It is indeed a commonplace among students of the Alpine world that seasonal emigration was the best way of optimizing labour during the slack winter months, while permanent emigration provided a crucial safety valve in a marginal environment where limited resources tended to be rapidly outstripped by demographic growth. In the cybernetic jargon favoured by ecological anthropologists, emigration was one of the 'servomechanisms' whereby a viable balance between population and resources could be achieved or restored. And in Malthus's model, too, emigration was granted a major role as one of the variables which could fundamentally affect the economic and demographic structure of upland communities and turn them into 'open' systems.

By contrast, the importance of immigration has been usually played down. It is of course acknowledged that the boundaries of Alpine communities were regularly crossed by a trickle of in-marrying spouses (mainly wives) from neighbouring villages. But, as far as proper migratory movements are concerned,[1] the more or less tacit assumption is that, after the end of the medieval colonization of the high valleys, people from the lowlands had clearly little incentive to try and settle in the snow-bound and increasingly overpopulated uplands. The general impression one receives from the literature is, therefore, that the overflow of seasonal and permanent emigrants moving to the plains was the only form of long-distance spatial

---

[1] On the need to distinguish between proper migration and what he calls 'micro-mobility', see Poussou, 'Les mouvements migratoires en France', pp. 19–21.

mobility. In the mountains, it has been authoritatively stated, 'l'émigration se fait toujours dans le sens descendant'.[2] This, however, proves to be a rather simplistic and ultimately misleading picture. As this chapter will show, long-distance immigration did exist, and its impact on the ecology, demography and social structure of many Alpine districts cannot be underrated.

In the Alps immigration is commonly presented as a relatively recent development, a consequence of the changes which marked, after 1850, the end of the age of autarky.[3] The 'railway revolution', the growth of the hydro-electric industry and the beginnings of tourism, it is maintained, not only disturbed the traditional patterns of rural life but also attracted large numbers of workers from outside, many of whom eventually settled in the mountains. This view is essentially correct in so far as it links immigration to the availability of industrial (or, in any case, non-agricultural) jobs. What can easily be called in question is the claim that sizable flows of migration towards the Alpine valleys and other mountain areas can only be observed after the end of the so-called age of autarky.

It is worth remembering that, in his seminal study of proto-industrialization in the highlands of Canton Zurich, Rudolf Braun found that the districts which in the seventeenth and eighteenth centuries saw the rise of cottage industry had been endemically affected by substantial emigration, the product of social and economic mechanisms which pushed surplus population out of their communities. With the expansion of the textile industry, however, these districts 'lost their push-force and even developed a certain pull-force of immigration'.[4] The hypothesis that proto-industrialization could generate immigration has now been corroborated by more recent research conducted on other Swiss localities,[5] and we can expect further evidence pointing in this direction to come out in the next few years. But the popularity which the study of proto-industry is currently enjoying should not obscure the fact that in many parts of the Alps mobility and immigration had been stimulated well before the rise of cottage industry (and, indeed, even more massively) by mining.

Mining has a very long history in the Alps, archaeological remains showing that copper was mined on a fairly large scale already in the Bronze Age. By studying the finds in the galleries, the ore-washing areas and the associated settlements, it can be established that in the

---

[2] Veyret-Verner, 'Équilibre démographique', p. 338.
[3] See e.g. Guichonnet, 'Développement démographique', p. 173.
[4] Braun, 'Protoindustrialization and demographic changes', pp. 302–5.
[5] See e.g. C. Pfister, 'Menschen im Kanton Bern', p. 491.

Austrian region of Salzburg copper mining started as early as the eighteenth century B.C. and reached its peak some centuries later in the Late Bronze Age. In the same period substantial mining activities are also attested in Tyrol. But smaller deposits were worked all over the Alps, although only a few of them appear to have been sufficiently productive to meet more than local requirements.[6]

The economic and commercial significance of Alpine copper mining in the Bronze Age is strongly emphasized in the archaeological litera-ture. Since copper was recoverable, beyond the border of the Alpine region, only in parts of Germany and Italy, the Alps almost inevitably became a focal point in the economy of a large territory. Copper min-ing, however, suddenly declined with the introduction of iron in the eighth century B.C., which favoured the rise of the mining districts where the richest iron deposits in the Alps are found, namely the easternmost regions of Styria, Carinthia and Slovenia. But, at least in the Salzburg region, the decline of copper mining was counter-balanced by the growth of salt mining in localities like Hallstatt and Hallein-Dürrnberg. The mining of precious metals developed some-what later, but the Romans certainly knew the silver mines of Carin-thia; and if Strabo and Pliny are to be believed, large-scale gold mining was practised in several districts of the Western Alps. Indeed, the desire to get control of the gold mines of the Salassi was, according to Strabo, one of the main reasons behind the Roman conquest of the Aosta Valley.[7]

When historians, geographers and anthropologists more or less con-sciously subscribe to the Braudelian notion that in the mountains the tempo of history has been regulated by immutable environmental constraints, the picture they have in mind is that of an essentially agrarian society. Their attention is therefore focussed on the powerful influence exerted on mountain farming by the climatic and edaphic factors which are at the core of the ecological model outlined in Chapter 1. Cursory as it is, the brief reference which has been made to the origins and early development of Alpine mining is a useful corrective to that 'obsession with food-getting' which has led particu-larly ecological anthropologists to neglect natural resources which can-not be eaten and yet may prove decisive in moulding the economic, social and demographic structure of a community.[8] In large sectors

---

[6] Pauli, *The Alps,* pp. 244–5.

[7] Pliny, *Nat. Hist.* 33, 78; Strabo, *Geog.* 4, 6, 7. See also Jervis, *Tesori sotterranei,* p. 135; Gribaudi, *Il Piemonte nell'antichità classica,* pp. 299–307; and for a recent overview Pauli, *The Alps,* pp. 23–8.

[8] Cf. Ellen, *Environment, subsistence and system,* p. 100.

of the Alps the exploitation of mineral deposits has been, along with husbandry, one of the 'basics of living' for centuries or even millennia, and this obviously cannot be ignored in a balanced account of the relationships between population and natural resources in Alpine and, more generally, mountain environments. For historically the connections between mining and mountains (still betrayed by the two German words for 'mining', *Bergbau* and *Montanwesen*) have been very strong indeed, mineral deposits being characteristically located in mountainous, wooded, agriculturally marginal regions.[9]

It has been argued that similar environmental settings, coupled with a number of basic organizational requirements of the mining industry, tend to produce a set of distinctive features which vary only a little from one mining district or community to another, whatever the stage of economic and technological development.[10] One of the most important of these features is that the discovery of a new vein pushes miners to areas which are either not yet settled or have only a few inhabitants, and since prehistoric times the Alps have been no exception. As we have noticed in the preceding chapter, it was the discovery of copper deposits in the Tyrolese valleys which caused the establishment of the first high-altitude settlements in that part of the Alps. And it appears, to quote another example, that both in Hallstatt and on the Dürrnberg the salt mines were largely worked by immigrant labour.[11]

These two examples show that some of the most typical ecological and demographic effects of mining in modern times – immigration and the foundation of new settlements in isolated, inaccessible areas – are already detectable in Alpine prehistory. What is more, the very names of the localities we have mentioned (Hallstatt, the Dürrnberg, Tyrol, all places where mining was still thriving over two thousand years later) immediately suggest the existence of long-term lines of continuity. But once again, as with the problem of the beginnings of *Alpwirtschaft* discussed in Chapter 6, an emphasis on similarity and continuity should not be allowed to obscure the existence of the equally significant elements of diversity and discontinuity. Thus, although the importance of Alpine mining in pre-Roman and Roman times cannot be doubted, it is not completely clear whether it is strictly comparable (in terms of organization, scale and demographic impact,

---

[9] See especially Molenda, 'Mining towns', pp. 168–71. Cf. also Lewis, 'Industrialization in two highland societies', on Wales and Appalachia; and Godoy, 'Mining', on the Andes.

[10] Bulmer, 'Sociological models of the mining community', p. 61; Godoy, 'Mining', pp. 205–8.

[11] Pauli, *The Alps*, pp. 255–7.

for instance) with the full-fledged industry of the fifteenth and six-teenth centuries. What we know of the evolution of mining in the Alps since the Middle Ages points, in fact, to a number of crucial discontinuities.

In the Middle Ages mining appears to have mostly been a small family business. Even in the Austrian Alps, the rich iron deposits of Styria and Carinthia were exploited, at least until the thirteenth or fourteenth century, by people who were far from earning their living exclusively from their work with a shovel or pick. The Styrian and Carinthian *Eisenbauern* were primarily farmers and for them mining was a secondary, though not unimportant, activity.[12] This is not to say that in this period mining can be described as an 'autarkic industry'. These farmer-miners may well have devoted less time to mining than to their agricultural endeavours, but they certainly did not work in the mines just to satisfy the needs of their families or even of the local communities. Production was definitely market-oriented.[13] We may wonder, however, whether in terms of scale and organization medieval mining had much to share with the big indus-trial enterprises which came into being in the early modern period. It would seem, in particular, that the second half of the fifteenth cen-tury (which was characterized by a number of major technological innovations) marked a watershed in the history of Alpine mining. This impression is, indeed, strongly reinforced by what we know about the demographic consequences of mining.

The demographic impact of mining

Beginning in about 1460 Central Europe witnessed a sudden rise of mineral production, largely due to technological improvements which permitted the exploitation of what had previously been marginal mines. The invention of better methods of drilling, drainage and venti-lation led to the intensification of silver and gold mining,[14] and for many Alpine districts this had far-reaching ecological and demo-graphic effects. As Michael Mitterauer has pointed out,[15] in that period gold and silver mining required a more centralized organization than salt or iron mining, and a much higher number of workers. The rise of gold and silver mining therefore stimulated massive waves

---

[12] Mitterauer, 'Produktionsweise im österreichischen Montanwesen', pp. 287–8.
[13] Mitterauer, 'Produktionsweise im österreichischen Montanwesen', p. 291.
[14] Perroy, *Le Moyen Âge*, pp. 559–62.
[15] Mitterauer, 'Produktionsweise im österreichischen Montanwesen', pp. 236–7.

of immigration and the growth of towns whose spatial structure was very different from that of the dispersed settlements of the medieval *Eisenbauern*.

The Austrian Alps provide the most spectacular examples of changes brought about by the intensification of mining. Let us consider, for instance, the Gastein Valley, in the Salzburg region, which became one of the main centres of silver mining. In 1456 this valley only counted 298 households, that is about 1,800 inhabitants at most. In 1497 the number of its inhabitants had already increased to 3,000, and in the course of the sixteenth century it reached the figure of 5,000, of whom at least 1,200 were miners.[16] Similar patterns can be found in many other parts of Salzburg, Carinthia and Styria, but the most striking instances of rapid demographic growth come from Tyrol, whose mines acquired gigantic proportion and were probably the biggest in Central Europe. In 1554 the mines of Falkenstein near Schwaz employed 7,500 workers, and the whole district of Schwaz about 11,500. In a few decades, Schwaz had turned from a small village into the second largest city of Austria after Vienna, its population having reached a total of nearly 20,000 inhabitants.[17]

As one can easily infer from these figures, in the Austrian Alps the demographic and economic impact of mining was exceptionally pronounced. Mainly because of the immigration of large numbers of miners from southern Germany, the population of Tyrol grew from about 70,000 people in 1427 to 110,000 one century later and 140,000 in 1600; and it has been estimated that in the early sixteenth century at least one-quarter of the inhabitants of this region lived on mining.[18] It is therefore understandable that the mines of Tyrol, Salzburg, Carinthia and Styria have almost monopolized the attention of economic historians – all the more so in view of the crucial role played by the Tyrolese silver mines in favouring the ascendancy of the Habsburg dynasty.[19] Yet it would be inaccurate to assume that substantial mining activities and large-scale immigration were confined to the Austrian Alps.

Waves of immigration spurred by the growth of the mining industry seem to have been especially frequent on the Italian side of the Eastern Alps. Well-documented examples are offered by the small Fersina

---

[16] Klein, 'Die Bevölkerung Österreichs', p. 75; Mitterauer, 'Produktionsweise im österreichischen Montanwesen', p. 237.

[17] Sombart, *Der moderne Kapitalismus*, vol. 2.2, pp. 791–2; Klein, 'Die Bevölkerung Österreichs', pp. 85–6; Mitterauer, 'Produktionsweise im österreichischen Montanwesen', p. 237.

[18] Klein, 'Die Bevölkerung Österreichs', p. 86.

[19] For a recent overview, see Kellenbenz, 'Der mittlere Alpenraum'.

Valley, in the Trentino region, which in the early sixteenth century hosted over 1,000 immigrants,[20] and by the village of Riva d'Agordo, in the mountains of Veneto, whose population increased steeply from less than 150 people in 1584 to 855 sixty years later.[21] But serious attempts were also made to develop the mining industry in the Central and Western Alps. As early as the mid-fifteenth century both the Dukes of Savoy and the Dukes of Milan were already encouraging mineralogical researches in the mountainous areas of their states, and the existence of numerous mines in Savoy, Piedmont and Lombardy is solidly attested in the sixteenth century.[22] In this early period the importance of mining was admittedly still moderate, and so were its economic and demographic effects. In the late sixteenth century, however, and even more in the eighteenth century, several mines in the Central and Western Alps could rival in size with those in the Eastern Alps, which had in the meantime suffered a certain decline. In the Piedmontese Alps, mines were worked on a large scale in the Lanzo Valley, in the Orco Valley, in parts of the large Aosta Valley, in the Anzasca Valley, and above all in the Chiusella Valley.[23] But an excellent demonstration of the impact which mining could have on an Alpine community is provided by Alagna itself.

Very little is known about the origins of mining in Alagna, but it was probably in the 1530s that the gold mines began to be worked by the Scarogninis, a family of entrepreneurs from the lower Sesia Valley. A more intensive exploitation seems, however, to have started in 1634, when the Spanish government (which then ruled the State of Milan, of which the Sesia Valley was part) gave these mines in concession to Giorgio d'Adda, a Milanese nobleman related to the Scarogninis. Like most mining entrepreneurs of his day, he recruited specialists from outside (mainly from Germany and Tyrol) and so probably did his successors, who continued to work the mines until the end of the Spanish rule in 1707. Whether local men were also employed is not clear, but in any case it is unlikely that in this period mining could seriously affect either Alagna's economy or its demography. Immigrants have left very scant traces in the extant parish registers. And when the mines were visited by a local magistrate

[20] Riedman, 'Bergbau im Fersental', p. 180.
[21] Vergani, 'Una comunità mineraria di montagna', pp. 615–16.
[22] Prato, *La vita economica in Piemonte*, p. 250; Fanfani, 'L'industria mineraria lombarda', pp. 161–79.
[23] On the mining industry on the Italian side of the Alps from the sixteenth to the eighteenth century, see Cima, 'Strategie tecnologiche', pp. 211–21 and map 2. On the Piedmontese Alps, see also Prato, *La vita economica in Piemonte*, pp. 250–4, and Blanchard, *Les Alpes Occidentales*, vol. 6.2, pp. 496–503.

in the 1650s, a decade of peak productivity, he found only 23 workers.[24]

Things began to change after 1707, when Alagna and its mines were annexed to the Piedmontese state. From the very first years of Piedmontese rule, the parish registers unmistakably point to a fairly substantial flow of immigrants, coming partly from the various mining districts of the Piedmontese Alps and partly from several areas of Central and Northern Europe: Flanders, Bohemia, Tyrol, Denmark, Hanover and above all Saxony.[25] However, a real mining boom started only in the 1750s, when the Piedmontese government decided to give further impulse to the industry. The mines of Alagna were selected as particularly promising, and their management was entrusted to the *'soldati minatori'*, a newly created branch of artillery-men specialized in mining and mainly recruited from the Andorno and Chiusella Valleys. But since these soldiers could only furnish about a third of the required labour force, the government also encouraged the immigration of civilians. Designated in our sources as 'voluntary miners' (*minatori volontari*), some of these civilians were employed on piece-work. But most of them received regular wages and were paid roughly the same as the soldiers. Lower wages were paid to those workers (often women and children) who were engaged on a daily basis to perform less skilled or less heavy tasks.[26]

The effects of this new policy are most strikingly demonstrated by the dramatic surge of births, deaths and marriages recorded in Alagna (see Figure 7.1), which suggests that the immigrants who settled in the village were numbered by the hundreds. This is confirmed by balance sheets and other documents preserved in the Royal Library in Turin, which show that in the 1750s between 300 and 350 workers were simultaneously employed in the Alagna mines.[27] Not all these

[24] For a fuller account of the history of mining in Alagna and its consequences, see Viazzo, 'Ethnic change in a Walser community', pp. 204–40. For the period before 1707, see also Fanfani, 'L'industria mineraria lombarda', pp. 168–225.

[25] D. Molenda has noticed that 'especially in the initial stage of their existence the population of mining towns was extremely varied from the nationality point of view'. It is also worth noting that Saxony was for centuries the most important reservoir of skilled miners in Europe. In Bosnia and Serbia the word 'Saxon' (*Sas*) actually became synonymous with 'miner'. See Molenda, 'Mining towns', pp. 179–80.

[26] Very detailed information on the development of the Alagna mines and on their organization is provided by the report which the director of the state mines, N. S. de Robilant, sent to the Piedmontese minister G. B. Bogino in 1754: 'Relazione di Risoluzioni ... nella coltura delle miniere della Valle di Sesia', BRT, St.P. 751/2, esp. fols. 1–29. See also Robilant, *De l'utilité des voyages*, pp. 13–14 and plates 1–6; Barelli, *Cenni di statistica mineralogica*, pp. 442–50; and Prato, *La vita economica in Piemonte*, pp. 251–2.

[27] See especially 'Bilancio per la cultura delle Regie Miniere ... a tutto Decembre 1758', BRT, St.P. 751/1.

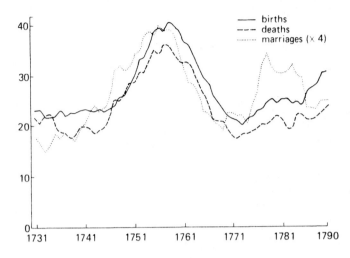

Figure 7.1 Births, deaths and marriages in Alagna 1731–1790
Note: Nine-year moving averages

workers were immigrants. But many men brought along wives, children and other relatives who were not engaged in mining, and an estimate of about 400 immigrants (with a sex ratio rather unbalanced in favour of males) should not be too far from the truth. The *libri status animarum* indicate that the 'host' population consisted of about 850 people.[28] Immigrants, old and new, may therefore have represented nearly one-third of the total population of Alagna in those years, and perhaps even more.

Throughout the 1750s Alagna hummed with activity, and life was not infrequently stirred up by turmoils to which the village had not previously been accustomed. These could range from the occasional brawl between miners, whose tragic end is recorded in the death register, to more serious affairs like the mutiny which broke out in 1759, when the soldiers rioted asking for higher wages.[29] But this decade had witnessed a typically short-lived mining boom, as the curves of Figure 7.1 show so vividly. By 1757 the disappointing pro-

[28] It should be noticed that the *status animarum* only enumerate the *de jure* population, which includes the locals who were temporarily absent as well as permanent immigrants but not temporary immigrants. See Bellettini, 'Gli Status Animarum', pp. 7–8; and Bodo and Viazzo, 'Gli status animarum come fonte storico-demografica', p. 10.

[29] A letter sent by the minister Bogino to one of the directors of the mines (published by Tonetti, *Museo storico*, pp. 9–10) informs us that a detachment of the army had to intervene to put down the mutiny and arrest the six leaders of the revolt.

ductivity of the Alagna mines was already giving cause for concern, and in 1763 it was decided to reorganize the activity on a more modest basis. A few years later, in the early 1770s, the mines were given back in concession to petty private entrepreneurs. A certain number of miners remained, but the great majority of them left Alagna for good.

It is evident that in the eighteenth century Alagna displayed many of the distinctive features of a mining town.[30] The most obvious of these features are of course the rapid pace of the population growth experienced by the village in the 1750s, the crucial role played by immigration and, no less significantly, the sudden exodus of the miners after 1763. The mining boom may well have been shorter-lived here than elsewhere, but more or less the same pattern can be found in many other mining districts in the Alps. In Tyrol itself, the massive intensification promoted in the course of the sixteenth century led fairly rapidly to the virtual exhaustion of many deposits by the early 1600s. Even if Tyrol as a whole was to remain a rather important mining area for at least another two centuries, the effects of the decline of the industry are clearly visible. In 1645 the population of Schwaz had dropped to only 7,500 inhabitants, and some of the lesser mining towns had faded into insignificance.

What we have seen about Tyrol or, on a smaller scale, about Alagna leaves no doubt as to the importance of the short-term economic, ecological and demographic consequences of mining. The Alpine mines could clearly prove a powerful pole of attraction for workers coming from very distant regions and also stimulate a considerable amount of mobility from one Alpine district to another. Yet it would seem that in a local perspective the effects of mining were bound to be ephemeral. When the industry fell into decay, the miners would move away and what had been busy mining centres would revert to their previous economic conditions.

This is of course largely true. However, a more accurate analysis of the aftermath of Alagna's mining boom and the results of a few recent studies of other Alpine mining communities reveal a rather more complex picture. Even in those localities which experienced a pronounced process of 'de-industrialization', to use Mitterauer's term,[31] some of the ecological and social-structural consequences of mining could be long lasting. Moreover, these studies suggest that

---

[30] For a useful characterization of the 'mining town' in a Central European context, see Molenda, 'Mining towns'.
[31] See especially Mitterauer, 'Auswirkungen von Urbanisierung', p. 61.

Alpine mining populations may have departed in some important respects from the sociological and demographic models of the mining community which have been put forward in the last ten or fifteen years. They raise, in short, a number of questions which appear to be well worth exploring. And to do so, a useful first step is to consider in some detail a topic which has been too often neglected by most studies of mining communities, namely the relationship between the local population and immigrant miners.

Immigrants and locals

In the Alps as anywhere else the mining industry was characterized by the high mobility of skilled workers, often travelling in groups and over long distances. These groups, as the case of Alagna shows, could include married men, women, children and elderly relatives of the miners. Nevertheless, immigrant miners were typically unmarried men of prime working age, whose arrival obviously tended to affect the demographic structure of the population in the districts where they temporarily settled. One of the localities we have previously mentioned, the Gastein Valley, provides an instructive example. In 1497, when mining was thriving and the population of the valley was rapidly growing because of continuous immigration, the sex ratio was severely unbalanced. For every 100 men there were only 68.3 women. If we consider the various settlements in the valley, the effects of mining and immigration are even more evident, for Hofgastein had a ratio of 100 men to 63.1 women, whereas the agricultural settlement of Rotten, which had been virtually unaffected by mining, had a ratio of 100 men to 101.7 women. Two centuries later, in 1690, when mining had lost much of its importance and many workers had left, the sex ratio was far more balanced, men outnumbering women only by 100 to 96.6.[32]

Such a massive 'supply' of unmarried men can of course be expected to have an impact on the local marriage market – particularly, one would surmise, in communities like Alagna, where heavy male emigration tended to create a surplus of women and was largely responsible for unusually high levels of female permanent celibacy. That in Alagna this impact was indeed considerable is shown by Table 7.1. Endogamy rates, which had exceeded 90 per cent throughout the seventeenth century, dropped very markedly in the eighteenth, plunging to just over 55 per cent in the 1750s. The shift from high

---

[32] Mitterauer, 'Auswirkungen von Urbanisierung', pp. 70–1.

Table 7.1. *Marriages in Alagna 1701–1800*

	Total	Endogamous	Exogamous	Between outsiders	Endogamy rate
	(1)	(2)	(3)	(4)	(2)/(1)
1701–10	63	58	5	0	92.1
1711–20	55	44	11	0	80.0
1721–30	47	37	6	4	78.7
1731–40	46	38	7	1	82.6
1741–50	63	54	6	3	85.7
1751–60	101	56	14	31	55.4
1761–70	54	39	11	4	72.2
1771–80	64	48	7	9	75.0
1781–90	70	57	6	7	81.4
1791–1800	51	40	5	6	78.4
Total	614	471	78	65	76.7

Source: APA, *Libri matrimoniorum*.

to low endogamy rates observed 'diachronically' in Alagna is reminiscent of the 'synchronic' contrast between agrarian and mining communities in the Tyrolese Ziller Valley. In the fifty years between 1751 and 1800 the endogamy rate of the agrarian and rather isolated village of Tux was as high as 88.6 per cent, whereas in the mining community of Zell am Ziller the proportion of marriages in which both bride and groom were born locally was only 36.7 per cent.[33]

At first glance, figures like these would seem to demonstrate that immigration inevitably led to the breakdown of the strictly endogamic regime which was so common a feature of Alpine communities. Yet, if we examine the data more carefully, we discover that in Alagna the dramatic fall of endogamy rates was largely due to the steep increase in the number of marriages between outsiders. In the course of the eighteenth century exogamous marriages only accounted for less than 15 per cent of all marriages involving a local man or woman, and even in the 1750s the ratio between exogamous and endogamous marriages was just 1 to 4. This indicates that, although the proportion of endogamous marriages (the 'endogamy rate') strongly declined, nevertheless there was not much intermarriage. The low values of the endogamy rate are more a symptom of the mobility of miners than of any real interpenetration between locals and immigrants through marriage.

[33] Troger, *Bevölkerungsgeographie des Zillertales*, pp. 57–60.

This is an interesting finding. But no less intriguing is what emerges from a further and more detailed examination of the exogamous marriages. The analysis of the 1690 listing of Hofgastein's households carried out a few years ago by Mitterauer showed that miners tended more frequently than other men to marry wives older than themselves, and that in several cases the age gap was abnormally wide.[34] Very much the same pattern can be detected in eighteenth-century Alagna. If we consider the 30 exogamous marriages celebrated in this century for which the age of both spouses is known, we find that over half of the immigrants who married local women were younger than their wives. By contrast, when we turn to endogamous marriages we see that the proportion was lower than 25 per cent. Furthermore, in 6 cases the local wives were older than their immigrant husbands by ten years or more, and in 2 cases the age gap was over twenty years. These wide age gaps partly reflect a certain tendency for immigrant miners to marry oldish widows, often with children – in itself an interesting fact, since this was unusual among the locals. But, even if we exclude widows, we still find that the age of the Alagnese women who married immigrant miners was, on average, much higher than that of those who married endogamously: 28.2 years as compared to 24.4.[35]

These may well be small numbers, but they certainly suggest that a social boundary separated the immigrants from the local population. The existence of some degree of intermarriage shows of course that such a boundary was sometimes crossed, but this seems to have occurred in rather unusual circumstances. It is indeed difficult to avoid the conclusion that both in Alagna and probably also in Hofgastein most miners, if they managed to find a local wife at all, had to settle for a second-rate marriage: their bride would be a middle-aged spinster, a widow with children, or rather frequently (at least in Alagna) a woman who had been born out of wedlock.

This raises two related, if rather different questions. Did the social boundary revealed by the study of intermarriage coincide with an occupational boundary running across the local population itself? And to what extent did the availability of industrial jobs created by mining affect the previous occupational and migratory patterns of the local men? Studies of proto-industrial communities in several parts of the

---

[34] Mitterauer, 'Auswirkungen von Urbanisierung', pp. 71–2.
[35] A Kolmogorov-Smirnov two-tailed two-sample test of the differences in the age at first marriage between women married to local men (N = 459) and women married to immigrants (N = 42) was significant at the 97.5 per cent level.

Alps have suggested that the growth of cottage industry led the local populations away from agriculture and pastoralism and also caused the end of seasonal emigration.[36] The case of the mining industry might, however, be different. A recent study of one of the villages of the Fersina Valley, for instance, has established that from the fourteenth century up to at least the second half of the eighteenth century mining remained the monopoly of foreign miners mainly coming from Carinthia and Tyrol. Interestingly, this study also shows that in spite of the absence of any major ethnic or linguistic boundary (this valley, though on the Italian side, is inhabited by a German-speaking population) intermarriage between local women and miners was extremely rare.[37]

In Chapter 5 we have seen that also in Alagna mining was entirely left, in the late nineteenth and early twentieth centuries, to immigrant workers. On the basis of some eighteenth-century evidence it is tempting to guess that the situation must not have been much different in the more remote past. It seems significant, for example, that the proceedings of the Pastoral Visitation of 1760 (one of the years of the boom) report only that the men from Alagna worked in the building industry and that most of them emigrated abroad. There is no hint that they might have been involved in mining.[38] Moreover, although cases of local men earning their livelihood by working as miners are from time to time attested either by the extant pay rolls or by other documents, nevertheless their number appears to have been very limited indeed. Yet it would clearly be hazardous to conclude, on this evidence alone, that the economy and demography of the local population was scarcely affected by the growth of mining.

The most convenient and effective way of roughly assessing the impact of the growth of mining on the local patterns of seasonal emigration is, of course, to look at the seasonality of births and see whether there are signs of change in the course of the eighteenth century. Needless to say the analysis and interpretation of Alagna's demographic records is less straightforward for the eighteenth century than it is for other periods less affected by immigration. In particular, the fall in endogamy rates was obviously paralleled by a marked increase in the number of births of babies having one or both parents from

---

[36] See e.g. Braun, 'Protoindustrialization and demographic changes', pp. 302–5, and Mitterauer, 'Formen ländlicher Familienwirtschaft', p. 235.
[37] Sebesta, 'Mito e realtà della Valle dei Mocheni', pp. 126, 135–6.
[38] ASDN, 1–315, fol. 10v.

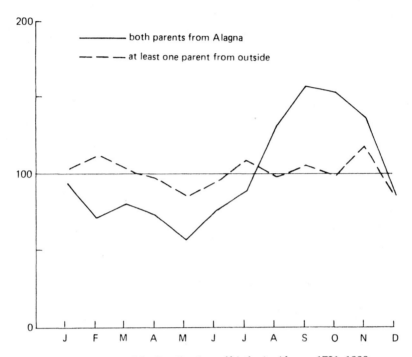

Figure 7.2 Monthly distribution of births in Alagna 1731–1800
Note: For method used in calculating the values plotted on this graph, see
note to Figure 6.1

outside. Their proportion begins to exceed 20 per cent in the 1730s
and reaches 34.4 per cent two decades later. It is therefore necessary
to separate the births of babies whose parents were both natives of
Alagna from the births of babies having at least one parent from outside (which meant, in the vast majority of cases, that the father worked
in the mines). This simple exercise, as Figure 7.2 shows, is sufficient
to demonstrate that the old pattern was still detectable and also that
a sharp contrast existed between the local men engaged in seasonal
emigration and the immigrant miners who lived in Alagna throughout
the year. Seasonality remains pronounced even if we examine it more
stringently, by concentrating on the 1750s and 1760s and by excluding
first births from computation, so as to remove the influence of the
seasonality of weddings (see Figure 7.3). On the other hand, both
Figure 7.2 and even more Figure 7.3 show very clearly that in the

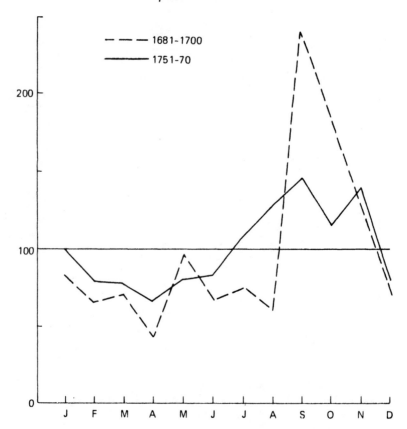

Figure 7.3 Monthly distribution of 2nd- and higher-order births in Alagna,
1681–1700 and 1751–1770

Note: Births of children having both parents from Alagna (1681–1700: N = 350;
1751–1770: N = 368). For method used in calculating values, see note to
Figure 6.1

eighteenth century the strength of seasonal concentration fails to attain
the exceedingly high values which had been customary before. This
is an indication that, especially in the years of the boom, the impact
of the growth of mining on local emigration patterns was far from
negligible.

There are various ways in which the growth of the mining industry
might have affected emigration in Alagna. From the rather scanty
evidence we possess, we gather that food provisions were essentially

secured by merchants from outside. We can nonetheless surmise that a few men may have decided to stay at home in order to increase the agro-pastoral productivity of their land in times of strong demand for food supplies. But the growth of the mining industry offered several other opportunities. Thus, the task of supplying and repairing the tools which were needed in mines and foundries was entrusted to two Alagnese blacksmiths, Pietro Ronco and Cristoforo Giordano.[39] Even more predictably, the Piedmontese government resorted to local contractors to build new houses to lodge the miners and new plants to process the ore. In 1753 alone, the aim of the management of the Alagna mines was to have no less than fifteen new buildings completed by the end of the year. This datum in itself is sufficient to demonstrate that in the 1750s local demand for skilled builders must have been very high.[40]

Indirect involvement with mining seems to have been the main cause of the temporary decline of seasonal emigration. The number of locals working as miners was apparently very small, as we have noticed, and the reason may be that the wages paid to miners were unlikely to appeal to many Alagnese men. Highly skilled workers were well paid (between 350 and 450 Piedmontese *Lire* per year) and the salaries of the managers could be very high indeed: in 1758 the director of the mines was paid 1,642.5 *Lire* per year, while the salaries of accountants and other clerks ranged between 600 and 700 *Lire*. The ordinary miners, however, received only 233 *Lire*.[41] This sum, though not really very low, was slightly less than the average industrial wages of that period and could not compete with the much higher earnings of skilled builders.[42] It is significant, in this respect, that mining was undertaken almost exclusively by members of the poorest local families.[43]

However, the exploration of networks of social relations centred on local people who at some stage were closely involved with mining reveals a number of situations that straddle these boundaries between locals and immigrants, rich and poor, miners and non-miners. Let us consider, for instance, the case of a petty contractor, the *impresaro*

[39] 'Relazione di Risoluzioni ... nella coltura delle miniere della Valle di Sesia', BRT, St.P. 751/2, fol. 33r.
[40] 'Notta delle Fabbriche ... alle miniere della Valla di Sesia', BRT, St.P. 751/2.
[41] 'Bilancio per la cultura delle Regie Miniere ... a tutto Decembre 1758', BRT, St.P. 751/1.
[42] Cf. Prato, *La vita economica in Piemonte*, pp. 451–63.
[43] See the list of families aided by the Charity of the Poor (ASD, 64 B/2), discussed in Viazzo, 'Ethnic change in a Walser community', p. 269.

Pietro Jachetti, as he is designated in the documents which provide the starting-point for the reconstruction of his social and economic relations.[44] Jachetti was no wealthy man, but, thanks to the substantial deposit given on his behalf by two fellow villagers he had managed, in 1759, to secure a contract to haul, crush and transport the ore extracted from one of the gold mines. (A deposit was needed because capital equipment was provided by the government.) However, his enterprise soon proved a failure and in 1760 the two sureties decided to take over the business from Jachetti. Interestingly enough, these sureties were Pietro Ronco and Cristoforo Giordano, the two blacksmiths who a few years earlier had themselves entered an important contract with the management of the mines. But an examination of Pietro Jachetti's network shows that he was closely linked to a number of other people having something to do with mining, whether they were locals or immigrants. Thus, we discover that as early as 1755 the director of the mines had been the godfather of one of Jachetti's daughters, that in 1759 Jachetti's only sister married a miner from the Chiusella Valley, and that his wife's sister was married to a middle-range manager of the mines coming from Turin. As for his three daughters, they all married miners. One was an Alagnese, while the others were a second-generation immigrant and a newcomer from Tyrol.

Cases like that of the Jachettis help us arrive at a more subtle and correct understanding of intermarriage in eighteenth-century Alagna, for they show that a minority of families closely involved with mining and miners were much more exposed to the risk of exogamy, as it were, than the rest of the local population. In fact, families like the Jachettis display virtually the same pattern of marriage alliances as the immigrants' families. During the second half of the eighteenth century two-thirds of the daughters of immigrants who got married took new immigrants as husbands. The remaining ones tended, like their brothers, either to marry second-generation immigrants or to marry into Alagnese families whose members were engaged in mining. Most of the 'exogamous' marriages occurring after the end of the boom were therefore occupationally endogamous.

This is an important indication that in the course of the eighteenth century the distinction between 'local' and 'immigrant' becomes increasingly blurred. By 1788 nearly 20 per cent of the inhabitants of Alagna bore, in fact, surnames which had been introduced into the village by recent immigration. In the hamlets clustered around

---

[44] 'Rinontia d'Impresa ... da Pietro Giachetti', AFA, B4.

the church, where most of them lived, these people formed the majority of the population. Yet a boundary continued to exist and it was probably stronger than in the years of the boom. Most of those local men who in the 1750s and early 1760s had stayed at home (either to work in the mining industry or to meet the increased local demand for builders) went back to the traditional pattern of seasonal emigration. Some of them, on the other hand, continued to work in the mines and became part of the sub-community of miners, which gradually acquired the traits of a self-reproducing group. The size of this sub-community varied over time with the changing fortunes of the mining industry, which went through a series of minor booms followed by periods of depression. But it never disappeared, and retained a distinct identity until the early decades of the twentieth century, when the occupational, social, ethnic and even spatial boundary which had crossed Alagna for two centuries began to lose its significance.

The consequences of immigration

The example of eighteenth-century Alagna illustrates one of the most widespread and important consequences brought about by mining and immigration in the Alps, namely the formation of groups of predominantly immigrant origin displaying a considerable degree of continuity and distinctiveness over time. In some places these groups included only a portion of the population. This was the case of villages like Alagna or Zell am Ziller, a Tyrolese mining centre whose social and occupational composition has been analyzed by Mitterauer. A listing of 1779 reveals that in addition to farmers and servants (the two usual social categories in rural Austria), there lived in this village also a sizable number of people descending from the miners who had settled in the area in the sixteenth and seventeenth centuries. Partly still engaged in the declining mining industry, partly working as muleteers or petty tradesmen, they formed a group which is in many ways reminiscent of Alagna's sub-community of immigrants and miners.[45] In those settlements which had virtually come into being because of mining, on the other hand, immigrants and their descendants could represent the overwhelming majority of the population. This was, for instance, the case of Riva d'Agordo, where mining remained the prevailing economic activity for over three centuries.

It is also important to notice that especially in the Austrian Alps

---

[45] Mitterauer, 'Formen ländlicher Familienwirtschaft', pp. 206–7.

many immigrant miners managed to acquire a cottage and a small agricultural holding. In some parts of Tyrol, Salzburg and Carinthia this resulted in a rapid and sometimes very marked increase in the number of 'cottagers', that is of people who were neither farmers nor servants but combined the running of their dwarf farms or garden plots with some form of wage-earning activity.[46] Similar effects can be observed in areas not directly touched by immigration but for which mining represented a source of subsidiary income. One such area is the Unterinntal, a Tyrolese valley lying between the two mining districts of Schwaz and Hall. In the heyday of silver mining the Unterinntal had supplied manpower to the Schwaz mines and in the seventeenth century (as implied by their designation in local records as *'operarii in monte salinario'*) a substantial number of men from the valley worked in the salt mines of Hall. Access to the flow of cash assured by industrial employment encouraged an unusually high rate of holding subdivision, which in turn resulted in a large proportion of cottagers in the population. In the eighteenth century, when the mines of Hall began to decline, the rate of subdivision also slowed down and there was even a tendency for the number of holdings to shrink.[47]

All these examples indicate that mining, even where it declined fairly rapidly, caused important changes in the composition of the population of many Alpine communities and deeply affected the local patterns of landownership and social stratification. Particularly in localities like Zell am Ziller, as Mitterauer has emphasized,[48] the process of 're-agrarianization' was far from being complete. The economic position of those miners who decided or were forced to stay was, however, highly vulnerable. Since mining remained their primary source of income, a crisis of the industry could leave them without sufficient resources. In some extreme instances they turned into beggars, but more frequently they managed to survive by working as agricultural day-labourers for local landed families.[49] Indeed, a typical feature of those Alpine communities where a 'guest' population of miners lived side by side with a 'host' community of local farmers was the development of a symbiotic, if unbalanced, relationship between the two groups.[50]

---

[46] Klein, 'Die Bevölkerung Österreichs', p. 53.
[47] Fliri, *Bevölkerungsgeographische Untersuchungen*, pp. 10, 22.
[48] Mitterauer, 'Formen ländlicher Familienwirtschaft', p. 207.
[49] A series of *status animarum* compiled in the first half of the nineteenth century shows that the immigrants who had settled in Alagna for good experienced a considerable degree of occupational instability. In the death registers some of them are significantly designated as 'miner and day-labourer'.
[50] Mitterauer, 'Formen ländlicher Familienwirtschaft', pp. 240–1.

The situation was quite different in a locality like Riva d'Agordo, whose sustained demographic growth (from less than 150 inhabitants in 1584 to 855 in 1645 and 1,130 in 1766) had been entirely powered by mining. The population was here much more homogeneous than in Alagna or Zell am Ziller, mining being almost the only occupation: in 1766 no less than 315 out of 347 adult men were listed as mine workers, and just 11 as agricultural workers. A few years later, however, the industry suffered a major crisis and by 1779 only 173 men were still employed in the mines, while the number of men listed as agricultural workers had greatly increased. It would seem that in these years the whole community of Riva 'is moving into the agro-pastoral sector to exploit fields, meadows and animals as fully as possible, this sector functioning as a sort of "lung" in times of economic crisis'.[51] But the very high population density made possible by mining was obviously out of proportion with the meagre agricultural and pastoral resources of Riva's territory. To alleviate the pressure of the population upon the land, the men of Riva soon had to turn – apparently for the first time in the history of the village – to seasonal emigration.

The miners of Riva d'Agordo were not unique in resorting to seasonal emigration in times of hardship. The intensification of seasonal emigration recorded in several other mountainous districts of Veneto in the second half of the eighteenth century was largely due to the decline of mining and metallurgical activities. Roughly in the same period, the members of the 'mining sub-community' of Zell am Ziller also turned increasingly to seasonal emigration.[52] This is a useful reminder that for mining communities a massive exodus was not the only possible response to severe crises. Seasonal emigration could provide, in some circumstances, a viable alternative. Moreover, it can be presumed that some adaptive demographic changes also occurred. Unfortunately, very little is known of the demography of Alpine mining communities (or sub-communities) in their various stages of development, and this also makes it difficult to assess whether they conformed to the general models of demographic behaviour which have been proposed for mining populations.

Perhaps the most important conclusion reached by a number of studies of nineteenth-century mining populations has been that they had higher fertility than the rural dwellers from the surrounding

[51] Vergani, 'Una comunità mineraria di montagna', p. 643.
[52] Troger, *Bevölkerungsgeographie des Zillertales*, p. 43; Mitterauer, 'Formen ländlicher Familienwirtschaft', p. 206.

countryside.[53] As has been recently remarked, 'the general thesis regarding high fertility of miners remains to be tested cross-culturally for contemporary populations'.[54] But it would also be interesting to test this notion, and its accompanying hypotheses, for mining populations in a more distant past. To be sure, not all these hypotheses can be expected to apply to mining populations of the seventeenth or eighteenth centuries.[55] Yet, some of them might prove fruitful and help identify important differentials in demographic behaviour.

For instance, one of the hypotheses which have been put forward to explain the higher birth rates displayed by nineteenth-century mining populations is that infant mortality was heavier. This, it has been argued, led to higher marital fertility, either because the interruption of lactation shortened birth intervals or because more children were conceived in a conscious attempt to obtain a targetted surviving family size.[56] The evidence is, however, rather conflicting, and there is very little in the literature on Alpine mining communities that can either support or refute these assertions. It is nonetheless intriguing that in Alagna infant mortality was, in the period 1731–1800, much higher among the children having one or both parents from outside than among the children whose parents were both native-born. An infant mortality rate of 262.6 per thousand, compared to a rate of only 186.8 per thousand for the children of local couples, indicates that the children of miners had a distinctly more unfavourable mortality experience.[57]

Another major hypothesis is that the higher fertility of nineteenth-century mining populations was the consequence of their higher levels of nuptiality. The miners' ability to get married could of course be seriously hampered by the very structure of the employment. Migration, in particular, was typically biased by age and sex, since mining

---

[53] See Wrigley, *Industrial growth and population change*; Friedlander, 'Demographic patterns'; and especially Haines, *Fertility and occupation*.

[54] Godoy, 'Mining', p. 205.

[55] One hypothesis is, for instance, that mining communities retained for a longer period attitudes favouring high fertility because their physical and social isolation 'also insulated the population from slow changes in societal norms'. Haines, *Fertility and occupation*, p. 51. Such differential attitudes to family limitation can scarcely be expected before the nineteenth century.

[56] See Haines, *Fertility and occupation*, p. 150.

[57] These rates have been calculated by relating the number of deaths under one year of age as recorded in the death registers to the number of births. They are preferable to estimates based on family reconstitution, because a sizable proportion of the miners' children who died before completing their first year had not been born in Alagna. The absolute numbers are the following: 268 infant deaths out of 1,435 for the children of local couples; 120 infant deaths out of 457 for the children of miners.

towns attracted large numbers of single, young adult men. However, Dov Friedlander has argued that the imbalanced age-sex distribution strongly contributed to the lowering of women's marriage age. Moreover, it has been found that permanent celibacy could eventually turn out to be lower among miners than in the rest of the population, implying that they had better economic opportunities to set up a family than other categories of male workers.[58] The scattered shreds of evidence from the Alpine area we have examined in this chapter certainly suggest a few interesting qualifications. The argument concerning women's low marriage age advanced by Friedlander, for instance, may well hold true for the closely knit and occupationally homogeneous mining communities which have guided the typological efforts of sociologists and anthropologists.[59] But the situation could be significantly different in localities like Hofgastein, the Fersina Valley or Alagna, where miners were separated from the rest of the local population by social, occupational and (in Alagna) also ethnic boundaries. Here, the structural imbalances brought about by immigration could have relatively unimportant effects on the marriage market. Also, we have seen that the local wives of immigrant miners could be expected to marry at a later age than other local women.

Nevertheless, the hypothesis that miners may have had a better chance to get married than other categories of men deserves to be seriously considered, particularly in an Alpine context. It is especially relevant to notice that in Austria most miners came from the ranks of the non-inheriting sons of peasant families. These men would, as a rule, never marry and would always be subject to the authority of a household head, who could be their father, their elder brother, or a stranger if they became servants. For these men, as Mitterauer has stressed, 'movement into wage-labour in mining represented in many ways a personal emancipation'.[60] One of the main aspects of this 'emancipation' from the authority of the household head was in fact that miners, unlike servants, were entitled to marry. Since they did not have to wait until their fathers died or retired, miners could (in principle, at least) get married and establish a household of their own at an earlier age than the farmers' heirs. Although the benefits of becoming a miner are most evident in an area of impartible inheritance such as Austria, the same set of hypotheses is well worth

---

[58] See Friedlander, 'Demographic patterns', p. 44, and Haines, *Fertility and occupation*, pp. 23–7.

[59] See Dennis *et al.*, *Coal is our life*; Bulmer, 'Sociological models of the mining community'; and Godoy 'Mining'.

[60] Mitterauer, 'Produktionsweise im österreichischen Montanwesen', p. 313.

testing in the rest of the Alps, for we have seen that there are good reasons to believe that nuptiality tended to be low even in those Alpine regions where systems of partibility prevailed.

One of the concomitants of the low levels of nuptiality which characterized the Alps should predictably be a high proportion of illegitimate births. The figures presented in Chapter 4 show, however, that the relationship between nuptiality and illegitimacy was more complex than is usually assumed and that regional variations were very marked, illegitimacy being really high only in the eastern provinces of Austria. To this problem we shall go back in the next chapter. But it is relevant to notice here that it is widely accepted that nineteenth-century mining populations were characterized by a rather moderate incidence of illegitimacy. Indeed, the most comprehensive of the demographic models of nineteenth-century mining populations, the one proposed by Michael Haines, ignores illegitimate fertility altogether.[61] Alpine mining communities may have been, in this respect, considerably different. A detailed study of illegitimacy in Alagna over three centuries has revealed a decisive connection between illegitimacy, mining and immigration;[62] and in eighteenth-century Zell am Ziller it was the miners and their descendants who prominently accounted (as in Alagna) for a level of illegitimacy which was higher than in most other parts of Tyrol.[63] This link between mining and illegitimacy is all the more intriguing in the light of the data now emerging from rich Austrian sources recently studied by Mitterauer, where the 'infamous miners' (*ehrlosen Bergknappen*) are presented in the main as responsible for sudden epidemics of illegitimacy.[64] The evidence from Alagna shows that it would be simplistic to imagine that in areas affected by predominantly male migration illegitimacy was merely a matter of itinerant workers seducing local girls and then moving away. But Mitterauer seems to be right when he contends that a big lacuna in all discussions of illegitimacy in historic Europe has been the lack of attention paid to the role of highly mobile wage-earners such as lumberjacks and above all miners.

These findings on illegitimacy emphasize once again the importance of the mobility of workers stimulated by mining. It is probably true that in the long run the most important consequences of mining and immigration were social-structural.[65] But the long-term demographic

---

[61] See Haines, *Fertility and occupation*, p. 37.
[62] See Viazzo, 'Illegitimacy and the European marriage pattern', pp. 104–14.
[63] Mitterauer, 'Familienformen und Illegitimität', p. 159.
[64] Mitterauer, *Ledige Mütter*, p. 90.
[65] As suggested by Mitterauer, 'Formen ländlicher Familienwirtschaft', p. 207.

and ecological effects were also far from negligible. The ways in which the populations of mining districts adapted to the changed circumstances brought about by the rise of the industry and its decline certainly deserve to be more extensively studied than has been the case so far. It is clear, on the other hand, that mining did not produce a generalized growth of the Alpine population. This sets it apart from other agents of demographic growth such as proto-industrialization and the so-called 'agrarian revolution', which are believed to have drastically altered the balance of population and resources and to have caused, in the late eighteenth and early nineteenth centuries, a substantial increase in the population of all parts of the Alps. Having discussed the effects of mining and immigration, it is therefore time to turn to this period of rapid ecological and demographic change, which provides a unique opportunity to test some of the theoretical issues examined in this book and in particular the hypothesis that nuptiality acted as a crucial homeostatic mechanism.

8

Population, resources and homeostatic regulation

The changing balance of population and resources

The discussion of Alpine migration patterns contained in the last two chapters has shown that many widespread notions concerning both emigration and immigration are in need of major modification, and that a number of important problems must be considered more carefully than has been the case so far. One such problem is whether permanent emigration actually played a more decisive role than other coping devices used by Alpine populations to strike a viable balance with their resources. The best way of tackling this problem is to verify whether upland communities could approach a homeostatic condition in which mechanisms lowering fertility kept natural increase within tolerable limits, thereby reducing the significance of permanent emigration as a safety valve. Some evidence has already been presented in Chapter 6. But it is now time to examine in a more comprehensive manner both this question and, more generally, the Malthusian model outlined in Chapter 2.

As we have seen, the foundation of Malthus's argument is that in mountain areas the ceiling of resources is easily reached, all the more quickly when for some reason mortality sharply declines, as had apparently been the case in the Swiss Alps in the course of the eighteenth century. It is therefore in the mountains that the check of nuptiality should be expected 'to prevail to an unusual extent'. Indeed, the figures collected by Muret on Leysin and other mountainous parishes of Canton Vaud offered an impressive example of how effective the check of nuptiality could be as a homeostatic mechanism. Although he was unable to rely on detailed data for other regions, Malthus nevertheless presumed that in the mid-eighteenth century most Swiss mountain villages 'must resemble in a great measure the

178

alpine parishes of the Pays de Vaud in the extraordinary health of the people, and the absolute necessity of the preventive check'.[1] An indirect confirmation seemed to come from the diverging trends displayed by the various natural regions of Switzerland during the eighteenth century. While in the flat parts population had substantially increased, there was reason to believe that in the mountains it had remained nearly stationary.[2]

This is only partly correct, however. Modern research has established that towards the middle of the eighteenth century large portions of Alpine Switzerland actually approached a stationary state characterized by low mortality, low nuptiality and relatively low overall fertility. But in the early nineteenth century, when Malthus was writing his chapter on the checks of population in Switzerland, the population of the Swiss highlands had already started to grow. It is true that the pace of growth had not been as quick as in the *Mittelland*, the Swiss plateau. Growth rates had nevertheless been rather substantial also in the mountains, for it can be estimated that between 1800 and 1850 the population of Alpine Switzerland grew from 466,000 to 614,000 people, at an annual rate of 5.5 per thousand.[3]

What had been the causes of this growth? Malthus would most probably have attributed it to the breakdown of the preventive check brought about by what he calls the 'introduction of manufactures'. As is well known, in the last pages of his chapter on Switzerland Malthus quotes at length the opinion of a peasant he had met in a village of the Swiss Jura, where a manufacture had been established some years earlier. The facility of providing for a family and of finding early employment for children, the peasant reported, had greatly encouraged early marriage; but 'the same habit had continued, when, from a change of fashion, accident, and other causes, the manufacture was almost at the end'. The peasant had no doubt that the misery now experienced by the village was rooted in the habit of early marriages, which 'might really, he said, be called *le vice du pays*'.[4]

Rudolf Braun's seminal studies of economic and demographic change in the highlands of Canton Zurich[5] would seem to confirm

---

[1] Malthus, *Essay on population*, p. 211.
[2] Malthus, *Essay on population*, p. 212.
[3] Estimates based on Bickel, *Bevölkerungsgeschichte der Schweiz*, p. 135, and Mattmüller, 'Landwirtschaft und Bevölkerung'. In the same period the population of non-Alpine Switzerland grew from about 1,210,000 to 1,780,000 people, at an annual rate of approximately 7.5 per thousand.
[4] Malthus, *Essay on population*, p. 214.
[5] See especially Braun, *Industrialisierung und Volksleben*, and 'Protoindustrialization and demographic changes'.

that early forms of industrialization were the main force behind population growth in the mountains of Switzerland. There are, however, two serious difficulties. The first difficulty concerns one of the central arguments in the theory of proto-industrialization, namely that the development of cottage industry not only favoured but even required earlier and more frequent marriage, and that the resulting increase in nuptiality was the decisive mechanism promoting population growth.[6] The evidence from the Swiss highlands is, in fact, rather conflicting. It is worth noting that Braun himself, whose work has done so much to win acceptance for this interpretation, has never offered statistical evidence for a drop in marriage age in the hilly regions of Canton Zurich.[7] And the most recent reconstitution study of a Swiss proto-industrial Alpine area actually suggests that the mean age at marriage went up for both men and women.[8] This indicates that the relationships between proto-industrialization and nuptiality need further investigation, particularly in areas such as the Alps, where domestic industry was often simply part of the total range of economic activities. It might well be that in such circumstances nuptiality was severely constrained, as Guttmann and Leboutte have contended,[9] by changes in the agricultural and pastoral sectors, which could compel couples to wait until a late age before marrying.

A second major point is that the degree of penetration of proto-industry into the Swiss Alps, and more generally into the Alpine region, should not be overestimated. It is of course true that in the second half of the eighteenth century the portion of the population employed in the cotton industry was higher in Switzerland than in any other country. The number of persons employed at the end of the century may have ranged between 150,000 and 200,000, and con-

---

[6] On the demographic implications of proto-industrialization, see Mendels, 'Proto-industrialization', pp. 249–53; Levine, 'Demographic implications of rural industrialization'; and Medick, 'Proto-industrial family economy', pp. 304–9.

[7] Braun's argument is, however, borne out by the results of U. Pfister's recent analysis of demographic change in the districts of Canton Zurich where the proportion of spinners was highest. Pfister has found that in the second half of the eighteenth century population growth is mainly explained, in these districts, by an increase in marriage rates. Before 1750, on the other hand, population growth appears to have been determined primarily by changes in mortality. Moreover, no relationship between population growth and proto-industrialization can be detected in those districts in which cotton weaving (rather than spinning) was the dominant activity. See U. Pfister, 'Proto-industrialization and demographic change'.

[8] Kurmann, *Das Luzerner Suhrental*, p. 91. For a partly similar pattern in a part of the Italian Western Alps, see Ramella, *Terra e telai*. Cf. also the recent remarks by Mitterauer, 'Formen ländlicher Familienwirtschaft', pp. 239–40, on the diversity of nuptiality regimes displayed by proto-industrial communities in the Austrian region of Vorarlberg.

[9] Gutmann and Leboutte, 'Rethinking protoindustrialization'.

temporary observers report that in many rural areas only one-third of the population depended on agriculture or pastoralism, the other two-thirds being occupied in industry.[10] But these areas were mostly concentrated in hillside districts like the Zurich highlands, rather than in the Alpine zone proper. This is not to deny that in some Alpine cantons cottage industry was an important economic force. Glarus is perhaps the best-known example. But there is little doubt that on the whole the economy of the Swiss Alps remained essentially agrarian,[11] and that proto-industrialization can therefore scarcely account for the population growth recorded in the late eighteenth and early nineteenth centuries.

Once it is accepted that the economy of the Swiss Alps remained essentially agrarian, the only possible conclusion is that population growth was stimulated (or at least made possible) by a considerable increase in the local agricultural or pastoral resources. This hypothesis has been advanced by several writers, both for Switzerland and for other parts of the Alps.[12] But its most cogent and theoretically elegant formulation is to be found in Netting's recent work on Törbel, which is of special interest not simply because it provides one of the few adequate analyses of population dynamics in an Alpine locality, but also because it represents the most accomplished attempt to demonstrate that in the Alps the balance between population and resources was homeostatically regulated by a set of social servomechanisms.

By reconstructing the history of Törbel's population over three centuries, from the late seventeenth century up to our days, Netting has been able to establish that it has been characterized by long periods of stability and by a relatively narrow range of fluctuations in growth – two features, he writes, that 'suggest the operation of finely tuned homeostatic mechanisms in the local ecosystem'.[13] Homeostasis, however, does not mean unchanging equilibrium. In the first three-quarters of the eighteenth century the population of Törbel remained virtually constant, which 'is just what one might expect if the local community had arrived at a kind of equilibrium with its environment and limited productive resources'.[14] But in the last quarter of the century the village population began to grow. In less than one hundred

---

[10] Bickel, *Bevölkerungsgeschichte der Schweiz*, pp. 53–4.

[11] Cf. Mattmüller, 'Landwirtschaft und Bevölkerung', and C. Pfister, 'Menschen im Kanton Bern', p. 491. On the rather limited importance of proto-industrial activities in the French Alps, see Poitrineau, 'Aspects spécifiques', p. 111.

[12] See e.g. Bickel, *Bevölkerungsgeschichte der Schweiz*, p. 53; Klein, 'Österreichs Bevölkerung 1754–1869', pp. 48–55; and Cole and Wolf, *The hidden frontier*, pp. 111–15.

[13] Netting, *Balancing on an alp*, p. 112.

[14] Netting, *Balancing on an alp*, p. 96.

years it more than doubled, from 280 inhabitants in 1775 to 590 in 1867, at an annual growth rate of 8 per thousand.

The main factor behind this growth was, if Netting's analysis is correct, falling mortality. The crude death rate dropped from about 28–30 per thousand in the mid-eighteenth century to just 20 per thousand in the first half of the nineteenth century. Interestingly, this decline in mortality was accompanied by an increase in both the celibacy rate and the average age at marriage, particularly for women. The old socio-economic regulators were apparently still at work. But, although they acted as a brake on population growth, they did not stop it altogether. Falling mortality caused an increase in the average duration of marriages, which in turn led to an increase in the mean number of children per marriage, from 3.8 in the first half of the eighteenth century to 4.9 one hundred years later. What is more, there are also signs of increasing fertility within marriage, a change which Netting chiefly attributes to improvements in the mothers' diet.

Such improvements are, according to Netting, one of the effects we should expect from an event of capital importance for Törbel, namely the introduction of the potato, which took place in the late eighteenth century and brought about a dramatic, 'even revolutionary change in the local ecosystem'.[15] The introduction of the potato and the consequent expansion of local resources are, for Netting, the ultimate cause of the growth of Törbel's population, which simply adjusted to the ecosystem's increased carrying capacity. The decline of nuptiality did not stop this adjustment process, but made it quite gradual and so helped prevent any serious degradation of the environment or any major deterioration of living standards.

Although he is obviously aware that we cannot expect to find in a single mountain peasant community the same causal factors that powered the rise of population on a whole continent, nevertheless Netting stresses the fact that 'the general shape of population growth in many parts of Europe is not unlike that of Törbel'.[16] Indeed, the case of Törbel invites a number of interesting comparisons. Netting himself suggests some similarities with the case of England. But the pattern detected by Netting in Törbel is more closely reminiscent of the process observed in France, where in this period falling mortality was initially counteracted by an increase in both marriage age and celibacy rate. As in Törbel, in France too this 'traditional' homeostatic mechanism proved insufficient to control population growth fully.[17]

---

[15] Netting, *Balancing on an alp*, p. 159.
[16] Netting, *Balancing on an alp*, p. 97.
[17] Wrigley, 'Marital fertility in nineteenth-century France'.

But whereas in France it apparently became imperative to resort to family limitation, in Törbel there is no evidence of birth control, which suggests that thanks to the beneficial effects of the 'potato revolution' the inhabitants of Törbel could afford to retain unlimited fertility within marriage. It is well worth noting that Törbel also departs, in spite of significant similarities, from the Irish model as described in K. H. Connell's classic study,[18] for in Törbel the introduction of the potato caused no abrupt decrease in age at marriage or proportion of celibates.

Broad comparisons like these are no doubt interesting, but it is perhaps more relevant to observe that Törbel's population curve looks very similar to that of Alpine Switzerland as a whole. The estimates most recently worked out by Mattmüller indicate that the eighteenth century was a period of very slow growth, followed by a rapid acceleration of the rate of growth in the first half of the nineteenth century.[19] These estimates for the Central Alps appear to support the widely held notion (mainly based on data from the Western Alps) that a two-phase development of this kind was characteristic of the whole Alpine area. If we add that many students of the Alps have little doubt in regarding the introduction of the potato as the prime mover, we see that there are good reasons to believe that the process observed and analyzed by Netting is, to a very large extent, representative of the demographic history of the Alps in the eighteenth and early nineteenth centuries. However, other evidence would seem to suggest otherwise. In order to shed some light on this question, it will be necessary to consider in greater detail a few features of the Swiss Alps in this period. But it will then also be necessary to extend, if only briefly, our analysis to other parts of the Alps so as to see whether the indications emerging from the Swiss evidence can be safely generalized or whether there were, on the contrary, significant regional variations.

Regional demographic patterns, 1700–1850

The Swiss Alps
As Netting has recently observed, one of the main reasons why he thought that Törbel could provide an excellent setting for his research

[18] K. H. Connell, *The population of Ireland*. It should be noticed that Connell's argument linking Irish population growth to a dramatic increase in nuptiality made possible by the introduction of the potato has now been questioned by a number of scholars. For a recent discussion, see Connolly, 'Marriage in pre-famine Ireland'.

[19] Mattmüller, 'Landwirtschaft und Bevölkerung', estimates that between 1700 and 1800 the population of Alpine Switzerland increased from 408,000 to 466,000 people, at an annual growth rate of approximately 1.3 per thousand.

was that it 'seemed by all accounts a representative Alpine village whose peasants had lived since at least the eleventh century A.D. on the returns of agro-pastoral subsistence pursuits carried on within their demarcated territory'.[20] It is in fact very likely that through most of its history Törbel has been, to use the terminology of Swiss economic historians, one of those 'autarkic' communities which, although not completely self-sufficient, nevertheless displayed a considerable degree of economic closure. But how representative was an agro-pastoral community like Törbel of the Swiss Alps as a whole in the period we are considering? For about fifty years Swiss economic historians have strongly emphasized the significance of the transformation, in the seventeenth and eighteenth centuries, of many 'autarkic' communities into pastoral villages. The distinct impression one receives from the literature is, indeed, that by the middle of the eighteenth century the dominant type of community in the Swiss Alps was purely pastoral in orientation. The cultivation of rye and barley, we are told, had almost entirely disappeared, since fields were now predominantly devoted to the production of hay. As a consequence, the villages of the *Hirtenland*,[21] the pastoral region, were heavily dependent on the commerce of livestock or dairy products and on the purchase of grains.[22]

It would therefore seem that a community like Törbel (and, presumably, its demographic evolution) can hardly qualify as typical. There are, however, two important points to be noticed. The first point is that the position of pre-eminence which the *Hirtenland* occupies in Swiss historiography is now being questioned by a growing number of scholars.[23] As one of them has cogently argued, such a pre-eminence is largely explained by the fact that, in the second half of the eighteenth century, pastoral communities were the dominant form in the mountainous zones of the cantons which were already part of the Swiss Confederation. Little attention has been paid to the predominance of 'autarkic' agro-pastoral communities both in Valais and in the Grisons, which only joined the Confederation in the early nineteenth century, and in the valleys of Ticino, which at that time

---

[20] Netting, 'Alpine village as ecosystem', p. 227.

[21] The term *'Hirtenland'* was first used in the late eighteenth century by K. V. von Bonstetten in his *Briefe über ein schweizerisches Hirtenland*, but acquired a technical sense among Swiss historians with the publication in 1938 of R. Bircher's *Wirtschaft und Lebenshaltung im schweizerischen 'Hirtenland'*.

[22] For a recent and authoritative discussion of these issues, see Braun, *Das ausgehende Ancien Régime*, pp. 58–109. See also Bergier, *Wirtschaftsgeschichte der Schweiz*, pp. 88–98.

[23] See e.g. Budmiger, 'Das Land der Walser', pp. 26–7; Mathieu, 'Ein Land von Hirten und Sennen?'; and C. Pfister, 'Bevölkerung, Wirtschaft und Ernährung', pp. 364–9.

was a subject territory. Yet these regions – marginal as their position may be within Swiss historiography – constitute together well over three-quarters of the Swiss Alps.[24]

The second important point to be stressed is that the growth of the pastoral sector at the expense of mountain agriculture can scarcely account, of itself, for the substantial rise of Swiss Alpine population. As pastoralism was less labour-intensive than mixed farming, this resulted in a marked tendency towards unemployment. Therefore, in the eighteenth century the *Hirtenland* was on the verge of suffering a substantial loss of population through massive emigration of people who could not find work in the mountains, when two all-important changes occurred. The first change was, in some districts, the penetration of cottage industry, stimulated by the state of overpopulation of the *Hirtenland* and by the consequent availability of cheap labour. The second and more pervasive change was, as in the 'autarkic' zone, the introduction of the potato.[25]

The main demographic consequence of the rapid increase in food supply and other economic resources brought about by cottage industry and by the cultivation of the potato was, of course, that instead of stagnation or decline Alpine Switzerland witnessed a period of unprecedented growth. One of the best-studied and most instructive cases is that of the Entlebuch, a predominantly pastoral district of Canton Lucerne which also experienced a certain degree of proto-industrialization. The population of this valley, which in the mid-seventeenth century was about 5,500, had already grown to nearly 10,000 in 1745, to reach in 1850 the figure of 16,963. And Silvio Bucher's work leaves little doubt that this long period of sustained growth was made possible by the introduction of the potato, which began to be cultivated in the Entlebuch as early as the first years of the eighteenth century.[26]

The Entlebuch is probably the first Swiss district into which the potato was introduced. Interestingly, its cultivation was apparently started (as was also the case in other Swiss localities) by people belonging to the poorer sectors of the population, who had been granted temporary usufruct of tiny plots carved out of the communal land.[27] Because of their small size and marginal location, these plots could not be expected to support a household for a long time if barley or

---

[24] Mathieu, 'Ein Land von Hirten und Sennen?', pp. 14–5.
[25] See Matmüller, 'Landwirtschaft und Bevölkerung', and Head-König *et al.*, 'Évolution agraire'.
[26] Bucher, *Bevölkerung des Amtes Entlebuch*, pp. 107–12, 165–71.
[27] Bucher, *Bevölkerung des Amtes Entelbuch*, p. 169.

some other mountain grain were cultivated. In view of its greater sturdiness and higher productivity per unit of land, the potato was, on the other hand, an eminently suitable crop. As Bucher has documented, by 1782 no less than 98 per cent of all households were planting potatoes.[28] In other localities the progress of the potato was slower, and it is significant that its adoption came later in the 'autarkic' communities than in the *Hirtenland*, where the signs of overpopulation and pauperization (due to the changes which had occurred in the agrarian structure) had become manifest at an earlier stage.[29] But sooner or later, as Netting has shown, spells of bad weather and serious harvest failure forced even the largest grain-producing villages and the better-off strata in the population to adopt the new crop, that some had long regarded as 'a food stuff fit only for swine'.[30]

From what we have just seen, it seems fairly clear that the introduction of the potato was mainly a response to situations of overpopulation caused by subsistence crises, by transformations in the economy and agrarian structure, or more generally by a marked decline of mortality. Yet it is remarkable that the potato, once adopted by increasingly large sectors of the Swiss Alpine population, sustained a substantial growth without causing any serious decline in living standards or a degradation of the land. The careful and highly sophisticated analysis of an agricultural census of Canton Berne taken in 1847 has recently enabled Christian Pfister to estimate that in those years food production was sufficient to satisfy the nutritive requirements of the inhabitants of the upper zones, and that the potato had actually brought about a critical quantitative improvement in local peasant diets without undermining the nutritional balance.[31] These findings not only confirm the conclusions arrived at by Bucher in his pioneering nutritional analysis of peasant diet in the Entlebuch,[32] but also give considerable support to the main contentions advanced by Netting on the basis of the Törbel material.

In spite of the very considerable economic differences to be found between the various Swiss upland communities, it would also seem that the process of decline of nuptiality described for Törbel was quite common. We may perhaps expect nuptiality to have increased in most areas affected by an expansion of cottage industry (although this is, as we have seen, far from certain). But in the pastoral villages nuptiality

---

[28] Bucher, *Bevölkerung des Amtes Entlebuch*, p. 176.
[29] Mattmüller, 'Landwirtschaft und Bevölkerung'.
[30] Netting, *Balancing on an alp*, pp. 162–3.
[31] C. Pfister, 'Bevölkerung, Wirtschaft und Ernährung'.
[32] Bucher, *Bevölkerung des Amtes Entlebuch*, pp. 161–71.

appears to have generally declined. A recent reconstitution study of Andermatt (a high-altitude pastoral community in Canton Uri) reveals, as far as marriage age is concerned, roughly the same pattern as in Törbel. The brides' age at their first marriage gradually increased from about 24 years in the first half of the eighteenth century to 27.3 years in the early nineteenth century.[33] No data on celibacy are available for Andermatt, but the evidence concerning pastoral villages collected by Hanspeter Ruesch suggests that in the early decades of the nineteenth century permanent celibacy was rising – an increase that Ruesch himself interprets as an attempt to control, or at least slow down, population growth.[34]

This sketchy discussion seems therefore to allow us to conclude that Törbel, though not fully representative of the Swiss Alpine world, nevertheless experienced a process of demographic growth which was similar (not only in its general shape but also in its dynamics and underlying causes) to that of most upland communities. It may look at first sight surprising that nuptiality declined somewhat in a period marked by an expansion of resources. But this makes sense in view of the parallel changes which occurred in mortality and, probably, marital fertility. Moreover, it appears that the population of Törbel, and more generally of the Swiss Alps, gradually came to adjust to the new potential of the environment – which is, indeed, what the homeostatic models put forward by ecological anthropologists would predict.[35] It remains to be seen, however, whether this was true of the whole of the Alpine area. To investigate this problem, it will be particularly instructive to consider the main features displayed in the same period by the population history of the Austrian Alps.

The Austrian Alps
The body of received wisdom about Alpine historical demography – and in particular the notion that the eighteenth century was for the Alps a period of slow growth followed by a rapid acceleration in the first half of the nineteenth century – is still largely based on such works as Wilhelm Bickel's *Bevölkerungsgeschichte der Schweiz*, published in 1947, and Raoul Blanchard's monumental study of the Western Alps, completed in 1956. No comparable work exists for the Eastern Alps, but until a few years ago there seemed to be no reason

---

[33] Zurfluh, 'Urseren 1640–1830', pp. 311–13.
[34] Ruesch, 'Die Demographie der Alpen', p. 172.
[35] See e.g. Zubrow, 'Demographic anthropology', pp. 12–13. For a more extensive discussion of the problem of declining nuptiality in a context of increasing resources, see Chapter 10 below, pp. 269–71.

Upland communities

Table 8.1. *Population growth in Austria and Alpine Switzerland 1700–1850*

Year	Alpine Switzerland		Non-Alpine Austria		Alpine Austria	
	Pop.	r	Pop.	r	Pop.	r
1700	408,000		725,000		1,395,000	
		1.3		5.2		2.8
1800	466,000		1,216,000		1,848,000	
		5.5		7.4		2.8
1850	614,000		1,758,000		2,122,000	

Note: r is the annual growth rate per thousand.
Sources: Switzerland: Mattmüller, 'Landschaft und Bevölkerung', and Bickel, *Bevölkerungsgeschichte der Schweiz*, p. 135. Austria: Klein, 'Die Bevölkerung Österreichs', p. 105.

to doubt that the course of population history had been essentially the same all over the Alps and that the potato had played the same pivotal role in the eastern districts (where it was introduced towards the end of the eighteenth century) as in the other sectors of the Alpine crescent.

Thanks to Kurt Klein's systematic efforts to assemble all the available evidence on the evolution of the Austrian population before the mid-nineteenth century,[36] we are now able to see that the Austrian Alps offer, in fact, quite a different picture from the Swiss highlands. To be sure, as far as the eighteenth century is concerned there are important similarities. In both Austria and Switzerland the Alpine area grew at a much slower pace than in the adjacent lowlands. But in the first half of the nineteenth century growth was definitely weaker in the Austrian Alps than in Switzerland, as Table 8.1 shows. In such regions as Carinthia or Upper Austria the rate of growth was very modest, and in Salzburg and Tyrol there is hardly any sign of growth at all.

In the first half of the nineteenth century only Vorarlberg and Styria, of all the Austrian Alpine *Länder*, saw a sizable increase in their population: 35.9 per cent in Vorarlberg, 22.5 per cent in Styria. The case of Vorarlberg is however rather anomalous, not only because of the practice of partible inheritance (a trait which sets Vorarlberg apart from all the other Alpine regions of Austria)[37] but also because of

---

[36] Klein, 'Österreichs Bevölkerung 1754–1869', and 'Die Bevölkerung Österreichs'.
[37] With the notable exception of Western Tyrol, which is – interestingly enough – the only part of Tyrol to show signs of population growth in this period. See Klein, 'Österreichs Bevölkerung 1754–1869', pp. 53–4, and Keller, 'Die Bevölkerungsentwicklung im Ausserfern', pp. 355–6.

Table 8.2. *Population growth in Styria 1700–1850*

Year	Alpine Styria		Non-Alpine Styria	
	Pop.	Index	Pop.	Index
1700	155,400	100.0	268,400	100.0
1782	168,645	108.5	347,131	129.3
1850	186,456	120.0	440,600	164.2

Source: Klein, 'Österreichs Bevölkerung 1754–1859', p. 52.

the importance acquired by domestic industry in the villages of the Rhine valley and of the Bregenzerwald, where population growth was much more substantial than in the communities of the high valleys, which had retained a predominantly agrarian economy.[38] As for Styria, intra-regional differences were no less remarkable (as Table 8.2 shows) and actually provide a striking demonstration that the population of mountainous districts was growing much more slowly than either in the Austrian lowlands or in Alpine Switzerland.

Migration certainly played a part in causing these notable regional and intra-regional differences. But Austrian scholars agree that the decisive factor was the distinctive agrarian structure of the mountain areas. In the lowlands, a combination of institutional and economic factors (and in particular the introduction of new forms of intensive cultivation like viticulture, which favoured a shift from impartible to partible inheritance)[39] provided the basis for fast population growth. In the mountains, on the other hand, impartibility remained the rule. Impartibility, it is emphasized, entails late and infrequent marriage, and this in turn explains the lower fertility levels of the highlands and their slower rate of growth.[40]

Detailed information on fertility in the Austrian Alps before 1850

---

[38] Klein, 'Österreichs Bevölkerung 1754–1869', pp. 54–5.

[39] Cf. Mitterauer, 'Formen ländlicher Familienwirtschaft', pp. 223–5.

[40] Klein, 'Die Bevölkerung Österreichs', pp. 100–1; Findl and Helczmanovski, *The population of Austria*, p. 23; Mitterauer, 'Auswirkungen der Agrarrevolution', pp. 261–3; Pickl, 'Wirtschaft und Gesellschaft in den Ostalpenländern', pp. 76–86. Towards the middle of the nineteenth century Lower Austria displayed crude marriage rates higher than 8 per thousand and crude birth and death rates in the region of 38 and 34 per thousand respectively. In the Alpine provinces, by contrast, crude marriage rates ranged between 4.5 and 6 per thousand, while crude birth rates ranged between 27 and 30 per thousand and were almost completely offset by similar levels of mortality. Cf. Bolognese-Leuchtenmüller, *Bevölkerungsentwicklung*, Tables 3, 21, 29 and 36.

Table 8.3. *Crude birth, death and marriage rates in Tux (Tyrol) 1751–1850*

	CBR	CDR	CMR
1751–1800	26.2	24.6	5.6
1801–50	22.4	21.7	4.1

Source: Troger, *Bevölkerungsgeographie des Zillertales,* pp. 67–85.

is unfortunately rather scanty.[41] But nuptiality was so low that it can be safely assumed that overall fertility must have been fairly moderate. The most interesting point is perhaps that both marriage age and celibacy rates, which were already high in the eighteenth century (higher, it would seem, than in the previous century), apparently climbed throughout the first half of the nineteenth century. The population pyramids derived from the listings collected by Michael Mitterauer and his associates suggest that during this period the I_m declined from values in the region of 0.350–0.400 to values of 0.300 or less.[42]

The Austrian case offers a fascinating variant of the pattern observed in Törbel, where changes in nuptiality had proved insufficient to stop population growth. Whether in Austria marriage operated as a homeostatic mechanism is, however, open to question. It is true, on the one hand, that in the first half of the nineteenth century both mortality and overall fertility had dropped to very low levels indeed. In the eight Tyrolese communities studied by Troger and by Lässer, crude death rates ranged between 20 and 25 per thousand, and in the high valleys in particular they were not dissimilar to those still to be found in the early twentieth century.[43] As Table 8.3 shows, the figures concerning one of these communities, Tux in the upper Ziller Valley, are reminiscent of those for Leysin, the Swiss Alpine parish which Malthus had selected as the best illustration of his princi-

[41] Most of what we know comes from the pioneering attempts at family reconstitution made in the 1940s and early 1950s by F. Fliri, E. Troger and some other members of the Innsbruck school of historical geography. The impression is that marital fertility was generally high, but unfortunately these studies (besides concerning just a handful of Tyrolese villages) allow only crude comparisons with later reconstitution studies of other Alpine localities. Research is now in progress, however, on a Styrian village. See P. Becker, 'Traces on mountains'.

[42] These values have been estimated on the basis of the data assembled by Schmidt-bauer, 'Daten'. For a general discussion, see Mitterauer 'Auswirkungen der Agrar-revolution', pp. 261–2.

[43] See Troger, *Bevölkerungsgeographie des Zillertales,* p. 85, and Lässer, *St. Leonhard im Pitztal,* p. 48.

ples. It seems plausible that in this and in other Austrian communities marriage was performing exactly the same function of dampening overall fertility to adjust to the drop in mortality.

The model of homeostatically regulated stationary population proposed by Malthus assumed, however, that resources were unchanging. But this can scarcely apply to the Austrian Alps, where in this period the introduction of clover had greatly increased the profitability of stock-breeding while the spreading of the potato as a major crop had made it possible, it has been claimed, 'to feed three or four times as many people from the same acreage of land'.[44] Between 1750 and 1850 the Austrian Alps had in fact gone through an agrarian revolution which had been, in many crucial respects, very similar to that experienced by the Swiss Alps or even by the lowlands of Austria. But these changes clearly produced different responses.

One important point stressed by Mitterauer in his study of the effects of the agrarian revolution on family structures is that particularly in its first phase, which lasted until about the middle of the nineteenth century, the agrarian revolution generated an increased demand for farm-hands. In lowland Austria such a demand was mostly met through hiring labourers. This resulted in a considerable swelling of the numbers of cottagers, who – unlike servants – were able to marry and would combine the cultivation of tiny plots of land they owned with work for wages. In the Alpine region, by contrast, farmers resorted either to unmarried brothers and children or to servants.[45] In a few mountain areas a certain rise in the number of small independent holdings can probably be detected.[46] But in general, the much lower proportion of cottagers to be found in the highlands is an indication that the labour market was differently structured and that the rule of impartibility was obeyed far more strictly than in the lowlands.[47]

As one can easily see, the marked tendency to restrict marriage displayed by the Austrian Alpine communities in the first half of the nineteenth century was instrumental in increasing the number of unmarried siblings and servants. Demographically, the main consequence was that overall fertility considerably declined. But it is important to notice that there was also a massive surge in illegitimate births, which progressively came to account for an ever bigger share of total fertility and were to reach a peak in the second half of the nineteenth

[44] Mitterauer, 'Auswirkungen der Agrarrevolution', pp. 243–4.
[45] Mitterauer, 'Auswirkungen der Agrarrevolution', pp. 249–50.
[46] Cf. Cole and Wolf, *The hidden frontier*, pp. 149–51.
[47] See Pickl, 'Wirtschaft und Gesellschaft in den Ostalpenländern', pp. 53–60.

century.[48] And this, Mitterauer has argued, was not just because of the higher proportion of people at risk, but also because illegitimate children were a welcome addition to the rural lower strata, from which the farmers could draw servants.[49]

Thus, Austrian scholars seem to imply that impartibility actually prevented mountain populations from adjusting to the new opportunities created by the introduction of the potato and to a lesser degree by the other effects of the agrarian revolution. This is in sharp and intriguing contrast to the prediction that populations tend to expand to the limit of their food supply, and the impression one receives is that impartibility was rigidly enforced not so much because local communities had reached the ceiling of their resources but to assure the reproduction of the existing pattern of social and economic stratification. This vindicates the importance of inheritance systems and more generally of social structure in affecting population growth. The practice of impartibility was perhaps obeying imperatives which were more social-structural in nature than environmental.

The Western Alps

The data presented in the previous section show that in the first half of the nineteenth century the Austrian Alps were gradually acquiring those distinctive demographic features that we have noted in Chapter 4, namely a very low nuptiality and an exceedingly marked propensity on the part of unmarried women to produce illegitimate offspring. What about the French Alps? The problem of the chronological and structural origins of what we have called the 'French model' is, as we shall see, rather complex, and its solution by no means obvious. In order to tackle it correctly, it is essential to frame the question within the general context of the demography of the Western Alps, taking into account both the French and the Piedmontese sides. And to do so, it is first necessary to examine the general evolution of the population in this part of the Alps.

As we have noticed, the widespread opinion that the demographic history of the Alps was characterized by slow growth in the eighteenth century and then by a rapid population increase until about 1850 owes much to Raoul Blanchard's regional study of the French and Piedmontese Alps. In fact, we have just seen that the Austrian Alps departed quite considerably from this allegedly all-Alpine pattern. But there

---

[48] See especially Mitterauer, 'Familienformen und Illegitimität', and *Ledige Mütter*, pp. 92–100; and also Pickl, 'Wirtschaft und Gesellschaft in den Ostalpenländern', pp. 82–4.
[49] Mitterauer, 'Auswirkungen der Agrarrevolution', p. 263.

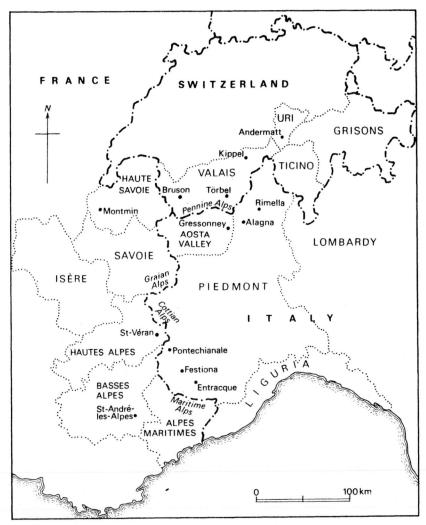

Map 3 The Western Alps

are reasons to believe that the case of the Western Alps, too, should be carefully reconsidered.

To be sure, for the eighteenth century Blanchard offered a rather chequered picture, marked by divergent trends in the three major regions covered by his study. A comparison between a census taken in 1734 and later enumerations seemed to establish beyond doubt that the eighteenth century had been, for the Piedmontese Alps, 'un

Table 8.4. *Population growth in the Western Alps 1806–1848*

	1806	1848	
Southern French Alps	424,000	481,600	(+ 13.6%)
Northern French Alps	477,000	593,600	(+ 24.4%)
Piedmontese Alps	250,000	340,400	(+ 36.3 %)
Total	1,151,000	1,416,000	(+ 23.0%)

Source: Blanchard, *Les Alpes Occidentales*, vol. 7, pp. 530–47.

siècle d'expansion démographique'.[50] He believed, on the other hand, that in the same period the Southern French Alps had experienced stagnation or even decline, whereas the Northern French Alps had apparently displayed a contrast between the growth of the low valleys and the essential stability of the population of the high valleys. During the first half of the nineteenth century, however, growth had been general all over the Western Alps, as shown by Table 8.4.

Some important limitations of Blanchard's pioneering study are well known. From an historical-demographic point of view, it is especially relevant to stress that it rests on very uneven evidence, particularly as far as the eighteenth century is concerned: while for the Piedmontese Alps he was able to rely on the 1734 census (which was generally deemed to be of the highest quality) and to some extent also on a later census taken in 1774, his documentation on the population of the French Alps is flimsy. If we add that Blanchard's interest in demography greatly increased from the 1930s, when he wrote the first volumes of his work, to the early 1950s, when he published the two volumes on the Piedmontese side, we can understand why his analysis of the population history of the Piedmontese Alps is much more detailed and informative than the sections on the demography of the French Alps, which remain rather impressionistic. In a different vein, it should also be mentioned that Blanchard's work, though covering most of the Western Alps, leaves out the Aosta Valley as well as the cluster of Piedmontese valleys south of Monte Rosa which form a transitional zone between the Western and the Central Alps.

In spite of these limitations, Blanchard's main points have been widely accepted, and have indeed received some support from a number of works published in the last thirty years. Bernard Janin's study of the Aosta Valley indicates, for instance, that between 1734 and 1848 the population of this area grew very much in the same

[50] Blanchard, *Les Alpes Occidentales*, vol. 6.1, pp. 319–30.

way as that of the Piedmontese Alps, although at a considerably slower rate; and the data recently summarized by Bernard Bonnin suggest that in the eighteenth century the population of many villages of the French Alps, and above all of villages situated in the high valleys, tended to stagnate or even to decline.[51] It would therefore seem warranted to conclude that Blanchard was right in arguing that the first decades of the nineteenth century had witnessed a turning-point, marked by a rapid acceleration of the growth rate in the Piedmontese Alps and by a shift away from the stagnation of the previous century in the French Alps.

There are, however, two important caveats. It is necessary not to forget, for one thing, that the first years of the nineteenth century probably represent a trough in the population curve of the Western Alps, which were badly affected by the ravages of the Napoleonic wars. As Blanchard himself had to admit, the forced adoption of the 1806 census as a basis for comparison is likely to produce a distorted and exaggerated impression of growth.[52] Thus, one is entitled to suspect that in the French Alps the first half of the nineteenth century may have been more a period of demographic recuperation than one of genuine growth. In the case of the Piedmontese Alps and of the Aosta Valley, on the other hand, the existence of at least a long-term upward trend would seem undeniable. The data assembled by Blanchard and by Janin indicate, in fact, that between 1734 and 1848 the population of these two regions increased by 67 and 29 per cent respectively (see Table 8.5). But here too there is a major difficulty, for it seems now certain that the 1734 enumeration (which was made for taxation purposes) severely underestimates the population of many an Alpine district, sometimes by 40 or 50 per cent.[53]

It is interesting to note that the reliability of other eighteenth-century censuses is also open to doubt. This is especially the case of the 1774 census, which was taken for military purposes and tends to overestimate the number of the inhabitants of mountain villages. On the whole, the distortion was perhaps less serious in 1774 than in 1734, but in some villages it could still be very substantial: to give just one

[51] Janin, *Le Val d'Aoste*, pp. 169–71; Bonnin, 'Les migrations dans les hautes terres dauphinoises', pp. 41–3. The data published in 1960 by R. Rousseau suggest, however, that in the second half of the eighteenth century the population of Savoy grew at a considerably faster rate than implied by Blanchard. See Rousseau, *La population de la Savoie*, pp. 220–1.
[52] Blanchard, *Les Alpes Occidentales*, vol. 7, pp. 530–1.
[53] For a discussion of the reliability of eighteenth-century Piedmontese censuses, and in particular of the enumerations of 1734 and 1774, see Albera *et al.*, 'Movimenti migratori'.

Table 8.5. *Population growth in the Piedmontese Alps and
in the Aosta Valley 1734–1848*

	Piedmontese Alps		Aosta Valley	
Year	Pop.	Index	Pop.	Index
1734	203,500	100.0	62,889	100.0
1806	250,000	122.9	72,100	114.6
1838	322,500	158.5	78,110	124.2
1848	340,800	167.5	81,082	128.9

Sources: Piedmontese Alps: Blanchard, *Les Alpes Occidentales*,
vol. 6.1, pp. 319–46. Aosta Valley: Janin, *Le Val d'Aoste*,
pp. 169–71, 542–3.

example, the 1774 census overestimates the population of Pontechianale, in the high Varaita Valley, by more than 40 per cent. Further
research is obviously needed, but the fact that the eighteenth-century
censuses are proving less reliable than it was previously assumed
suggests that in the period under observation the population growth
of the Piedmontese Alps and of the Aosta Valley, if there was growth
at all, may have been less spectacular than that implied by Blanchard
and by Janin. The legitimacy of this surmise seems to be confirmed
by the recent finding that from the beginning of the seventeenth century to the middle of the nineteenth century the total population of
one of the mountainous districts south of Monte Rosa (the large Sesia
Valley, of which Alagna is part) remained remarkably stable.[54]

Besides making it difficult to chart population growth, the unre-
liability of the eighteenth-century censuses renders any calculation
of demographic rates rather hazardous. Pontechianale provides a telling illustration. In the 1730s the average number of births recorded
every year in this locality was just under 49, whereas the number
of deaths was approximately 42. Since the 1734 census attributes to
Pontechianale 1,117 inhabitants, we obtain a crude birth rate of 43.8
and a crude death rate of 38.3 per thousand. In the 1770s the average
number of both births and deaths had declined slightly, but according
to the 1774 census Pontechianale now numbered no fewer than 2,045
people! Because of this gross overestimation, the resulting birth and
death rates are exceedingly low: only 20.2 and 16.9 per thousand.
In fact, the data contained in the proceedings of the Pastoral Visitations
suggest that both in 1734 and in 1774 the population of Pontechianale
consisted of about 1,400 individuals and, consequently, that crude

---

[54] Cf. Viazzo, 'Popolazione della Valsesia'.

Table 8.6. *Crude birth and death rates in the*
Alpine regions of the Kingdom of Sardinia in
the decade 1828–1837

	CBR	CDR
Aosta Valley	32.7	28.8
Maurienne	32.8	28.9
Tarentaise	30.4	24.6
Savoy	32.1	24.5
Piedmontese Alps	35.5	28.9

Source: Janin, *Le Val d'Aoste*, p. 175.

birth rates hovered between 30 and 35 per thousand and crude death rates between 25 and 30 per thousand.[55]

It is worth noting that estimates which can be derived from data available for two other villages of the southern Piedmontese Alps – Entracque, in the high Gesso Valley, and Elva, in the high Maira Valley – reveal for the eighteenth century crude birth and death rates that are close to those found in Pontechianale.[56] No less interesting is the fact that these ranges appear to be very much the same as those recorded during the first half of the nineteenth century not only in Pontechianale (where in 1838 the birth rate was 34.2 and the death rate 25.7 per thousand) but in the whole of the Western Alps, as Table 8.6 and further data furnished by writers like Eandi, Muttini-Conti, Janin, van de Walle and Blanchard himself make abundantly clear.[57]

These data show, of course, that significant spatial variations existed. In the French Alps both natality and mortality tended to be lower than in Piedmont. But in the French Alps themselves there were considerable differences between the demographic regime of,

[55] Cf. Albera *et al.*, 'Movimenti migratori'.
[56] The figures concerning Entracque presented in this and in the next chapter have been worked out on the basis of data collected by R. Bassani and available at the Department of History, University of Turin. The analysis has been conducted in collaboration with Dr D. Albera and has been mainly focused on the *status animarum* of 1730. In this year crude birth and death rates may be estimated in the region of 32 and 30 per thousand respectively. Half a century later, in 1780, the estimated values were 33.7 and 26.1. For Elva, crude birth and death rates can be estimated with some degree of confidence for the period 1731–50 on the basis of the series published by Dao, 'Ricerca storica su Elva', pp. 87–9, and prove to be in the region of 31 and 25 per thousand.
[57] Eandi, *Statistica*, pp. 269–78; Blanchard, *Les Alpes Occidentales*, vol. 6.1, pp. 325–6; Muttini-Conti, *La popolazione del Piemonte*, pp. 135–53; Janin, *Le Val d'Aoste*, pp. 172–6; É. van de Walle, *The female population of France*, pp. 235–40, 331–3.

say, the Maurienne or the Tarentaise and the very low rates recorded in the Ubaye region, which had already puzzled Blanchard.[58] As for the Piedmontese side, it is evident that birth and death rates were highest in the Maritime Alps and lowest in the Pennine Alps, with the Cottian and Graian Alps somewhere in between. Perhaps more important, however, is the finding that throughout the Western Alps natality and mortality were consistently lower in the high valleys than in the low valleys and in the surrounding plains. The low levels of mortality are particularly striking. As Blanchard had already noticed, there can be little doubt that 'au XIXe siècle on mourait moins en montagne que dans les régions déprimées', mortality being 'toujours inferieure à celle des régions basses et parfois dans des proportions extraordinaires'.[59] A comparison between the mortality levels of such high-altitude villages as Pontechianale, Entracque and Elva and those of a lower-altitude village like Martiniana Po, where crude death rates could exceed 40 per thousand,[60] suggests that this was probably true of the eighteenth century as well. The general impression is therefore that in the period under consideration the Western Alps, and especially the high valleys, displayed largely the same demographic system as the other parts of the Alps surveyed in this chapter. Yet there is an important difference – an Alpine anomaly, one would be tempted to say. It concerns a variable which most previous studies have overlooked, namely nuptiality.

A few years ago, the first results of ethnographic inquiries conducted in the high Varaita Valley suggested that in the 'traditional past' this part of the Cottian Alps might have been characterized by rather higher levels of nuptiality than could be expected in an Alpine area. It appeared that in the years before the First World War both men and women married at an early age, and the older villagers were adamant in asserting that permanent celibacy was a highly unusual status for both sexes.[61] Subsequent historical investigations focused on the commune of Pontechianale[62] have corroborated this ethnographic evidence. In the course of the nineteenth century men had tended to marry at 25 or 26 years of age or less, while the brides' mean age at marriage hovered between 20 and 23 years. Furthermore, a listing of inhabitants compiled in 1807 and preserved in the commu-

---

[58] See the section devoted to 'L'étrange démographie de l'Ubaye' in Blanchard, *Les Alpes Occidentales*, vol. 5.2, pp. 738–40.
[59] Blanchard, *Les Alpes Occidentales*, vol. 7, pp. 543–4.
[60] Dossetti, 'Aspetti demografici', pp. 87–91.
[61] Albera, 'I giovani e il matrimonio', pp. 98–103.
[62] See Albera, 'Systèmes familiaux'.

nal archive seems to confirm that in the past permanent celibacy was very uncommon: in that year only 5.7 per cent of all the men of Ponte-chianale aged over 50 years, and only 8.8 per cent of all women in the same age group, had never been married. (Very similar propor-tions are recorded by another listing of 1826.)

In the light of the admittedly scanty information offered by the available literature on the nineteenth century,[63] the case of Pontechia-nale, far from being exceptional, seems to be quite representative of nuptiality trends on the Italian side of the Maritime and Cottian Alps. (In the Graian and, even more, in the Pennine Alps nuptiality was apparently lower.) Once again, there is reason to believe that the same trends were already discernible in the eighteenth century. For Entracque, in the Maritime Alps, it can be estimated that in 1730 the singulate mean age at marriage was as low as 23.15 years for men and 20.06 years for women,[64] while celibacy rates were strikingly reminiscent of those found in Pontechianale nearly one century later: 4.9 per cent of all men aged 50 years or more and 8.1 per cent of all women in the same age group.

What is more, there is evidence that nuptiality could also be very high, by Alpine standards, on the other side of the Western Alps. In an article published in 1977, Étienne van de Walle noticed that in the three *départements* of Isère, Hautes-Alpes and Basses-Alpes per-manent celibacy rates appeared to have changed only slightly between the eighteenth century and the first half of the nineteenth century.[65] This suggests that the nuptiality of French Alpine populations was already fairly high before the turn of the eighteenth century. Such an impression is now reinforced by the results of Anne M. Jones's family reconstitution study of Montmin, a village in Savoy, as well as by Alain Collomp's most recent suggestion that in the mountains of Haute-Provence nuptiality actually declined somewhat in the course of the nineteenth century. Jones's research shows that in Montmin marriage was consistently early throughout the seventeenth and eight-eenth centuries, mean ages ranging between 23.72 and 25.99 for men and between 21.84 and 24.32 for women. Collomp, on his part, has

---

[63] See Eandi, *Statistica*, pp. 267–86; Muttini-Conti, *La popolazione del Piemonte*; Dossetti, 'Aspetti demografici', p. 101. Cf. also Livi-Bacci, *History of Italian fertility*, map 4.24.

[64] The 'singulate mean age at marriage' (SMAM) is an estimate of the mean age at first marriage derived from the proportion of each age group not yet married as shown by a census. It was first proposed in 1953 by Hajnal, 'Age at marriage and proportions marrying'.

[65] É. van de Walle, 'La nuptialité des Françaises', pp. 456–62.

estimated that in eighteenth-century Haute Provence the mean age at first marriage was in the region of 25 years for men and 22 years for women, and has contended that the rate of permanent celibacy was low both at the local and at the regional level.[66]

It is obviously very difficult to say whether, and to what extent, nuptiality acted homeostatically. The picture is still too fragmentary. For the time being we can only detect a general tendency for overall fertility to be higher in those regions where nuptiality too was higher. Yet we have seen that even in localities where the brides' age at marriage was very low and celibacy infrequent, birth rates could remain well below the threshold of 38–40 per thousand. The impression one receives is that in the Western Alps natality was potentially very high, but that this potential often failed to be exploited fully. In Montmin complete progeny accounted for only 65–75 per cent of the Hutterite standard schedule,[67] and in eighteenth-century Entracque, where the reproductive potential of the population was very high indeed, levels of marital fertility were even lower: in 1730 an I_m of 0.751 was matched by an I_g not exceeding 0.570. The latter value, it may be observed, is very similar to the ones for Pontechianale in 1807 ($I_g = 0.610$) and in 1826 ($I_g = 0.559$).

These findings inevitably bring us back to the question of the origins of the 'French model' set at the beginning of this section. As we have seen in Chapter 4, it has been known for some time that in the 1830s the southern regions of the French Alps had already been characterized by low levels of marital fertility and by fairly high nuptiality. This would seem to be the obvious consequence of the early adoption of family limitation practices which is typical of France as a whole. However, the data we have just examined indicate that in the first half of the nineteenth century this allegedly 'post-traditional' pattern can also be found on the Piedmontese side, where family limitation is believed to have started only in the late nineteenth and early twentieth centuries. What is more, the cases of Entracque and Montmin suggest that a coexistence of low marital fertility and high nuptiality may have been the basic feature of a demographic pattern of long

---

[66] See Jones, 'Population dynamics', and Collomp, 'From stem family to nuclear family', p. 79. Cf. also Collomp, 'Tensions, dissections, and ruptures', p. 157. It should be noticed, however, that higher ages at marriage (in the region of 27–8 years for both men and women) are reported for eighteenth-century Saint-Véran by Espagnet, 'Saint-Véran en Queyras', quoted by Fauve-Chamoux, 'Le fonctionnement de la famille-souche', p. 629. See also note 68 below.

[67] Jones, 'Population dynamics'.

standing, most clearly visible in the southern sector of the Western Alps but also detectable in some parts of the northern sector.[68]

Spatial variations in fertility: some determinants

One remarkable result of the analysis of Alpine fertility patterns carried out in Chapter 4 was that in the second half of the nineteenth century overall fertility was low all over the Alps, but the weight of its components could vary significantly from one region to another. The rapid survey attempted in this chapter indicates that this was already the case well before 1850. This raises an important question. If overall fertility tended to be uniformly moderate in spite of varying levels of nuptiality, what other factors were at work to check fertility?

This is no easy question to answer, partly because of its intrinsic complexity and even more because of the present paucity of reliable data. One of the factors most likely to explain differentials in fertility between the various major Alpine regions is of course breast-feeding, but so far this crucial issue has been largely neglected. Although very little is known about the actual duration of lactation and its variations between different places and over time, nevertheless breast-feeding seems to have been the norm in the Western Alps, whereas it was highly unusual in the Austrian Alps.[69] The Swiss Alps, on the other hand, are something of an enigma. The scanty and rather anecdotal evidence reviewed by Netting has led him to conclude, albeit tentatively, that breast-feeding 'was considered vital to the infant's health

---

[68] It is interesting to note that in the 1830s levels of nuptiality seem to have varied quite considerably in the seven districts of Savoy. In the period 1828–37, the median age at marriage (including remarriages) ranged from 23.6 to 26.3 years for women and from 26.4 to 29.1 for men. In the district of which Montmin was part, the province of Annecy, the median ages were 24.2 years for women (the second lowest in the whole region) and 28.5 years for men. Variability appears to have been greater than in the western Piedmontese Alps, where median values only ranged between 22.0 and 23.2 years for women and between 27.1 and 28.4 years for men. See Regno di Sardegna, *Informazioni statistiche*, vol. 2, p. 351. Some information on nuptiality trends in Savoy can be derived from the 1838, 1848 and 1858 censuses. Unfortunately, in these censuses data are presented in ways that make direct comparison difficult or utterly impossible. The strong impression one receives is, however, that in the course of the first half of the nineteenth century nuptiality declined markedly. Rates of permanent celibacy seem to have increased, and in the 1850s the mean age at marriage probably exceeded 27 years for women and 30 years for men. See Regno d'Italia, *Censimento degli Antichi Stati Sardi*, vol. 3, especially pp. 19–21, 43–5.

[69] This at least was the situation in the second half of the nineteenth century. On the Western Alps, see Rollet, 'Allaitement, mise en nourrice et mortalité infantile', and Livi-Bacci, *History of Italian fertility*, p. 256. On the Austrian Alps, see Fliri, *Bevölkerungsgeographische Untersuchungen*, p. 54; and Knodel and van de Walle, 'Breastfeeding, fertility and infant mortality', p. 118.

and was routinely sustained for several years'.[70] But such a claim is difficult to accept, for although it certainly fits well with the relatively low levels of infant mortality reported for a number of Swiss localities, it cannot be easily reconciled with marital fertility rates which were among the highest recorded in Europe.[71]

As has been recently observed,[72] the realization that lactation has played a primary role in the demography of pre-industrial Europe sets new tasks for the social and demographic historian. Thus, it can be expected that in the next few years a growing number of researchers will try to determine what caused mothers in the Western parts of the Alps to undertake prolonged periods of breast-feeding while those in the Austrian Alps did not, and to evaluate more accurately how far differences in feeding practices can explain fertility differentials. However, breast-feeding is only one of the several factors which may be presumed to have contributed to lowering natural fertility. Particularly in the Alps, the prolonged absence of husbands through migration is certainly a major influence to be taken into account. Moreover, in those areas where the alps were individually managed – such as Montmin and, indeed, Pontechianale and Entracque – the importance of the period of separation imposed on married couples by the requirements of pastoral activities should not be overlooked. And finally, when faced by extreme instances of low fertility, we can hardly avoid considering the possibility of conscious restriction on births.

Unfortunately, so far these topics have been rather poorly investigated. But it should be emphasized that, even when reasonably good and detailed information is available, the question of determining which factor was decisively affecting fertility may still prove difficult to disentangle. In order to explore a few dimensions of this complex problem, it will be useful to consider some evidence brought to light by my own study of Alagna and to compare it with the data provided by two other family reconstitution studies concerning high-altitude villages and covering the period 1700–1850, namely Netting's study of Törbel and Zurfluh's study of Andermatt. It is interesting to note that until a few decades ago Alagna shared not only with Törbel but also with Andermatt, which is another Walser colony, the same dialect and largely the same material culture. But its demographic history was, as we shall see, very different.

---

[70] Netting, *Balancing on an alp*, pp. 155–7.
[71] For evidence on the coexistence of short birth spacing, high marital fertility and yet moderate infant mortality, see e.g. Bucher, *Bevölkerung des Amtes Entlebuch*, pp. 73–5; Zurfluh, 'Urseren 1640–1830', pp. 315–19; and Kurmann, *Das Luzerner Suhrental*, pp. 96–112.
[72] Wilson, 'Proximate determinants', pp. 227–8.

In the first fifty years of the eighteenth century Alagna offered a clear example of a low-pressure demographic regime, with birth rates fluctuating between 25 and 30 per thousand and death rates not exceeding 25 per thousand. There were apparently two main factors accounting for the low birth rates. The first factor was nuptiality. Admittedly, the mean age at first marriage for women, though fairly high (24.8 years), was lower than in other parts of the Alps in the same period (and also lower, incidentally, than it was in Alagna in the period between the two world wars). In eighteenth-century Alagna young brides of 20 years of age or less were not unusual, and several cases of child brides marrying at 13 or 14 are also recorded. But celibacy rates – and here lies perhaps the main difference from such villages as Pontechianale or Entracque – were very high: about one-sixth of all men and, above all, one-third of all women failed to marry. It is therefore celibacy, more than late marriage, that accounts for an I_m which was, in 1738, as low as 0.387.

However, if nuptiality was low, marital fertility was, in its turn, not very high by eighteenth-century standards, and illegitimate fertility was definitely low. In 1738 the value of I_g was 0.702 and that of I_h 0.005. We may note that these values are remarkably close to those displayed by the Swiss Canton Ticino in 1888 (see Table 4.7). In her important article on the influence of migration on fertility, Francine van de Walle has maintained that the significantly lower marital fertility of Ticino *vis-à-vis* such cantons as Valais and Uri was essentially due to the existence in Ticino of massive seasonal emigration.[73] Since Alagna was characterized by exactly the same pattern of massive seasonal emigration of men as most valleys in Ticino, it is conceivable that this factor largely explains why in the first half of the eighteenth century women were (as Figure 8.1 shows) less fertile in Alagna than in Törbel or in Andermatt.

In the second half of the eighteenth century marital fertility continued to be lower in Alagna than in Törbel and Andermatt. Figure 8.2 shows, however, that marital fertility decreased fairly substantially in all three parishes, which is rather puzzling. At all events, as far as Alagna is concerned it is interesting to observe that overall fertility remained very much the same as before, since the decline in marital fertility was offset (as we can see from Table 8.7) by improvements in nuptiality. In fifty years the I_m index climbed from less than 0.400 in 1738 to 0.509 in 1788 – a change which is explained not so much by variations in the brides' ages at marriage, which were extremely modest (see Table 8.8), as by a substantial drop in celibacy rates.

[73] F. van de Walle, 'Migration and fertility in Ticino', p. 461.

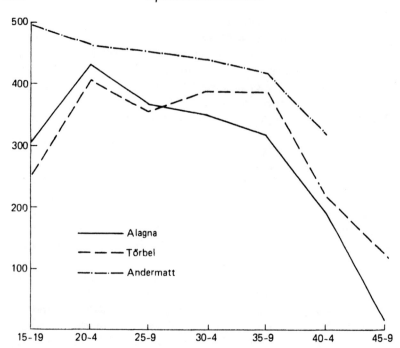

Figure 8.1 Age-specific marital fertility rates in Alagna, Törbel and Andermatt, 1701–1750

It is important to notice that the fertility and nuptiality pattern found in Alagna in the late eighteenth century is very similar to the one displayed by the southern regions of the French Alps in the 1860s,[74] and yet there is no convincing sign of contraceptive behaviour. Birth control, however, may have started to play a significant role in the first half of the nineteenth century. In this period, as Figure 8.3 shows so strikingly, Alagna's demography departs very markedly from that of Törbel and Andermatt. In both these localities nuptiality declined somewhat, but this was more than compensated by considerable increases in marital fertility. In Alagna, on the contrary, nuptiality went up, especially in the second quarter of the century. In 1838 the I_m reached the value of 0.565. But marital fertility, as Figure 8.3 shows, dropped to very low levels indeed – so low, in fact, that it is difficult not to explain them as due to conscious family limitation.

Particularly in a village like Alagna, where emigration was so important, a plausible alternative hypothesis is that changes in the emigration pattern may have resulted in longer periods of spousal

[74] See Table 4.8.

Table 8.7. *Fertility indices in Alagna 1738–1838*

	I_f	I_g	I_h	I_m
1738	0.275	0.702	0.005	0.387
1788	0.300	0.570	0.021	0.509
1838	0.242	0.420	0.011	0.565

Note: The values of I_f, I_g and I_h have been calculated by relating the data on women by age and marital status provided by the *status animarum* of 1738, 1788 and 1838 to the mean annual number of births (total, legitimate, illegitimate) in the 15-year period centred on the year in which the *status animarum* was compiled.

Sources: APA, *Libri status animarum* and *Libri baptizatorum*.

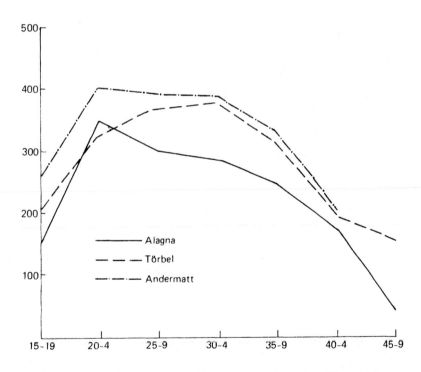

Figure 8.2 Age-specific marital fertility rates in Alagna, Törbel and Andermatt, 1751–1800

Table 8.8. *Mean age at first marriage in*
Alagna 1701–1980

Period	Men	Women
1701–50	28.33	24.75
1751–1800	27.57	24.64
1801–50	27.05	24.38
1851–1900	27.19	24.20
1901–50	29.31	26.06
1951–80	28.58	24.91

Source: 1701–1865: Family Reconstitution Study.
1866–1980: ACA, Marriage registers.

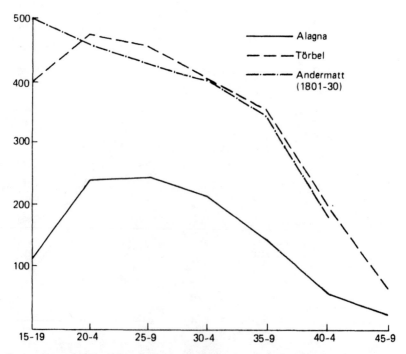

Figure 8.3 Age-specific marital fertility rates in Alagna, Törbel and Andermatt,
1801–1850

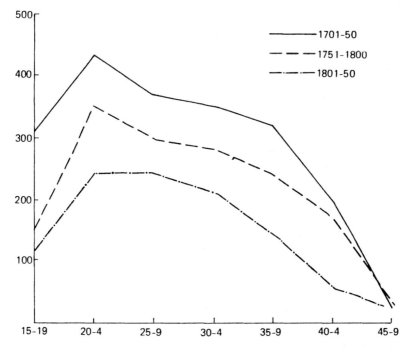

Figure 8.4 Age-specific marital fertility rates in Alagna 1701–1850

separation. However, there is no direct evidence that such changes
actually occurred. Moreover, this hypothesis cannot easily account
for the decline in the mean age of mothers at last birth or the increase
in the length of the ultimate birth interval, which (as Table 8.9 shows)
are both rather substantial and make a striking contrast to the stability
displayed by Törbel. Finally, in the first half of the nineteenth century
there is a clear change in the shape of the fertility curve, as one can
see both from Figure 8.4 and from the values of the Coale and Trussell's
m presented in Table 8.10.[75]

When the number of births is small, as is almost inevitably the

[75] The model devised by Coale and Trussell is defined in such a way that if a schedule
of observed age-specific fertility rates displays exactly the same shape as the standard
schedule of 'natural fertility' calculated in 1961 by L. Henry, then the value of m
is zero. If the observed fertility rates decline more steeply than is the case in the
standard, the value of m increases. If, on the other hand, the rate of the decline
in fertility with age is lower than in the standard, m will be negative. See Coale
and Trussell, 'Model fertility schedules', and 'Two parameters', and the recent discussions of some of the limitations of this model by Broström, 'Practical aspects',
and by Wilson *et al.*, 'What is natural fertility?'

Table 8.9. Some features of completed families in Alagna and Törbel, 1701–1850

	1701–50		1751–1800		1801–50	
	Alagna	Törbel	Alagna	Törbel	Alagna	Törbel
Number of completed families	75	30	103	45	112	87
Mean number of births:						
(a) completed families	6.7	5.3	5.2	6.0	3.3	5.9
(b) reconstituted families	4.8	3.8	3.9	4.7	3.2	4.9
(c) difference	1.9	1.5	1.3	1.3	0.1	1.0
Percentage of completed families with nine or more births	27	28	18	22	3	24
Mean age of mothers at birth of last child (years)	41.4	42.4	40.0	42.7	36.7	41.4
Mean birth intervals (months):						
(a) penultimate	32.9	34.6	38.8	39.6	36.8	31.3
(b) ultimate	41.1	40.7	42.9	44.7	53.3	38.5
(c) difference	8.2	6.1	4.1	5.1	16.5	7.2

Note: 'Completed' families are those in which the wife reaches age 45 during marriage or in which marriage is known to have lasted 30 years or more. By 'reconstituted' families I mean, following Netting (Balancing on an alp, p. 132), families 'remaining resident in the village so that family reconstitution and reproductive histories are possible'.
Sources: Alagna: Family Reconstitution Study. Törbel: Netting, Balancing on an alp, Tables 6.11 and 6.18.

Table 8.10. Coale-Trussell parameters of marital fertility, Alagna 1701–1850

Period	N of births	M	m	T
1701–50	478	0.842	−0.185	1.804
1751–1800	521	0.670	−0.198	4.187
1801–50	357	0.598	0.271	2.318

Notes: Parameters have been estimated by the maximum likelihood method proposed by Broström, 'Practical aspects', and on the basis of a five-point fit using data for ages 20 to 44. The estimation procedure is weighted by the number of births in each age group. 'T' is the Pearson chi-square goodness of fit statistic based on the number of births and is distributed as chi-square with 3 degrees of freedom: values of 'T' greater than 7.81 are significant at the 95% level.

case with family reconstitution studies of single parishes, random variation can be expected to be quite large. The results obtained by using the Coale-Trussell model (even in its improved versions) must therefore be treated with a great deal of caution.[76] Nevertheless, the figures in Table 8.9 certainly do not contradict the hypothesis that in the first half of the nineteenth century conscious family limitation had begun to be practised in Alagna. It should also be noticed that in Alagna there was apparently a tendency for married men to be absent more frequently and, probably, for longer periods in their younger age.[77] One should consequently expect seasonal and temporary emigration not only to strengthen the intervals between births but also to make it impossible for many couples to concentrate their childbearing in the early years of marriage. This tendency would indeed seem to be reflected by the negative values of m between 1701 and 1800. In the first half of the nineteenth century, however, the value of m becomes positive, which indicates that, although fertility rates for the younger ages declined very steeply, the rates for the older ages dropped even more sharply.

In the next chapter we shall again touch upon the decline of fertility experienced by Alagna in the first half of the nineteenth century and discuss some of its more intriguing aspects. But the data examined so far are sufficient to demonstrate that in this village nuptiality fluctuated rather substantially over time and that its relationship with fertility was not static. It is especially evident that in the period between the two world wars nuptiality was much lower than one hundred years earlier. Rather than being a 'traditional' feature of the local social structure, the low nuptiality of the 1930s appears to be related to a progressive deterioration of Alagna's economic fortunes and to changes which occurred in its ethnic and social composition.[78] Nor can the low nuptiality of those years be seen as a response to environmental imperatives. As early as the first half of the nineteenth century the old homeostatic mechanism, control over marriage, had

---

[76] One of the advantages of the maximum likelihood estimation method (see note to Table 8.10) is that it is possible to calculate approximate confidence regions for the parameters. In the case of Alagna, these suggest that parameter estimates are subject to a variation of about ±0.2 for m at the 95 per cent confidence level.

[77] This was a feature of the traditional pattern of male emigration as remembered by the oldest living villagers in Alagna. That this was also the case in the period considered here is indirectly suggested by an analysis of birth seasonality by age group and, more directly, by the detailed *status animarum* compiled in the summer of 1788, which shows that the proportion of absent men was highest among the husbands aged 20 to 29 years (about 75 per cent) and then declined with age to just over 40 per cent among husbands aged 50 to 59 years.

[78] See Viazzo, 'Ethnic change in a Walser community', pp. 307–14.

probably already been replaced by other means of achieving a balance between population and resources.

'The dependence of the births on the deaths'

Much work clearly remains to be done on the ways in which nuptiality, emigration, breastfeeding practices and direct birth control contributed to check fertility. But further research is no less badly needed on the factor which more than any other can be supposed to have forced Alpine populations to adopt these 'adaptive strategies', namely low mortality. As Malthus had emphasized, the case of Leysin and more generally of the Swiss Alps did not simply show the importance of marriage as a preventive check; it also demonstrated, in his view, that there existed a fundamental 'dependence of the births on the deaths'[79] – or, as modern demographers would put it, that 'the central factor in demographic homeostasis is the force of mortality'.[80] The evidence rapidly surveyed in this chapter reveals, in fact, that the low levels of overall fertility displayed by the Alpine area were matched by even lower levels of mortality, and there are indications that major adjustments in nuptiality and fertility were made imperative by changes in mortality. When and why the low-pressure regime we find in the eighteenth century came into being, however, we do not know for certain.

As we have briefly mentioned in the course of Chapter 6, there is a considerable amount of disagreement about some crucial aspects of mortality in the Alps during the poorly documented period which goes from the medieval colonization to the end of the seventeenth century. Some scholars have argued that upland regions were less subject to the impact of epidemics, and in particular of bubonic plague, than the surrounding lowlands. The main reasons would have been the greater isolation of mountain areas, the lower density of their settlement and, as far as bubonic plague is concerned, the fact that fleas (the vectors of the plague bacillus) cannot flourish at high altitude because of the cold temperature.[81] Yet it is certain that the mountains were not immune to the visitation of epidemic diseases, including

[79] Malthus, *Summary view*, p. 212.
[80] Lesthaeghe, 'Social control', p. 528.
[81] Cf. Zimpel, 'Entwicklung der Walserkolonien', p. 133; Zurfluh, 'Gibt es den *homo alpinus?*', p. 240; and especially Bergier, 'Le cycle médiéval', pp. 224–6. It should be noticed, however, that Alpine regions might have been more vulnerable to plague in its pneumonic form. While bubonic plague is transmitted by fleas (or lice), pneumonic plague is communicated from man to man and is essentially associated with cold weather or cold climates. See Biraben, *Les hommes et la peste*, pp. 12–15.

plague. The Austrian historian Othmar Pickl, for instance, has maintained that in the fourteenth century about one-third of the inhabitants of Styria and Carinthia were wiped out by the Black Death, and Klein believes that mortality was actually higher in the mountainous parts of these regions.[82] Even if estimates have been in some cases grossly exaggerated,[83] there is then little doubt that in more recent times many Alpine districts were disastrously affected by plague epidemics. Thus, if Alagna managed to escape the great plague of 1630–2, the neighbouring village of Riva Valdobbia was struck very severely, the infection killing 240 out of about 1,000 inhabitants. The death toll was no less severe in Entracque, where in the year 1630 as many as 658 deaths were recorded from a population of probably just over 3,000 people.[84]

As in most parts of Europe, also in the Alps the virulence of epidemics seems to have subsided in the course of the eighteenth century, and this might be largely responsible for the decline of mortality observed in a number of Alpine localities, from Leysin to Törbel. But epidemics are not the only possible cause of mortality crises. Indeed, in ecological perspective perhaps a more important question is whether unusually high mortality was likely to occur frequently because of famine and relative states of overpopulation. Using impact simulation models based upon monthly temperature and precipitation series derived from his impressive scrutiny of Swiss sources, Christian Pfister has recently been able to investigate the effects that specific weather patterns and climatic regimes had on Alpine production levels between the early sixteenth century and the middle of the nineteenth century.[85] His general conclusion has been that at least until the end of the seventeenth century the agrarian ecosystems of the Swiss highlands were highly vulnerable to climatic shocks and that their carrying capacity was therefore rather unstable, its upper limit being a function not only of land and technology but also of climatic fluctuations. The main implication of this, Pfister has argued, is that peaks of high

---

[82] See Pickl, 'Wirtschaft und Gesellschaft in den Ostalpenländern', pp. 48–53, and Klein, 'Die Bevölkerung Österreichs', pp. 93–4.

[83] Cf. e.g. the implausible figures for the Aosta Valley accepted by Janin, *Le Val d'Aoste*, pp. 133–4.

[84] The impact of the plague on the population of Riva Valdobbia is discussed by Viazzo, 'Popolazione della Valsesia', p. 128. The number of deaths in Entracque is derived from Bassani, 'Una comunità del Cuneese', p. 241, whereas the number of inhabitants (3,106 in 1612) is provided by Gribaudi, 'Valle del Gesso', p. 371. On plague epidemics in the Swiss Alps during the sixteenth and seventeenth centuries, see Eckert, 'Boundary formation and diffusion of plague', and Mattmüller, *Bevölkerungsgeschichte der Schweiz*, vol. 1, pp. 228–59.

[85] See C. Pfister, 'Changes in stability', and especially his two-volume book *Das Klima der Schweiz*.

mortality caused by subsistence crises must have been an endemic feature of Alpine demography.[86]

This prediction would seem to be confirmed by the relatively well-documented effects of the harsh climatic worsening of the 1690s, when mortality crises are reported from several parts of upland Switzerland.[87] According to Pfister, in the second half of the seventeenth century the upper limit of the carrying capacity of Alpine ecosystems had been raised by a succession of decades mainly characterized by favourable climatic conditions, and the size of many human and animal local populations had presumably approached the upper limit. When in 1687 temperature suddenly declined, and a frequent occurrence of wet springs and summers made things worse, 'population and herd size were reduced by Malthusian forces to the lower carrying capacity'.[88]

In Pfister's view, this state of endemic instability was radically altered by the advent of the potato. Prior to the introduction of the new crop, the main weakness of the Alpine agrarian ecosystems had been their lack of flexibility, for a high frequency of cold and wet spells (particularly between April and October) ineluctably led to a simultaneous slump in grain, fruit, hay and cheese production. As a consequence, substitutions in the highlanders' diet were difficult or utterly impossible. The potato, on the other hand, was a sturdier crop than summer grains, harvest failures being unlikely even in adverse meteorological conditions. Thus, the incorporation of the potato into Alpine ecosystems, besides increasing productivity, made them more flexible and therefore more resistant to climatic stress. Though still affecting to some extent the carrying capacity of Alpine ecosystems, climatic fluctuations no longer triggered immediate demographic effects in the form of mortality crises.[89]

We may note that the set of explanations and the temporal sequence proposed by Pfister seem to fit rather well with what we know of the evolution of mortality in Törbel. In this village death registers are unfortunately unavailable before 1687, but from that year onwards it can be established that 'crisis mortality, defined as a death toll of more than double the annual average, affected Törbel in 1690, 1693, 1704, 1718, 1728, 1763, 1803, 1831, 1881, and 1918'.[90] These crises, Netting has stressed, never came close to the mortality reported for

---

[86] C. Pfister, 'Changes in stability', p. 292.
[87] Cf. Mattmüller, *Bevölkerungsgeschichte der Schweiz*, vol. 1, pp. 260–307.
[88] C. Pfister, 'Changes in stability', p. 292.
[89] C. Pfister, *Das Klima der Schweiz*, vol. 2, pp. 106–9.
[90] Netting, *Balancing on an alp*, p. 116.

some French communities in the seventeenth century.[91] Nevertheless, crisis years are fairly numerous. But if we consider their distribution over time, we see that they are concentrated in the late seventeenth and early eighteenth centuries, and then tend to become increasingly rare.

In Alagna, Pontechianale and Entracque, on the other hand, remarkably few crisis years are attested much before the introduction of the potato, which apparently took place only in the very last years of the eighteenth century.[92] In the eighty-five years between 1715 (when the extant series of death registers starts) and 1800, we find in Alagna just one year in which the number of burials was more than twice the expected annual average.[93] Only one crisis year was also experienced by Pontechianale between 1733 and 1800, and none by Entracque throughout the eighteenth century.[94] This discrepancy with the case of Törbel and with Pfister's predictions may partly be explained by the marked differences which existed between villages like Entracque, Pontechianale and especially Alagna, whose economies were critically dependent on emigration, and an agrarian community like Törbel, which approached much more closely the assumptions which underlie Pfister's models.

It is perhaps worth noting that in Alagna the potato, though becoming an important part of the diet, never completely supplanted rye, which the locals seem to have held in much higher esteem. Even in the early twentieth century, I was told, the portion of land planted with potatoes was no larger than the portion allocated to the cultivation of rye. This is in marked contrast to other communities in the Sesia Valley itself. In Rimella, for instance, the penetration of the potato was so pervasive that the older villagers are adamant that in the past no grains were cultivated – only potatoes.[95] This suggests

[91] The classic study of subsistence and mortality crises in seventeenth-century France is Meuvret, 'Les crises de subsistances'. See also Meuvret, 'Demographic crisis', pp. 513–19.

[92] On the introduction of the potato into the southern Piedmontese Alps, see the report written in 1802 by Prefect De Gregori, published in Sacco, *La provincia di Cuneo*, p. 185. For the Sesia Valley, see Sottile, *Quadro della Valsesia*, p. 10.

[93] In 1788 there were 50 deaths, a number which corresponds to a crude rate of 55 per thousand and is 2.39 times higher than the eleven-year moving average centred on 1788.

[94] Series of annual numbers of deaths are provided by Albera *et al.*, 'Movimenti migratori', for Pontechianale, and by Bassani, 'Una comunità del Cuneese', pp. 241–9, for Entracque.

[95] Personal communication from Professor P. Sibilla. It is worth noting that in 1847 the proportion of cultivated land planted with potatoes ranged, in the highland districts of Canton Berne, between 31 and 68 per cent (as compared to 14–24 per cent in the lowland districts), but could exceed 90 per cent in some high-altitude communities. Cf. Head-König *et al.*, 'Évolution agraire', p. 255.

that in a village like Alagna the potato could not be expected to have the 'revolutionary' effects it apparently had in Törbel. In fact, during the first half of the nineteenth century the population of Alagna displays, in spite of the recent introduction of the potato, a certain decline – again in contrast with the growth of Rimella and other agrarian communities of the Sesia Valley.[96]

It also seems clear that in the eighteenth and early nineteenth century mortality declined rather more markedly in Törbel than in Alagna. As we have seen, in Törbel the crude death rate dropped from about 28–30 per thousand in the mid-eighteenth century to just 20 per thousand in the first decades of the nineteenth. In Alagna the crude death rate also reached 20 per thousand in the 1830s, but throughout the eighteenth century it had ranged only between 22 and 25 per thousand. From a different angle, this stability of mortality at low levels is confirmed by the fact that for the people born in Alagna in the first half of the eighteenth century the expectation of life at birth was very much the same as for their fellow villagers born in the second half of the century. If we follow the two cohorts of women born in the years 1716–50 and 1751–85, we find that infant mortality rates were remarkably similar (165 and 169 per thousand respectively), and so was life expectancy: 42.6 years for the older cohort, 41.6 for the younger one.[97]

The several differences which exist between Törbel and Alagna invite two general considerations. Some of the evidence reviewed in this section would seem to suggest that in the eighteenth century, partly because of the declining virulence of epidemics and partly because of the beneficial effects of the introduction of the potato, a transition occurred from a relatively high-pressure 'crisis' regime to a low-pressure 'homeostatic' regime.[98] The case of Alagna, however, indicates that some caution is needed before this impression can safely be generalized, for we have seen that in this village mortality crises were already rare before the potato began to be cultivated. Moreover, as we have briefly noticed in Chapter 6, traces of low-pressure regime are already detectable in Alagna as early as the turn of the sixteenth century, when crude birth rates ranged between 25 and 30 per thousand and the age at marriage for both men and women was on average as high as in the eighteenth century. Although this is bound to remain

---

[96] Cf. Sibilla, *Una comunità walser*, pp. 55–84, and Viazzo, 'Popolazione della Valsesia', pp. 122–3.

[97] These estimates have been obtained through family reconstitution. The size of the two cohorts is similar: 358 for the period 1716–50, and 344 for the period 1751–85.

[98] For a relevant discussion of these two regimes, see Macfarlane, *Resources and population*, pp. 292–312.

simply a guess owing to the loss of the death registers, it is tempting, and certainly plausible, to surmise that in those days mortality too was already rather low.

The second general consideration is that the differences which Alagna and Törbel display in spite of their ethnic and also geographical closeness provide one further demonstration of the extreme diversity of the Alpine world. Clearly one can hardly expect to find the same demographic characteristics in a spectrum of communities ranging from tendentially autarkic villages like Törbel to villages where the backbone of the economy was cottage industry, the commerce of live-stock or, as in the case of Alagna, labour migration. But it is important to stress that these economic distinctions appear to have been them-selves cross-cut by major demographic variations between altitudinal zones. We have noticed, in particular, that Blanchard's inspection of a large body of statistical data on the French and Piedmontese Alps had convinced him that in the nineteenth century mortality was much lower in the mountains than in the surrounding lowlands. More-over, evidence from both the Western Alps and Austria suggested that a gradation could be detected within the boundaries of the Alpine region itself, mortality being generally more moderate in the high valleys than in the communities located at lower altitudes.

This impression has now been reinforced by recent research con-ducted on the Swiss Alps. Anselm Zurfluh's study of Andermatt has shown that in this high-altitude settlement in Canton Uri life expec-tancy was much higher than in Silenen, a low-altitude village in the same canton studied some years ago by Jürg Bielmann. In the second half of the eighteenth century and in the first decades of the nine-teenth, life expectancy was 38–9 years in Andermatt as compared to only 27–30 years in Silenen.[99] The first results of a major study of all the communities of Canton Berne between 1760 and 1860 also point in the same direction. The 195 parishes of this canton have been subdivided into four altitudinal zones, and the analysis of six censuses taken between 1764 and 1856 has not only revealed that crude death rates remained lowest in the most elevated zone through-out this period but has also brought out a striking inverse correlation between altitude and mortality.[100]

These marked differences highlight, once again, some of the elements which make any generalization about the Alps and their

[99] Cf. Zurfluh, 'Urseren 1640–1830', p. 319, and Bielmann, 'La population du Pays d'Uri', 456–8.
[100] See C. Pfister, 'Bevölkerung, Wirtschaft und Ernährung', pp. 369–70.

demography not simply difficult but, in some cases, positively misleading. Uri, to take a useful example, is a mountain canton *par excel-
lence* and the whole of its territory belongs to the Alpine region. Yet
its settlements are located at widely different altitudes and in the period we are considering their economic and demographic features also
differed very substantially. (The economy of high-altitude villages like
Andermatt, it should be remembered, was predominantly pastoral,
its agricultural component being far less pronounced than in villages
like Silenen.) Zurfluh is therefore right when he argues that historical
demographers, instead of looking for a single Alpine demographic
pattern, should take full account of the existence of important variations more or less directly related to altitude.[101]

Once these differences in levels of mortality are recognized, however, they still need to be explained. Some evidence provided by Zurfluh himself for Uri suggests that the dynamics of subsistence crises
may have differed according to altitude. The villages of the high valleys, it would seem, were less vulnerable to direct subsistence crises
than lower-altitude communities because of their lesser dependence
on grains, even if their economic bases could be badly hit by meteorological conditions damaging grass.[102] But a more important factor was,
in Zurfluh's view, infant mortality, which was distinctly lower in
Andermatt than in the communities of the low valleys.[103]

Detailed studies comparing levels of infant mortality in a mountain
district and in the adjacent plains, or in different villages within the
same mountain district, are unfortunately still very rare.[104] But what
data we possess certainly indicate a general tendency for infant mortality to be lower in the uplands. A recent study by Breschi and Livi-Bacci
has shown that in the 1830s Savoy was the region with the lowest
rates of infant mortality in the whole Piedmontese state: only 177
per thousand compared to 250–70 per thousand in the agricultural
districts of the Piedmontese plains.[105] Interestingly, the rates recorded
in Savoy in these years are very close to those found in Montmin
in the course of the seventeenth and eighteenth centuries, which

---

[101] Zurfluh, 'Urseren 1640–1830', p. 323.
[102] Zurfluh, 'Gibt es den *homo alpinus*?', pp. 246–9.
[103] See Zurfluh, 'Urseren 1640–1830', p. 319.
[104] One such comparative study (on the area near Lake Como) is now being conducted
       by Professor R. Merzario. Preliminary results communicated at the seminar 'Sulla
       storia della famiglia europea' (Florence, 1986) suggest that rates of infant mortality
       were considerably lower in the mountainous parts of this area than in the plains.
[105] Breschi and Livi-Bacci, 'Stagione di nascita', pp. 90–1.

Table 8.11. *Infant mortality rates (IMR) in Switzerland between 1867 and 1871: ranking of Alpine cantons*

Canton	IMR	Ranking
Ticino	149	1
Valais	169	2
Grisons	175	3
Obwalden	201	4
Nidwalden	216	5
Uri	221	7
Schwyz	255	13
Glarus	292	22

Note: The total number of Swiss cantons is 24. The infant mortality rate for the whole of Switzerland between 1867 and 1871 was 246 per thousand.
Source: F. van de Walle, *One hundred years of decline*, Table 4.10.

ranged between 154 and 216 per thousand.[106] Similarly low values also characterized the demography of Alagna throughout the eighteenth century, as we have seen. Rates were probably somewhat higher in some parts of the Swiss and, even more, of the Austrian Alps. But here too it is likely that infant mortality was less severe than in the lowlands. It is indeed striking to discover that in the years around 1870 the five Swiss cantons with the lowest levels of infant mortality were all part of the Alpine region (see Table 8.11).

Zurfluh has contended that this general tendency could be mainly explained by altitude itself. The cold Alpine climate, he has suggested, made infants less vulnerable to bronchial and pulmonary diseases. In addition, water was less contaminated than in the lowlands, and this reduced the probability of gastro-intestinal disorders.[107] This hypothesis obviously requires to be further corroborated. But it is of considerable interest – not least because it turns upside down the argument (first advanced in the late nineteenth century and apparently still popular in some circles) according to which infant mortality

[106] Jones, 'Population dynamics'. A note of caution is suggested, however, by the much higher rates of infant mortality (329 per thousand in the period 1739–49) which have been reported for another community in Savoy by Hudry, 'La démographie d'une commune de montagne', quoted by Guillaume and Poussou, *Démographie historique*, p. 139.

[107] Zurfluh, 'Urseren 1640–1830', p. 319. Similar hypotheses have been put forward by C. Pfister, 'Bevölkerung, Wirtschaft und Ernährung', p. 370.

would grow with altitude.[108] One point well worth stressing is that the relationships between altitude and infant mortality have greatly changed over time. In her analysis of the 1870 census of Switzerland, Francine van de Walle has shown that in that year there was a rather strong negative correlation between infant mortality and altitude: the correlation coefficient between infant mortality rate and 'high altitude' (defined as the percentage of the population of a district living in communes situated over 1,000 m) was −0.434. A negative correlation was still detectable in 1888 ($r = -0.343$), but by 1910 infant mortality had reversed its relation to altitude, the coefficient being then +0.101 – a change which is indicative of the rapid worsening of the economic and sanitary conditions of the mountains relative to the increasingly urbanized plains.[109]

Van de Walle's figures clearly support the contention that in the past babies and young children had a more favourable mortality experience in the mountains than in the plains.[110] But they also remind us that the variable 'altitude', besides having a direct climatic component, could proximate for a variety of different factors. Breschi and Livi-Bacci, for example, have found that in the various regions of the Piedmontese state a correlation existed between low infant mortality and high levels of literacy, and have tentatively suggested that the widespread literacy of Savoy might be an indication (or perhaps even a cause) of higher standards of infant and child care.[111] In a rather different perspective, the importance of factors other than altitude in affecting infant mortality in an Alpine context is demonstrated by the finding that in Alagna infant mortality was substantially lower, in the period 1731–1800, among those children whose parents were both native-born than among the children of immigrant miners.[112] Nevertheless, the impression remains strong that the main cause of

[108]	For a useful discussion of this argument and its fallacies, see Imhof, 'Unterschiedliche Säuglingssterblichkeit', pp. 361–6.

[109]	See F. van de Walle, *One hundred years of decline*, Table 4.7. The data presented by Bolognese-Leuchtenmüller, *Bevölkerungsentwicklung*, Tables 36 and 40, show that a very similar evolution can be detected in Austria. In 1850 infant mortality was much heavier in Lower Austria (360 per thousand) than in the Alpine regions, where rates per thousand ranged from 210 in Carinthia to just under 300 in Salzburg. In 1910 the situation had been completely reversed: infant mortality was lowest in Lower Austria (175 per thousand) and highest in Carinthia, where rates had remained stationary in the neighbourhood of 200 per thousand.

[110]	It is worth noting that V. Fildes, *Breasts, bottles and babies*, p. 265, has recently suggested that artificial feeding, especially when milk-based foods were used, was more likely to succeed in cold climates, because of the lower risk that milk and other foods might rapidly become sour and contaminated, making infants more susceptible to gastro-intestinal diseases.

[111]	Breschi and Livi-Bacci, 'Stagione di nascita,' p. 99.

[112]	See Chapter 7 above, p. 174.

the low levels of infant mortality found in the Alpine valleys resided in the very 'healthiness' of the environment.

Conclusions

The material presented in this chapter shows that, while marital fertility could be very high, overall fertility was fairly low all over the Alps from at least the first decades of the eighteenth century, and so were both adult and infant mortality. All this indicates that the model proposed by Guichonnet in 1975 must be substantially revised, and adds strength to the alternative position held by scholars like Lichtenberger, who have argued that the Alps were traditionally characterized by a 'low-pressure' demographic regime and that a balance of low levels of both fertility and mortality was achieved through the check of nuptiality.[113] There are, however, two qualifications to be made. The first one is that what we have throughout this book termed 'Alpine region' actually consisted of different ecological and altitudinal zones – fertility, nuptiality and mortality being, as a rule, distinctly lower in the high valleys than in the low valleys and in the adjacent hills and plains. The second major qualification is that, although the importance of nuptiality can scarcely be disputed, the example of the Western Alps (where birth and death rates were relatively moderate in spite of high levels of nuptiality) shows that other regulatory mechanisms could be at work.

There is little doubt, in particular, that the role of emigration within the demographic system of the Alps should be reconsidered in this perspective. The notion of emigration as a social and demographic 'servomechanism' is not new in Alpine studies, but most scholars have regarded emigration as just a safety valve, a device through which Alpine areas disposed of excess population. The relations between emigration and fertility have been (apart from few remarkable exceptions such as Francine van de Walle's 1975 paper on Ticino) nearly ignored. Yet permanent emigration could often result in severely unbalanced sex ratios and impinge on overall fertility through reducing nuptiality, while seasonal and temporary emigration directly affected marital fertility. In Alagna or in the valleys of Canton Ticino, the prolonged absence of husbands further depressed birth rates which were already kept down by low nuptiality. In such regions as the Maritime and Cottian Alps, seasonal and temporary emigration could offset the potential effects of high nuptiality and was probably the single most important check on overall fertility.

[113] See Chapter 2 above, p. 42.

The evidence surveyed in this chapter allows another conclusion, which is of considerable relevance to anthropological theory and practice. As we have seen in the Introduction, the American anthropologist Melvyn Goldstein has argued that Himalayan populations were part of a homeostatic system where low nuptiality facilitated the sustenance of major civilizations without either destroying the productive capacity of the environment or causing chronic starvation and large-scale emigration.[114] As is typical of anthropological studies, Goldstein's approach was based on the analysis of recent social and economic changes and his conclusions were predicated on a set of assumptions about the past. The advantage offered by research on the Alps is that contentions of this kind can be checked, to some extent at least, against a diachronic background. There is no doubt that our survey of the available evidence broadly supports the argument, advanced by writers as different as Malthus and Goldstein, that in mountain areas nuptiality acted as a crucial homeostatic mechanism. But it also shows that levels of nuptiality could vary to a rather large degree from one region to another and over time. The implication is that the picture of traditional Alpine nuptiality derived from the anthropological literature is somewhat deceptive and needs to be revised. The two postulates on which it rests – that similar ecological imperatives must invariably produce similar responses and that recent changes must have been preceded by a long period of static equilibrium – are too rigid and, in the last analysis, untenable.

Another point made by Goldstein raises comparative issues of considerable anthropological relevance. He reports that the low nuptiality systems found in the Himalayas were 'linked traditionally to primogeniture . . . so that land fragmentation was impossible'.[115] This point, which has also been made by other anthropologists who have worked in the Himalayas,[116] is strongly reminiscent of arguments put forward by a number of anthropologists for the Alpine area. However, the results of our investigation clearly suggest that students of the Alps (and indeed of any other mountain area) should keep a wary eye on the common assumption that systems of partible inheritance inevitably result in high nuptiality and rapid population growth and are therefore maladaptive. In many parts of the Central and Western Alps characterized by partibility, nuptiality could be as low as in the Austrian Alps. And even where nuptiality was higher, as in some

---

[114] Goldstein, 'Social matrix of Tibetan populations', p. 102. For a rather different view, see Macfarlane, *Resources and population*.
[115] Goldstein, 'Social matrix of Tibetan populations', p. 102.
[116] Cf. e.g. Carrasco, *Land and polity in Tibet*.

sectors of the Western Alps, population growth was far from being as rapid as might have been expected.

Nevertheless, one of the reasons why the Austrian case is so fascinating is that it suggests the hypothesis that a custom prescribing impartibility can make a demographic system less elastic than others in homeostatically adjusting to increased resources – or may perhaps even prevent it from adjusting at all. It is worth noting that the function of nuptiality is usually seen as that of a brake, the unwritten assumption being that in mountain environments resources are always inevitably scarce. A rather different, and more sophisticated, view holds that nuptiality can also work the other way. Thus, nuptiality can be expected to rise after a mortality crisis (in order to restore population to its previous level) or when resources are on the increase. One of the most interesting features of the demographic evolution of Törbel described by Netting is that it shows that even in a context of increasing resources nuptiality may well decline. But Netting's study also strengthens the widespread conviction that the size of population will eventually tend to adjust to resources. In Austria, however, this might not have been the case.

Commenting on Wynne-Edwards's theory of animal dispersion, which has influenced some of the leading theorists of nuptiality as a central regulatory mechanism,[117] the British anthropologist Mary Douglas has argued that when we deal with human populations and their regulatory mechanisms the focus of inquiry should be shifted from subsistence to prestige, for 'the kind of relation to resources that is sought is more often a relation to limited social advantages than to resources crucial to survival'.[118] Of special relevance is one of the examples quoted by Douglas, who notes that in order to maintain their social and economic advantages the Nambudiri Brahmins allow only one son to marry, so as the estates are not divided. The similarities between some aspects of what might be called the 'strategies of social reproduction' pursued by this Indian group and, in the Alpine context, by the Austrian *Bauern* are intriguing, and it seems reasonable to suspect, as has already been hinted, that in the Austrian Alps nuptiality may have been blocked well below carrying capacity so as to permit the perpetuation of a given kind of social structure.

Douglas's contention has important implications and lays bare one

---

[117] See especially Wrigley, *Population and history*, pp. 39–44, and Dupâquier, 'De l'animal à l'homme', pp. 181–93. See also Le Roy Ladurie, 'Homme-animal, nature-culture', pp. 554–67; and for a recent discussion, Bideau, 'Autoregulating mechanisms'.

[118] Douglas, 'Population control', p. 272.

fundamental element of diversity which exists in the anthropological approaches to the study of the relationships between environment, population and social structure. The 'cultural-ecological' approach pioneered by Julian Steward deserves the credit for having established the set of correlations between environmental factors, subsistence patterns and forms of social organization which are at the core of models such as the one outlined in Chapter 1. The so-called 'neo-functionalists' have, for their part, made these models more comprehensive and dynamic by introducing the concept of ecosystem and by focusing the attention on the ways in which resources and population are kept in balance by a number of homeostatic mechanisms. Though less obviously deterministic than cultural ecologists, the proponents of the ecosystemic approach (which has a similar counterpart in historical demography) can nonetheless be criticized for overstating the importance of environmental constraints and treating both population and, even more, social structure as mere dependent variables. The charge that their notion of social structure befits animal communities far better than human populations may not seem too unfair when one considers that the central concepts of ecosystem and homeostatic regulation have been borrowed from biology.

On the other hand, the British school of social anthropology, of which Mary Douglas is a leading exponent, has traditionally granted to social structure not just an analytical but also an explanatory primacy. The shortcomings of this approach are well known – not least its failure to recognize the importance of environmental factors in constraining or even moulding some crucial sectors of social structure.[119] Moreover, most members of the British school have shared with the proponents of the ecosystemic approach a dangerous tendency to regard local communities as self-contained units of analysis. Nevertheless, a shift of the focus of inquiry 'from subsistence to prestige', to use Douglas's phrase, is helpful in directing the attention to the fact that the processes whereby social structures are reproduced may well follow imperatives which are not fully consonant with the expectations of models of ecological and demographic homeostasis – a point also made by Marxist anthropologists and by an historical demographer strongly influenced by British anthropology like Ron Lesthaeghe.[120] Although the merits of the ecological models which

---

[119] See Forde, 'Ecology and social structure', p. 26.
[120] See e.g. Friedman, 'Marxism, structuralism and vulgar materialism', pp. 457–60, and Lesthaeghe, 'Social control'.

have been our starting-point can scarcely be denied, a more balanced conceptualization of the relationships between environment, population and social structure is required, and this is what the last part of this book will try to provide.

9

The domestic domain

Anthropological models of the Alpine household

Over the last few decades, the emergence of common areas of research on the border between history and anthropology has led many anthropologists to acquire greater familiarity with the methods and techniques of historical demography. For their part, historical demographers are now paying more attention to the work of anthropologists, and the growing emphasis they are placing on nuptiality is likely to further increase their interest in a number of topics which have long been of primary significance in the anthropological investigation of social structure. As E. A. Wrigley has recently observed, if it is recognized that marriage was central to European population history, then 'questions such as the transmission of property between successive generations, authority structures within the family, patterns of co-residence and support, the institution of service, inheritance customs, and cognate matters, can scarcely fail to attract study'.[1]

Indeed, the results of our historical survey indicate that in order to shed more light on several important yet elusive aspects of Alpine demography it is necessary to examine in more detail what Jack Goody has called 'the domestic domain',[2] and in particular the nexus linking inheritance systems to nuptiality and family formation. Both historians and anthropologists have widely assumed that impartible inheritance will produce low levels of nuptiality and a predominance of stem-family households, whereas partibility should result in early marriage, moderate rates of permanent celibacy, and a high proportion of nuclear families. As far as nuptiality is concerned, however, this

[1] Wrigley, 'Population history', p. 210. [2] Goody, Production and reproduction.

assumption is hardly borne out by the Alpine evidence, for marriage could be as late and infrequent in the Swiss and Italian Alps, which were mostly characterized by various forms of partibility, as it was in the Austrian Alps, where undivided land inheritance was generally practised.

This would seem to confirm the view that populations facing similar ecological problems are ultimately forced, whatever their cultural and legal traditions, to converge on similar demographic solutions. However, such a generalization is in its turn challenged by the surprisingly high levels of nuptiality recorded in many parts of the Western Alps well before the inception of birth control – a finding which is all the more surprising if we consider that nuptiality was highest in the Provençal-speaking valleys, which are believed to have shared with the rest of Provence a custom of 'preferential legacy' akin to impartibility. The case of the Western Alps shows, therefore, that the marriage patterns observed in the Alpine area cannot easily be explained by either inheritance customs or environmental constraints. This realization has important implications for the study of family formation and calls for a reassessment of the various models of the Alpine household proposed by historians, geographers and, more explicitly, social anthropologists.

Competing models of household structure in the Alps go back, in anthropology, to the early 1960s. As we have seen, in 1962 Wolf had reported that the two villages of the Eastern Alps where he had conducted his research, though sharing the same ecological setting, had contrasting inheritance customs and, consequently, divergent forms of family organization: impartible inheritance and a stem family system in German-speaking St Felix, partibility and nuclear families in the neighbouring Romance community of Tret. This contrast in inheritance and family forms was, for Wolf, a local manifestation of 'a cultural contrast between populations with Germanic traditions and those of Mediterranean cultural provenance'.[3] But only one year later, in 1963, Burns contended that a predominance of single-heir inheritance and stem family organization was to be expected all over the Alps, because in mountain areas the quantity of family land was rarely if ever capable of supporting more than one household, and its subdivision would therefore be inevitably disastrous.[4]

A common feature of these two models is that inheritance and household composition are viewed as two sides of the same coin, but they differ markedly in the relative weight assigned to culture and

[3] See Wolf, 'Cultural dissonance', and 'Inheritance of land', p. 103.
[4] Burns, 'The Circum-Alpine area', p. 143.

environment. It is worth noting that Burns's perception of the question was obviously influenced by his fieldwork experience in Saint-Véran, a Provençal-speaking village in the French Alps. Both legal and social historians have emphasized that in the south of France the prevalence of Roman law allowed fathers to dispose of as large a part of their patrimonies as they liked by making a will. Fathers were thus able to fight fragmentation by favouring one child, who would succeed to the headship of the parental house and inherit virtually the whole of the family land.[5] An anthropologist of 'diffusionist' persuasion would have concluded that the stem family system found in Saint-Véran had its bases in the legal traditions of Provence. Instead, Burns boldly presented Saint-Véran and its family system as representative of a distinctively Alpine culture area, whose unity derived from the environmental constraints which are typical of mountainous regions.

The trouble with both Wolf's and Burns's arguments was that the evidence offered by the literature and by their own field researches was essentially 'qualitative' and sometimes utterly impressionistic. The limitations of a purely qualitative approach became evident to social anthropologists when, at roughly the same time as family historians, they began to count and measure the domestic groups of the communities where their fieldwork was carried out. This is most strikingly demonstrated by the developments of Wolf and Cole's study of St Felix and Tret. A census of all households revealed that in St Felix the proportion of stem families was surprisingly low – only 9.2 per cent. There were good reasons to believe that in the past stem families had been more frequent. But in the mid-1960s they were, ironically, slightly less numerous than in Tret. What is more, Cole and Wolf discovered that for over one hundred years nuptiality had been as low in Tret as in St Felix. And further research showed that, contrary to the expectation that partibility should result in greater land fragmentation, the size of the holdings was more or less the same in both villages.[6]

This rather disconcerting finding led Wolf and Cole to conclude that, in those mountain areas where custom prescribed the division of property, the ecological imperative of maintaining viable estates created an endemic contradiction between the ideology and the practice of inheritance. Such a contradiction could be resolved only by family strategies which aimed at the elimination of all but one of the potential heirs and cumulatively produced, so to speak, a system

---

[5] See e.g. Le Roy Ladurie, 'Structures familiales', pp. 840–3, and Flandrin, *Familles*, pp. 75–81.
[6] Cole and Wolf, *The hidden frontier*, pp. 202, 234–6.

of impartible inheritance in disguise. This explained why in a village like Tret marriage had been so late and infrequent, and it could be surmised (as a corollary of the general argument) that in the past stem families had been the prevailing residential arrangement in Tret no less than in St Felix. Though rather more flexible and sophisticated because of its 'strategic' component, Cole and Wolf's ingenious reasoning eventually came to provide influential support to the ecological argument first advocated by Burns.

It should be noticed that both Burns and, subsequently, Cole and Wolf regarded the viability of the estates to be the crucial goal of mountain peasantry and, indirectly, the critical determinant of family structure. Yet, a quite different but equally plausible ecological theory of household formation might be advanced. A characteristic feature of mountain farming, as has been repeatedly stressed in this book, is the unusually delicate balance between tillage and stock-raising, and the consequent need to tend carefully both the animals in the alps and the fields situated at lower altitudes. Moreover, in order to minimize the risks of complete crop failure and secure a fairly constant annual yield, it is common practice to scatter tiny plots in locations of varying microclimatic condition. It seems legitimate to deduce that such a spatial dispersion of resources requires a sizable number of people working together as a productive unit. This, in turn, should be expected to encourage the formation of households containing relatives beyond the nuclear family, or even of large joint family households where two or more married couples live together.

This argument is, in fact, almost a commonplace among anthropologists who have worked in mountain areas as diverse as the Andes and the uplands of Japan.[7] In Alpine studies, however, it can be found in the work of some geographers,[8] but has been curiously ignored by most anthropologists. The only notable exception is an article published in 1979, where Saunders presented the results of his own fieldwork and provided a useful survey of the ethnographic literature produced in the previous fifteen years. As we have briefly seen in Chapter 4, Saunders subscribes to Burns's contention that the stem family was dominant throughout the Alps. But he also attempts to reconcile Burns's emphasis on land scarcity with a recognition of the significance of labour requirements as a determinant of

---

[7] See e.g. Befu, 'Ecology, residence and authority', p. 29, and Webster, 'Native pastoralism', p. 124.
[8] See Cholley, *Les Préalpes de Savoie*, pp. 399–400; and more recently Siddle and Jones, 'Family household structures', p. 29.

household composition. Of all household forms, the stem family would be, for Saunders, the one best adapted to the Alpine environment, because on the one hand it commanded a larger labour force than the nuclear family, but on the other it was smaller than the joint family and did not put undue pressure on the family land, which he assumes to have been invariably in short supply.[9]

A major implication of this model is that systems of household formation other than the one generating stem families would be ecologically 'maladaptive', and therefore unlikely to have existed in the Alps. But a few recent anthropological studies suggest that the Alpine area displayed a greater variety of family forms than intimated by Saunders. Although the authors have failed to provide conclusive evidence, two cases of joint family system have been reported for the Valtellina, in the Italian Central Alps, and for the Fersina Valley, the German-speaking district in the Trentino region which has been mentioned several times in preceding chapters.[10] Furthermore, the existence of a system of simple household formation has been solidly documented by Netting for nineteenth-century Törbel.

The merits of Netting's study of household dynamics in Törbel have already been discussed at some length.[11] But it is relevant to add that it demonstrates, among other things, that in the Alps the problem of maintaining viable estates could have more than one solution. It is a *leit-motiv* of Alpine anthropology that in the mountains a viable homestead must include a finely balanced combination of meadowland, pastures, woodland and ploughland, and that single-heir inheritance acts to preserve this optimal ecological combination, which would be threatened by subdivision.[12] The example of Törbel shows that, if the process of inheritance was sufficiently flexible and mechanisms of land consolidation were at hand, a system of bilateral partibility could prove as effective as one of strict impartibility, and the formation of neolocal independent households was no threat.

Nevertheless, Netting's study raises a number of questions. Once it is accepted that a newly married couple could command sufficient resources to establish an independent household, it still remains to be clarified, for instance, how they managed to meet the demanding labour requirements of mountain farming. Furthermore, in Törbel marriage was late and the proportion of people never marrying very

---

[9] Saunders, 'Social change', pp. 210–11.
[10] On the Valtellina, see Benetti *et al., Uomini delle Alpi*, pp. 17–109; on the Fersina Valley, Sellan, 'Système familial', p. 49.
[11] See Chapter 4 above, pp. 97–8.
[12] See especially Wolf, *Peasants*, p. 75.

high. This is a precious indication that low nuptiality was not necessarily either the cause or the effect of a stem family pattern. But it would also seem to confirm that for Alpine populations, whatever the system of household formation, a strict control over nuptiality remained inescapable. Yet we have seen that in some parts of the Alps nuptiality could be relatively high, which suggests that the dominant views about the interaction between ecology, demography and family formation need to be reconsidered. In the following sections of this chapter an attempt will therefore be made to explore, however tentatively, the relations between household structure and such variables as nuptiality, marital fertility, emigration, and the social organization of mountain farming. Before tackling these issues, however, it will be useful to supplement the scanty quantitative information on household composition provided by the anthropological literature with the data which have recently emerged from the analysis of historical sources. And we shall start from the area for which such data are at present more copiously available, namely the Western Alps.

Family forms in the Western Alps

It is indeed appropriate to start our survey from the Western Alps, for some of the most influential studies of Alpine family structure come from this region. Saint-Véran and 'Valbella', the two villages where Burns and Saunders conducted their anthropological fieldwork, are both located in the southern ranges of the Western Alps. And also in the Western Alps lies the community of Saint-André-les-Alpes, whose inheritance and family system has been minutely examined by the French historian Alain Collomp and is widely regarded as one of the clearest instances of stem family organization in the historical and ethnographic literature. In a long series of studies focussed on the years between 1640 and 1793, Collomp has argued that various strategies were pursued by the inhabitants of this village in the mountains of Haute-Provence to prevent or reduce the fragmentation of family property and has emphasized the role of the Provençal custom of 'preferential legacy'. Fathers, he reports, 'chose one of their children, invariably a son if there was at least one male inheritor, and most frequently the oldest, and made him "the inheritor of the house". He would marry and stay with his wife and children under the parental roof.'[13] It is worth noting that one of the stated aims both of

---

[13] Collomp, 'Tensions, dissentions, and ruptures', p. 151.

Collomp's earlier publications[14] and of Saunders's 1979 article was to test (and reject) the controversial 'null hypothesis' put forward by Peter Laslett, who had stressed the methodological necessity of assuming that family organization had always and invariably been nuclear unless the contrary could be proven.[15] Saunders had been fortunate enough to find in 'Valbella' a village census taken in 1905, and had discovered that extended and multiple households accounted for no less than 29 per cent of all households.[16] This finding has since been confirmed by a more recent anthropological study of Festiona, a large settlement belonging to the commune of 'Valbella'. As we have briefly seen in Chapter 4, Adriana Destro's analysis of a listing of 1877 has established that in that year nearly 26 per cent of Festiona's 232 households were either extended or multiple.[17]

Collomp's researches on Saint-André, on the other hand, are not based on census-like sources (which are unfortunately unavailable for the period 1640–1793) but on notarial records. These records can nevertheless be subjected to some degree of quantitative analysis, which indicates that complex households in which a married son lived with his parents must have been very numerous. In addition, Collomp has been able to find and analyse four eighteenth-century listings from as many communities in the uplands of Provence, and in all cases the proportion of complex households turns out to be very high indeed: 41.7 per cent in the village of Saint-Martin-Vésubie (1718), 42.5 per cent in Mirabeau (1745), 41.4 per cent in Péone (1787) and 41.8 per cent in Guillaumes (1788).[18]

The impression that in the Western Alps complex households represented a very common residential arrangement is further reinforced by what we know of household composition in a number of other localities, including Montmin, Entracque, Pontechianale and Alagna, the four communities whose nuptiality pattern has been examined in some detail in the last chapter. It is unfortunate that no listing is available for Montmin in the period covered by the family reconstitution study, which extends from 1613 to 1792, but a listing compiled in 1832 records a proportion of complex households as high as 37.3 per cent. Remarkably, a listing also survives for 1561, and the proportion of complex households which can be estimated for that year is

---

[14] See Collomp, 'Famille nucléaire et famille élargie', and 'Ménage et famille'.
[15] Laslett, 'Preface', p. xi.
[16] Saunders, 'Social change', pp. 222–9.
[17] Destro, *L'ultima generazione*, pp. 111–23.
[18] See Collomp, 'Ménage et famille', p. 785, and 'From stem family to nuclear family', p. 72.

Table 9.1. *Household composition in Alagna 1734–1980*

Year	Population	Number of households	MHS	1	2	3	4	5	4+5
1734	890	189	4.71	14.3	9.0	42.8	19.6	14.3	33.9
1738	835	188	4.44	13.8	8.5	47.9	16.0	13.8	29.8
1749	845	184	4.59	10.9	6.0	50.0	19.0	14.1	33.1
1760	822	172	4.78	11.0	7.6	48.3	15.7	17.4	33.1
1764	906	197	4.60	12.7	6.1	45.2	20.8	15.2	36.0
1778	887	184	4.82	6.5	7.1	52.2	16.3	17.9	34.2
1788	872	199	4.38	10.6	5.5	46.7	19.6	17.6	37.2
1833	740	182	4.07	14.8	4.9	51.1	14.3	14.8	29.1
1838	728	179	4.07	12.8	6.7	48.6	15.1	16.8	31.9
1841	705	175	4.03	15.4	7.4	44.0	14.9	18.3	33.2
1848	688	188	3.66	17.0	6.4	48.4	16.0	12.2	28.2
1879	634	162	3.91	13.0	3.7	53.7	15.4	14.2	29.6
1935	499	167	2.99	20.5	9.0	56.0	10.8	3.6	14.4
1980	428	161	2.66	28.9	4.4	62.9	2.5	1.3	3.8

Key: MHS = mean household size; type 1 = solitaries; type 2 = no-family households; type 3 = simple-family households; type 4 = extended-family households; type 5 = multiple-family households.
Note: For details on the household typology, see note to Table 4.9.
Sources: 1734–1935: APA, *Libri status animarum*. 1980: my own census.

strikingly similar: 38.1 per cent.[19] Proportions remain very high when we turn to the Piedmontese side of the Western Alps, for we find that in 1730 about one-quarter of the households of Entracque were either extended or multiple and that these two types accounted for 40 per cent of Pontechianale's households in 1826. Finally, as Table 9.1 shows, the long-term persistence of high proportions of complex households is impressively demonstrated, for Alagna, by a rich series of *status animarum*.

It would be unwarranted to draw definite conclusions from figures which only refer to a handful of villages and are mostly derived from cross-sectional analyses of single listings. Nevertheless, they strongly suggest that up to the early twentieth century the social structure of a large number of upland communities in the Western Alps was characterized by proportions of complex households ranging from

[19] Jones, 'Extending the family'.

perhaps 25 to 40–45 per cent.[20] It may be interesting to observe, by way of comparison, that, in the sample of 30 English pre-industrial communities used by Laslett and Wachter, proportions ranged from nought to 25 or at most 28 per cent.[21] No less importantly, the overwhelming majority of complex households in England were of the 'extended' type. In the Western Alps, by contrast, the proportion of multiple households was considerable, which indicates that co-residence of married children with members of the parental generation was widespread.

However, high proportions of complex households are still no proof that the stem family was the dominant type, for they might well be the product not so much of a stem family system as of a joint family system in which two or more married sons were allowed to stay in the parents' household – Le Play's 'patriarchal family'. This is a major ambiguity, and it should be realized that in the Western Alps these two systems of household formation can prove difficult to distinguish from one another, particularly when listings happen to be the only reliable sources. It is relevant to note, in this respect, that Hajnal has recently argued that two essential characters of joint family systems are represented by an early age at first marriage for both sexes and by a pronounced tendency for newly married couples to start life together in a household in which members of the parental generation are in charge.[22] These two criteria are in fact sufficient to distinguish clearly a joint family system from the system found in most parts of north-western Europe or in an Alpine locality like Törbel (where marriage was late and entailed the formation of a new household) but not from the stem family system which allegedly prevailed in the Western Alps. Burns, Saunders and Collomp have all stressed

[20] Data on household composition are, to my knowledge, available for about twenty communities of the Western Alps. In addition to the localities that have just been mentioned, proportions of complex households generally ranging between 25 and 40 per cent (but sometimes exceeding 50 per cent) have also been documented for Chevaline and Entrevernes, two small villages in the vicinity of Montmin, and on the Piedmontese side for Prali, Mussello, Sambuco and two pre-Alpine communities in the district of Biella (Mosso and Rongio di Masserano). See Jones, 'Extending the family'; Ravis Giordani, 'Introduction'; Ramella, 'Famiglia, terra e salario'; and the results of unpublished research by D. Albera on Sambuco and Rongio di Masserano. Apart from Törbel (which is located, like Alagna, in the zone of transition between the Western and the Central Alps), the only exception is paradoxically represented by Saint-André-les-Alpes, where a listing of 1836 records only a proportion of 9.9 per cent. However, Collomp advances a number of reasons which plausibly suggest that in the first decades of the nineteenth century the household structure of Saint-André had undergone substantial changes and had acquired rather atypical features. See Collomp, 'From stem family to nuclear family', pp. 74–80.

[21] Laslett *et al.*, 'English evidence on household structure', pp. 70–1.

[22] Hajnal, 'Two kinds of household formation', pp. 68–72.

that fathers retained authority within their houses until old age, most often until their death, and that marriage was in no way timed to coincide with the heir's succession to headship.[23]

This is not to say that this variant of the stem family system (which is usually termed 'patricentric' by anthropologists)[24] can be classified as a joint family system. It is a distinctive feature of joint family systems that new households are normally produced by fission, a mechanism which is incompatible with a stem family system. Moreover, in a population exhibiting a stem family system the cohabitation of two or more married sons can only be attributed to anomalous and temporary circumstances. Under a joint family system, by contrast, this is the pattern of co-residence that all domestic groups whose growth is not affected by adverse demographic, economic or physical factors should be expected to display at some point. But it is well known that, even if we leave aside other kinds of constraints, demography alone can drastically limit the frequency with which joint families occur and the length of time during which they remain in a joint phase, and consequently the incidence of joint families appearing in a listing.[25]

Since stem and joint family systems can generate very similar distributions of household types, the problems of interpretation raised by a listing are potentially quite serious. Nevertheless, the ideological foundations of the two systems (as well as their supposed ecological rationales) remain very different, and the central importance assigned to the stem family by some prominent students of Alpine social structure certainly justifies the effort of further investigating this issue. The evidence is scanty, but certain relevant points can be usefully clarified by examining in some detail the cases of Saint-André-les-Alpes and Alagna.

Stem and joint family systems: two case-studies

Most of those who have studied societies where extended and multiple family households were frequently encountered, have tended to play down the significance of proportions of nuclear families which, though lower than in north-western Europe, could still be substantial. (In

---

[23] Burns, 'The Circum-Alpine area', p. 144; Saunders, 'Social change', pp. 213–22; Collomp, 'Tensions, dissentions, and ruptures', p. 151.

[24] See Goldschmidt and Kunkel, 'The structure of the peasant family', p. 1073. This form of stem family is substantially different from the stem family practices analysed by Arensberg and Kimball for Ireland and by Berkner for a lowland region of Austria, where the heir was allowed to marry only on the retirement of the father. Cf. Arensberg and Kimball, *Family and community in Ireland*, pp. 122–44, and Berkner, 'Stem family and developmental cycle'.

[25] See Wheaton, 'Family and kinship', pp. 614–15.

most of the Western Alpine communities surveyed in the preceding section, for example, nuclear families accounted for about 50 per cent or more of all households at any point in time.) The 'synchronic' dominance of nuclear families has generally been dismissed as simply a result of the mortality of parents, and it has been assumed that the formation of new households at marriage was a rare or even exceptional event. This is, however, an assumption which requires testing, if the ecological and demographic correlates of stem and joint family systems are to be more correctly understood.

Collomp's well-known analysis of all the 1,254 marriage contracts drawn up in Saint-André between 1638 and 1792 is, in this respect, very instructive. The result of his painstaking investigation was that 568 of these contracts envisaged the newly married couple living together with the parents of one of the spouses, and that in the case of the 686 couples who did not live under the parental roof, three-quarters of the bridegrooms had lost their fathers before the marriage took place and could not, therefore, live with them.[26] These figures leave little doubt that the majority of couples, if it were not for demographic constraints, would start their married life in a complex family household. But it is also clear that neolocal marriages did occur, and accounted for perhaps one-quarter of all marriages.

This is by no means a negligible proportion, and in his more recent papers Collomp has indeed increasingly recognized the importance of neolocality. By reconstructing horizontal genealogies, he has often been able to gain information about all the children in a group of brothers, and the impression he has received is that when a father or a widowed mother had several sons to marry off, they did their best to enable all of them to marry and settle in the village. As an example of what he calls the 'fairness' of the system, Collomp quotes the case of a widow who 'settled the two eldest sons at Saint-André in their own houses, while she lived with the third with a patrimony probably much reduced by the gifts she had made'.[27]

We have already noticed that in the stem family system of the Provençal Alps, as described by Collomp as well as by Burns and Saunders, marriage was not timed to coincide with succession to headship. Heirs could therefore marry at a relatively early age. Indeed, if Collomp is correct in his estimates of marriage age in Haute-Provence, before 1800 men married on average at 25 years and women at 22.[28] But another major demographic consequence of the 'fairness'

---

[26] Collomp, 'Alliance et filiation', p. 445.
[27] Collomp, 'Tensions, dissentions, and ruptures', p. 157.
[28] Collomp, 'From stem family to nuclear family', p. 79.

of this system was a low rate of permanent celibacy, both at the local and at the regional level. 'In Haute-Provence, there were no bachelors, at least until the end of the eighteenth century, the only exceptions being those unable to marry because of some physical or mental defect, and even deaf-mutes married.'[29]

Thus, as Collomp himself concludes, 'eighteenth-century Haute-Provence was unlike other preferential legacy regions at the time in which the eldest son kept the bulk of his parents' estate and the younger one (and even his sisters) was sacrificed, being condemned to celibacy and working for his father and then for his eldest brother'.[30] This goes a long way towards explaining one puzzling feature of Alpine demography, namely the seemingly paradoxical co-existence in the Western Alps of early and almost universal marriage with inheritance customs which are generally believed to depress nuptiality. Moreover, Collomp's evidence – and in particular cases like that of the widow who married off her two eldest sons and lived with the third – shows that the formation of stem families might have been due to welfare reasons as much as to inheritance strategies fighting the fragmentation of the patrimony.

Finally, it is not even certain that the set of rules governing household formation in Saint-André can be uncompromisingly described as a stem family system. One of the drawbacks of the study of marriage contracts is that it is difficult, or utterly impossible, to define the composition of the domestic groups. A contract informs us that a newly married couple agreed to live together with the parents of one of the spouses, but is usually silent about the other members of the household. A crucial question is therefore left without a definite answer: 'Le choix du père se limite-t-il à un seul de ses fils pour demeurer avec lui après mariage?.... Certes quelques contrats sont, dans ce sens, privilégiés: par exemple les deux fils d'un "ménager" épousant le même jour deux soeurs et restant vivre tous deux en communauté avec leur père.'[31]

The only way of investigating this question in a systematic manner is to turn to census-like sources. Though regrettably lacking in Saint-André, listings are available for other communities on both sides of the Western Alps. The next few pages will thus present some of the evidence emerging from these sources, and special consideration will be given to the case of Alagna, which I have been able to study more comprehensively. A full analysis of the system of household formation

[29] Collomp, 'Tensions, dissentions, and ruptures', p. 157.
[30] Collomp, 'Tensions, dissentions, and ruptures', p. 157.
[31] Collomp, 'Famille nucléaire et famille élargie', p. 973.

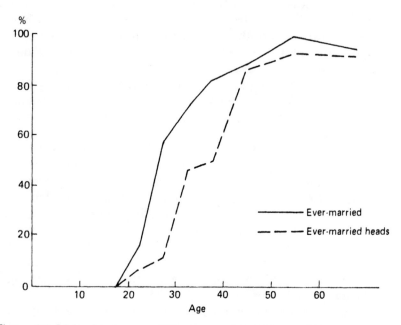

Figure 9.1 Males by age, marital status and headship position in Alagna, 1838

in Alagna would inevitably plunge us into a morass of details and is clearly beyond the scope of this chapter. But a number of issues can be tested or illustrated adequately by focussing on a single listing, the *status animarum* of 1838, which offers a valuable vantage point partly because of its very good quality and partly because it can be collated with other listings compiled in the same period.

A simple but effective way of expressing the relation between nuptiality and family formation has recently been proposed by Hajnal and consists in plotting the rate of ever-married men and that of ever-married male heads of households by age group.[32] Figure 9.1 shows that although in the first half of the nineteenth century the mean age at first marriage of Alagna's men was rather late – just over 27 years[33] – marriage hardly coincided with the attainment of headship. This implies that neolocal marriages must have been infrequent. But

[32] Hajnal, 'Two kinds of household formation', pp. 85–6.
[33] The mean age at first marriage for the period 1801–50 established through family reconstitution is almost exactly the same as the 'singulate mean age at marriage' estimated on the basis of the *status animarum* of 1838: 27.05 and 27.10 years respectively.

Table 9.2. *Married men aged 20–39 by household type in Alagna, 1838*

Age group	'Simple'		'Extended'		'Multiple'		Total	
	N	%	N	%	N	%	N	%
20–9	2	9.1	1	4.5	19	86.4	22	100.0
30–9	9	30.0	9	30.0	12	40.0	30	100.0

Source: APA, *Status animarum* of 1838.

a more precise estimate of the incidence of neolocality can be obtained by distributing married men by age group and household type. This gives a quick but useful impression both of residence at marriage and, at the same time, of the effects of the mortality of parents in the course of the developmental cycle of the various households. The results of this exercise are presented in Table 9.2 and confirm that neolocal marriages were in fact exceedingly rare.[34]

However, further refinements are possible. If we consider more closely the 52 married men aged from 20 to 39 years living in Alagna in 1838, we discover that they included one husband from the neighbouring village of Riva Valdobbia (who is described as a plasterer and lived in an extended household with his wife and his mother-in-law) and five second-generation immigrants belonging to what we have termed the 'sub-community' of miners. Interestingly, of these five men, three lived in simple family households. Although their number is very small, it is tempting to surmise that for the members of this 'sub-community' neolocal marriage and residence in nuclear families were a more common experience than among the rest of the population. It seems no accident that these three men had all established independent households while their fathers were still alive.

This may have been due to the fact that miners were landless wage-earners and that their families did not constitute work-groups. Or, more probably, to the fact that most miners could only afford to live in small tenements. Be that as it may, if we exclude the immigrant miners and take into account only the 46 local men, the rarity of neolocal marriages comes out even more clearly. As Table 9.3 demonstrates, the proportion of young couples spending the first years of their married life outside multiple households was negligible. But a more vivid perception of the dynamics of household formation can be gained by examining the case of two of the eight local men under 40 years

[34] The distribution is exactly the same for women: 86.7 per cent of all married women aged 15 to 24 years lived in multiple households, while the proportion dropped to 40 per cent for those aged 25 to 34 years.

Table 9.3. *Local married men aged 20–39 by household type in Alagna, 1838*

Age group	'Simple' N	%	'Extended' N	%	'Multiple' N	%	Total N	%
20–9	1	5.3	0	0.0	18	94.7	19	100.0
30–9	7	25.9	8	29.6	12	44.4	27	99.9

Source: See Table 9.2.

of age who headed a nuclear family: the brothers Cristoforo and Antonio Ferraris.

Cristoforo and Antonio belonged to an unusually large set of brothers,[35] and in 1833 they lived (as shown by Figure 9.2) in a very complex household containing three married brothers. By 1838, however, this household had spawned three nuclear families. The split had presumably been triggered by the marriage of two more brothers: Antonio, who moved to a house owned by his wife, and Lorenzo, who brought his wife into the parental household. Finally, we see that in 1841 Lorenzo himself has established an independent household. But he has been replaced, so to speak, by Pietro, and the parental household remains therefore in a 'joint' phase marked by the co-residence of at least two married brothers.

This 'diachronic' close-up reveals that five out of six brothers started their married life in a multiple household and confirms that for the cohort of men born in the late eighteenth and early nineteenth centuries neolocal marriage was a very uncommon experience. But we may wonder how representative the case of the Ferraris family was, in other respects, of Alagna's system of household formation. It is important to observe, on the one hand, that the timing of fission apparently departed from the normal pattern, for, if we consider all the local married men whose fathers were still alive, we find that in 1838 the three brothers Giuseppe, Cristoforo and Antonio Ferraris were the only ones to head independent nuclear families. All the others either lived with their fathers or had married uxorilocally and lived in complex households with their wives' relatives. It would seem that the very size of the Ferraris family was the cause of the early fission of some brothers. Otherwise, a strong tendency for fission not to take place before the death of the father can be detected throughout the series of *status animarum*, at least until the mid-nineteenth

---

[35] Giovanni Ferraris had nine children, and all six sons survived to maturity. Of the three daughters, two had already died in 1833, whereas the third had left the parental household at marriage.

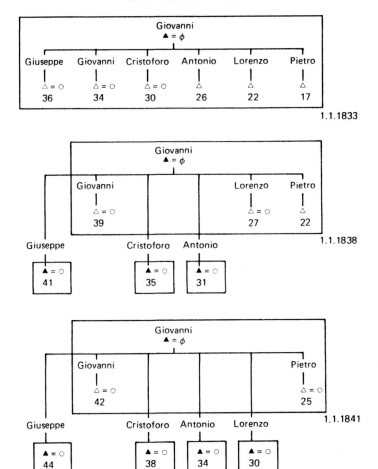

Figure 9.2 The household of Giovanni Ferraris and its fission, 1833–1841

century. In 1738, for instance, a certain Petrus Prato was the only man in Alagna to head a nuclear family while his father was still alive, and to denote his highly unusual condition he is designated in the listing as *'filius separatus'*.[36]

There is little doubt, on the other hand, that the case of the Ferraris family illustrates a widespread tendency towards the formation of

[36] The usage of the term 'separated' to mark out the rare cases of sons heading independent households while their father was still alive is also reported for the village of Guillaumes in the 1780s by Collomp, 'From stem family to nuclear family', p. 73. It should be noticed that in Alagna these cases became less rare in the second half of the nineteenth century (as indicated by the *status animarum* of 1879) and were the rule by 1935.

Table 9.4. *Number and proportion of joint family households in Alagna*
1734–1980

Year	N of joint households	% of all households	% of all multiple households
1734	6	3.2	22.2
1738	5	2.7	19.2
1749	4	2.2	15.4
1760	11	6.4	36.7
1764	10	5.1	33.3
1778	9	4.9	27.3
1788	6	3.0	17.1
1833	4	2.2	14.8
1838	6	3.4	20.0
1841	9	5.1	28.1
1848	3	1.6	13.0
1879	3	1.9	13.0
1935	0	0.0	0.0
1980	0	0.0	0.0

Sources: See Table 9.1.

joint households. Table 9.4 shows that although their number and proportion could undergo substantial variations from one census to another, as might be expected from a small community, instances of joint family households are recorded by all the *status animarum* before 1935. (There are, incidentally, 10 cases of households containing three or more married brothers.) To be sure, the proportion of joint households is never very high, but this is hardly surprising in view of the severe constraints imposed by Alagna's demography. Mortality was relatively mild: it can be estimated that between 1700 and 1850 at least two-thirds of all males survived to maturity, and those who reached marriageable age still had a favourable life expectancy. But the mean number of children per couple was, even before the sharp decline of the first half of the nineteenth century, fairly modest. Consequently, it cannot be expected that a large proportion of couples should have produced more than one son surviving to the age of marriage. Moreover, some of the 'surplus' sons married into households without male heirs or left the village as permanent emigrants. Finally, and perhaps most crucially, in Alagna marriage was rather late and a sizable number of men remained celibate.

All in all, the low-pressure demographic regime of Alagna greatly limited the 'visibility' of joint households. Estimates are very arduous.

But it seems safe to state that if fission had always taken place at the death of the father, as is the case with many joint family systems, then the incidence of this household form in the listings would have been even lower.[37] In Alagna, however, there was a distinct tendency for two or more married sons not to split as long as at least one parent was still alive. The death of the surviving parent often precipitated the fission of the household, but it was not infrequent that married brothers decided to stay together for a few more years or, in some cases, even for decades. About 35 per cent of all instances of joint family are in fact *frérèches*.[38]

In a different but no less important perspective, it should finally be stressed that the experience of spending the first years of their marriage in a joint family household was shared by the majority of Alagna's younger couples. In 1838, over half of all married men under 30 years of age and their wives lived in joint families, and the proportion easily exceeded two-thirds in 1760. It seems therefore legitimate to conclude that the system of household formation found in Alagna was unmistakably a joint family system. This is an interesting conclusion for more than one reason. It suggests, first of all, that an early age at marriage, though obviously very important to maximize the number of co-resident couples, is not as essential to the definition of a joint family system as the other criteria set by Hajnal: the virtual absence of neolocality; a rule allowing two or more married sons to stay in the parental households; and fission as the only mechanism leading to the formation of new households. Secondly, the case of Alagna shows that contrary to what is usually maintained in the anthropological literature,[39] a pattern of bilateral partible inheritance is not incompatible with the formation of patrilocal joint families. Thirdly, the evidence from Alagna provides an empirical demonstration that caution is needed before attributing the high proportions of complex households recorded in several communities of the Western Alps to the predominance of a stem family system.

It is of course still impossible to know how frequently systems of household formation similar to that of Alagna were encountered in

[37] If we apply eighteenth-century Alagna's nuptiality and mortality parameters (SMAM = 28 years; e_{28} = 32) to the set of rules and assumptions adopted by Wheaton, 'Family and kinship', pp. 614–15, and further assume that all families were wealthy enough to support a joint family arrangement, the expected proportion of households in a joint phase recorded in a census is only 1.56 per cent.

[38] In only 12 of the 76 cases of joint family recorded by the *status animarum* were both father and mother still alive. In 14 cases (18.4 per cent) only the father survived, and in 23 cases (30.3 per cent) only the mother. The other 27 cases (35.5 per cent) were *frérèches*.

[39] See Goldschmidt and Kunkel, 'The structure of the peasant family'.

the Western Alps. But it is most likely that a joint family system existed in Montmin. It is relevant to note that in 1925 a serious and perceptive scholar like Cholley asserted that in the part of Savoy where Montmin is located, the social structure of upland communities had been traditionally dominated by large 'patriarchal families'. The persistence of this form of domestic organization, he argued, had been favoured by the advantages enjoyed by joint families in meeting the labour requirements of mixed mountain farming.[40] The preliminary data on Montmin and other villages of Savoy published a few years ago by Siddle and Jones, and the more detailed information recently made available for two hamlets of Montmin, certainly appear to corroborate this claim.[41]

As for the Provençal Alps, it is at least possible to observe that the interpretation of census data, if it is difficult for the historical demographer, can prove no easier for the anthropologist, even when these data refer to a comparatively recent past. We have seen that archival research carried out by both Saunders and Destro has established that towards the turn of the nineteenth century the Provençal-speaking village of 'Valbella', in the Piedmontese Alps, displayed high proportions of complex households. But Saunders's contention that the stem family was the dominant pattern is contradicted by Destro's ethnographic analysis of inheritance and family formation practices.[42] And research still in progress on Sambuco, a village situated in the same valley, indicates that in the nineteenth century large joint families and *frérèches* were far from infrequent.[43]

The same is true of Entracque in 1730 and Pontechianale in 1826. Although the analysis of the listings hints at a slightly higher incidence of neolocality, in these two communities the system of household formation was apparently very similar to that of Alagna, as Figure 9.3 also suggests. It would be probably too much to turn the received wisdom upside down and deny that stem family systems existed in the Western Alps. Nevertheless, it is sufficiently clear that in Provençal-speaking communities like Entracque, Pontechianale, Sambuco and perhaps 'Valbella' itself the stem family hardly represented, to use Michel Verdon's notion, the 'limit of growth' of the domestic

---

[40] Cholley, *Les Préalpes de Savoie*, pp. 399–400.
[41] Cf. Siddle and Jones, 'Family household structures', pp. 14–21; Jones, 'Extending the family'; and Siddle, 'Grid of inheritance', p. 131.
[42] See Destro, *L'ultima generazione*, pp. 62–135, and Albera, 'Systèmes familiaux', pp. 8–14.
[43] The analysis of a census of 1858 by D. Albera has revealed a proportion of joint households comparable to those found in Alagna (3.8 per cent). Research is now being extended to other nineteenth-century listings.

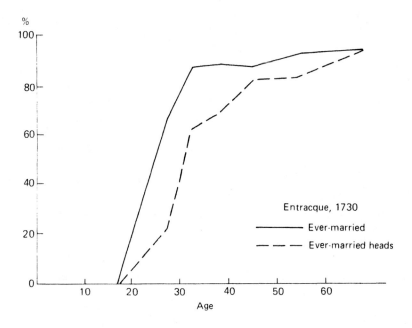

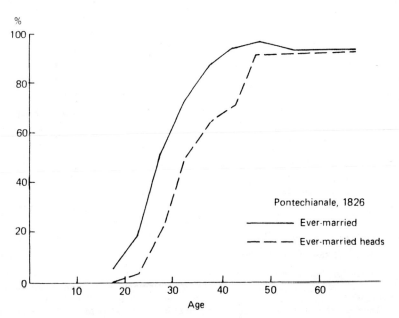

Figure 9.3 Males by age, marital status and headship position in Entracque (1730) and in Pontechianale (1826)

groups,[44] and that their systems of household formation are more accurately characterized as joint family systems.

'Hungarian' patterns in the Alps?

In 1963 Robert Burns claimed that one distinguishing feature of the Alpine culture area was the dominance of the stem family, which stood 'in marked contrast to the joint family of the Mediterranean'.[45] The evidence presented in the previous section shows, on the contrary, that in the Western Alps joint families did exist. And it will have been noticed that particularly in villages like Entracque, Pontechianale and Montmin, where nuptiality was very high, the total configuration comprising both the marriage pattern and the system of household formation is remarkably close to the 'Mediterranean' type, or tendency, as recently defined by Laslett and other writers.[46] At first glance, this might be regarded as an indication that the Western Alps were more heavily affected by Mediterranean influences than other parts of the Alps. But the not dissimilar case of Alemannic Alagna (and, probably, that of the Fersina Valley) is a warning that any theory phrased in broad cultural or ethnic terms is unlikely to prove successful, and also that more attention should be paid to a variable which has often been neglected by students of family forms, namely marital fertility.

Indeed, what makes the systems found in Entracque, Pontechianale and Montmin intriguingly similar to the one found in Alagna is not simply the tendency towards the formation of joint households but also the rather low fertility displayed by the couples residing in these joint households. Although the relations between fertility and family forms have been strangely neglected, as we have just noticed, some scholars have nonetheless argued that joint family organization tends, for a variety of reasons, to favour high fertility.[47] By contrast, in these Alpine villages a joint family system appears to be associated with low fertility, which suggests that this kind of family form could in fact depress fertility – or even that low fertility might be a precondition to the formation (and viability) of joint households.

In order to explore this set of questions, it is very useful to consider the similarities with the 'Hungarian' pattern which has become classic

[44] Cf. Verdon, 'Stem family', p. 91.
[45] Burns, 'The Circum-Alpine area', p. 143.
[46] Laslett, 'Family and household as work group', pp. 516–35. See also Macfarlane, 'Demographic structures'; Smith, 'People of Tuscany'; and Hajnal, 'Two kinds of household formation'.
[47] The classic statement of this argument is Davis, 'Institutional patterns', pp. 34–7.

in the historical-demographic literature thanks to the work of Rudolf Andorka and his associates. As Andorka and Faragó have shown, in the first half of the nineteenth century the Hungarian region of Transdanubia was characterized by a joint family system as well as by very early marriage and low celibacy rates. Perhaps the most interesting point made by the two Hungarian scholars is that 'contrary to the opinion expressed in demographic literature, the high proportion of extended and multiple households was correlated to a relatively low level of marital fertility'.[48] This correlation is explained, according to Andorka and Faragó, by a peasant strategy which allowed young people to marry and live in the parental household on the condition that marital fertility was kept low, so as to control the number of the members of the household and the ratio between producers and consumers. As we have seen in Chapter 8, marital fertility was relatively low also in Montmin, Entracque and Pontechianale, not to mention Alagna. Andorka and Faragó have no doubt that in the Hungarian villages of Transdanubia low fertility was due to the widespread early practice of birth control. In the Western Alps it might have been mainly due to prolonged lactation and to the effects of temporary and seasonal emigration,[49] but the similarity between the two systems remains impressive and instructive.

The case of Alagna actually invites some further considerations. One distinctive feature of the pattern of family limitation which Andorka and Faragó describe for Transdanubia is that low levels of fertility should already be expected in the first years of marriage, when young married couples are most likely to co-reside with members of the parental generation and to be under their authority.[50] What is remarkable in Alagna is that between 1801 and 1850 the fertility rates for the younger age intervals (15–19 and 20–4) did in fact drop to very low levels and that this was largely due to the steep increase in the mean length of the first birth interval among women married at less than 20 years of age, from 22.5 months in 1701–50 and 21.1 months in 1751–1800 to no less than 54.2 months in the first half of the nineteenth century. These very young brides, who were

---

[48] Andorka and Faragó, 'Pre-industrial household structure in Hungary', p. 306.

[49] In a recent discussion of the effects of seasonal and temporary emigration of men in the French Alps, Poitrineau, 'Aspects spécifiques', p. 114, has observed that 'leurs absences prolongées parfois par enjambement de plusieurs retours saisonniers (c'est souvent le cas pour les jeunes mariés) présente l'avantage, dans un contexte d'où la contraception est exclue, d'espacer les naissances et de réduire quelque peu la tension démographique'.

[50] As Andorka has remarked, this explains why the fertility curve cannot be expected to display a pronounced concavity. See Andorka, 'Un exemple de faible fecondité', p. 37.

obviously the ones most likely to spend a long period of their married life in the joint household headed by their parents-in-law, could therefore be expected to wait, on average, more than four years before having their first child. No less interestingly, the length of the first birth intervals declined with age and was shortest among brides of 30 years or more, whose chances of marrying men who had already attained household headship was greatest.[51] All this clearly suggests that in the first years of marriage the younger couples practised family control or, alternatively, that the younger husbands now tended to spend most of these years away from their family. In either case, it would seem that the relations between family forms and 'fertility strategies' deserve to be more carefully investigated than has been the case so far, and the joint families of the Alpine area are likely to prove a useful laboratory for the historical demographer.

Labour requirements and household composition

Once it has been established that in the Western Alps joint families did exist, it still remains to be explained why. Some of the reasons advanced by Andorka and Faragó for the Hungarian regions where this family form was particularly frequent are reminiscent of the arguments put forward by those anthropologists who have singled out labour requirements as the most powerful determinant of the formation of joint family households. The gist of these arguments is that joint families will tend to contain a larger number of adults of prime working age than other kinds of households, and that this will enable them to work the family estate without resorting to costly hired labour, to maintain larger herds, and so forth. In certain circumstances joint families will therefore possess several organizational advantages, and it has indeed been contended that these advantages should prove especially 'adaptive' in mountain areas, where a greater division of labour is needed to exploit varied types of land.

However, the general applicability of this reasoning to the Alps is immediately challenged by the existence of alternative forms of domestic organization such as the stem family and, most critically,

---

[51] In the 1801–50 period the mean length of the first birth interval declines from 54.2 months for the women married at 15 to 19 years of age (N = 18; s.d. = 33.3), to 26.6 months for those married at age 20 to 24 (N = 33; s.d. = 24.3), 20.6 months for those married at age 25 to 29 (N = 30; s.d. = 12.1), and 16.5 months for women married at 30 years or more (N = 10; s.d. = 14.0). This pattern is remarkably similar to the one reported for the Swedish parish of Alskog by D. Gaunt, 'Family planning', pp. 37–57, who also believes that the longer protogenesic intervals displayed by the younger brides is explained by pressures exerted by the parental generation.

the nuclear family system found by Netting in Törbel. This does not necessarily mean that anthropologists are wrong in expecting mountain farming and household structure to be functionally interdependent, but their models clearly need to be refined. And a useful first step in this direction is to pay attention to a variable whose relationship with family structure has not been so far systematically investigated.

It is an anthropological tenet that joint families are, to use Marshall Sahlins's words, 'adjusted to working spatially separated resources'.[52] On the other hand, as Sahlins himself has shown in his influential study of contrasting family patterns in Fiji, if resources are not spatially separated joint families have no real *raison d'être*. Alpine agro-pastoral systems provide extreme examples of spatial separation between crucial spheres of activity (the crop fields and the high-altitude pastures) and it is well known that the allocation of labour became highly problematic during the summer, when demand was greatest in both the agricultural and pastoral sectors. If the alps had to be individually managed by each family, then complex households appear to have been the only viable kind of family organization.[53] But there was, of course, the widespread alternative solution of having the animals communally tended by small teams of specialists, who relieved the whole community of a series of very time-consuming tasks.[54] It seems no accident that in Törbel, which offers the best-documented case of nuclear family organization in the Alpine region, animals were communally tended, whereas in localities like Alagna, Montmin, Entracque and Pontechianale the alps were individually managed.

This argument is, at present, very difficult to test, mainly because of the scarcity of quantitative evidence on family forms outside the Western Alps. But it is encouraging that the very few studies containing enough information seem to confirm that a correlation existed between household organization and modes of alp management. In Tarasp, a Romansh-speaking community of the Swiss Alps, four censuses spanning the period 1670–1834 reveal a preponderance of fairly small and structurally simple domestic groups, with proportions of extended and multiple households comparable to those found in nineteenth-century Törbel. And in Tarasp, as in Törbel, animals were tended by a small team of hired herdsmen.[55] By contrast, in the large Tyrolese village of Villgraten, where the alps were privately owned

[52] Sahlins, 'Land use and extended family', p. 461.
[53] Vincze, 'Peasant animal husbandry', p. 398.
[54] Netting, *Balancing on an alp*, pp. 64–5.
[55] See Mathieu, 'Haushalt, Verwandte und Nachbarn', pp. 168, 175–6, and *Bauern und Bären*, pp. 54–77, 134–40.

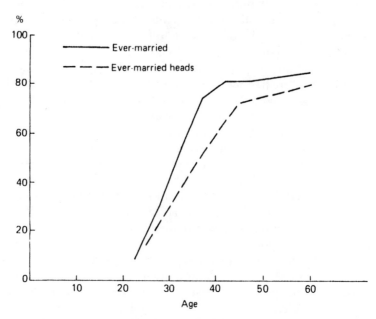

Figure 9.4 Males by age, marital status and headship position in Villgraten, 1781

and individually managed, the proportion of complex households was very high. A listing of 1781 shows that 21.6 per cent of all households were extended and 17.8 multiple, and there is little doubt that household formation closely approached Hajnal's joint family system. A first indication comes from Figure 9.4, which shows that in Villgraten marriage hardly coincided with the attainment of headship. No less significantly, the data recently published by Mitterauer and his associates, though still not providing a full picture, demonstrate that *frérèches* and households containing more than one married son were frequently recorded.[56]

Even when the cases of Tarasp and Villgraten are taken into account, the evidence remains too fragmentary to authorize any confident conclusion. What is more, the hypothesis that different family forms were correlated with different ways of managing pastoral resources brings us back to a classic riddle in Alpine ethnography and human geography, namely the identification of the causes of the highly irregular

---

[56] Schmidtbauer, 'Changing household', pp. 364–6; Mitterauer, 'Formen ländlicher Familienwirtschaft', pp. 209–13. The values plotted in Figure 9.4 have been estimated on the basis of the data provided by Schmidtbauer, 'Daten'.

geographical distribution of individual and communal alp management.[57] Nevertheless, this hypothesis is certainly worthy of further consideration. And the fact that a joint family system can be found at the heart of the Austrian Alps strengthens the suspicion that family forms which at first sight might look typically 'Mediterranean' may actually be rooted in the distinctive ecological features of the Alpine area.

If this attractive hypothesis is to be tested seriously, however, some of its underlying assumptions must be carefully scrutinized. While strongly suggesting the importance of alp management as a variable affecting labour requirements and household composition, the case of a village like Alagna is also a reminder that the ethnographic and demographic reality could be far more complex than students of upland societies have often assumed. For one thing, the contrast between the amount of labour commanded by domestic groups under a system of joint family formation and under other systems should not be exaggerated. The mean size of Alagna's households was fairly small, as we have seen from Table 9.1, and in the course of their developmental cycle most households passed through protracted nuclear phases. Secondly, agriculture and pastoralism were not the only economic activities in which Alpine populations could engage, as shown for instance by the enormous importance acquired by seasonal emigration in Alagna. It is obvious that in the Alps, and especially in those villages where men were away during the summer, the labour requirements of seasonal emigration interacted with those of mountain farming and could arguably be even more critical in shaping household structure.

In view of the common recognition that 'the ability to adjust to the migrants' absence is a crucial factor in the decision to migrate in the first place',[58] it is rather surprising that students of Alpine emigration have so far failed, to my knowledge, to test in any systematic way a number of claims which have been advanced about the degree of compatibility between migration and diverse forms of family organization. In particular, the finding that in rural areas all over the world migrants tend to come from large families has mostly been taken as evidence that complex households are better able than nuclear families to promote (or allow) emigration.[59] One anthropologist has indeed sharply asserted that heavy emigration 'is clearly not consistent with a social organization which stresses the nuclear family as the

[57] See Chapter 3 above, pp. 59–61.
[58] J. Connell *et al.*, *Migration from rural areas*, p. 47.
[59] J. Connell *et al.*, *Migration from rural areas*, pp. 45–7.

Table 9.5. *Number and proportion of temporary absents aged 15–49 by sex and household type in Alagna, 1788*

| Household type | Men | | Women | | % Absent | |
	Present	Absent	Present	Absent	Men	Women
'Simple'	33	38	84	4	53.5	4.5
'Extended'	14	25	46	2	64.1	4.2
'Multiple'	20	44	63	3	68.8	4.5

Note: These data refer only to households headed by people of local descent (N = 137)
Source: APA, *Status animarum* of 1788.

basic domestic group'.[60] For the historian of Alpine emigration, these claims are admittedly difficult to test, since the required information is generally lacking. But a few useful indications can be derived from those listings (unfortunately, only a minority) which mark out the villagers who were temporarily absent from the parish when the census was taken.

Of all the listings preserved in the parish archive of Alagna, the *status animarum* compiled in the summer of 1788 is the only one to furnish this vital piece of information. A first inspection quickly shows that seasonal emigrants tended to come from the larger and structurally more complex households: the mean size of the 96 households with at least one member listed as temporarily absent was 5.34, compared to only 3.49 for the 103 households unaffected by emigration; and nearly two-thirds of all emigrants came either from extended or from multiple households. Alagna was apparently no exception to the general trend. But it should be noted that in 1788 about 20 per cent of all households were headed by immigrant miners. More robust conclusions can therefore be reached by focussing only on the households headed by people of local descent, and also by excluding from our computation the weaker local households (types 1 and 2 in the Laslett-Hammel classificatory scheme), whose contribution to seasonal emigration was negligible.

The results of this finer-grained analysis are presented in Table 9.5, which brings out a smooth correlation between propensity to migrate and household complexity. Still, the possibility cannot be ruled out that such a correlation reflects not so much the better ability of complex households to cope with the migrants' absence as their tendency to contain a higher proportion of bachelors and young husbands. It is

---

[60] Solien de Gonzales, 'Family organization', p. 1274. For a similar claim, see Pasternak *et al.*, 'Conditions favouring extended family', p. 121.

Table 9.6. *Proportion of temporary absents among married men aged 30–49 by type of household in Alagna, 1788*

Household type	% absent	N present	N absent	Total
'Simple'	44.4	15	12	27
'Extended'	50.0	9	9	18
'Multiple'	60.0	8	12	20

Note: See Table 9.5.
Source: See Table 9.5.

Table 9.7. *Mean number of men and women aged 15–49 by household type in Alagna, 1788*

Household type	Men	Women	Total	Absent men	N households	MHS
'Simple'	1.01	1.26	2.27	0.54	70	4.27
'Extended'	1.11	1.37	2.48	0.71	35	4.80
'Multiple'	2.00	2.06	4.06	1.38	32	6.90

Note: See Table 9.5.
Source: See Table 9.5.

a well established point in the literature on emigration from rural areas that 'almost anywhere, migration concentrates extremely heavily on villagers aged 15–30',[61] and in Chapter 8 we have noticed that this was certainly true of Alagna, where bachelors also tended to migrate more frequently than married men. A simple way of removing this bias consists in restricting our attention to the older married men. This leaves us with quite small numbers. But the impression one receives from Table 9.6 is that married men living in nuclear families, or in the smaller extended families, were in fact more likely to stay at home than those living in larger and more complex households.

However, in order to better assess the differential ability of Alagna's households to adjust to the absence of men, it is helpful to move a step further and relate the number of emigrants to the total labour force commanded by the households of which they were members. The summary indices presented in Table 9.7 are very rough. (It hardly needs to be stressed that particularly in agro-pastoral economies both children under 15 years of age and elderly people could contribute

[61] J. Connell *et al.*, *Migration from rural areas*, p. 39.

substantially to family labour.) Nevertheless, this table shows that not only simple-family households but also extended households contained, on average, just one man of prime working age. If the husband decided to migrate, his wife often remained the only able-bodied member of the household and could scarcely be expected to cope successfully with the tasks of mountain farming, all the more so when she was encumbered with young children or aged relatives.

It is therefore remarkable that over half of the men living in simple or extended families were temporarily absent. But we have seen that in Alagna it was common practice to hire day-labourers and hay-mowers, to recruit female servants for the alp season and (more rarely) to resort to some form of co-operation with relatives and neighbours. This is a reminder that a productive activity, as has been rightly intimated, 'can be accomplished by a variety of household types depending on how production is socially organized'.[62] More specifically, it suggests that for the men of Alagna (and no doubt for many other Alpine emigrants)[63] it could be more profitable to hire day-labourers and seasonal servants than to renounce emigration.

But it should not be forgotten that for my informants in Alagna – and most probably also for their ancestors – it was self-evident that recourse to hired workers had to be reduced as much as possible or, ideally, avoided altogether. In a community where domestic groups were forced to strike a difficult balance between the labour requirements of seasonal emigration and those of mountain farming, a system of joint household formation had therefore more than one *raison d'être*. It may well have been a legacy of the Walser mode of colonization, which had the private ownership and individual management of the alps as one of its most prominent features. But it is conceivable, though very difficult to prove, that a tendency for joint families to emerge and persist was further strengthened by the growth of seasonal emigration. It is interesting to note, in this respect, that in the summer of 1788 the seven adult men who lived in *frérèches* were all away from Alagna – a tiny number, but perhaps an indication that the rewards of emigration could encourage married brothers to delay fission beyond the point at which most joint families would break up.

All in all, the case of Alagna appears to support Robert Wheaton's contention that joint families, more than any other kind of household, 'must be united around some common economic project'.[64] Unfortu-

[62] Yanagisako, 'Family and household', p. 174.
[63] See e.g. Fontaine, 'Effets déséquilibrants du colportage', pp. 20–1.
[64] Wheaton, 'Family and kinship', p. 174.

Table 9.8. *Animal wealth and household composition in Villgraten, 1781*

	N households	% multiple	% extended
Agrarian population			
0–4 cattle	103	1.9	14.6
5–6 cattle	71	14.1	22.5
7–9 cattle	116	21.6	20.7
10–14 cattle	105	25.7	22.9
15+ cattle	40	47.5	27.9
Non-agrarian population			
0–4 cattle	68	7.4	27.9
5+ cattle	19	26.3	21.1
Total	522	17.8	21.6

Source: Schmidtbauer, 'Changing household', p. 364.

nately, the available evidence does not allow us to test for Alagna the related claim that wealth represented a crucial precondition to the formation of joint families – or, more generally, that the structural complexity of households tends to increase with wealth. But two of the localities which have been mentioned in this chapter provide data that point in this direction. The number of animals possessed by each household is accurately recorded for Montmin in 1561, and the correlation between household size and animal wealth has proved very strong.[65] Even more spectacular are the figures on Villgraten published by Peter Schmidtbauer and reproduced in Table 9.8. We have seen that in Villgraten the proportion of multiple households was very high. But this proportion, Schmidtbauer observes, 'becomes even more striking if one breaks down the households according to wealth'.[66]

Whether wealth was the cause of structural complexity is, however, an open question, for under a regime of partible inheritance (and both Montmin and Villgraten had such a custom) the larger amount of animals and land controlled by joint families might well depend on the fact that property has not yet been divided among the heirs. It may be hard to dispute that in mountain environments the management of the several integrated herding and cultivating cycles 'is optimized by a larger domestic group with centralized authority, encouraging subordinate families to remain until they are ready to

[65] See Siddle, 'Grid of inheritance', pp. 130–3.
[66] Schmidtbauer, 'Changing household', p. 366.

Table 9.9. *Household structure and population composition in three eighteenth-century Austrian mountain communities*

Locality	Year	Household types		Population	
		% multiple	% extended	% servants	% lodgers
Villgraten (E. Tyrol)	1781	17.8	21.6	10.8	5.6
Zell am Ziller (Tyrol)	1779	2.2	48.2	13.7	26.8
Metnitz (Carinthia)	1757	1.2	20.4	36.0	5.0

Sources: Schmidtbauer, 'Changing household', pp. 364–5, and Mitterauer, 'Formen ländlicher Familienwirtschaft', pp. 194–7.

sacrifice this joint affluence'.[67] Sooner or later fission did nevertheless take place, and it is not obvious that the resulting smaller households were significantly less affluent than the original joint household.

What Table 9.8 positively shows is that manpower was mainly recruited through kinship and marriage. Along with the existence of a system of partible inheritance, this makes Villgraten rather similar to most Western Alpine communities – and quite dissimilar to the majority of Austrian upland communities, where farmsteads remained undivided and the required labour force was essentially provided either by servants or by lodgers and day-labourers. Table 9.9 presents a comparison between three Austrian communities which are representative of as many different patterns of labour force recruitment, and reveals that these patterns were closely related to differences in the composition of the population as well as in the structure of domestic groups.

Perhaps the most striking contrast to emerge from this table is the one between the high frequency of multiple households in Villgraten and the exceedingly low proportions recorded in both Zell am Ziller and Metnitz. If by 'stem family' we mean a residential arrangement in which a married son co-resides with his parents (rather than the transmission of an undivided farm to one heir), it is clear that in Zell am Ziller and Metnitz the incidence of stem families must have been negligible. To some extent, this may have been due to a tendency for parents to establish separate households on retirement. But it should be noted that in Alpine Austria retirement was less early and frequent than in the lowlands. As in Provence, fathers retained headship until old age, often until their death. In Austria, however, marriage was dependent on succession and therefore took place either

[67] Webster, 'Native pastoralism', p. 124.

on the father's death or when he was very old, thereby reducing chances of co-residence.[68]

If we turn to the composition of the population of the three communities, we find that in Zell am Ziller the proportion of servants was almost as low as in Villgraten. But in Zell, as we have seen in Chapter 7, the decay of the mining industry had provided the farmers with a supply of cheap labour. One-quarter of Zell's population consisted of lodgers, and they were mainly miners or descendants of miners who survived by working on a more or less casual basis for local landed families. This is a pattern found in other declining mining centres, and in a region like the Austrian Alps (where mining powerfully moulded the history of so many communities) its significance cannot be underestimated. There is, however, little doubt that the dominant practice was to resort to servants, who were especially numerous in Carinthia. A community like Metnitz, where servants represented 36 per cent of the total population, was by no means exceptional. But Mitterauer has forcefully argued that a very high number of servants was a general feature of upland Austria and that this was explained by the specific requirements of an agrarian economy where stock-raising was more important than elsewhere. In grain-producing areas, and even more in viticultural communities, farmers tended to have fewer living-in servants and to resort to day-labourers for the peak periods. In the Alpine zone, on the other hand, the prevalence of livestock farming required a large permanent labour force.[69]

This Austrian evidence prompts a few final considerations. The first one is that the greater number and proportion of living-in servants found in upland regions is a further demonstration that the distinctive labour requirements of mountain farming critically affected the size and composition of Alpine households. Mitterauer is certainly correct in contending that the dynamics of household formation are better understood when they are studied in their ecological context.[70] Similar labour requirements, however, did not necessarily result in identical forms of family and work organization. Varying patterns of inheritance and succession could generate very different household structures, as shown by the striking contrast between the joint families of Villgraten and the households of Carinthian localities like Metnitz, where domestic labour was mainly supplied by servants.

---

[68] See Fliri, *Bevölkerungsgeographische Untersuchungen*, p. 27, and Held, 'Rural retirement', p. 231.

[69] Mitterauer, 'Formen ländlicher Familienwirtschaft', p. 201.

[70] Mitterauer, 'Formen ländlicher Familienwirtschaft', pp. 188–200.

In this respect, it is worth noting that the emphasis which has rightly been placed on servants should not lead to the conclusion that in Austria relatives were, if we except rather unusual communities like Villgraten, an unimportant source of labour. The fact that the farmers' children often left home only when they were well into their thirties[71] indicates that efforts were made to keep at least some children other than the heir on the farm. But at some point in time, perhaps when the father died and was succeeded by the heir apparent, most of them eventually left home and were replaced by servants. Some remained, but they were not allowed to marry, had little or no authority, and in many cases their status could hardly be distinguished from that of a servant.

Indeed, a striking feature of Austrian listings is that not only distant relatives but also brothers and sisters of the head are often designated merely as 'servants'. As we have repeatedly noticed, low nuptiality was common to most parts of the Alps and it was frequently the case that unmarried siblings lived in the same household with a married brother. But the ethnographic evidence available for several communities (including Alagna) strongly suggests that outside Austria their status was generally much higher.[72] It is significant, in particular, that bachelors could often be the recognized heads of the household, even when the domestic group comprised a younger married brother. This would be unimaginable in the Austrian Alps, where it was not their kin relationship but the specific working role played by the head's unmarried siblings that defined their membership in the household.

Such a sharp contrast in the structure of authority within the household is perhaps the clearest indication of the extent to which the harsh system of impartible inheritance found in the Austrian Alps affected the domestic domain. But it should not be forgotten that the inheritance process, as Cole and Wolf have remarked, 'worked simultaneously at two levels: at the level of the domestic group and at the level of the village as a whole, in the public domain'.[73] As we have just seen, one of the major structural implications of impartibility in Austria was that it created a local élite of farmers and, at the same time, provided this élite with a labour force of disadvantaged siblings. In the final pages of Chapter 8 we noticed that there were reasons to believe that a social-structural mechanism of this kind was the key

---

[71] Mitterauer, 'Gesindedienst und Jugendphase', p. 189.

[72] Sellan, 'Système familial', p. 57, even argues that in the Fersina Valley 'le célibataire jouit de prestige tant au sein du groupe domestique que dans la communauté villageoise'.

[73] Cole and Wolf, *The hidden frontier*, p. 205.

to make sense of the rather anomalous pattern of population growth displayed by the Austrian Alps in the late eighteenth and early nineteenth centuries. This is a problem of considerable significance, which requires to be discussed in greater detail than has been possible so far. Having completed our forcedly sketchy exploration of the domestic domain, in the next and final chapter we shall therefore turn to examine the implications of divergent inheritance customs for patterns of social stratification in upland communities and their impact on the relationships between population and environment.

10

Upland communities

Inheritance customs and population growth

Inheritance customs have often been invoked to explain not only the variations in family structure displayed by European peasant societies, but also their demographic evolution. As H. J. Habakkuk recognized in a classic article published over thirty years ago, it is 'difficult in the extreme to disentangle the effects of the rules of succession from many other circumstances that influence population growth'. But in general he was inclined to believe that the single-heir system tended to retard population growth, and division to promote it. By maintaining a fixed number of openings on the land, he remarked, impartible inheritance curbs nuptiality and encourages the permanent emigration of those children who have no prospect of inheriting land and getting married. Partible inheritance, on the other hand, can be expected to favour local settlement and higher marriage rates, and therefore to result in more rapid population growth.[1]

This argument provides a challenging perspective on the study of the relations between environment, population and social structure in a region like the Alps. Let us consider, in particular, the question of permanent emigration. As we have repeatedly noticed, most students of mountain societies have seen permanent emigration as a way of relieving demographic pressure – a mechanism which either directly (by removing excess population) or indirectly (by reducing nuptiality) prevented population from exceeding the carrying capacity of a given territory. By contrast, Habakkuk regards it to be less a function of density than of social structure. 'The division areas,' he

[1] Habakkuk, 'Family structure and economic change', p. 6. For a general discussion of this issue, see Berkner and Mendels, 'Inheritance systems'.

writes, 'may have tended to have the densest population in relation to their capacity, but they are populations which it was difficult in normal times to induce permanently to leave the area.' In order to make up the difference between what the land could provide and what was required to survive, the inhabitants of division areas were forced to emigrate on a seasonal or temporary basis. But they were tethered to their homeland, for it was in their native village that they were entitled to some land through inheritance and had the best chances of getting married. On the contrary, areas with impartible inheritance may have been less densely populated, but the limited prospects of non-heirs made the bulk of the population more capable of permanent movement.[2]

The paucity of reliable quantitative evidence on permanent emigration before the mid-nineteenth century makes these claims difficult to test for the Alpine area in historic times. It is nevertheless worth noting that similar opinions have been expressed by many of the scholars who have investigated the causes of mountain depopulation in more recent times.[3] Also, this argument appears to be supported by Netting's detailed analysis of permanent emigration from Törbel, which has revealed that before 1850 the number of individuals leaving the village for good was quite small. It can be estimated that in the eighteenth and early nineteenth centuries less than 10 per cent of all people surviving to maturity emigrated, and many of them were women who moved to a neighbouring community at marriage and were replaced by a roughly equal number of in-marrying wives from outside. Although Törbel's system of partible inheritance is not adduced by Netting as the sole cause of the limited extent of permanent emigration, he certainly believes that it was a major contributory factor and suggests that 'in situations where land is passed on by primogeniture ... a great deal more mobility can be expected'.[4]

However, other evidence we possess on Alpine permanent emigration provides rather more conflicting indications. For the Western Alps, the best source of information is probably a census taken by the Piedmontese government in 1782, which shows that in the second half of the eighteenth century permanent emigration from the moun-

---

[2] Habakkuk, 'Family structure and economic change', p. 8.
[3] Of special interest are the contrasting views expressed by the group of geographers and agrarian economists who studied the depopulation of the Italian Alps in the period between the two world wars, summarized by Giusti, 'Note riassuntive', p. liv.
[4] Netting, *Balancing on an alp*, p. 77.

tain districts of Piedmont was generally moderate.[5] The highest incidence (3.8 per cent) was to be found in the Aosta Valley, where 2,602
individuals out of a total population of 69,089 were recorded as permanently absent. Since in the Piedmontese Alps partible inheritance was
the rule, this would seem to corroborate Habakkuk's argument. But
variations from one community to another could be very substantial
indeed. Interestingly, of all the communities of the Aosta Valley, the
one with the highest number of permanent emigrants was Gressoney,
the Walser colony whose emigration pattern has been discussed in
Chapter 6. In 1782 the resident population of Gressoney consisted
of 1,077 people and the number of permanent emigrants amounted
to no less than 212. It can therefore be reckoned that Gressoney had
lost through emigration over 15 per cent of its population.

Unfortunately, the 1782 census contains no information on the Sesia
Valley. It is, however, very likely that in Alagna the incidence of
permanent emigration was nearly as high as in Gressoney. This is
indirectly suggested by the severely unbalanced sex ratios that emerge
from all the eighteenth- and nineteenth-century *status animarum*, in
which women consistently outnumber men by 15 to 30 per cent. And
a precious direct confirmation is provided by a note written in 1764
by the parish priest, who gives an estimate of about 110 permanent
absentees.[6] In that year, the population of Alagna consisted of 502
women and only 404 men, and of these men just 250 or so were
over 20 years of age. These figures indicate that in Alagna, where
permanent emigrants were mostly males of adult age, between perhaps one-fourth and one-third of all men surviving to maturity left
the village for good.

The cases of Törbel, Gressoney and Alagna provide extreme examples of the range of variation displayed by Alpine permanent emigration. But it is important to add that the contrast is no less striking
if we consider seasonal emigration. The monthly distribution of births
exhibited by Törbel leaves no doubt that seasonal emigration was

---

[5] 'Stato della popolazione delle Persone e delle Bestie del Ducato d'Aosta resultante
dalla Consegna Generale del 1782.' AST, II Sez. (Finanze), 2^a arch., cap. 79, n. 14.
On this census, and on the less complete one taken in 1734, see Prato, *La vita economica
in Piemonte*, pp. 43–4, who notes the limited extent of permanent emigration from
the mountainous zone, 'i figli della quale si inducono sempre mal volentieri ad un
definitivo distacco dalla terra natia'. This is essentially in agreement with the results
of the more recent study by Levi, 'Mobilità della popolazione', who emphasizes
the seasonal or temporary character of migration from the mountains of Piedmont
and Savoy in the eighteenth century and plays down the role of immigrants from
the mountains in producing the urban growth of Turin.

[6] Cf. Viazzo and Bodo, 'Emigrazione e immigrazione ad Alagna', pp. 12–13.

practised.[7] But the scale was incomparably smaller than in Alagna (or, one may safely assume, than in Gressoney). This suggests, for one thing, that a steady and substantial flow of permanent emigration could be not so much an alternative to seasonal emigration as a consequence of it. Also, it seems no accident that permanent emigration happened to be so high from villages like Alagna or Gressoney, where emigration offered far greater rewards and opportunities than in Törbel. However, what makes the contrast particularly striking and instructive is the fact that the two Walser settlements south of Monte Rosa were not only of the same linguistic and ethnic stock as Törbel, but also shared the same custom of strict partible inheritance. Yet the demographic and economic role of emigration could hardly have been more different.

No less instructive are the results of Mitterauer's recent attempt to estimate, on the basis of listings of inhabitants, the intensity of permanent emigration from a fairly large number of Austrian communities. The simple method used by Mitterauer consists of calculating the ratio between the size of the age group 2–11 and the size of older age groups. These ratios are, of course, very rough indicators of the effects of migration. But it seems nonetheless significant that of all the Alpine localities in Mitterauer's sample, the highest rate of 'cohort depletion' is found in the only community where custom prescribed partibility, namely Villgraten, which also displayed by far the most unbalanced sex ratio. (In 1781, women outnumbered men by 111 to 100.) Another locality exhibiting signs of sizable permanent emigration was, interestingly enough, Zell am Ziller in 1779 – a finding which comes as no surprise to Mitterauer, in view of the decline of the mining industry, which in that period was driving many miners away from Zell or turning them into seasonal migrants. In all the other Alpine localities, however, there is no indication that permanent emigration had significantly affected the age pyramid.[8]

The local-level evidence provided by Mitterauer brings support to what had been asserted by a number of other writers on the basis of admittedly crude regional statistics, namely that before the middle of the nineteenth century permanent emigration had played a rather minor role in the Austrian Alps, and that in any case it had affected division areas like Vorarlberg or West Tyrol much more seriously than the single-heir regions.[9] This is not to say that the population of

[7] Cf. Netting, *Balancing on an alp*, pp. 151–2.
[8] Mitterauer, 'Formen ländlicher Familienwirtschaft', pp. 308–10. On the decline of mining and its effects in Zell am Ziller, cf. Chapter 7 above, pp. 171–3.
[9] Klein, 'Österreichs Bevölkerung', pp. 53–5; Keller, 'Die Bevölkerungsentwicklung im Ausserfern', pp. 365–9; Lichtenberger, *The Eastern Alps*, p. 7.

the villages with impartible inheritance (which represented the vast majority) was immobile. Although more detailed research is needed to clarify this issue, it is likely that many non-inheriting children left not only their households but also their villages and moved to other places to take jobs as servants or agricultural labourers. But it would seem that they only rarely went outside the Alpine zone.

The impression that the model outlined by Habakkuk scarcely applies to the Alpine area is further strengthened by what we have seen about nuptiality. The extensive evidence discussed in this book has shown that until the Second World War a pattern of late marriage and high celibacy rates was dominant in most Alpine regions whatever the inheritance system. It would seem all too easy, at this point, to conclude that as far as the Alps are concerned, the hypothesis of a crucial link between inheritance systems and demographic patterns should be discarded. In spite of highly dissimilar inheritance rules, the demography of a Swiss village like Törbel appears to have differed very little from that of a typical Austrian upland community both in terms of nuptiality and in terms of net migration. However, if we consider the evolution of population over the long term, the picture changes dramatically. It becomes apparent, in particular, that in the course of the late eighteenth and early nineteenth centuries the population of Törbel (and more generally of the Swiss Alps) greatly increased, whereas that of most Austrian mountain districts remained almost stationary.

The first aim of this final chapter will be to tackle this puzzling question and to reconsider from a somewhat different angle the possibility that the very marked difference in the rate of population growth displayed by the Swiss and Austrian Alps can be traced back to the prevalence of differing customs of inheritance. Since so far this demographic contrast has been little investigated by Swiss and Austrian scholars, precise comparative analyses are still lacking and any explanatory argument is bound to be highly tentative. Nevertheless, an attempt will be made to examine the relationship between inheritance and nuptiality in a less static way than has been the case in the previous chapters. Special attention will be devoted, in this context, to a comparison between the demographic implications of the system of social and economic stratification which was predominant in the Austrian Alps and the system found in Swiss localities like Törbel, which experienced rapid population growth.

The demographic history of Törbel, however, differed rather substantially from that of other Swiss mountain communities. Though less immediately visible than the major contrast between the Swiss and the Austrian Alps, these differences raise a number of intriguing and theoretically significant questions. In order to shed some light on these questions, it will be necessary to assess the importance of a variety of economic and social-structural factors. This will entail, among other things, a reconsideration of the notion of 'closed corporate community', a form of communal organization which is believed to have been particularly frequent in mountain areas and to possess a set of structural properties which are essential to an understanding of Alpine demographic history. The claim that corporate communities tended to have closed populations will be evaluated, as will the other claim that this type of community structure was a variable crucially affecting the interaction between outside economic forces and local systems of social stratification, and thereby impinging on the relation between population and resources.

Alpine patterns of social stratification

The argument advanced by Habakkuk still provides a convenient framework for research on the relations between inheritance systems and demographic patterns. Since the early 1970s, however, a growing number of anthropologists and historians have intimated that the elegant but rigid dichotomy which is at the core of this argument is inadequate to capture the complexity and flexibility of inheritance processes, and therefore to predict their consequences. Following the lead of anthropologists like Fredrik Barth and Pierre Bourdieu, many scholars have tried to demonstrate that peasants, far from blindly following the dictates of inheritance rules, could break these rules if they thought that this was in their interest. A new orthodoxy has indeed emerged, according to which 'inheritance laws and customs are things that the peasant must deal with in planning a strategy which will reach his goals; they do not determine the goals of the strategy'.[10]

If inheritance customs do not determine the peasant's goal, however, the ecological imperatives of the harsh mountain environment apparently do. This is, at least, what has been argued by a number of historians and social anthropologists who have used the notion of family strategy in their studies of peasant communities in mountain areas such as the Pyrenees, the Massif Central, the Alps and the uplands of Northern Portugal. As one of them has recently concluded, 'the goal in mountain regions of Europe seems to be the same ... the preservation of viable landed patrimonies through the avoidance

[10] Berkner and Mendels, 'Inheritance systems', p. 216.

of partition'.[11] As a consequence, in mountain areas a system of inheritance which is partible in theory can be expected to function as an impartible one in practice.

It is difficult not to receive the impression that the notion of family strategy, while freeing these scholars from the excessive legalism that had previously plagued the study of peasant inheritance patterns, has led them to a sophisticated but curiously inflexible form of environmental determinism. As we have just seen, the evidence on Alpine nuptiality presented in this book suggests that a certain degree of environmental determinism may well be justified. But a model positing that similar environmental constraints are inexorably conducive to essentially similar family and inheritance strategies cannot adequately account for some of the more puzzling features of Alpine demographic and ecological history.

As I have argued elsewhere,[12] one major problem with this model is that 'family strategies' have been mostly considered in isolation from a number of crucial constraints, as if peasant families had a completely free hand on their land and were simply playing a 'minimax' game with the environment. Yet, even a quick look at the origins and evolution of inheritance patterns in the Austrian Alps makes one wonder whether the integrity of the farm was the aim of the peasantry, as is usually assumed, or rather the aim of the dominant power-holders. Although the evidence is at times conflicting and some questions have not yet been satisfactorily settled, there is little doubt that the dominance of impartible inheritance in the Austrian Alps is not so much the outcome of peasant 'adaptive strategies' as the legacy of the prevailing mode of colonization in this area. In the Austrian Alps, as we have seen in Chapter 3, colonization was generally later than in the other sectors of the crescent and took place in a period of growing market involvement. It was therefore in the landlords' interest to ensure the persistence of landed holdings capable of producing a surplus which could be marketed in the lowlands. As a consequence, impartibility was furthered and the holding could not, in any case, be divided without the lord's express consent.

It should be stressed that all over the Alps – and Austria was no exception – peasants generally enjoyed a greater degree of freedom from the landlords' political and legal jurisdiction than the inhabitants of the adjacent plains. Particularly those colonists who settled in the

---

[11] O'Neill, 'Dying and inheriting', p. 73. Cf. Cole and Wolf, *The hidden frontier*, pp. 174–205; Fine-Souriac, 'La famille-souche pyrénéenne', p. 483; and Lamaison, 'Stratégies matrimoniales', p. 722.

[12] Viazzo, 'Anthropology, family history and the concept of "strategy"'.

high valleys were offered very favourable conditions, as the case of the Walser shows. Even in medieval times they were more frequently tenants than serfs. However, in the Western and even more in the Swiss Alps, upland communities were able to free themselves from any obligation to the feudal lords at a much earlier date than in Austria, where the latter retained a considerable amount of power until the mid-nineteenth century. Indeed, starting from the sixteenth century the Austrian Alps experienced a major process of rationalization of the manorial system, whereby the landlords (aided by the growing fiscal needs of the Habsburg state) made great efforts to regroup earlier scattered holdings into viable farms to be let out on emphyteutic tenure. They therefore insisted on impartibility and strongly discouraged the building of cottages.[13]

These efforts are reflected in legislation. If we consider Tyrol, for example, we find that in the early sixteenth century norms were still quite permissive. Thus, the *Landesordnung* of 1532 stated that partition was allowed if the estate was large enough that the farmer would be able to settle or marry off more than one of his children onto it.[14] But in the following centuries impartibility was increasingly favoured, and especially since the middle of the eighteenth century the legislation sought to prevent the partition of land altogether, in order to maintain a viable peasantry. As Hermann Wopfner has noticed, these measures enjoyed a greatly varying degree of success. In those areas of Tyrol where for some reason a custom of partible inheritance was solidly entrenched (such as West Tyrol or localities like Villgraten), they apparently had little or no impact. In most other areas, however, they critically reinforced a pre-existing practice of impartibility.[15]

The imposition of impartibility from above has been regarded by some scholars as marking a worsening of the peasants' lot. But it should not be overlooked that the aim of these measures was also that of creating a strong peasantry. In fact, Hermann Rebel has recently argued that Austria witnessed not so much a weakening of the peasants' bargaining position *vis-à-vis* their landlords as what he calls a process of 'bureaucratization of property and family relations', which amounted to co-option of the household heads by higher authority and profoundly affected both family life and the pattern of social stratification. Briefly, his argument is that the household was made the

---

[13] Cf. e.g. Rebel, *Peasant classes*, pp. 3–42; Fox, 'Peasants as bureaucrats?', pp. 216–17; and Pickl, 'Wirtschaft und Gesellschaft in den Ostalpenländern', pp. 51–6.

[14] Partition was permitted if 'Hof oder gut so ansechlich wäre, dass der Bawmann seiner Kinder mer dann eins darauf setzen oder verheyraten möchte'. This regulation is quoted by Wopfner, 'Güterteilung und Übervölkerung', p. 211.

[15] Wopfner, 'Güterteilung und Übervölkerung', pp. 212–13.

lowest instance of the hierarchy of state absolutism and that the household head, the *Bauer*, became more tied to higher authority than to fellow household members. This exacerbated the division between hereditary tenants and their dispossessed siblings, whose chances of acquiring a holding were exceedingly slight. As Rebel remarks, a division between these two categories 'had existed before the formation of the early Habsburg state, but under strict orders of impartibility of tenant holdings, of emphyteusis, and of contractual accountability, the functions of this social division were greatly expanded and its meaning radically altered'.[16]

Although some of Rebel's contentions appear rather debatable, and others probably apply better to the region he has studied in detail (Upper Austria) than to other parts of the Austrian Alps, nevertheless he has certainly brought out very effectively the basic feature of social stratification in Austrian communities – namely the fact that the crucial economic and social cleavage divided not the village population into richer and poorer households, but actually each household against itself.[17] This has an important implication. It is almost a commonplace to consider the practice of impartibility and the formation of stem families as a peasant strategy whose aim was to maintain the family property intact while at the same time 'keeping the family name on the land'. But Rebel has rightly objected that in Austria 'the chief purpose of the stem family was not to preserve the integrity of the "family property"; it did not seek to assure the future of all the children, nor indeed of the "stem" or "lineage"'.[18] The rich material analysed by Mitterauer and his associates shows, in fact, that farms tended to remain undivided for very long periods but their occupants could change quite frequently.[19] Clearly the farm came first and enjoyed a continuity of its own, independently of the vicissitudes of its occupants.

A sharp contrast is provided, in this respect, by the communities of Valais and more generally by the Swiss Alps. One major difference is that between the end of the thirteenth and the end of the sixteenth centuries the peasant populations of the Swiss Alps successfully fought domination by expansionist noble families. Indeed, the various small independent states which are now part of Switzerland (Valais, the Grisons and the Swiss Confederation itself) originated as alliances of peasant cantons and communes to resist infringements of their

---

[16] Rebel, *Peasant classes*, p. 167.
[17] For a useful discussion of Rebel's book, see Fox, 'Peasants as bureaucrats?'.
[18] Rebel, *Peasant classes*, p. 168.
[19] See e.g. Sieder and Mitterauer, 'The reconstitution of the family life course'.

hard-won autonomy by secular and ecclesiastical lords.[20] A second difference is that in the Swiss Alps inheritance customs mostly prescribed partibility. In a number of areas (and notably in Valais) partibility was especially strict, each heir having right to an equal share of the estate regardless of age and sex. Because women were entitled to inherit equally with men, a new estate was formed with each marriage.

If followed in practice, a custom of strict partibility should generate a process whereby wealth moves continuously through the local community. Particularly if the poor had fewer children (either through lower fertility or through higher infant and child mortality), a systematic levelling of wealth would result. There are, however, a number of ways in which the effects of inheritance rules could be by-passed and a concentration of wealth and prestige in relatively few hands could be maintained over time. One strategy might consist, of course, in limiting fertility through contraception so as to prevent fragmentation among numerous offspring. But a concentration of wealth, as McGuire and Netting have remarked, could also be maintained 'by a marital strategy in which the rich took pains to marry only each other, in which they married later in life than the rest of the population, and in which more children remained celibate so that their property would revert to their married siblings' offspring'.[21]

If these propositions are to be tested with any rigour, detailed demographic data must be matched carefully with information about wealth distribution. Even when the required sources are available (which is not often the case), this is a demanding task and good studies are consequently very rare. Students of Alpine society are therefore greatly indebted to Ellen Wiegandt and to Robert Netting and Randall McGuire for two excellent analyses of the relation between demography, inheritance and stratification in two communities of Valais: Törbel, and the French-speaking village of Mase.[22] Both these studies are mainly focussed on the second half of the nineteenth century, since their key-sources (a series of tax rolls providing information on land ownership) are only available for that period. This is a regrettable limitation. But the results are nonetheless very interesting and highly relevant to the problems discussed in this chapter. They show, first of all, that greater wealth was not correlated with lower marital

[20] See Kohn, *Nationalism and liberty*, pp. 18–19, and also Wiegandt, 'Inheritance and demography', pp. 134–6.
[21] McGuire and Netting, 'Leveling peasants?', p. 277.
[22] See Wiegandt, 'Inheritance and demography' on Mase; and McGuire and Netting, 'Leveling peasants?' on Törbel. For a similar but less complete analysis of economic stratification in Montmin, see Siddle, 'Grid of inheritance', pp. 128–39.

fertility. Wiegandt has actually found that in Mase it was the richer couples who tended to have more numerous offspring. Secondly, wealth did not prove to be a dominant factor in the selection of marriage partners. Thirdly, no significant relation was detected between wealth and nuptiality. Fourthly, it has emerged that siblings did in fact receive essentially equal shares of the parental estates. And finally, the correlation between a father's wealth and his son's wealth at the same age was very weak. As a result, both Törbel and Mase come out in this period as remarkably egalitarian communities. The differences between the richest and poorest in the two villages were relatively small, and wealth tended not to remain concentrated among a few families through time but to move up and down throughout the community.

Social structure and nuptiality: statics vs. dynamics

The Austrian communities studied by Rebel, and Swiss villages like Törbel or Mase provide extreme examples of two radically different systems of social stratification. We may wonder, however, whether such a difference is of any relevance in the search for an explanation of the contrasting patterns of population growth displayed by the Austrian and Swiss Alps in the eighteenth and nineteenth centuries. At first glance, it would indeed seem that nuptiality was hardly correlated to variations in social structure. The finding that in Törbel individuals from richer and poorer families tended to marry at the same age and had approximately the same chances of remaining celibate is of considerable sociological interest, for it suggests that there was no significant attempt on the part of the richer families to maintain their social standing over time through what we might call 'nuptiality strategies'. Yet in nineteenth-century Törbel marriage was on average just as late, and celibacy rates just as high, as in most Austrian upland communities.

However, our perception of the relation between patterns of social stratification and patterns of nuptiality (and population growth) drastically changes when we look at nuptiality in a different and more dynamic perspective. The evidence surveyed in previous chapters has shown that a considerable amount of work has been devoted to the measuring of nuptiality in the Alps. But it is essential not to lose sight of the fact that apart from marriage age, the measures which have been usually employed – be they celibacy rates, the Princeton index of proportion married (I_m) or simply crude marriage rates – are all *relative* measures. Useful as those rates and indices are, in certain circumstances they can easily produce a static picture and lead to paradoxical conclusions.

If we consider once again the case of Törbel, we find that in the second half of the nineteenth century the mean age at first marriage was about two years higher than one century before for both men and women. Even more significantly, the proportion of individuals reaching 20 years of age who never married had increased from 20 to 33 per cent.[23] There seems therefore to be no doubt that from the middle of the eighteenth century nuptiality had severely declined. Yet, if we consider the *absolute* number of people getting married in Törbel, we find that in this period it increased considerably, and so did the number of estates, for we have seen that a new estate was formed with each marriage. The reason is, of course, that between the middle of the eighteenth century and the end of the nineteenth century the population of Törbel more than doubled, and the proportions of people never marrying therefore refer to cohorts of very different size. The number of people born in Törbel in the period 1750–99 was in fact just over 50 per cent of those born between 1850 and 1899, and the number of those who eventually got married just over 60 per cent.

Since the total amount of productive land worked by the people of Törbel and Mase remained essentially the same, as Netting and Wiegandt both stress, the average amount of land owned by each individual (or household) steadily declined. The distribution of wealth remained highly egalitarian, but the whole village population went through what Netting and Wiegandt call a process of general downward mobility. However, the balance between population and resources did not necessarily deteriorate, for 'another process was taking place that in part counteracted (and in part was responsible for) population growth: intensification of production ... The nineteenth century was a period of technical change in Alpine agriculture. As potatoes became a principal crop and garden vegetables slowly replaced beans, more nutrients could be produced on the same land area.'[24] Moreover, as human population increased, so did cattle population. In both Törbel and Mase, the ratio between the number of cattle and the number of people fluctuated somewhat, but did not decrease.[25]

It is interesting to note that Wiegandt calls to task Cole and Wolf

---

[23] Cf. Netting, *Balancing on an alp*, pp. 132–5.

[24] Wiegandt, 'Inheritance and demography', p. 139.

[25] Cf. Wiegandt, 'Inheritance and demography', p. 139, and Netting, *Balancing on an alp*, pp. 26–7.

for arguing that population pressure pushes people to break the rule of partibility, her contention being that partible inheritance can be a perfectly viable ecological strategy, provided that yields also increase.[26] Indeed, some of the data provided by Wiegandt herself and by Netting, as well as by Pfister on the highlands of Canton Berne,[27] strongly suggest that in spite of population growth the agricultural and pastoral output *per capita* remained remarkably constant. This, however, was achieved through an increase in the age at marriage and in the proportion of celibates which, though not amounting to a break of the rule of partibility, nevertheless slowed down both the fragmentation of village land and the rate of population growth. That the output *per capita* remained almost constant is an indication that at least in some parts of the Alps local ecosystems really were, to use Netting's phrase, 'as finely calibrated and dependable as an old Swiss watch'[28] – and that nuptiality worked as a surprisingly precise homeostatic mechanism.

This is in marked contrast with what was apparently happening in the Austrian Alps, where population remained almost stationary and fragmentation was (apart from rather exceptional cases) very limited. It has sometimes been suggested that in the second half of the eighteenth century the population of the Austrian uplands had virtually reached its ceiling. This is, however, hard to accept. As Mitterauer has remarked, the 'agrarian revolution' and in particular the introduction of the potato made it possible to feed a much greater number of people from the same acreage of land.[29] This was often the case in the lowlands of Austria. But the new potential was exploited only to a limited extent in the mountains, where the formation of cottages was strongly discouraged both by external power-holders and by the local farming élite, and the number of what Mitterauer calls 'potato-people' consequently remained quite small. While in a village like Törbel social-structural factors were opposing minimum resistance to the adjustment of both population and nuptiality to the increased carrying capacity of the ecosystem, in Austria efforts were made to maximize the comparative economic advantages of the various districts and ecological zones. Thus, hillside districts typically experi-

---

26 Wiegandt, 'Inheritance and demography', pp. 138–9.
27 C. Pfister, 'Bevölkerung, Wirtschaft und Ernährung'. It should be noticed, however, that in the highlands of Canton Berne the ratio between the number of cows and the number of inhabitants appears to have decreased rather markedly. Cf. C. Pfister, 'Changes in stability', p. 294.
28 Netting, *Balancing on an alp*, p. 89.
29 Mitterauer, 'Auswirkungen der Agrarrevolution', pp. 243–4, and 'Formen ländlicher Familienwirtschaft', p. 254.

enced a substantial development of viticulture, which resulted in a faster rate of land subdivision, an increase in the number and proportion of cottagers, a 'relaxation' of nuptiality and rapid population growth. In the mountains, on the other hand, and particularly in wet areas such as north-western Tyrol, emphasis was increasingly placed on dairy-farming. Two major counterparts of this economic development were, predictably, a further growth in the number of unmarried servants, and demographic stagnation.[30]

Contrasting communities

The social-structural factors examined in the two previous sections help make sense of the broad contrast between the demographic history of the Swiss and Austrian Alps in the eighteenth and nineteenth centuries. But if we look at the map of population growth from a shorter distance, it becomes apparent that significant differences existed within both the Swiss and the Austrian Alps (as, indeed, within all the other major sectors of the Alpine crescent). These differences have received particular attention from Swiss scholars, who have long been puzzled by the fact that while most Swiss cantons greatly increased the number of their inhabitants, the population of a few other cantons remained nearly stationary or even declined. In 1947 Bickel had already offered, on the basis of the scanty evidence available at that time, some tentative explanations.[31] Over the last few decades, many more data have come from a spate of regional and local studies. As Mattmüller remarked some years ago, however, the detailed information furnished by recent studies makes the search for an explanation even more complex, 'because often very great differences are observed between two localities no more than a few kilometres apart'. But he also added that the small-scale contrasts between communities or districts belonging to the same region and sharing largely the same institutional and ecological setting might ultimately provide an important methodological advantage by reducing the number of intervening variables.[32]

This has been demonstrated recently by the enlightening results of Christian Pfister's comparative study of two districts of the Bernese Oberland: the eastern district of Oberhasli, whose population increased between 1764 and 1846 at the fast annual rate of 1.1 per

---

[30] Cf. Wopfner, 'Güterteilung und Übervölkerung', pp. 208–10, and Pickl, 'Wirtschaft und Gesellschaft in den Ostalpenländern', pp. 76–86.

[31] Bickel, *Bevölkerungsgeschichte der Schweiz*, pp. 111–72.

[32] Mattmüller, 'Études de démographie historique', p. 455.

cent, and the western district of Saanen, which only displayed a growth rate of 0.2 per cent. The demography of the Oberhasli was closely reminiscent in a number of crucial respects of that of Törbel. Pfister does not provide data on nuptiality. But an important similarity is that this district experienced, like Törbel, a sharp decline of mortality and possibly also a certain increase in marital fertility. Even more remarkably, the substantial surplus of births generated by these demographic changes was mostly absorbed, as in Törbel, by the local ecosystem: the annual rate of net migration amounted to only 0.15 per cent, without any sign of deterioration in the diet and living standards of those who remained. In contrast, Saanen displayed lower fertility, a rather heavier mortality and – most interestingly – a net migration rate which was twice as high as in the Oberhasli.[33]

These demographic differences are regarded by Pfister to be due to marked differences in the economy. The geographical features of the two districts were, he stresses, fundamentally similar. But the Oberhasli had retained what Pfister calls a 'dynamic balance' between the agricultural and the pastoral sectors, whereas Saanen had turned into a classic instance of *Hirtenland*. (It was, indeed, a visit to Saanen that in the late eighteenth century prompted Karl Viktor von Bonstetten to coin this term, which has subsequently acquired a technical meaning among Swiss historians.) As Pfister writes,

in the period of the boom in the cheese market in the eighteenth century hay-fields were converted to pastures, whereby the capacity to support cattle over the winter was reduced in order to increase capacity in the summer. The pastures were overstocked by large herds of cows which were leased in the spring by cattle-farmers in the lowlands, and from the milk was produced hard cheese which sold very well in the market.[34]

This was clearly a major economic and ecological transformation. The agricultural census of Canton Berne taken in 1847 shows, in fact, that in Saanen the amount of land *per capita* devoted to the cultivation of cereals and potatoes was just $500m^2$, whereas in 'autarkic' districts like the Oberhasli it still exceeded $1,000m^2$ in spite of much faster population growth. But it is interesting and indeed essential to note that such a transformation was closely interwoven with significant changes in the social structure of these communities, for 'the system favoured the richer cattle-farmers, who could undertake the risk of the lease, and must have encouraged speculative land purchases, which deprived the lower strata of their small fields and gardens and

[33] C. Pfister, 'Bevölkerung, Wirtschaft und Ernährung', pp. 374–82.
[34] C. Pfister, 'Bevölkerung, Wirtschaft und Ernährung', p. 382.

thus of their basis for subsistence'.[35] In the course of the eighteenth century, pastoral communities like those of the Saanen district thus became far more inegalitarian than they had previously been. As Bonstetten had already recognized, in the *Hirtenland* 'poverty was the child of wealth, as inequality arose and many lost land and work'.[36] The relatively small edge that some families or individuals had over their fellow villagers enabled them to grasp the new opportunities offered by the growing demand for hard cheese and to secure a privileged position within the more rigid system of social stratification which was coming into being.

This system was still very different from the one which was typical of Austrian upland communities. Nevertheless, the new social and economic order of the *Hirtenland* apparently played a similar role in preventing population from adjusting the new potential brought about by the introduction of the potato. This is not to say that in the *Hirtenland* this innovation had no significant demographic effects. As we have seen in Chapter 8, the poorer strata increasingly resorted to the new crop, which was probably decisive (as Mattmüller has contended)[37] in at least hindering a decline of the population. But the potato did not enable pastoral communities to avoid a rather more severe emigration than that experienced by the 'autarkic' communities, and a greater degree of pauperization.[38]

Thus, the comparison between Saanen and the Oberhasli, while revealing a number of very significant contrasts between these two areas, confirms at the same time the importance of the introduction of the potato in the ecological and demographic history of the Alpine area in the eighteenth and nineteenth centuries. It allowed, on the one hand, 'autarkic' communities like Törbel or the villages of the Oberhasli to absorb most of the surplus births resulting from the sharp decline of mortality. But it also enabled the pastoral communities of the *Hirtenland* to stem the exodus of those who were losing 'land and work' and to retain a population which was generally stationary but could even grow at a slow rate. These two types of community, however, were both essentially agrarian. In less agrarian communities the role of the potato may be expected to have been less important, and the pattern of demographic development quite different.

This was presumably the case for those communities where seasonal emigration had long represented the backbone of the economy, and

---

[35] C. Pfister, 'Bevölkerung, Wirtschaft und Ernährung', p. 382.

[36] Bonstetten, *Briefe über ein schweizerisches Hirtenland*, p. 99, quoted by Braun, *Das ausgehende Ancien Régime*, p. 81.

[37] Mattmüller, 'Landwirtschaft und Bevölkerung'.

[38] On pauperization, see C. Pfister, 'Bevölkerung, Wirtschaft und Ernährung', p. 381.

permanent emigration was not simply an outlet for surplus population but a source of attractive opportunities. It is interesting to note, in this respect, that between 1775 and 1850 the population of Törbel grew at an annual rate of 0.8 per cent. By contrast, the population of both Alagna and Gressoney steadily declined at a rate of approximately 0.3–0.4 per cent. At first glance, it may seem paradoxical that this decline broadly coincided with the introduction of the potato. But we have seen that in Alagna (and, one suspects, also in Gressoney) the potato, though gradually becoming an important part of the diet, never supplanted rye and never brought about the 'revolutionary change in the local environment' which Netting has described for Törbel.[39]

Opposite trends characterized certain proto-industrial communities, whose population grew at such a fast rate that it can be only explained by substantial immigration. Pfister's study of the demographic evolution of Canton Berne has shown, among other things, that, while 'agrarian growth' tended to take place at a rate of 1 per cent at most, proto-industrial areas could grow (especially in the Jura) at rates sometimes exceeding 4 per cent.[40] We have already observed that proto-industry was more heavily concentrated either in the Jura or in hillside districts such as the Zurich Oberland and some parts of Vorarlberg rather than in the Alpine zone proper. Its significance in promoting the population growth of the Alps should therefore not be exaggerated. Nevertheless, the presence of proto-industrial activities clearly lies behind the rise of population in a number of Alpine districts, particularly the Swiss Canton Glarus. Moreover, the very fact that proto-industry failed to penetrate into most high valleys leads to a few more questions about the role of social structure in affecting the relationship between environment and population.

These questions have been raised most clearly by the Swiss historian Rudolf Braun, at first in his studies of proto-industrialization and demographic change in Canton Zurich,[41] and more recently in his general account of the economic and social history of eighteenth-

---

[39] Cf. Chapter 8 above, pp. 213–14.

[40] C. Pfister, 'Menschen im Kanton Bern', p. 491.

[41] Braun, *Industrialisierung und Volksleben*, and 'Protoindustrialization and demographic changes'. It is perhaps worth mentioning that, although it is generally assumed that closed corporate communities are more widespread and stronger in mountain areas than in the plains, Braun's study is rather confusingly concerned with an area in which corporate community structure happened to be far stronger in the flatter districts than in the adjacent highlands. It should be added that the 'highlands' of Canton Zurich are more accurately characterized as a hilly zone, and they are generally excluded from the Alpine region proper. Nevertheless, they are known as the Zurich *Oberland*, and Braun uses the term 'highlands'.

century Switzerland.[42] The studies focused on Canton Zurich are best-known because of Braun's pioneering argument that population growth was generated by proto-industrialization through an increase in nuptiality. But it should be stressed that Braun was at least as interested in the *preconditions* of proto-industrialization as in its social and demographic consequences. The baffling problem he was facing was to explain why cottage industry, which had become the dominant activity in the highlands, had gained no foothold in the farming districts of the flatter parts of the canton, despite the fact that the latter were situated mostly nearer the city of Zurich (which was the centre of the putting-out system) and had therefore advantages in terms of transportation and communication.

To make sense of this seeming paradox, Braun points out that the communities in the flatter districts of Canton Zurich were marked by rigid regulations concerning the right of using common property and of being a member of the community. Such regulations had a twofold effect: they kept newcomers out and prevented too great an expansion from within. These barriers had been erected to guarantee the livelihood of the members of agrarian communities whose economy was based on the traditional three-field system of cultivation. But they were responsible, Braun suggests, for keeping off the cottage industry, which would have caused a disruption of the traditional social and economic order. By contrast, at the beginning of industrialization the highlands of this Canton were still sparsely settled, commons were small or non-existent, and there were few, if any, legal provisions to prevent settlement. As a result, cottage industry could not be kept out. Although the districts which experienced proto-industrialization could differ considerably in many respects, he remarks, 'they all shared the common feature that their socioeconomic structure as well as their legal and institutional framework furthered – or at least could not hinder or prevent – the growth of cottage industry'.[43]

Braun's contention is therefore that in Canton Zurich the degree of penetration of cottage industry varied with the rigidity of communal structures – or, as an anthropologist would probably say, with the presence or absence of 'closed corporate communities'. In his more recent work, Braun has further developed this argument and has intimated that this was also true of the Alpine zone proper. What is more, he has suggested that communal structures should be seen

---

[42] Braun, *Das ausgehende Ancien Régime*.
[43] Braun, 'Protoindustrialization and demographic changes', p. 309. The importance of the variable strength of communal regulations is also emphasized by U. Pfister in his recent re-analysis of the development of cottage industry in Canton Zurich. See U. Pfister, 'Proto-industrialization and demographic change'.

as an important variable to account for the uneven penetration of commercial pastoralism. This is a highly relevant argument in itself. But it also leads us back to a number of important questions which were raised in the first chapters of this book.

The Alpine 'closed corporate community': a reassessment

The notion of 'closed corporate community' was proposed in 1955 by Eric Wolf to designate the dominant form of village social organization in the mountainous areas of twentieth-century Latin America. Wolf noticed that lowland village communities generally lacked a formalized corporate structure. Little attempt was made to restrict membership, and there was no legal provision to prohibit or limit sale of land to outsiders. The highland communities, on the other hand, tended to acquire the form of a corporation. A large proportion of the village land was owned in common, and the rest was usually available only to people born within the community and could not be alienated to outsiders. This restriction, Wolf observed, could be further strengthened by forcing community members to marry endogamously. Another distinctive characteristic of the corporate communities was the presence of mechanisms whereby differences in power and wealth were levelled. And in contrast to the 'open' communities of the lowlands, which permitted 'free permeation by outside influences', the highland communities used their institutional barriers to resist changes and innovations imposed from the outside.[44]

After the publication of Wolf's first articles on this subject, it gradually became apparent that not only in Latin America but also in Europe and Asia communal forms conforming to Wolf's definition were more frequently encountered by anthropologists in the mountains than in the plains. In 1963 the closed corporate community was singled out by Burns as one of the distinctive features of the Alpine area *vis-à-vis* the surrounding lowlands,[45] and a few years later Rhoades and Thompson emphasized the 'many points in common between the Swiss and Sherpa communities ... and Wolf's "closed corporate peasant community"'.[46] This has led some anthropologists (including Burns, Rhoades and Thompson, and Netting) to suggest that the persistence of corporate communities in the uplands, and

[44] For a characterization of the closed corporate community, see Wolf, 'Types of Latin American peasantry', 'Closed corporate peasant communities', and *Peasants*, pp. 86–7. An account of the origins and development of this concept has been recently provided by Wolf himself, 'Vicissitudes of closed corporate community'.
[45] Burns, 'The Circum-Alpine area', pp. 145–8.
[46] Rhoades and Thompson, 'Adaptive strategies', p. 548.

probably also their origin, are due to their being eminently adaptive to the requirements of agro-pastoral economy in mountain environments. Other anthropologists, however, would object that 'the relationship between man and habitat in mountainous areas does not produce particular institutions, but results rather in an adaptation and a combination of general institutional elements which fit the natural environment'.[47] Wolf himself has pointed out that closed corporate communities are to be found in a variety of historical and geographical contexts ranging from colonial Java to manorial Europe,[48] and has argued that their longer persistence in the mountains is explained by their marginal location, which has made their destruction more costly or more difficult for the larger society.[49]

In spite of different views on its origin, both camps tend nevertheless to consider the closed corporate community as a constant in the social organization of upland populations, if not necessarily one of its specific features. Also, there is a general agreement that the closed corporate community possesses a number of demographic properties. As we have seen, because of its structural characteristics this kind of community is expected to cause high rates of village endogamy and to discourage or utterly prevent immigration. But it may be further argued (although opinion is, on this issue, rather divided) that corporate regulation also prevents or at least tends to slow down permanent emigration. As Netting has noticed, community membership with its attendant rights in a range of vital resources generally depended not only on birth but also on residence. Thus, people leaving their native village for good lost these rights and in a strongly corporative environment were unlikely to acquire similar rights elsewhere. This, it is suggested, was hardly an incentive to emigration.[50] According to Netting, structural closure tends therefore to result in demographic closure. Since the territorial boundaries of the various communities also tend to be unchanging and some equilibrium between population and resources has to be reached, the implication is that nuptiality

---

[47] Berthoud, 'Dynamics of ownership', p. 120.

[48] According to Wolf, the closed corporate community was often 'a child of conquest', or in any case the result of the attempt by power-holders to seize resources, concentrate population and make village units collectively responsible for tribute and corvée labour. See especially Wolf, 'Closed corporate peasant communities', pp. 7–8, and *Peasants*, pp. 81–95. This argument is challenged by Netting, 'What Alpine peasants have in common'. For an intermediate view on the origin and persistence of closed corporate communities in the Alps, see Poppi, 'Kinship and social organization', p. 61.

[49] Wolf, 'Types of Latin America peasantry', p. 457. For a similar argument, see Berthoud, 'Dynamics of ownership', p. 120.

[50] Netting, 'Eine lange Ahnenreihe', p. 195.

(in view of the limited extent of migration allowed by the model) can be expected to be the crucial regulatory mechanism.

Demographically, the ecosystemic model of the closed corporate community proposed by Netting is of course very similar to the one worked out by Malthus on the basis of Muret's data for Leysin. As we have seen in the course of this book, it provides a useful and attractive ideal type. But how closely, and how frequently, was this model approached in the real world? As Netting himself has remarked, in the last few decades the findings of historical demographic research have made the notion of the immobile village population highly suspicious.[51] But he is certainly justified in arguing that his detailed study of Törbel demonstrates that in the Alps it was possible for village communities to be little affected not only by immigration but also by emigration, and that the ability of local populations to adjust homeostatically to resources could be very considerable indeed. The results of Pfister's study of the demography and ecology of the highlands of Canton Berne increase our confidence that Törbel was not an anomaly, but was in fact representative of the kind of community which was largely responsible for the growth of Swiss Alpine population in the late eighteenth and nineteenth centuries.

Our investigation has shown, however, that the demographic history of Törbel markedly departed from that of other kinds of Alpine community. This creates something of a dilemma. As we have seen, the ecological arguments advanced by most anthropologists imply that closed corporate structures were a constant in upland social organization. If this was really the case, the demographic variations observed in the Alps can scarcely be traced back to this ubiquitous social-structural feature. Alternatively, the closed corporate community might have been a variable, and should be tested as such. The first point to be ascertained is, therefore, whether in the Alpine area this form of social organization was actually as pervasive as anthropologists have maintained. This is a complex question, and a comparison between Törbel and Alagna will once again be useful to clarify some of its aspects.

At first glance, Alagna appears to conform less strictly than Törbel to the classic Latin American type of the closed corporate community, whose boundaries coincide with those of the village. However, the scaffolding of Alagna's traditional social structure consisted (as we have briefly noticed in Chapter 4) of a variety of corporate groups. Indeed, the commune of Alagna came into existence gradually as a federation of 'alp corporations' which were essentially conterminous

[51] Netting, *Balancing on an alp*, pp. 76–82.

with the village's four wards and controlled the resources of the small valleys at whose feet the four clusters of hamlets were situated. As in many other Alpine localities, these corporations (which had each a governing body elected by the assembly of the household heads) had functioned at first as rent-paying units and later, when the feudal lords sold the possessions they had in the territory of Alagna, as purchasing units.[52]

'Enduring organizations of rights and duties held by a stable membership',[53] the four wards which made up the commune and parish of Alagna can legitimately be seen as constituting as many closed corporate communities quite similar to Törbel. (It is relevant to note that although in the late nineteenth century Törbel had a larger population than Alagna, until 1750 it was still a small village of just over 200 inhabitants and was therefore of roughly the same size as each one of Alagna's wards.) For a long time, the land controlled by each alp corporation and by the corresponding ward was actually recorded in cadastral registers as the common property of that corporation viewed legally as a single unit. But in fact the undivided land (*allmaina*) consisted only of the woodland and of the higher pastures where sheep and goats were grazed. The far more important lower pastures were, on the contrary, divided out among the members of the corporation, and the resulting 'family alps' were privately owned and individually managed by each household.

This leads us to a point of considerable significance. Anthropologists have been impressed by the finding that 'in the Andes and Himalayas, as well as in the Alps, communal tenure is associated with high-altitude zones where grazing and gathering (e.g. firewood collecting) are done'.[54] This has been explained by arguing that communal tenure promotes optimum production from a range of resources which include forests and, critically, the summer pastures. As Netting has stressed, common grazing lands are the more viable option because of the labour economies they allow: 'A handful of men can herd the animals of an entire village, milk them, and produce cheese in bulk. The rest of the population is thereby freed for the vital summer task of haying ... A diffuse resource such as an alp both loses productive

---

[52] For a more extended discussion of Alagna's corporate groups, see Viazzo, 'Ethnic change in a Walser community', pp. 155–6, 173–85. A perceptive account of the similar pattern of corporate social structure found in Rimella is provided by Sibilla, *I luoghi della memoria*, pp. 45–60.

[53] This is the definition of closed corporate communities formulated by Wolf, *Peasants*, p. 86.

[54] Brush, 'Introduction', p. 130.

value if it is split into private parcels and requires a considerably increased labour input due to the duplication of effort.'[55]

As we have seen in Chapter 1, this contention is central to the bold argument advanced by Netting and other ecological anthropologists, according to which the economic advantages of communal herding would entail communal tenure of the high-altitude zones, and communal tenure would in its turn entail the closed corporate community as the only adaptive form of village social organization. The comparison between Alagna and Törbel brings out the fallacy of assuming that what is ecologically adaptive or economically rational must therefore be inevitable, and also reveals an ambiguity in the notion of communal tenure which has plagued the anthropological literature. There is little doubt that in Alagna there was communal tenure of the alps. Only members of the alp corporation had access to the pastures (and to the forests) controlled by the corporation itself. And yet, the alps were divided out among the various households and managed individually.

Indeed, if on the one hand it is undeniable that communal forms approaching the closed corporate community were found almost everywhere in the Alps, it is no less clear that they were not rigidly associated with systems of communal herding, and that they exercised a greatly varying extent of control over their members. It would therefore seem that the closed corporate community is better seen as a variable rather than as a constant in Alpine social organization. This raises two questions. The first one is whether the differential strength of corporate regulations can help explain the variable degree of demographic and economic closure exhibited by Alpine communities. The second and more general one concerns the relation between demographic and economic closure.

In order to tackle these questions, it is first necessary to distinguish between the various kinds of migration and to consider the economic context within which migration took place. If we consider the agrarian communities of an area like Upper Valais, where partible inheritance endowed all natives with rights in communal resources and recourse to live-in servants was negligible, it may well be that the barriers erected by each community against the settlement of outsiders restricted immigration from neighbouring villages and 'increased the benefits of producing and reproducing in the home community', as Netting has argued.[56] However, what we are dealing with here is short-distance mobility rather than proper migration. As we have

---

[55] Netting, 'What Alpine peasants have in common', p. 141.
[56] Netting, *Balancing on an alp*, p. 71.

seen, in the Alps as a whole a more typical and important form of mobility consisted in long-distance emigration towards the plains. And the evidence we have examined in Chapter 6 clearly suggests that the advantages provided by community membership could hardly be very effective in preventing seasonal emigrants from leaving their homeland for good if the opportunities offered by the mainly urban contexts where they worked were good enough.[57]

The same probably applies to the ability of closed structures to prevent immigration outside an agrarian context. It is interesting to note that in the late sixteenth century Riva d'Agordo displayed all the marks of the closed corporate community,[58] but this scarcely enabled the members of this community to stem the massive immigration of miners which was to alter the economy and the demography of the valley so radically. The same is true, of course, of Alagna. But it should be acknowledged that, in the case of mining, pressures from outside were often exceptionally hard to resist. In Tyrol, the development of the mining industry was promoted by very powerful capitalist families from southern Germany, in particular by the Fuggers, and was strongly supported by the state. In the early sixteenth century, as has been noted, 'Tyrol provided a substantial part of the wealth that filled the Habsburg coffers and underwrote the pan-European ascendancy of the dynasty'.[59] In Alagna and in Riva d'Agordo mining was also directly promoted by the Piedmontese and by the Venetian governments.

On the other hand, the attempts by urban-based merchants to develop commercial pastoralism in the uplands or to establish a putting-out system in rural areas, although supported by powerful commercial interests, were not directly endorsed by central governments. It is therefore conceivable that these attempts may have encountered greater difficulties in overcoming the resistance of closed corporate communities. According to Braun, as we have seen, this was the reason why cottage industry gained a foothold in the

[57] It should not be forgotten, however, that, even when they left the mountains, Alpine emigrants were still likely to move in a strongly corporative social environment, where economic crises could easily lead cities to restrict immigration and naturalization, or to close them altogether. We have seen in Chapter 6 that in 1556 the City Council of Berne issued an edict whereby measures were taken against the immigration of men from Alagna and Gressoney. And it is also worth noting that, in the years in which Melcher Bodmer became a citizen of Zurich, naturalization fees were on the increase. In 1543 he had to pay 20 *Gulden*, in addition to 10 *Gulden* to be accepted into the powerful stone-masons' guild – in total 30 *Gulden*, that is to say approximately one-half of a stone-mason's yearly earnings. Only two years later, naturalization was closed. See Stucki, *Geschichte der Familie Bodmer*, pp. 31–4.

[58] Cf. Vergani, 'Una comunità mineraria di montagna', p. 616.

[59] Cole and Wolf, *The hidden frontier*, p. 38.

highlands of the canton of Zurich rather than the villages of the flatter districts. And he also believes that the uneven penetration of industrial activities into the mountainous Canton Glarus is primarily explained by the same reason. In Glarus, Braun suggests, the lack of proto-industrial development in districts like the Sernftal was due to the existence of rigid corporate communities comparable to those of the lowlands of Canton Zurich, whereas in places like the Linthal, where communal regulations were very loose, cottage industry thrived.[60]

No less significant are the implications of Braun's argument for an understanding of the rise of commercial pastoralism. As we noticed in Chapter 8, a growing number of Swiss scholars are now questioning the position of pre-eminence which the *Hirtenland* has been granted in Swiss historiography. While they concede that commercial pastoralism prevailed on the northern side of the Swiss Alps, these scholars rightly observe that in the drier 'intra-Alpine zone' (which includes Valais, Ticino and the Grisons) the so-called 'autarkic' communities were markedly dominant. Echoing the arguments already advanced in the 1940s by Richard Weiss, however, some of them simply tend to attribute the spatial distribution of these two forms of upland economy to environmental differences and to single out the amount of precipitation as the critical determinant.[61] Although it would be ill-advised to underestimate the importance of the 'comparative advantages' offered by the various zones, this is unlikely to be the whole story. As we have seen, in the Bernese Oberland commercial pastoralism became dominant in a district like Saanen but hardly affected, in spite of very similar physical and climatic characteristics, the communities of the Oberhasli.

Braun's contention is that social-structural factors, and especially communal regulations, could prevent external entrepreneurs from maximizing a region's comparative advantages for commercial purposes. In this respect, his lengthy discussion of the case of Canton Uri is particularly enlightening. In Uri, he remarks, 'the major part of the inhabitants were smallholders (so-called *Stümpler*) with three to seven cattle, who were able to impose the regulations necessary to protect their agricultural and pastoral resources against the rich families and also against outside persons and capital'. One crucial provision was that the alps, despite being understocked and therefore poorly exploited, could not be leased to outsiders. Nor was the exploitation of the alps increased by cattle being bought in spring, summered

---

[60] Braun, *Das ausgehende Ancien Régime*, p. 37.
[61] Cf. Weiss, *Volkskunde der Schweiz*, p. 105, and more recent Mathieu, 'Ein Land von Hirten und Sennen?', and especially Budmiger, 'Das Land der Walser'.

there, and sold in the autumn at a higher price. Such a form of supplemental exploitation, which was the rule in other regions, was forbidden by regulations of the closed corporate community (*Marktgenossenschaft*), which prescribed that only cattle which were wintered over might be pastured on the alps. This, Braun comments, was one of the measures which had been taken by the closed corporate community 'in order to achieve an agreement of interests between the richer and poorer members, that is to prevent members with more capital and credit from overburdening the alps with purchased cattle'.[62]

The case of Uri is interesting in more than one way. For one thing, it provides another example of an Alpine local ecosystem approaching very closely the model outlined in Chapter 1. Secondly, it shows that a strong corporate structure and a set of provisions preventing penetration from outside could indeed be essential to keep the delicate balance between animal population and hay production which is at the core of the notion of *Alpwirtschaft*. Thirdly, it confirms that the closed corporate community is better treated as an organizational variable rather than as a constant feature of Alpine social structure. Braun emphasizes that the communities of Canton Uri were unusual in their ability to enforce the strict regulations of their statutes. This entails that in the Swiss Alps not all *Marktgenossenschaften* (or similar corporate bodies) were equally capable of fulfilling those 'protective' functions which Wolf had posited as one of the main characteristics of the closed corporate community. Fourthly, the case of Uri is a reminder that closed corporate communities were aimed not only at preventing foreign intrusions into the local economy but also at maintaining an egalitarian pattern of social stratification.

As we have seen, Wolf had suggested that one of the distinctive features of the Andean closed corporate community was the presence of mechanisms whereby differences in power and wealth among the members were levelled. In Latin America this was achieved either through periodic reallotments of land or, typically, through various forms of wealth redistribution taking place on the occasion of *fiestas*. As Wiegandt and Netting have shown, Alpine closed corporate communities like Mase and Törbel could indeed be highly egalitarian. But their analyses indicate that the egalitarian nature of these communities resulted less from wealth-levelling mechanisms similar to those described by Wolf than from the working of partible inheritance. The case of Uri suggests, however, the potential significance of communal regulations such as the clause prohibiting a cattle owner to 'carry'

[62] Braun, *Das ausgehende Ancien Régime*, pp. 76–7.

more animals on the pastures than he could winter – a rule which was apparently strictly obeyed in Törbel. Moreover, Netting and Mc-Guire have rightly directed attention to another mechanism which in closed corporate communities usually had levelling effects, namely the credit system. In Törbel, they have noted, 'land hunger ... did not in itself provide opportunities for capital accumulation because the rich seldom advanced loans for land purchase. Since medieval times, there is documentary evidence that loans were provided by the corporate community itself'.[63]

It is worth observing, in this connection, that in Switzerland the revised settlement law of 1874, while transferring important political prerogatives from the citizens to the resident community, left the closed corporate community of the citizens with the right to administer the Charity of the Poor.[64] In contrast, the administrative reforms that followed the unification of Italy in 1861 marked the end of Alagna's Charity (the *Almosna der Ormu*) as well as of the other similar funds, whose administration had for centuries been handled locally by the various corporate groups. By 1879 they had been dismantled, and their functions had been transferred to the new charitable institutions established by the new state. As I have shown elsewhere,[65] providing relief for the village poor had been just one of the many tasks of these local charities, which had been instrumental in supporting emigration by advancing on favourable terms the money a villager might need for travel expenses, to get a son apprenticed, and so on. Their disappearance was almost certainly related to the spread of usury (one of the great plagues of Italian rural society in the late nineteenth century)[66] and led, through usury, to a more pronounced stratification within Alagna's population.

Sketchy as they are, these remarks are indicative of how important the availability of communal credit facilities could prove to be in Alpine communities, whatever their economic orientation. They also bring support to the thesis that the dissolution of closed corporate communities resulted in increased stratification. But it should be stressed that the credit system did not function as a levelling mechanism in all Alpine closed corporate communities. A study published some years ago shows, for instance, that in the Fassa Valley (in the Italian Eastern Alps) communal regulations severely limiting the settlement of outsiders were internally matched by a credit system which nullified the

[63] McGuire and Netting, 'Leveling peasants?', p. 283.
[64] Barber, *The death of communal liberty*, p. 215.
[65] Viazzo, 'Ethnic change in a Walser community', pp. 302–4.
[66] Cf. Sereni, *Il capitalismo nelle campagne*, pp. 243–5.

levelling effects of partible inheritance. The credit system was, in fact, instrumental in producing the concentration of land in the hands of relatively few families, which in turn paved the way to the commercialization of pastoral activities.[67]

It is relevant to note that the literature on the closed corporate community contains attempts to relate different patterns of allocation of power to varying degrees of penetration of outside forces leading to economic change. It has been suggested, in particular, that at either extreme in the spectrum (that is, where feudal lords are powerful and control vital resources, and where communities are egalitarian) the emergence of outward-oriented individuals or groups is likely to be stifled. 'It is in the middle range of the spectrum of allocation of power – that is, where there is a somewhat unequal distribution of power – that some peasants may have sufficient resources, given proper opportunities, to establish links with groups or institutions outside the village'.[68] This is what seems to have happened in the Fassa Valley or in Saanen, where an inegalitarian pattern of social stratification made the institutional barriers of the closed corporate community unable to resist external pressures.

All in all, the Alpine evidence surveyed in this chapter suggests that 'strong' corporate structures were in fact capable of vigorously resisting outside economic forces and, in some circumstances, of maintaining not only a comparatively closed economy but also a largely closed population. The relation between 'weak' corporate structures and migration was, on the other hand, mediated by the kind of economic change which external forces had brought about. Both the growth of cottage industry in the highlands of Canton Zurich and the development of the *Hirtenland* appear to have been favoured by the weakness of communal structures. But the former kind of 'open' economy caused a decrease in emigration and even encouraged immigration from agrarian areas; the latter, as the example of Saanen suggests, resulted in underemployment and high rates of emigration. It would therefore seem that a 'strong' corporate community was able to prevent or slow down emigration not so much directly (because of the rights it conferred to its members) as indirectly through the resistance it opposed to economic changes which might jeopardize the living standards of some villagers and force them to leave.

[67] Poppi, 'Kinship and social organization', pp. 84–5.
[68] Smith, '"Modernization" and the corporate community', p. 150.

A summary of conclusions

In 1980 Alan Macfarlane remarked that it was 'a pleasing irony that one of the "hardest" of the social sciences, concerned with the analysis of numbers of births, marriages and deaths, should be nudging us towards that realization of the importance of "culture" which, so some have argued, is the special contribution of anthropology'. Recent research in historical demography had in fact demonstrated the existence in pre-industrial Europe of broad regional differences in demographic systems and family structures, and 'looking from a very long distance' one could not help being struck by the association between the cultural and ethnic subdivisions of traditional Europe and the demographic map which was gradually emerging. It seemed more than a pure coincidence, to Macfarlane, that the boundary between western and eastern European marriage patterns detected by Hajnal roughly followed the Slav/non-Slav division, and that in Western Europe a demographic frontier separated the southern regions where Roman culture and law were dominant from the Germanic regions to the north.[1]

It is certainly reassuring for anthropology that the findings of historical demographers appear to vindicate the usefulness of the 'culture area' approach which Conrad Arensberg had recommended in the early 1960s for the anthropological study of the peoples of the Old World.[2] However, more refined information which has become available in the last few years shows that significant demographic differences existed not only between the major cultural regions of Europe but also within them. We may therefore wonder whether the scale

---

[1] Macfarlane, 'Demographic structures', pp. 1, 14.
[2] Arensberg, 'The Old World peoples'.

of Macfarlane's map is not too large, or at least whether that is the only map which anthropologists and historical demographers should use. It is interesting to note, in this respect, that Macfarlane has rightly contended that the north-south divide revealed by Hajnal or the demographic 'fault' line running across western Europe cannot be explained by reference to environmental features, for these areas are too vast and their physical characteristics too diverse.[3] Yet, environmental factors might prove relevant to make sense of smaller-scale variations. And the possibility cannot be ruled out that populations of different cultural background but facing similar ecological problems may have been forced to adopt similar demographic solutions.

Although the centrality of the notion of 'culture' in anthropology can scarcely be denied, many anthropologists have emphasized the importance of assessing the extent to which specific aspects of culture and social organization can be explained 'in terms of the functions they serve in adapting local populations to their environments'.[4] Indeed, a number of anthropologists who have worked in mountain areas of Europe have argued that, in the process of adapting to life in the mountains, upland populations (though ultimately of lowland derivation and sharing common traditions with their lowland counterparts) have modifed these traditions to a very large extent and in very similar ways. It is evident, for instance, that characteristic land use patterns and technological arrangements had to be developed in order to cope both with altitude, which entails lower productivity than in the plains, and with a range of topographic conditions causing wide variation in the agricultural potential within the same area. Thus, it has been suggested that 'an upland cultural ecotype can be identified which cuts across the culture areas and linguistic zones which have traditionally been used to classify populations in Europe'.[5]

As we have repeatedly noticed in this book, it is a tenet among ecological anthropologists that the fundamental goal of populations living in mountain environments must have been the preservation of viable landed patrimonies through the avoidance of partition. One corollary of this statement is that in mountain areas stem family organization should be expected to prevail whatever the legal, cultural and ethnic background of a population. But another, no less important corollary is that the practice of impartibility should result in low levels of nuptiality and, consequently, in low levels of both fertility and

---

[3] Macfarlane, 'Demographic structures', p. 7.
[4] Orlove, 'Ecological anthropology', p. 240.
[5] Cole, 'Inheritance processes', pp. 117–18.

mortality. A major feature of the 'upland ecotype' should therefore
be represented by a low-pressure demographic regime characterized
by moderate birth and death rates.

Inhabited by a large number of ethnic and linguistic groups, ranging
from Provençal-speakers in the Western Alps to Germanic and Slavonic populations in the northern and eastern sectors of the crescent,
the Alpine area provides a unique 'laboratory' for anthropologists
to assess the relative importance of cultural and environmental factors
in shaping demographic behaviour. If the hypothesis suggested by
Macfarlane is correct, one should find in the Alps a variety of demographic regimes, related to different and culturally distinctive patterns
of nuptiality and family formation. If, on the other hand, ecological
anthropologists are right in arguing that the same upland ecotype
can be identified all over the Alps, then one should expect no significant variation in birth and death rates between the various Alpine
regions.

However, not all students of the Alps are prepared to concede that
the environmental constraints which are typical of mountain areas
should result in a low-pressure demographic regime. A number of
leading historians and geographers have in fact contended that the
opposite was true. Although opinion may differ between those who
stress the role of emigration as a safety valve and those who believe
that a demographic balance was maintained mainly through high mortality, these scholars essentially agree that in the past the fertility of
Alpine populations used to be very high, as 'a sort of response to
the permanent "challenge" of the mountain environment'.[6]

Indeed, it is indisputable that in the recent past the Alpine regions
displayed birth and death rates which, though not very high in absolute terms, were nevertheless considerably higher than in the plains.
As late as 1960, as we noticed in Chapter 4, the birth rates recorded
in a large proportion of Alpine districts still exceeded 20 per thousand
(a threshold which the adjacent lowland regions had crossed over
fifty years earlier), and the higher levels of mortality were more than
simply the effect of the faster process of population ageing experienced
by the uplands. The available evidence on life expectancy in Switzerland in the course of the twentieth century led two Swiss demographers to conclude that it was necessary to dispose of what they called
'the myth of the longevity of mountain people, the alleged result of
healthy and unpolluted life'. As a matter of fact, they argued, it was

---

[6] Guichonnet, 'Développement démographique', p. 158.

evident that particularly before the Second World War people died younger in the mountains than in the plains.[7]

Our investigation has demonstrated, however, that once we move back into the more distant past the whole picture changes radically. The results of a spate of studies conducted in the past ten years show that for at least two centuries, from the mid-eighteenth century to the Second World War, the levels of fertility and mortality had been remarkably similar all over the Alpine area, and significantly lower than in the surrounding flat regions. Crude birth rates rarely exceeded the level of 30 per thousand, while death rates typically ranged between 22 and 28 per thousand. The contrast with the high-pressure regime of many adjacent lowland areas, where crude birth and death rates could easily reach 35 or even 40 per thousand, is striking.

Sweeping generalizations of this kind obviously require some qualifications. One major qualification is that, although birth and death rates changed far less in the Alps than in the surrounding plains, nevertheless they were by no means constant over time. Further research is badly needed to shed light on the beginnings of the low-pressure regime observed in the Alps since the mid-eighteenth century. In some localities, low birth and death rates are already recorded in the late sixteenth century. But it would seem that in most parts of the Alps death rates dropped markedly in the course of the eighteenth century, partly because of the declining virulence of epidemics and partly because of the introduction of the potato, which made Alpine local ecosystems more flexible and more resistant to climatic stress. Such a decrease in mortality appears, in its turn, to have been followed by a decrease in overall fertility.

A second major qualification is that what we have termed 'Alpine area' actually consists of different ecological and altitudinal zones. Yet, one of the main findings of the comparative investigation undertaken in this book has been that both fertility and mortality were, as a rule, distinctly lower in the high valleys than in the low valleys or than in the neighbouring hilly districts. This is particularly clear in the case of infant mortality. Swiss evidence, corroborated by data from the rest of the Alps, shows that towards the middle of the nineteenth century there was a marked tendency for infant mortality to decrease with altitude. By the early twentieth century, however, this relation had been reversed, and in the period between the two world wars infant mortality rates were far higher in the upland regions than

[7] Hagmann and Menthonnex, 'Éléments de démographie alpine', pp. 222-4.

in the plains. This is a revealing indication of the rapid worsening of the economic and sanitary conditions of the mountains relative to the increasingly urbanized plains, which greatly accelerated after 1850 and has been responsible for a number of anachronistic assumptions about the demography of the Alps in the past.

It goes without saying that the variable 'altitude', besides having a direct climatic component, can proximate for a variety of social and economic factors. Nevertheless, the strong impression produced by the material reviewed in this book is that the main cause of low mortality resided in what Malthus had called the 'healthiness' of mountain areas. It would also seem that Malthus was right to think that the decline in birth rates recorded in the Swiss Alps in the course of the eighteenth century (which alarmed more than one contemporary observer) was simply an adjustment of fertility to the lower levels of mortality, and more generally a demonstration of the fundamental principle of the 'dependence of the births on the deaths'.

But in Chapter 2 we also noticed that according to Malthus the strikingly low levels of mortality recorded in the Swiss Alps could not possibly have been achieved and maintained, if favourable environmental conditions 'had not been accompanied by a proportionate action of the prudential restraint on marriage'.[8] Foreshadowing the models put forward nearly two centuries later by historical demographers and ecological anthropologists, Malthus suggested that the demography of Alpine populations was bound to work as a finely balanced homeostatic system, in which fertility was adjusted to mortality and resources through the regulatory functions of nuptiality. The testing of this hypothesis has been one of the main aims of this book, and especially interesting results have come out from a comparison between the demographic evolution of the Swiss Alps (which Malthus had used as a crucial case-study to demonstrate the validity of his principles) and that of the neighbouring Austrian Alps.

A first important outcome of this comparison has been the finding that, in spite of markedly different systems of inheritance, the Swiss and the Austrian Alps displayed very similar patterns of nuptiality. In both areas marriage was very late for both men and women, and rates of permanent celibacy exceedingly high. This would seem to support Malthus's contention that it is in mountain areas that the prudential check of marriage should be expected to prevail to a greater degree, and also the related view that in marginal areas like the Alps marriage patterns are shaped more decisively by environmental con-

---

[8] Malthus, *Summary view*, p. 214.

straints than by the formal properties of inheritance and succession rules. The decline in nuptiality recorded in both areas in the course of the eighteenth century also would seem to corroborate Malthus's other contention that, since in mountain environments resources tend to be fixed and cannot sustain population growth, then improvements in mortality necessarily entail a decline in nuptiality.

What Malthus had not forecast was the substantial expansion of resources made possible by the introduction of the potato, which in most Alpine districts took place towards the end of the eighteenth century. In these crucially changed circumstances, one would expect a 'relaxation' of nuptiality allowing population size to increase so as to adjust to resources. In the Austrian Alps, however, the introduction of the potato appears to have had little effect. The population of all its provinces either increased very little or stagnated. The population of the Swiss Alps, on the other hand, grew at a fast pace. But nuptiality, instead of increasing, continued to decline.

Although detailed comparative studies of these puzzling questions are still lacking, there is reason to believe that the key to solving them consists on the one hand in considering marriage patterns more dynamically than has generally been the case in Alpine studies, and on the other in examining nuptiality in the context of the sharply different systems of stratification found in Swiss and Austrian communities. Apart from marriage age, the demographic indicators which have usually been employed in the study of Alpine nuptiality all provide relative measures, ignoring variations in the size of cohorts over time. This may easily lead to paradoxical conclusions. Thus, the marked increase in the proportion of celibates recorded in Switzerland between 1750 and the late nineteenth century would seem to suggest that prospects for marriage were worsening. But, if we consider the absolute number of people getting married, we find that it increased considerably, and so did the number of estates. It is important to note that since the total amount of land remained essentially the same, the average amount of land worked by each individual (or household) steadily declined. Yet, the balance between population and resources did not necessarily deteriorate, owing to the beneficial effects of the introduction of the potato. Indeed, the fact that the agricultural output *per capita* appears to have remained virtually constant is an indication that nuptiality functioned as a surprisingly precise homeostatic mechanism.

As for the no less puzzling question of the differential impact of the introduction of the potato on population growth in the Swiss and Austrian Alps, it seems essential to observe that in Switzerland the cultivation of the potato was started by people belonging to the poorer stratum, who had been granted usufruct of tiny plots carved out of the communal land. By contrast, the new potential was exploited only to a limited extent in the Austrian mountains, where the formation of cottages was strongly discouraged both by the external power-holders and by the local farming élite. While in most parts of Switzerland social-structural factors were opposing minimum resistance to the adjustment of population and nuptiality to the increased carrying capacity of local ecosystems, in Austria marriage was sternly restricted in order to preserve a situation of 'static equilibrium', in which population size was blocked well below carrying capacity so as to permit the perpetuation of the existing social structure.

The same contrast between the social structure of Swiss and Austrian communities probably explains another major difference in their demography, namely the far larger share of total fertility accounted for by illegitimate births in Austria. What is most striking is that the levels of both nuptiality and overall fertility were very similar, while marital fertility was (at least in the second half of the nineteenth century) considerably lower in the eastern provinces of Austria than in the Swiss Alps or in western Austrian provinces like Tyrol and Vorarlberg. But in the eastern part of Austria lower marital fertility was almost perfectly counterbalanced by astonishingly high levels of illegitimacy.

The fact that in the Swiss and in the Austrian Alps a very similar level of overall fertility could be achieved through different combinations of legitimate and illegitimate fertility is an indication that, although the Alpine area as a whole displayed just one demographic *regime*, its regional subdivisions exhibited a range of significantly different demographic *systems*. An even more impressive demonstration of this variability is provided by the Western Alps. As we have seen in Chapter 4, it had been known for some time that since at least the 1830s the southern regions of the French Alps had been characterized by comparatively low levels of fertility and by levels of nuptiality which were unusually high by Alpine standards. This seemed to be the obvious consequence of the early adoption of family limitation practices which is typical of France as a whole. However, the data examined in this book indicate that in the first half of the nineteenth century this allegedly 'post-traditional' pattern can also be detected on the Piedmontese side, where family limitation is believed to have started only late in the century. What is more, an increasing amount of evidence suggests that a coexistence of low marital fertility and high nuptiality may have been the basic feature of a demographic pattern of long standing on both sides of the Western Alps.

These findings demonstrate that in mountain areas regulatory mechanisms other than nuptiality could be at work, and raise the question of the causes of the marked variations in nuptiality and fertility observed in the various Alpine regions. One factor most likely to have affected marital fertility is breastfeeding, which is believed to have been more usual in the Western than in the Eastern Alps. However, the effects of the long periods of spousal separation caused in many districts by male emigration also require to be carefully evaluated. And it would probably be a mistake to overlook the possibility that different systems of family formation may have been a variable of some importance in influencing fertility. Although any generalization would be premature, the evidence reviewed in Chapter 9 certainly suggests that in the Western Alps lower marital fertility was associated with systems of joint family formation. This implies that, contrary to what is generally maintained, this kind of family form could in fact depress fertility, or even that low fertility may have been (particularly in Alpine environments) a precondition to the formation and viability of joint households.

Treating household structure as a variable obviously runs counter to the assertion, advanced mainly by ecological anthropologists, that one of the distinguishing features of the Alpine area was the overwhelming predominance of the stem family. The evidence discussed in this book shows, on the contrary, that the Alps displayed a variety of family forms, ranging from classic instances of joint family system to the nuclear family system documented by Netting for nineteenth-century Törbel. It is intriguing that so far local systems of joint family formation have been attested more frequently in the Western Alps, which were mainly inhabited by Romance populations and were characterized by relatively high levels of nuptiality. Such a combination of household complexity and high nuptiality is remarkably close to what is generally termed a 'Mediterranean' type, and the possibility that household composition in the Western Alps may have been more heavily affected by Mediterranean cultural and legal influences is certainly worthy of being further explored.

Nevertheless, systems of joint family formation are also documented in a number of German-speaking localities. This is a warning that any theory phrased in broad cultural or ethnic terms is unlikely to prove successful. The comparison between Alagna and Törbel has been, in this respect, particularly instructive. The populations of these two villages were of the same ethnic stock, sharing the same Alemannic dialect, the same material culture and the same system of inheritance. Because of the different mode of colonization, however, the settlement pattern was very dissimilar, and so was the way in which agricultural and pastoral resources were managed. As a consequence, the management of agricultural and pastoral resources imposed very different labour requirements on the individual households. This contrast in the patterns of spatial and economic organization, it has been suggested, might be crucial to explain why Törbel displayed a system of nuclear household formation which had little in common with the joint family system found in Alagna.

On the other hand, the enormous importance of seasonal emigration in Alagna was a reminder that agriculture and pastoralism were not the only economic activities in which Alpine population could engage. It is obvious that in the Alps (and particularly in those villages where, as in Alagna, men were away during the summer) the labour requirements of seasonal emigration interacted with those of mountain farming and could arguably be even more critical in shaping household structure. Relevant material from my own research on Alagna was presented in the final section of Chapter 9, but any attempt at general statements was hampered by the surprising lack of studies testing for the Alpine area the various claims which have been advanced about the degree of compatibility between migration and diverse forms of family organization.

But this is only one aspect of the generally disappointing state of research and theorizing on the subject of Alpine emigration. In fact, one of the main contentions of this book is that the whole problem of the causes and consequences of emigration should be reconsidered. Most students of the Alpine world have taken it for granted that in the mountains population endemically tends to exceed the limits imposed by local resources, and have stressed the role of emigration as a way of disposing of surplus population. Therefore, Alpine emigration has been generally characterized and explained in terms of poverty and overpopulation. The evidence presented in this book has laid bare a number of major shortcomings in this approach, one of these shortcomings being a marked tendency to perceive emigration as a response to environmental imperatives as inevitable and unchanging as the environment itself. Yet it is salutary to remember that the migratory imbalance to which we are now accustomed is a relatively recent phenomenon. Until the fourteenth and fifteenth centuries, people were in fact more likely to move into the Alpine valleys than to leave them for good. And, even after the end of the medieval colonization, the social and demographic structure of a large number of Alpine districts continued to be affected by flows of immigration stimulated by the growth of the mining industry.

Another conclusion to emerge from the evidence examined in this book is that caution is needed before a rise in either seasonal or permanent emigration can be interpreted as a sign of overpopulation. Nor should emigration be seen as the obvious effect of poverty. Students of the Alps have been prone to assume that the inhabitants of barren high valleys were bound to be very poor, thereby confusing the poverty of the land, which was very real, with the poverty of the people in the mountains, which was simply potential. Perhaps the most serious consequence of equating emigration with poverty is that it obscures the complex nexus linking emigration to the social and economic structure of the Alpine community. In its various formulations, this equation either conveys the impression that all emigrants were equally poor and hopeless or, alternatively, that emigrants overwhelmingly belonged to the poorer stratum of upland society. A growing amount of evidence suggests, on the contrary, that the condition of the emigrants was not always miserable and that they actually tended to be recruited more from amongst the rich than from amongst the poor.

The discovery that all over the Alps birth rates tended to be moderate, and that a number of regulatory mechanisms were at work to keep natural increase within tolerable limits, obviously entails a revision of the widespread notion that permanent emigration was the only alternative to starvation. Indeed, the regulatory functions of permanent emigration itself should be carefully reconsidered in this new perspective. Since Malthus's days, most scholars have tended to regard restricted nuptiality and permanent emigration as two mutually exclusive mechanisms whereby mountain societies could keep their numbers in balance with their resources. This view seems, however, to overlook the fact that in the Alps permanent emigration was essentially a male affair, often resulting in severely unbalanced sex ratios. Unbalanced sex ratios were, in their turn, the first determinant of the extraordinarily high rates of female celibacy that represent one of the distinguishing features of the nuptiality patterns displayed by many Alpine districts *vis-à-vis* other variants of the European marriage patterns. Far from being an alternative to low nuptiality, permanent emigration could therefore be one of its main preconditions.

Finally, it should be stressed that, although seasonal and permanent emigration were found virtually everywhere in the Alps, it is becoming increasingly clear that their incidence could vary to a surprisingly large extent. Cases like that of Alagna provide a striking demonstration of the pervasive importance which emigration in its various forms could acquire in Alpine communities. But the results of recent studies of a number of Swiss localities are no less impressive in showing that in other parts of the Alps emigration could play a decidedly limited role both economically and demographically. To be sure, a high degree of economic and demographic closure could be attained more easily in a context of expanding agricultural resources, which allowed local ecosystems to absorb almost completely the natural increase without seriously deteriorating the living standards. Also, much depended on the characteristics of local communal structures, and on their ability to resist economic and political pressure from outside. Nevertheless, this variability suggests that, while it would be dangerous to accept the stereotypical image of the self-contained upland community, it would be equally wrong to assume that the economic and demographic closure of Alpine communities was always too weak to warrant the use of local ecosystems as legitimate and meaningful units of analysis and explanation.

Bibliography

Abelson, A. E., 'Altitude and fertility', *Human Biology*, 48 (1976), pp. 83–91.

Adams, J. W. and Kasakoff, A. B., 'Ecosystems over time: the study of migration in "long run" perspective', in E. F. Moran (ed.), *The ecosystem concept in anthropology* (Boulder, 1984), pp. 205–23.

Albera, D., 'I giovani e il matrimonio in una vallata alpina', unpublished dissertation, University of Turin, 1982.

'Systèmes familiaux dans les Alpes occidentales', unpublished Mémoire de D. E. A., University of Provence, 1986.

'Open systems and closed minds, or: the limitations of anthropological naivety. A native's view' (forthcoming in *Man*).

Albera, D., Dossetti, M. and Ottonelli, S., 'Società ed emigrazioni nell' alta Valle Varaita', *Bollettino Storico Bibliografico Subalpino*, 86. 1 (1988), pp. 117–69.

Allio, R., 'Emigrazione dalla Valle Maira tra Ottocento e Novecento', *Bollettino della Società per gli Studi Storici, Archeologici e Artistici della Provincia di Cuneo*, 93 (1985), pp. 131–6.

Anderson, R. T., *Modern Europe: an anthropological perspective* (Pacific Palisades, Cal., 1973).

Anderson, R. T. and Anderson, G., 'The replicate social structure', *Southwestern Journal of Anthropology*, 18 (1962), pp. 365–70.

Andorka, R., 'Un exemple de faible fécondité légitime dans une région de la Hongrie', *Annales de Démographie Historique*, 1972, pp. 25–53.

Andorka, R. and Faragó, T., 'Pre-industrial household structure in Hungary', in R. Wall, J. Robin and P. Laslett (eds.), *Family forms in historic Europe* (Cambridge, 1983), pp. 281–307.

Arbos, P., *La vie pastorale dans les Alpes françaises* (Grenoble, 1922).

Arensberg, C. M., 'The Old World peoples', *Anthropological Quarterly*, 36 (1963), pp. 75–99.

Arensberg, C. M. and Kimball, S. T., *Family and community in Ireland* (Cambridge, Mass., 1940).

Arnold, K., 'Der Umbruch des generativen Verhaltens in einem Bergbauern-gebiet', in H. Helczmanovszki (ed.), *Beiträge zur Bevölkerungs- und Sozialgeschichte Österreichs* (Vienna, 1973), pp. 403–48.

Bailey, F. G., 'Changing communities', in F. G. Bailey (ed.), *Gifts and poison. The politics of reputation* (Oxford, 1971), pp. 26–40.

'What are *Signori?*', in F. G. Bailey (ed.), *Gifts and poison. The politics of reputation* (Oxford, 1971), pp. 230–51.

Bailey, F. G. (ed.), *Gifts and poison. The politics of reputation* (Oxford, 1971).

Debate and compromise. The politics of innovation (Oxford, 1973).

Barber, B. R., *The death of communal liberty. A history of freedom in a Swiss mountain canton* (Princeton, 1974).

Barelli, V., *Cenni di statistica mineralogica degli Stati di S.M. il Re di Sardegna* (Turin, 1835).

Bascapè, C., *Novaria, seu de ecclesia novariensi libri duo* (Novara, 1612).

Bassani, R., 'Una comunità del Cuneese fra Sei e Settecento', unpublished dissertation, University of Turin, 1977.

Bates, D. G. and Lees, S. H., 'The myth of population regulation', in N. A. Chagnon and W. Irons (eds.), *Evolutionary biology and human social behavior. An anthropological perspective* (North Scituate, Mass., 1979), pp. 273–89.

Becker, H., 'Types and forms of the medieval settlement expansion process in the central parts of the south of the Eastern Alps', *Geographia Polonica*, 38 (1978), pp. 25–30.

Becker, P., 'Traces on mountains: reconstituting the families of an Alpine village (St. Lamprecht, Styria, 1600–1850)', paper presented at the AHC Second Annual Conference on 'History and computing' (London, 1987).

Befu, H., 'Ecology, residence and authority: the corporate household in Central Japan', *Ethnology*, 7 (1968), pp. 25–42.

Behar, C. L., 'Malthus and the development of demographic analysis', *Population Studies*, 41 (1987), pp. 269–81.

Bell, R. M., *Fate and honor, family and village. Demographic and cultural change in rural Italy since 1800* (Chicago, 1979).

Bellettini, A., 'Gli "status animarum": caratteristiche e problemi di utilizzazione nelle ricerche di demografia storica', in E. Sonnino (ed.), *Le fonti della demografia storica in Italia* (Rome, 1972), vol. 1, pp. 3–31.

Benetti, A., Benetti, D., Dell'Oca, A. and Zoia, D., *Uomini delle Alpi. Contadini e pastori in Valtellina* (Milan, 1983).

Bergier, J.-F., 'Le trafic à travers les Alpes et les liaisons transalpines du haut moyen âge au XVIIe siècle', in J.-F. Bergier *et al.*, *Le Alpi e l'Europa*, vol. 3, *Economia e transiti* (Bari, 1975), pp. 1–72.

'Le cycle médiéval: des sociétés féodales aux états territoriaux', in P. Guichonnet (ed.), *Histoire et civilisations des Alpes* (Toulouse and Lausanne, 1980), vol. 1, pp. 163–264.

Die Wirtschaftsgeschichte der Schweiz (Zurich and Cologne, 1983).

Berkner, L. K., 'The stem family and the developmental cycle of the peasant household: an eighteenth-century Austrian example', *American Historical Review*, 77 (1972), pp. 398–418.

Berkner, L. K. and Mendels, F. F., 'Inheritance systems, family structure, and demographic patterns in Western Europe, 1700–1900', in C. Tilly (ed.), *Historical studies of changing fertility* (Princeton, 1978), pp. 209–23.

Bernard, P. P., *Rush to the Alps. The evolution of vacationing in Switzerland* (Boulder, 1978).

Berthoud, G., *Changements économiques et sociaux de la montagne. Vernamiège en Valais* (Berne, 1967).

'Dynamics of ownership in the Circum-Alpine area', *Anthropological Quarterly*, 45 (1972), pp. 117–24.

Béteille, R., 'Tourisme et milieu rural montagnard: l'exemple du Pitztal (Tirol autrichien)', *Revue de Géographie Alpine*, 56 (1968), pp. 367–76.

Bickel, W., *Bevölkerungsgeschichte und Bevölkerungspolitik der Schweiz seit dem Ausgang des Mittelalters* (Zurich, 1947).

Bideau, A., 'Autoregulating mechanisms in traditional populations', in N. Keyfitz (ed.), *Population and biology* (Liège, 1984), pp. 117–31.

Bielmann, J., 'La population du Pays d'Uri au XVIIIe siècle', *Annales de Démographie Historique*, 1976, pp. 456–8.

Billigmeier, R. H., *A crisis in Swiss pluralism. The Romansh and their relations with the German- and Italian-Swiss* (The Hague, 1979).

Binz, L., 'La population du diocèse de Genève à la fin du moyen âge', in *Mélanges d'histoire économique et sociale en hommage au professeur Antony Babel* (Geneva, 1963), vol. 1, pp. 145–96.

Biraben, J.-N., *Les hommes et la peste en France et dans les pays européens et méditerranéens*, 2 vols. (Paris, 1975–6).

Bircher, R., *Wirtschaft und Lebenshaltung im schweizerischen 'Hirtenland' am Ende des 18. Jahrhunderts* (Zurich, 1938).

Blanchard, R., *Les Alpes Occidentales*, 7 vols. (Grenoble and Paris, 1938–56).

Bodo, M., 'Issime: alfabetizzazione e istruzione scolastica tra '700 e '800', *Walserglocken*, 13 (1982), pp. 36–9.

Bodo, M. and Viazzo, P. P., 'Gli status animarum come fonte storico-demografica: l'esempio di Alagna', *Novarien*, 11 (1981), pp. 5–29.

Bolognese-Leuchtenmüller, B., *Bevölkerungsentwicklung und Berufsstruktur, Gesundheits- und Fürsorgewesen in Österreich 1750–1918* (Vienna, 1978).

Bongaarts, J. and Potter, R. G., 'Fertility effect of seasonal migration and seasonal variation in fecundability', *Demography*, 16 (1979), pp. 475–9.

Bonnin, B., 'Les migrations dans les hautes terres dauphinoises au XVIIIe siècle', in P. Guillen (ed.), *Travail et migration dans les Alpes françaises et italiennes* (Grenoble, 1982), pp. 33–47.

Bonstetten, K. V. von, *Briefe über ein schweizerisches Hirtenland* (Basle, 1782).

Boserup, E., *The conditions of agricultural growth* (London, 1965).

Braudel, F., 'Histoire et sciences sociales: la longue durée', *Annales E.S.C.*, 13 (1958), pp. 725–53.

La Méditerranée et le monde méditerranéen à l'époque de Philippe II, 2nd edn, 2 vols. (Paris, 1966).

The Mediterranean and the mediterranean world in the age of Philip II, English edn of *La Méditerranée*, 2 vols. (London, 1972).

Braun, R., *Industrialisierung und Volksleben. Die Veränderungen der Lebensformen in einem ländlichen Industriegebiet vor 1800 (Zürcher Oberland)* (Zurich, 1960).

'Protoindustrialization and demographic changes in the Canton of Zurich', in C. Tilly (ed.), *Historical studies of changing fertility* (Princeton, 1978), pp. 289–334.

Das ausgehende Ancien Régime in der Schweiz. Aufriss einer Sozial- und Wirtschaftsgeschichte des 18. Jahrhunderts (Göttingen and Zurich, 1984).

Brennan, E. R., James, A. V. and Morrill, W. T., 'Inheritance, demographic structure, and marriage: a cross-cultural perspective', *Journal of Family History*, 7 (1982), pp. 289–98.

Breschi, M. and Livi-Bacci, M., 'Stagione di nascita e clima come determinanti della mortalità infantile negli Stati Sardi di Terraferma', *Genus*, 42 (1986), pp. 87–101.

Broström, G., 'Practical aspects on the estimation of the parameters in Coale's model for marital fertility', *Demography*, 22 (1985), pp. 625–31.

Brudner, L. A., 'The maintenance of bilingualism in southern Austria', *Ethnology*, 11 (1972), pp. 39–54.

Brush, S. B., 'Introduction to the symposium "Cultural adaptations to mountain ecosystems"', *Human Ecology*, 4 (1976), pp. 125–33.

Bucher, S., *Bevölkerung und Wirtschaft des Amtes Entlebuch im 18. Jahrhundert* (Lucerne, 1974).

Budmiger, G., 'Das Land der Walser', in G. Budmiger (ed.), *Die Walser* (Frauenfeld and Stuttgart, 1982), pp. 24–38.

Bulmer, M. J. A., 'Sociological models of the mining community', *The Sociological Review*, 23 (1975), pp. 61–92.

Burns, R. K., 'The ecological basis of the French Alpine peasant communities in the Dauphiné', *Anthropological Quarterly*, 34 (1961), pp. 19–35.

'The Circum-Alpine area: a preliminary view', *Anthropological Quarterly*, 36 (1963), pp. 130–55.

Butz, R., 'Extreme Entvölkerungsgemeinden in der Schweiz', *Geographica Helvetica*, 24 (1969), pp. 111–15.

Caffaro, M. G., 'Scolarità ed alfabetizzazione nelle Valli Valdesi tra Restaurazione ed Emancipazione: la Val Pellice', unpublished dissertation, University of Turin, 1983.

Carlen, L., 'Der Rat von Bern und die Krämer von Gressoney', *Wir Walser. Halbjahresschrift für Walsertum*, 5.2 (1967), pp. 28–30.

Rechtsgeschichte der Schweiz (Berne, 1968).

'Alpenlandschaft und ländliche Verfassung, besonders in Tirol, im Wallis und in den Walsersiedlungen', *Montafon*, 21 (1969), pp. 335–53.

Carol, H. and Senn, U., 'Jura, Mittelland und Alpen. Ihr Anteil an Fläche und Bevölkerung der Schweiz', *Geographica Helvetica*, 5 (1950), pp. 129–36.

Caroni, P., 'Zur Bedeutung des Warentransportes für die Bevölkerung der Passgebiete', *Schweizerische Zeitschrift für Geschichte*, 29 (1979), pp. 84–100.

Carrasco, P., *Land and polity in Tibet* (Seattle, 1959).

Carrier, E. H., *Water and grass. A study of the pastoral economy of southern Europe* (London, 1932).

Châtelain, A., *Les migrants temporaires en France de 1800 à 1914*, 2 vols. (Lille, 1976).

Cholley, A., *Les Préalpes de Savoie (Genevois, Bauges) et leur avant-pays* (Paris, 1925).

Cima, M., 'Strategie tecnologiche per l'industria alpina del ferro nei tre secoli dell'età moderna', *Ricerche Storiche*, 16 (1986), pp. 207–41.

Cipolla, C. M., *Literacy and development in the West* (Harmondsworth, 1969).

Coale, A. J., 'Factors associated with the development of low fertility: an historic summary', in *Proceedings of the World Population Conference, 1965* (New York, 1967), vol. 2, pp. 205–9.

Coale, A. J. and Treadway, R., 'A summary of the changing distribution of overall fertility, marital fertility, and the proportion married in the provinces of Europe', in A. J. Coale and S. C. Watkins (eds.), *The decline of fertility in Europe* (Princeton, 1986), pp. 31–181.

Coale, A. J. and Trussell, T. J., 'Model fertility schedules: variations in the age structure of childbearing in human populations', *Population Index*, 40 (1974), pp. 185–258.

'Finding the two parameters that specify a model schedule of marital fertility', *Population Index*, 44 (1978), pp. 203–13.

Cole, J. W., 'Inheritance processes in the Italian Alps', *Ethnohistory*, 24 (1977), pp. 117–32.

Cole, J. W. and Wolf, E. R., *The hidden frontier. Ecology and ethnicity in an Alpine valley* (New York, 1974).

Coleman, D. A., 'Marital choice and geographical mobility', in A. J. Boyce (ed.), *Migration and mobility. Biosocial aspects of human movement* (London, 1984), pp. 19–55.

'Population regulation: a long-range view', in D. A. Coleman and R. S. Schofield (eds.), *The state of population theory* (Oxford, 1986), pp. 14–41.

Collins, P. W., 'Functional analyses in the symposium "Man, culture, and animals"', in A. Leeds and A. P. Vayda (eds.), *Man, culture, and animals. The role of animals in human ecological adjustments* (Washington, 1965), pp. 271–82.

Collomp, A., 'Famille nucléaire et famille élargie en Haute Provence au XVIIIe siècle (1703–1734)', *Annales E.S.C.*, 27 (1972), pp. 969–75.

'Ménage et famille: études comparatives sur la dimension et la structure du groupe domestique', *Annales E.S.C.*, 29 (1974), pp. 777–86.

'Alliance et filiation en Haute-Provence au XVIIIe siècle', *Annales E.S.C.*, 32 (1977), pp. 445–77.

'Tensions, dissentions, and ruptures inside the family in seventeenth and eighteenth-century Haute-Provence', in H. Medick and D. W. Sabean (eds.), *Interest and emotion. Essays on the study of family and kinship* (Cambridge and Paris, 1984), pp. 145–70.

'From stem family to nuclear family: changes in the coresident domestic group in Haute Provence between the end of the eighteenth and the middle of the nineteenth centuries', *Continuity and Change*, 3 (1988), pp. 65–81.

Connell, J., Dasgupta, B., Laishley, R. and Lipton, M., *Migration from rural areas. The evidence from village studies* (Delhi, 1976).

Connell, K. H., *The population of Ireland 1750–1845* (Oxford, 1950).

Connolly, S. J., 'Marriage in pre-famine Ireland', in A. Cosgrove (ed.), *Marriage in Ireland* (Dublin, 1985), pp. 78–89.

Cook, N. D., *Demographic collapse. Indian Peru, 1520–1620* (Cambridge, 1981).

Cuatrecasas, J., 'Paramo vegetation and its life forms', in C. Troll (ed.), *Geoecology of the mountainous regions of the Tropical Americas* (Bonn, 1968), pp. 163–86.

Cuoco, F., 'Scolarità ed alfabetizzazione nelle Valli Valdesi tra Restaurazione ed Emancipazione: la Val Germanasca e la Bassa Val Chisone', unpublished dissertation, University of Turin, 1984.

Dao, E., 'Saggio di ricerca storica su Elva', *Bollettino della Società per gli Studi Storici, Archeologici e Artistici della Provincia di Cuneo*, 59 (1968), pp. 71–89.

David, J., Herbin, J. and Mériaudeau, R., 'La dynamique démographique de la zone de montagne française: le tournant historique des années 1970', *Espace-Populations-Sociétés*, 1986, pp. 365–76.

Davis, K., 'Institutional patterns favoring high fertility in underdeveloped areas', *Eugenics Quarterly*, 2 (1955), pp. 33–9.

Debiaggi, C., 'Gli artisti di Alagna', in E. Ragozza (ed.), *Alagna Valsesia, una comunità walser* (Borgosesia, 1983), pp. 225–46.

Denison, N., 'Sauris: a trilingual community in diatypic perspective', *Man*, n.s., 3 (1968), pp. 578–92.

Dennis, N., Henriques, F. and Slaughter, C., *Coal is our life. An analysis of a Yorkshire mining community* (London, 1956).

De Rossi, G., 'L'economia agraria alpina', in P. Guichonnet *et al.*, *Le Alpi e l'Europa*, vol. 2, *Uomini e territorio* (Bari, 1975), pp. 255–327.

Destro, A., *L'ultima generazione. Confini materiali e simbolici di una comunità delle Alpi Marittime* (Milan, 1984).

Deutscher, T. B., 'Carlo Bascapè and Tridentine Reform in the diocese of Novara (1593–1615)', unpublished Ph.D. dissertation, University of Toronto, 1978.

Dorfmann, M., 'Régions de montagne: de la dépendance a l'auto-développement?', *Revue de Géographie Alpine*, 71 (1983), pp. 5–34.

Dossetti, M., 'Aspetti demografici del Saluzzese: la popolazione di Martiniana Po dal 1770 al 1870', unpublished dissertation, University of Turin, 1970.

Douglas, M., 'Population control in primitive groups', *British Journal of Sociology*, 17 (1966), pp. 263–73.

Dupâquier, J., 'De l'animal à l'homme: le mécanisme autorégulateur des populations traditionnelles', *Revue de l'Institut de Sociologie de l'Université Libre de Bruxelles*, 2 (1972), pp. 177–211.

Eandi, G., *Statistica della provincia di Saluzzo* (Saluzzo, 1836).

Eckert, E. A., 'Boundary formation and diffusion of plague: Swiss epidemics from 1562 to 1669', *Annales de Démographie Historique*, 1978, pp. 49–80.

Ehmer, J. and Mitterauer, M., 'Zur Einführung', in J. Ehmer and M. Mitterauer (eds.), *Familienstruktur und Arbeitsorganisation in ländlichen Gesellschaften* (Vienna, 1986), pp. 7–30.

Ellen, R., *Environment, subsistence and system. The ecology of small-scale social formations* (Cambridge, 1982).

'Ecology', in A. Kuper and J. Kuper (eds.), *The Social Science Encyclopedia* (London, 1985), pp. 218–20.

Elsasser-Rusterholz, B. A., *Beiträge zur Siedlungs- und Wirtschaftsgeographie in den bündnerischen Walserkolonien* (Zurich, 1969).

Espagnet, M., 'Saint-Véran en Queyras (1735–1815), étude de démographie historique', unpublished Mémoire de maîtrise, EHESS (Paris), 1976.

Evans-Pritchard, E. E., 'Introduction', to R. Hertz, *Death and the right hand* (London, 1960), pp. 9–24.

Faidutti-Rudolph, A. M., *L'immigration italienne dans le Sud-Est de la France* (Gap, 1964).

Fanfani, A., 'L'industria mineraria lombarda durante il dominio spagnolo', in A. Fanfani, *Saggi di storia economica italiana* (Milan, 1936), pp. 161–253.

Fauve-Chamoux, A., 'Le fonctionnement de la famille-souche dans les Baronnies des Pyrénées du XVIIe siècle à la première guerre mondiale', in *Proceedings of the First Hispano-Luso-Italian Congress of Historical Demography* (Barcelona, 1987), pp. 627–32.

Febvre, L., *La terre et l'évolution humaine. Introduction géographique à l'histoire* (Paris, 1922).

A geographical introduction to history, English edn of *La terre et l'évolution humaine* (London, 1925).

'Un livre qui grandit: La Méditerranée et le monde méditerranéen à l'époque de Philippe II', *Revue Historique*, 74 (1950), pp. 216–24.

Fierro, A., 'Un cycle démographique: Dauphiné et Faucigny du XIVe au XIXe siècle', *Annales E.S.C.*, 26 (1971), pp. 941–59.

Fildes, V., *Breasts, bottles and babies. A history of infant feeding* (Edinburgh, 1986).

Fine-Souriac, A., 'La famille-souche pyrénéenne au XIXe siècle: quelques réflexions de méthode', *Annales E.S.C.*, 32 (1977), pp. 478–87.

Findl, P. and Helczmanovszki, H., *The population of Austria* (Vienna, 1977).

Firth, R., 'Bilateral descent groups: an operational viewpoint', in I. Schapera (ed.), *Studies in kinship and marriage* (London, 1963), pp. 22–37.

Flandrin, J.-L., *Families. Parenté, maison, sexualité dans l'ancienne societé* (Paris, 1976).

Fleury, M. and Valmary, P., 'Les progrès de l'instruction élémentaire de Louis XIV à Napoleon III d'après l'enquête de Louis Maggiolo (1877–1879)', *Population*, 12 (1957), pp. 71–92.

Flinn, M. W., *The European demographic system 1500–1820* (Brighton, 1981).

Fliri, F., *Bevölkerungsgeographische Untersuchungen im Unterinntal* (Innsbruck, 1948).

Fontaine, L., 'Les effets déséquilibrants du colportage sur les structures de famille et sur les pratiques économiques de la vallée de l'Oisans, 18e–19e siècles', European University Institute Working Papers No. 85/136 (Florence, 1985).

Forde, D., 'Ecology and social structure', *Proceedings of the Royal Anthropological Institute*, 1970, pp. 15–29.

Fox, T., 'Peasants as bureaucrats?', *Peasant Studies*, 12 (1985), pp. 215–25.

Franklin, S. H., *The European peasantry. The final phase* (London, 1969).

Frey, S., 'Die Herkunft der Familie aus dem Walserdorfe Alagna-Sesia', in F. Stucki, *Geschichte der Familie Bodmer von Zürich* (Zurich, 1942), pp. 1–22, 449–61.

Friedl, J., 'Benefits of fragmentation in a traditional society: a case from the Swiss Alps', *Human Organization*, 32 (1973), pp. 29–36.

Kippel. A changing village in the Alps (New York, 1974).

Friedl, J. and Ellis, W. S., 'Celibacy, late marriage and potential mates in a Swiss isolate', *Human Biology*, 48 (1976), pp. 23–35.

Friedlander, D., 'Demographic patterns and socioeconomic characteristics of the coal-mining population in England and Wales in the nineteenth century', *Economic Development and Cultural Change*, 22 (1973), pp. 39–51.

Friedman, J., 'Marxism, structuralism and vulgar materialism', *Man*, n.s., 9 (1974), pp. 444–69.

Frödin, J., *Zentraleuropas Alpwirtschaft*, 2 vols. (Oslo, 1940–1).

Furet, F. and Ozouf, J., *Reading and writing. Literacy in France from Calvin to Jules Ferry* (Cambridge, 1982).

Furrer, G. and Wegmann, D., 'Bevölkerungsveränderungen in den Schweizer Alpen 1950 bis 1970', *Mitteilungen der Österreichischen Geographischen Gesellschaft*, 119 (1977), pp. 52–65.

Gal, S., *Language shift. Social determinants of linguistic change in bilingual Austria* (New York, 1979).

Garnsey, P., 'Mountain economies in Southern Europe. Thoughts on the early history, continuity and individuality of Mediterranean upland pastoralism', in M. Mattmüller (ed.), *Wirtschaft und Gesellschaft in Berggebieten* (Basle, 1986), pp. 7–29.

Gaunt, D., 'Family planning and the pre-industrial society: some Swedish evidence', in K. Ågren *et al.*, *Aristocrats, farmers, proletarians. Essays in Swedish demographic history* (Uppsala, 1973), pp. 28–59.

Giordani, G., *La colonia tedesca di Alagna-Valsesia e il suo dialetto* (Turin, 1891).

Giusti, U., 'Note riassuntive', in INEA (Istituto Nazionale di Economia Agraria), *Lo spopolamento montano in Italia* (Milan and Rome, 1932), vol. 1, pp. xxxvi–lxiv.

Gluckman, M., 'The utility of the equilibrium model in the study of social change', *American Anthropologist*, 70 (1968), pp. 219–37.

Gnifetti, G., *Nozioni topografiche del Monte Rosa ed ascensioni su di esso* (Turin, 1845).

Godoy, R., 'Mining: anthropological perspectives', *Annual Review of Anthropology*, 14 (1985), pp. 199–217.

Goldschmidt, W. and Kunkel, E. J., 'The structure of the peasant family', *American Anthropologist*, 73 (1971), pp. 1059–76.

Goldstein, M. C., 'Fraternal polyandry and fertility in a high Himalayan valley in northwest Nepal', *Human Ecology*, 4 (1976), pp. 223–33.
  'New perspectives on Tibetan fertility and population decline', *American Ethnologist*, 8 (1981), pp. 721–38.
  'The transformation of the social matrix of Tibetan populations in the High Himalayas', in P. Baker and C. Jest (eds.) *Environmental and human population problems at high altitude* (Paris, 1981), pp. 101–5.
  Tsarong, P. and Beall, C. M., 'High altitude hypoxia, culture, and human fecundity/fertility: a comparative study', *American Anthropologist*, 85 (1983), pp. 28–49.

Golley, F. B., 'Historical origins of the ecosystem concept in biology', in E. F. Moran (ed.), *The ecosystem concept in anthropology* (Boulder, 1984), pp. 33–49.

Golzio, S., 'Il fattore demografico nelle zone alpine con particolare riguardo all'Italia', *Cronache Economiche*, 250 (1963), pp. 15–26.

Goody, J., 'Introduction', in J. Goody, J. Thirsk and E. P. Thompson (eds.), *Family and inheritance. Rural society in Western Europe 1200–1800* (Cambridge, 1976), pp. 1–9.
  Production and reproduction. A comparative study of the domestic domain (Cambridge, 1976).

Grasso, R., 'I movimenti della popolazione in Valsesia in relazione con l'andamento dell'industria, 1951–71', unpublished dissertation, State University of Milan, 1974.

Gribaudi, D., *Il Piemonte nell'antichità classica* (Turin, 1928).
  'Valle del Gesso', in INEA (Istituto Nazionale di Economia Agraria), *Lo spopolamento montano in Italia* (Milan and Rome, 1932), vol. 2, pp. 351–402.

Grigg, D. B., *Population growth and agrarian change. An historical perspective* (Cambridge, 1980).

Guibourdenche, H., 'Naissances et taux de natalité dans les Alpes du Nord', *Revue de Géographie Alpine*, 59 (1971), pp. 171–92.

Guichonnet, P., 'L'émigration alpine vers les pays de langue allemande', *Revue de Géographie Alpine*, 36 (1948), pp. 533–76.

'Le développement démographique et économique des régions alpines', in P. Guichonnet *et al.*, *Le Alpi e l'Europa*, vol. 2, *Uomini e territorio* (Bari, 1975), pp. 138–96.

'Le partage politique des Alpes aux XVIIe-XIXe siècles: les Alpes occidentales franco-italiennes', in P. Guichonnet (ed.), *Histoire et civilisations des Alpes* (Toulouse and Lausanne, 1980), vol. 1, pp. 266–310.

Guillaume, P. and Poussou, J.-P., *Démographie historique* (Paris, 1970).

Guillen, P., 'Introduction', in P. Guillen (ed.), *Travail et migration dans les Alpes françaises et italiennes* (Grenoble, 1982), pp. 1–4.

Guillet, D., 'Toward a cultural ecology of mountains: the Central Andes and the Himalayas compared', *Current Anthropology*, 24 (1983), pp. 561–74.

Guksch, C. E., 'Comment to Guillet', *Current Anthropology*, 24 (1983), pp. 567–8.

Gutmann, M. P. and Leboutte, R., 'Rethinking protoindustrialization and the family', *Journal of Interdisciplinary History*, 14 (1984), pp. 587–607.

Habakkuk, H. J., 'Family structure and economic change in nineteenth-century Europe', *Journal of Economic History*, 15 (1955), pp. 1–12.

Hagaman, R. M., Elias, W. S. and Netting, R. M., 'The genetic and demographic impact of in-migrants in a largely endogamous community', *Annals of Human Biology*, 5 (1978), pp. 505–15.

Hagmann, H.-M. and Menthonnex, J., 'Éléments de démographie alpine. Le cas de la Suisse, 1850–1970', *Schweizerische Zeitschrift für Geschichte*, 29 (1979), pp. 216–31.

Haines, M., *Fertility and occupation. Population patterns in industrialization* (New York, 1979).

Hajnal, J., 'Age at marriage and proportions marrying', *Populations Studies*, 7 (1953), pp. 111–36.

'European marriage patterns in perspective', in D. V. Glass and D. E. C. Eversley (eds.), *Population in history. Essays in historical demography* (London, 1965), pp. 101–43.

'Two kinds of pre-industrial household formation system', in R. Wall, J. Robin and P. Laslett (eds.), *Family forms in historic Europe* (Cambridge, 1983), pp. 65–104.

Hammel, E. A. and Laslett, P., 'Comparing household structure over time and between cultures', *Comparative Studies in Society and History*, 16 (1974), pp. 73–109.

Head-König, A. L., Hubler, L. and Pfister, C., 'Évolution agraire et démographique en Suisse (XVIIe-XIXe siècles)', in A. Fauve-Chamoux (ed.), *Évolution agraire et croissance démographique* (Liège, 1987), pp. 233–61.

Helbok, A., 'Zur Soziologie und Volkskunde des Alpenraumes', *Zeitschrift für Volkskunde*, 3 (1931), pp. 101–12.

Helczmanovszki, H., 'Die Entwicklung der Bevölkerung Österreichs in den letzen hundert Jahren nach den wichtigsten demographischen Komponenten', in H. Helczmanovszki (ed.), *Beiträge zur Bevölkerungs- und Sozialgeschichte Österreichs* (Vienna, 1973), pp. 113–65.

Held, T., 'Rural retirement arrangements in seventeenth- to nineteenth-century Austria: a cross-community analysis', *Journal of Family History*, 7 (1982), pp. 227–54.

Heppenstall, M. A., 'East Tyrol', in F. G. Bailey (ed.), *Debate and compromise. The politics of innovation* (Oxford, 1973), pp. 134–63.

Hertz, R., 'Saint Besse. Étude d'un culte alpestre', *Revue de l'Histoire des Religions*, 67 (1913), pp. 115–80.

Honigmann, J. J., 'Bauer and Arbeiter in a rural Austrian community', *Southwestern Journal of Anthropology*, 19 (1963), pp. 40–53.

'Survival of a cultural focus', in W. H. Goodenough (ed.), *Explorations in cultural anthropology* (New York, 1964), pp. 277–92.

'Rationality and fantasy in Styrian villagers', *Anthropologica*, 12 (1970), pp. 129–39.

Hudry, M., 'La démographie d'une commune de montagne aux XVIIe et XVIIIe siècles: Saint-Martin-de-Belleville (Savoie)', *Recueils des Mémoires et Documents de l'Académie de la Val d'Isère*, 1956, pp. 29–39.

Hufton, O., *The poor of eighteenth-century France, 1750–1789* (Oxford, 1974).

Hutson, S, 'Valloire', in F. G. Bailey (ed.), *Debate and compromise. The politics of innovation* (Oxford, 1973), pp. 16–47.

Ilg, K., 'Die heutige Lage des Walservolkstums in Vorarlberg', *Wir Walser. Halbjahresschrift für Walsertum*, 1.2 (1963), pp. 8–14.

Imhof, A. E., 'Unterschiedliche Säuglingssterblichkeit in Deutschland, 18. bis 20. Jahrhundert', *Zeitschrift für Bevölkerungswissenschaft*, 7 (1981), pp. 343–82.

ISTAT (Istituto Centrale di Statistica), *Censimento generale della popolazione, 1951. Dati sommari per comune* (Rome, 1956).

Censimento generale della popolazione, 1961. Dati sommari per comune (Rome, 1965).

Censimento generale della popolazione, 1971. Dati sommari per comune (Rome, 1973).

Secondo censimento dell'agricoltura, 1970. Dati sommari per comune (Rome, 1972).

Jacquard, A., 'Concepts of genetics and concepts of demography: specificities and analogies', in N. Keyfitz (ed.), *Population and biology* (Liège, 1984), pp. 29–39.

Janin, B., 'Le tourisme dans les Grandes Alpes italiennes: Breuil-Cervinia et Valtournanche', *Revue de Géographie Alpine*, 52 (1964), pp. 211–64.

Le Val d'Aoste. Tradition et renouveau (Grenoble, 1968).

Jervis, G., *I tesori sotterranei dell'Italia. Parte prima: Regione delle Alpi* (Turin, 1873).

Jochim, M., 'The ecosystem concept in archaeology', in E. F. Moran (ed.), *The ecosystem concept in anthropology* (Boulder, 1984), pp. 87–102.

Jones, A. M., 'Extending the family: family household structures and patriline continuity in Haute Savoie, 1561–1968', paper presented at the conference on 'Social reproduction: population, family and property' (Oeiras, 1983).

'Population dynamics in a marginal area of upland Europe: European or Mediterranean demographic regime?', paper presented at the conference on 'Family forms and demographic patterns in the Western Mediterranean' (Oeiras, 1984).

Jost, C., *Der Einfluss des Fremdenverkehrs auf Wirtschaft und Bevölkerung in der Landschaft Davos* (Berne, 1952).

Kellenbenz, H., 'Der mittlere Alpenraum. Aspekte der Kapitalverflechtung im Bunt- und Edelmetallbergbau', paper presented at the second conference on 'Le Alpi e l'Europa' (Lugano, 1985).

Keller, W., 'Die Bevölkerungsentwicklung im Ausserfern. Phasen und Komponenten von Zu- und Abnahme', *Mitteilungen der Österreichischen Geographischen Gesellschaft*, 117 (1975), pp. 364–79.

Khera, S., 'Social stratification and land inheritance among Austrian peasants', *American Anthropologist*, 75 (1973), pp. 814–23.

'Illegitimacy and mode of land inheritance among Austrian peasants', *Ethnology*, 20 (1981), pp. 307–23.

King, S. W., *The Italian valleys of the Pennine Alps* (London, 1858).

Klein, K., 'Österreichs Bevölkerung 1754–1869', *Mitteilungen der Österreichischen Geographischen Gesellschaft*, 113 (1971), pp. 34–62.

'Die Bevölkerung Österreichs vom Beginn des 16. bis zur Mitte des 18. Jahrhundert', in H. Helczmanovszki (ed.), *Beiträge zur Bevölkerungs- und Sozialgeschichte Österreichs* (Vienna, 1973), pp. 47–112.

Knodel, J. and van de Walle, E., 'Breastfeeding, fertility and infant mortality. An analysis of some early German data', *Population Studies*, 21 (1967), pp. 109–31.

Kohn, H., *Nationalism and liberty. The Swiss example* (London, 1956).

Kreis, H., *Die Walser. Ein Stück Siedlungsgeschichte der Zentralalpen*, 2nd edn (Berne, 1966).

Kullen, S., *Wandlungen der Bevölkerungs- und Wirtschaftsstruktur in den Wölzer Alpen* (Tübingen, 1972).

Kurmann, F., *Das Luzerner Suhrental im 18. Jahrhundert* (Lucerne, 1985).

Lamaison, P., 'Les stratégies matrimoniales dans un système complexe de parenté: Ribenne en Gévaudan (1650–1830)', *Annales E.S.C.*, 34 (1979), pp. 721–43.

Laslett, P., 'Preface', in P. Laslett and R. Wall (eds.), *Household and family in past time* (Cambridge, 1972), pp. ix–xii.

'Introduction: the history of the family', in P. Laslett and R. Wall (eds.), *Household and family in past time* (Cambridge, 1972), pp. 1–89.

'Family and household as work group and kin group: areas of traditional Europe compared', in R. Wall, J. Robin and P. Laslett (eds.), *Family forms in historic Europe* (Cambridge, 1983), pp. 513–63.

Laslett, P., Wachter, K. W. and Laslett, R., 'The English evidence on household structure compared with the outcomes of microsimulation', in K. W. Wachter *et al.*, *Statistical studies of historical social structure* (New York, 1978), pp. 65–87.

Lässer, A., *St. Leonhard im Pitztal. Bevölkerungsgeographische Untersuchung* (Innsbruck, 1956).

Le Roy Ladurie, E., *Times of feast, times of famine. A history of climate since the year 1000* (London, 1972).

'Structures familiales et coutumes d'héritage', *Annales E.S.C.*, 27 (1972), pp. 825–46.

'Homme-animal, nature-culture: les problèmes de l'équilibre démographique', in E. Morin and M. Piattelli-Palmarini (eds.), *L'unité de l'homme: invariants biologiques et universaux culturels* (Paris, 1974), pp. 553–94.

Lesthaeghe, R., 'On the social control of human reproduction', *Population and Development Review*, 6 (1980), pp. 527–48.

Levi, G., 'Mobilità della popolazione e immigrazione a Torino nella prima metà del Settecento', *Quaderni Storici*, 6 (1971), pp. 510–54.

Levine, D., 'The demographic implications of rural industrialization: a family reconstitution study of Shepshed, Leicestershire, 1600–1851', *Social History*, 1 (1976), pp. 177–96.

Lewis, H. M., 'Industrialization, class, and regional consciousness in two highland societies: Wales and Appalachia', in P. D. Beaver and B. L. Purrington (eds.), *Cultural adaptation to mountain environments* (Athens, Georgia, 1984), pp. 50–70.

Lichtenberger, E., 'Das Bergbauernproblem in den österreichischen Alpen: Perioden und Typen der Entsiedlung', *Erdkunde*, 19 (1965), pp. 39–57.

The Eastern Alps (Oxford, 1975).

'The crisis of rural settlement and farming in the high mountain region of continental Europe', *Geographia Polonica*, 38 (1978), pp. 181–7.

Liver, P., *Mittelalterliches Kolonistenrecht und freie Walser in Graubünden* (Zurich, 1943).

Livi-Bacci, M., *A history of Italian fertility during the last two centuries* (Princeton, 1977).

Loup, J., *Pasteurs et agriculteurs valaisans* (Grenoble, 1965).

Lurati, O., 'Alpwesen und Alpenwirtschaftung im Tessin', in L. Földes (ed.), *Viehwirtschaft und Hirtenkultur. Ethnographische Studien* (Budapest, 1969), pp. 756–77.

Macfarlane, A., *Resources and population. A study of the Gurungs of Nepal* (Cambridge, 1976).

The origins of the English individualism (Oxford, 1978).

'Demographic structures and cultural regions in Europe', *Cambridge Anthropology*, 6 (1980), pp. 1–17.

McGuire, R. and Netting, R. M., 'Leveling peasants? The maintenance of equality in a Swiss Alpine community', *American Ethnologist*, 9 (1982), pp. 269–90.

Macmillan Encyclopedia of Architects, 4 vols. (London, 1982).

Macherel, C., 'La traversée du champ matrimonial: un exemple alpin', *Études Rurales*, 73 (1979), pp. 9–40.

Malthus, T. R., *An essay on the principle of population*, 2nd edn [1803], in E. A. Wrigley and D. Souden (eds.), *The works of Thomas Robert Malthus*, 8 vols. (London, 1986).

A summary view of the principle of population [1830], in E. A. Wrigley and D. Souden (eds.), *The works of Thomas Robert Malthus*, 8 vols. (London, 1986).

Martin, A. F., 'The necessity for determinism. A metaphysical problem confronting geographers', *Publications of the Institute of British Geographers*, 17 (1952), pp. 1–11.

Martin, K., *Die Einwanderung aus Savoyen in das Allgäu und in einige angrenzende Gebiete* (Kempten, 1955).

Massey, D. S. and Mullan, B. P., 'A demonstration of the effects of seasonal migration on fertility', *Demography*, 21 (1984), pp. 501–17.

Mathieu, J., 'Haushalt, Verwandte und Nachbarn im alten Unterengadin (1650–1800)', *Ethnologica Helvetica*, 4 (1980), pp. 167–221.

'Ein Land von Hirten und Sennen? Inneralpine Wirtschaftsformen im 17.

und 18. Jahrhundert am Beispiel des Unterengadins', in J. Mathieu *et al.*, *Das Gebirge: Wirtschaft und Gesellschaft* (Lausanne, 1985), pp. 1–15.

Bauern und Bären. Eine Geschichte des Unterengadins von 1650 bis 1800 (Chur, 1987).

Mattmüller, M., 'Les études de démographie historique à l'Université de Bâle', *Annales de Démographie Historique*, 1976, pp. 453–6.

'Landwirtschaft und Bevölkerung in den Zentralalpen, 1500–1800', paper presented at the second conference on 'Le Alpi e l'Europa' (Lugano, 1985).

Bevölkerungsgeschichte der Schweiz: Die frühe Neuzeit, 1500–1700, 2 vols. (Basle, 1987).

Mauss, M. and Beuchat, H., 'Essai sur les variations saisonnières des sociétés eskimos. Essai de morphologie sociale', *Année Sociologique*, 9 (1904–5), pp. 39–132.

Mayer, K. B., *The population of Switzerland* (New York, 1952).

Medick, H., 'The proto-industrial family economy: the structural function of household and family during the transition from peasant society to industrial capitalism', *Social History*, (1976), pp. 291–315.

Mendels, F. F., 'Proto-industrialization: the first phase of the industrial process', *Journal of Economic History*, 32 (1972), pp. 241–61.

Menken, J., 'Seasonal migration and seasonal variation in fecundability: effects on birth rates and birth intervals', *Demography*, 16 (1979), pp. 103–19.

Mériaudeau, R., 'L'enfant, l'école et la montagne', *Revue de Géographie Alpine*, 69 (1981), pp. 69–125.

Merli-Brandini, P., 'Movimenti migratori fra i paesi alpini e perialpini', in P. Guichonnet *et al.*, *Le Alpi e l'Europa*, vol. 2, *Uomini e territorio* (Bari, 1975), pp. 221–54.

Meuvret, J., 'Les crises de subsistances et la démographie de la France d'ancien régime', *Population*, 1 (1946), pp. 643–50.

'Demographic crisis in France from the sixteenth to the eighteenth century', in D. V. Glass and D. E. C. Eversley (eds.), *Population in history. Essays in historical demography* (London, 1965), pp. 507–22.

Messerli B., Messerli, P., Pfister, C. and Zumbühl, H. J., 'Fluctuations of climate and glaciers in the Bernese Oberland, Switzerland, and their geo-ecological significance, 1600 to 1975', *Arctic and Alpine Research*, 10 (1978), pp. 247–60.

Meyer, W., 'Wüstungen als Zeugen des mittelalterlichen Alpwesens', *Schweizerische Zeitschrift für Geschichte*, 29 (1979), pp. 256–64.

Mitterauer, M., 'Produktionsweise, Siedlungsstruktur und Sozialformen im österreichischen Montanwesen des Mittelalters und der frühen Neuzeit', in M. Mitterauer (ed.), *Österreichisches Montanwesen. Produktion, Verteilung, Sozialformen* (Munich, 1974), pp. 234–315.

'Auswirkungen von Urbanisierung und Frühindustrialisierung auf die Familienverfassung an Beispielen des österreichischen Raums', in W. Conze (ed.), *Sozialgeschichte der Familie in der Neuzeit Europas* (Stuttgart, 1976), pp. 53–146.

'Familienformen und Illegitimität in ländlichen Gebieten Österreichs', *Archiv für Sozialgeschichte*, 19 (1979), pp. 123–88.

'Auswirkungen der Agrarrevolution auf die baüerliche Familienstruktur in

Österreich', in M. Mitterauer and R. Sieder (eds.), _Historische Familienforschung_ (Frankfurt a.M., 1982), pp. 241–70.

Ledige Mütter: zur Geschichte illegitimer Geburten in Europa (Munich, 1983).

'Gesindedienst und Jugendphase im europäischen Vergleich', _Geschichte und Gesellschaft_, 11 (1985), pp. 177–204.

'Formen ländlicher Familienwirtschaft. Historische Ökotypen und familiale Arbeitsorganisation im österreichischen Raum', in J. Ehmer and M. Mitterauer (eds.), _Familienstruktur und Arbeitsorganisation in ländlichen Gesellschaften_ (Vienna, 1986), pp. 185–323.

Molenda, D., 'Mining towns in Central-Eastern Europe in feudal times', _Acta Polonica Historica_, 34 (1976), pp. 165–88.

Moran, E. F., 'Limitations and advances in ecosystems research', in E. F. Moran (ed.), _The ecosystem concept in anthropology_ (Boulder, 1984), pp. 3–32.

Morassi, L. and Panjek, G., 'Strategie familiari in Val di Resia (sec. XIX)', paper presented at the conference on 'Strutture e rapporti familiari in epoca moderna' (Trieste, 1983).

Mortarotti, R., _I Walser nella Val d'Ossola_ (Domodossola, 1979).

Muret, J. L., _Mémoire sur l'état de la population dans le pays de Vaud_ (Yverdon, 1766).

Muttini-Conti, G., _La popolazione del Piemonte nel secolo XIX_ (Turin, 1962).

Netting, R. M., 'Of men and meadows: strategies of Alpine land use', _Anthropological Quarterly_, 45 (1972), pp. 132–44.

'What Alpine peasants have in common: observations on communal tenure in a Swiss village', _Human Ecology_, 4 (1976), pp. 135–46.

'Household dynamics in a nineteenth century Swiss village', _Journal of Family History_, 4 (1979), pp. 39–58.

'Eine lange Ahnenreihe. Die Fortdauer von Patrilinien über mehr als drei Jahrhunderte in einem schweizerischen Bergdorf', _Schweizerische Zeitschrift für Geschichte_, 29 (1979), pp. 194–215.

Balancing on an alp. Ecological change and continuity in a Swiss mountain community (Cambridge, 1981).

'Reflections on an Alpine village as ecosystem', in E. F. Moran (ed.), _The ecosystem concept in anthropology_ (Boulder, 1984), pp. 225–35.

Novak, V., 'Übersicht über Viehhaltungsformen und Alpwesen in Slowenien', in L. Földes (ed.), _Viehzucht und Hirtenleben in Ostmitteleuropa_ (Budapest, 1961), pp. 647–62.

Ohlin, P. G., 'Mortality, marriage, and growth in pre-industrial populations', _Population Studies_, 14 (1961), pp. 190–7.

O'Neill, B. J., 'Dying and inheriting in rural Trás-os-Montes', _Journal of the Anthropological Society of Oxford_, 14 (1983), pp. 44–74.

Orlove, B. S., 'Ecological anthropology', _Annual Review of Anthropology_, 9 (1980), pp. 235–73.

Parain, C., 'Esquisse d'une problématique des systèmes européens d'estivage à production fromagère', _L'Ethnographie_, n.s., 62–3 (1969), pp. 3–28.

Parry, M. L., 'Secular climatic change and marginal agriculture', _Transactions of the Institute of British Geographers_, 64 (1975), pp. 1–13.

Pasternak, B., Ember, C. R. and Ember, M., 'On the conditions favoring extended family households', _Journal of Anthropological Research_, 32 (1976), pp. 109–23.

Pauli, L., *The Alps. Archaeology and early history* (London, 1984).

Peattie, R., *Mountain geography. A critique and field study*, 2nd edn (New York, 1971).

Perroy, E., *Le Moyen Âge. L'expansion de l'Orient et la naissance de la civilisation occidentale* (Paris, 1955).

Pfeifer, G., 'The quality of peasant living in Central Europe', in W. L. Thomas (ed.), *Man's role in changing the face of the earth* (Chicago, 1956), pp. 240–77.

Pfister, C., 'Changes in stability and carrying capacity of lowland and highland agro-systems in Switzerland in the historical past', *Mountain Research and Development*, 3 (1983), pp. 291–7.

Das Klima der Schweiz von 1525–1860 und seine Bedeutung in der Geschichte von Bevölkerung und Landwirtschaft, 2 vols. (Berne, 1984).

'Bevölkerung, Wirtschaft und Ernährung in den Berg- und Talgebieten des Kantons Bern 1760–1860', in M. Mattmüller (ed.), *Wirtschaft und Gesellschaft in Berggebieten* (Basle, 1986), pp. 361–91.

'Menschen im Kanton Bern 1764–1980. Wandlungen in der Bevölkerungsentwicklung und -verteilung seit dem späten Ancien Régime', in *Der Mensch in der Landschaft. Festschrift für Georges Grosjean* (Berne, 1986), pp. 475–99.

Pfister, U., 'Proto-industrialization and demographic change: the canton of Zurich revisited' (forthcoming in *Journal of European Economic History*).

Pickl, O., 'Wirtschaft und Gesellschaft in den Ostalpenländern Kärnten und Steiermark bis zur Mitte des 19. Jahrhunderts', in M. Mattmüller (ed.), *Wirtschaft und Gesellschaft in Berggebieten* (Basle, 1986), pp. 38–101.

Planhol, X. de, 'Pression démographique et vie montagnarde (particulièrement dans la ceinture alpino-himalayenne)', *Revue de Géographie Alpine*, 56 (1968), pp. 531–51.

Poitrineau, A., *Remues d'hommes. Essai sur les migrations montagnardes en France aux XVIIe et XVIIIe siècles* (Paris, 1983).

'Quelques aspects spécifiques de l'économie montagnarde française à l'époque moderne', in M. Mattmüller (ed.), *Wirtschaft und Gesellschaft in Berggebieten* (Basle, 1986), pp. 102–22.

Poppi, C., 'Kinship and social organization among the Ladins of the Val di Fassa (Northern Italy)', *Cambridge Anthropology*, 6 (1980), pp. 60–88.

Poussou, J.-P., 'Les mouvements migratoires en France et à partir de la France de la fin du XVe siècle au début du XIXe siècle: approches pour une synthèse', *Annales de Démographie Historique*, 1970, pp. 11–78.

Prato, G., *La vita economica in Piemonte a mezzo il secolo XVIII* (Turin, 1908).

Prost, B., 'L'évolution démographique dans les zones de montagne (Vosges, Jura, Alpes du Nord)', *Espace-Populations-Sociétés*, 1986, pp. 355–63.

Rabell, C. A. and Assadourian, C. S., 'Self-regulating mechanisms of the population in a pre-Columbian society: the case of the Inca Empire', in *International Population Conference, Mexico 1977* (Liège, 1977), vol. 3, pp. 25–42.

Raffestin, C. and Crivelli, R., 'L'industrie alpine du XVIIIe au XXe siècle: défis et adaptations', paper presented at the second conference on 'Le Alpi e l'Europa' (Lugano, 1985).

Ramella, F., 'Famiglia, terra e salario in una comunità tessile dell'800', *Movimento Operaio e Socialista*, 1977, pp. 7–44.

Terra e telai. Sistemi di parentela e manifattura nel Biellese dell'Ottocento (Turin, 1984).

Rappaport, R. A., *Pigs for the ancestors. Ritual and ecology in a New Guinea people* (New Haven, 1968).

Ratzel, F., *Anthropo-Geographie, oder Grundzüge der Anwendung der Erdkunde auf die Geschichte*, 2 vols. (Stuttgart, 1882–91).

Ravis Giordani, G., 'Introduction', in G. Ravis Giordani (ed.), *Recherches sur l'organisation familiale et la parenté dans le Val Germanasca* (forthcoming).

Rebel, H., *Peasant classes. The bureaucratization of property and family relations under early Habsburg absolutism, 1511–1636* (Princeton, 1983).

Redfield, R., *The little community. Viewpoints for the study of a human whole* (Uppsala, 1955).

Regno d'Italia, *Censimento degli Antichi Stati Sardi* (Turin, 1862–4).

Regno di Sardegna, *Informazioni statistiche raccolte dalla Regia Commissione Superiore per gli Stati di Terraferma* (Turin, 1843).

Rhoades, R. E. and Thompson, S. I., 'Adaptive strategies in alpine environments: beyond ecological particularism', *American Ethnologist*, 2 (1975), pp. 535–51.

Riccarand, E. and Omezzoli, T., *Sur l'émigration valdôtaine* (Aosta, 1975).

Riedman, J., 'Bergbau im Fersental', in G. B. Pellegrini and M. Gretter (eds.), *La Valle del Fersina e le isole linguistiche di origine tedesca nel Trentino* (S. Michele all'Adige, 1979), pp. 175–86.

Riggenbach, R., *Ulrich Ruffiner von Prismell und die Bauten der Schinerzeit im Wallis*, 2nd edn (Brig, 1952).

Rizzi, E., 'La colonizzazione walser a sud del Rosa alla luce di nuovi documenti', *Lo Strona*, 5 (1980), pp. 27–38.

    Walser: gli uomini della montagna (Valstrona, 1981).

    'Sulla fondazione di Alagna', *Bollettino Storico per la Provincia di Novara*, 74 (1983), pp. 335–68.

Robilant, N. S. B. de, *De l'utilité et de l'importance des voyages et des courses dans son propre pays* (Turin, 1790).

Rollet, C., 'Allaitement, mise en nourrice et mortalité infantile en France à la fin du XIXe siècle', *Population*, 33 (1978), pp. 1189–1203.

Rousseau, R., *La population de la Savoie jusqu'en 1861* (Paris, 1960).

Ruesch, H., 'Die Demographie der Alpen zwischen 1650 und 1850', *Schweizerische Zeitschrift für Geschichte*, 29 (1979), pp. 159–80.

Sacco, I. M. (ed.), *La provincia di Cuneo dal 1800 ad oggi* (Turin, 1956).

Sahlins, M., 'Land use and the extended family in Moala, Fiji', *American Anthropologist*, 59 (1957), pp. 449–62.

Saunders, G. R., 'Social change and psychocultural continuity in Alpine Italian family life', *Ethos. Journal of the Society for Psychological Anthropology*, 7 (1979), pp. 206–31.

Sauter, M.-R., 'Des chausseurs moustériens au Bas Empire', *Schweizerische Zeitschrift für Geschichte*, 29 (1979), pp. 125–43.

Sauvy, A., *General theory of population* (London, 1969).

Schmidtbauer, P., 'Daten zur historischen Demographie', cyclostyled (Vienna, 1977).

    'The changing household: Austrian household structure from the seventeenth to the early twentieth century', in R. Wall, J. Robin and P. Laslett (eds.), *Family forms in historic Europe* (Cambridge, 1983), pp. 347–78.

Schofield, R., 'The relationship between demographic structure and environment in pre-industrial Western Europe', in W. Conze (ed.), *Sozialgeschichte der Familie in der Neuzeit Europas* (Stuttgart, 1976), pp. 147–60.

Schott, A., *Die deutschen Colonien in Piemont* (Stuttgart, 1842).

Schulte, A., *Geschichte des mittelalterlichen Handels und Verkehrs zwischen West-deutschland und Italien*, 2 vols. (Leipzig, 1900).

Scott Smith, D., 'A homeostatic demographic regime: patterns in west European family reconstitution studies', in R. D. Lee (ed.), *Population patterns in the past* (New York, 1977), pp. 19–51.

Sebesta, G., 'Mito e realtà della Valle dei Mocheni', in G. Marcuzzi and G. B. Pellegrini (eds.), *Atti del Convegno interdisciplinare sulle isole linguistiche tedesche delle Alpi meridionali* (Padua, 1983), pp. 125–39.

Sella, D., 'Au dossier des migrations montagnardes: l'exemple de la Lombardie au XVIIe siècle', in *Mélanges en l'honneur de Fernand Braudel* (Toulouse, 1973), vol. 1, pp. 547–54.

Sellan, G., 'Système familial et continuité culturelle: les Mocheni des Alpes italiennes', *Études Rurales*, 73 (1979), pp. 41–68.

Semple, E. C., *Influences of geographic environment on the basis of Ratzel's system of anthropo-geography* (New York, 1911).

Senn, U., 'Die Alpwirtschaft der Landschaft Davos', *Geographica Helvetica*, 7 (1952), pp. 265–350.

Sereni, E., *Il capitalismo nelle campagne (1860–1900)*, 2nd edn (Turin, 1968).

Sibilla, P., *Una comunità walser delle Alpi* (Florence, 1980).

   I luoghi della memoria. Cultura e vita quotidiana nella testimonianza del contadino valsesiano G. B. Filippa (1778–1838) (Anzola d'Ossola, 1985).

Siddle, D. J., 'Articulating the grid of inheritance: the accumulation and transmission of wealth in peasant Savoy 1561–1792', in M. Mattmüller (ed.), *Wirtschaft und Gesellschaft in Berggebieten* (Basle, 1986), pp. 123–81.

   'Cultural prejudice and the geography of ignorance: peasant literacy in south-eastern France, 1550–1790', *Transactions of the Institute of British Geographers*, n.s., 12 (1987), pp. 19–28.

Siddle, D. J. and Jones, A. M., 'Family household structures and inheritance in Savoy, 1561–1975', Liverpool Papers in Human Geography No. 11 (Liverpool, 1983).

Sieder, R. and Mitterauer, M., 'The reconstitution of the family life course: theoretical problems and empirical results', in R. Wall, J. Robin and P. Laslett (eds.), *Family forms in historic Europe* (Cambridge, 1983), pp. 309–45.

Smith, R. M., 'The people of Tuscany and their families in the fifteenth century: medieval or Mediterranean?', *Journal of Family History*, 6 (1981), pp. 107–28.

   '"Modernization" and the corporate medieval village community in England: some sceptical reflections', in A. R. H. Baker and D. Gregory (eds.), *Explorations in historical geography* (Cambridge, 1984), pp. 140–79.

Sölch, J., 'Raum und Gesellschaft in den Alpen', *Geographische Zeitung*, 37 (1931), pp. 143–68.

Solien de Gonzales, N. L., 'Family organization in five types of migratory wage labour', *American Anthropologist*, 63 (1961), pp. 1264–80.

Sombart, W., *Der moderne Kapitalismus*, 3 vols. (Munich and Leipzig, 1924–27).

Sottile, N., *Quadro della Valsesia* (Novara, 1803).

Spanna, M., 'Val Sesia', in INEA (Istituto Nazionale di Economia Agraria),

Lo spopolamento montano in Italia (Milan and Rome, 1932), vol. 1, pp. 135–77.

Spate, O. H. K., 'Environmentalism', in *International Encyclopaedia of the Social Sciences* (1968), vol. 5, pp. 93–7.

Steward, J., *Theory of culture change. The methodology of multilinear evolution* (Urbana, 1955).

Stoddard, D. R., 'Organism and ecosystem as geographical models', in R. J. Chorley and P. Haggett (eds.), *Models in geography* (London, 1967), pp. 511–48.

Stucki, F., *Geschichte der Familie Bodmer von Zürich* (Zurich, 1942).

Thieme, U. and Becker, F. (founders), *Allgemeines Lexicon der bildenden Künstler von der Antike bis zur Gegenwart*, 37 vols. (Leipzig, 1907–50).

Thomas, C. and Vojvoda, M., 'Alpine communities in transition: Bohinj, Yugoslavia', *Geography*, 58 (1973), pp. 217–26.

Thouret, J.-C., 'Pour une perspective géographique de l'étagement dans les grands systèmes montagneux', *Revue de Géographie Alpine*, 72 (1984), pp. 189–212.

Tomamichel, T., *Bosco Gurin. Das Walserdorf im Tessin* (Basle, 1953).

Tonetti, F., *Museo storico e artistico valsesiano* (Varallo, 1887).

Toscani, X., 'Le "Scuole della Dottrina Cristiana" come fattore di alfabetizzazione', in X. Toscani *et al.*, *Da Carlo Borromeo a Carlo Bascapè* (Novara, 1985), pp. 35–86.

Troger, E., *Bevölkerungsgeographie des Zillertales* (Innsbruck, 1954).

Troll, C., *Die tropischen Gebirge. Ihre dreidimensionale klimatische und pflanzengeographische Zonierung* (Bonn, 1959).

'The cordilleras of Tropical Americas. Aspects of climatic, phytogeographical and agrarian ecology', in C. Troll (ed.), *Geo-ecology of the mountainous regions of the Tropical Americas* (Bonn, 1968), pp. 15–56.

Troll, C. (ed.), *Geo-ecology of the mountainous regions of the Tropical Americas* (Bonn, 1968).

Tschudi, G., *Gallia Comata* (Constance, 1758).

UCCP (Unione delle Camere di Commercio del Piemonte), *I redditi dei comuni del Piemonte* (Turin, 1985).

Vayda, A. P. and McCay, B., 'New directions in ecology and ecological anthropology', *Annual Review of Anthropology*, 4 (1975), pp. 293–306.

Verdon, M., 'The stem family: toward a general theory', *Journal of Interdisciplinary History*, 10 (1979), pp. 87–105.

Vergani, R., 'Una comunità mineraria di montagna: Riva d'Agordo', in R. Romano and U. Tucci (eds.), *Economia naturale, economia monetaria* (Turin, 1983), pp. 611–48.

Veyret, P., 'Natural conditions', in M. Cépède and E. S. Abensour (eds.), *Rural problems in the Alpine area* (Rome, 1961), pp. 7–43.

'Alps. The people,' in *Encyclopaedia Britannica* (1964), vol. 1, pp. 678–9.

Les Alpes (Paris, 1972).

Veyret-Verner, G., 'Le problème de l'équilibre démographique en montagne', *Revue de Géographie Alpine*, 37 (1949), pp. 331–42.

'Population', in M. Cépède and E. S. Abensour (eds.), *Rural problems in the Alpine area* (Rome, 1961), pp. 158–82.

'Populations vieillies. Types, variétés des processus et des incidences sur la population adulte', *Revue de Géographie Alpine*, 49 (1961), pp. 433–56.

'L'évolution des méthodes de l'analyse démographique en montagne: l'exemple des Alpes Françaises', in *La pensée géographique française contemporaine. Mélanges offerts à André Meynier* (Saint-Brienc, 1972), pp. 407–14.

Viazzo, P. P., 'Ethnic change in a Walser community in the Italian Alps', unpublished Ph.D. dissertation, University of London, 1983.

'La scuola: alfabetizzazione e istruzione scolastica ad Alagna dal '500 ad oggi', in E. Ragozza (ed.), *Alagna Valsesia, una comunità walser* (Borgosesia, 1983), pp. 162–72.

'Due nuovi libri di antropologia alpina', *L'Uomo*, 8 (1984), pp. 301–6.

'L'evoluzione della popolazione della Valsesia dagli inizi del '600 alla metà dell'800', *Novarien*, 15 (1985), pp. 118–31.

'Anthropology, family history and the concept of "strategy"', paper presented at the Ninth International Economic History Congress (Berne, 1986).

'Illegitimacy and the European marriage pattern: comparative evidence from the Alpine area', in L. Bonfield, R. M. Smith and K. Wrightson (eds.), *The world we have gained. Histories of population and social structure* (Oxford, 1986), pp. 100–21.

Viazzo, P. P. and Albera, D., 'Population, resources and homeostatic regulation in the Alps: the role of nuptiality', in M. Mattmüller (ed.), *Wirtschaft und Gesellschaft in Berggebieten* (Basle, 1986), pp. 182–231.

Viazzo, P. P. and Bodo, M., 'Emigrazione e immigrazione ad Alagna, 1618–1848', *Wir Walser. Halbjahresschrift für Walsertum*, 18.2 (1980), pp. 9–15.

'"Visibilità" e "invisibilità" della presenza walser: alcune osservazioni storico-demografiche', in E. Rizzi (ed.), *Aspekte der Mittelalterforschung in Walsergebieten* (Anzola d'Ossola, 1985), pp. 147–65.

Vidal de la Blache, P., 'Les conditions géographiques des faits sociaux', *Annales de Géographie*, 11 (1902), pp. 13–23.

'Les genres de vie dans la géographie humaine', *Annales de Géographie*, 20 (1911), pp. 193–212, 289–304.

Vincze, L., 'Peasant animal husbandry: a dialectic model of techno-environmental integration in agro-pastoral societies', *Ethnology*, 19 (1980), pp. 387–403.

van de Walle, E., *The female population of France in the nineteenth century* (Princeton, 1974).

'La nuptialité des Françaises avant 1851, d'après l'état civil des décédées', *Population*, 32 (1977), Special issue in honour of L. Henry, pp. 447–65.

van de Walle, F., 'Migration and fertility in Ticino', *Population Studies*, 29 (1975), pp. 447–62.

One hundred years of decline. The history of Swiss fertility from 1860 to 1960 (forthcoming).

Webster, S., 'Native pastoralism in the South Andes', *Ethnology*, 12 (1973), pp. 115–33.

Weinberg, D., *Peasant wisdom. Cultural adaptation in a Swiss village* (Berkeley and Los Angeles, 1975).

Weiss, R., *Das Alpenwesen Graubündens* (Zurich, 1941).

Volkskunde der Schweiz (Zurich, 1946).

Häuser und Landschaften der Schweiz (Zurich, 1959).

Wheaton, R., 'Family and kinship in Western Europe: the problem of the joint family household', *Journal of Interdisciplinary History*, 4 (1975), pp. 601–28.

Wicki, H., *Bevölkerung und Wirtschaft des Kantons Luzern im 18. Jahrhundert* (Lucerne, 1979).

Wiegandt, E., 'Inheritance and demography in the Swiss Alps', *Ethnohistory*, 24 (1977), pp. 133–48.

Wilson, C., 'The proximate determinants of marital fertility in England 1600–1799', in L. Bonfield, R. M. Smith and K. Wrightson (eds.), *The world we have gained. Histories of population and social structure* (Oxford, 1986), pp. 203–30.

Wilson, C., Oeppen, J. and Pardoe, M., 'What is natural fertility?: The modelling of a concept', *Population Index*, 54 (1988), pp. 4–20.

Wolf, E. R., 'Types of Latin American peasantry: a preliminary discussion', *American Anthropologist*, 57 (1955), pp. 452–71.

'Closed corporate peasant communities in Mesoamerica and Central Java', *Southwestern Journal of Anthropology*, 13 (1957), pp. 1–18.

'Cultural dissonance in the Italian Alps', *Comparative Studies in Society and History*, 5 (1962), pp. 1–14.

Peasants (Englewood Cliffs, 1966).

'The inheritance of land among Bavarian and Tyrolese peasants', *Anthropologica*, 12 (1970), pp. 99–114

'Ownership and political ecology', *Anthropological Quarterly*, 45 (1972), pp. 201–5.

'The vicissitudes of the closed corporate peasant community', *American Ethnologist*, 13 (1986), pp. 325–9.

Wopfner, H., 'Güterteilung und Übervölkerung tirolischer Landbezirke im 16., 17. und 18. Jahrhundert', *Südostdeutsche Forschungen*, 3 (1938), pp. 202–32.

Wrigley, E. A., *Industrial growth and population change. A regional study of the coalfield areas of north-west Europe in the later nineteenth century* (Cambridge, 1961).

Population and history (London, 1969).

'Population history in the 1980s', *Journal of Interdisciplinary History*, 12 (1981), pp. 207–26.

'The fall of marital fertility in nineteenth-century France: exemplar or exception?', *European Journal of Population*, 1 (1985), pp. 31–60.

'Homeostatic regime', in C. Wilson (ed.), *The dictionary of demography* (Oxford, 1985), p. 97.

Wrigley, E. A. and Schofield, R. S., *The population history of England 1541–1871. A reconstruction* (London, 1981).

Wylie, L., 'Demographic change in Roussillon', in J. Pitt-Rivers (ed.), *Mediterranean countrymen* (Paris and The Hague, 1963), pp. 215–36.

Village in the Vaucluse, 3rd edn (Cambridge, Mass., 1974).

Wynne-Edwards, V. C., *Animal dispersion in relation to social behaviour* (Edinburgh and London, 1962).

Yanagisako, S. J., 'Family and household: the analysis of domestic groups', *Annual Review of Anthropology*, 8 (1979), pp. 161–205.

Zimpel, H.-G., *Der Verkehr als Gestalter der Kulturlandschaft* (Munich, 1958).

'Zur Entwicklung und zum heutigen Stand der Walserkolonien. Ein bevölkerungsgeographischer Beitrag', *Mitteilungen der Geographischen Gesellschaft in München*, 53 (1968), pp. 123–73.

Zinsli, P., *Walser Volkstum in der Schweiz, in Vorarlberg, Liechtenstein und Piemont*, 4th edn (Frauenfeld and Stuttgart, 1976).

Zubrow, E. B. W., 'Demographic anthropology: an introductory analysis', in E. B. W. Zubrow (ed.), *Demographic anthropology* (Albuquerque, 1976), pp. 1–25.

Zurfluh, A., 'Urseren 1640–1830, les populations des hautes vallées alpines: contribution à leur histoire démographique', *Schweizerische Zeitschrift für Geschichte*, 32 (1982), pp. 293–323.

'Gibt es den *homo alpinus*? Eine demographisch-kulturelle Fallstudie am Beispiele Uris (Schweiz) im 17.-18. Jahrhundert', in M. Mattmüller (ed.), *Wirtschaft und Gesellschaft in Berggebieten* (Basle, 1986), pp. 232–82.

Index

Printed in the United Kingdom
by Lightning Source UK Ltd.
102069UKS00001B/40